THE RAILWAY
SURVEYORS

THE RAILWAY SURVEYORS

*The Story of Railway
Property Management
1800-1990*

Gordon Biddle

LONDON

IAN ALLAN LTD
BRITISH RAIL PROPERTY BOARD

By the same author

The Canals of North West England (2 vols) with Charles Hadfield, 1970
Victorian Stations, 1973
The British Railway Station, with Jeoffry Spence, 1977
Pennine Waterway, 1977
Lancashire Waterways, 1980
Railway Stations in the North West, 1981
The Railway Heritage of Britain, with O.S. Nock and others, 1983
Great Railway Stations of Britain: Their Architecture, Growth and Development, 1986
The Railways Around Preston: An Historical Review, 1989

First published 1990

ISBN 0 7110 1954 1

Published by Ian Allan Ltd, Shepperton, Surrey
and British Rail Property Board, London; and
printed by Ian Allan Printing Ltd at their works at
Coombelands in Runnymede, England

Contents

List of Maps

Imperial and Metric Measures

	1 inch	=	2.54 cm
12 inches	= 1 foot	=	30.48 cm
3 feet	= 1 yard	=	0.9144 m
22 yards	= 1 chain	=	20.1168 m
10 chains	= 1 furlong	=	201.1680 m
8 furlongs	= 1 mile	=	1.6093 km
144 sq in	= 1 sq ft	=	0.0929 sq m
9 sq ft	= 1 sq yd	=	0.8361 sq m
4,840 sq yd	= 1 acre	=	0.4057 hectares

Foreword

By Sir James Swaffield CBE, RD, DL
Chairman, British Rail Property Board

Britain's railways have provided the material for one of the most written-about subjects in modern British history. The establishment of the original railway companies and their corporate development, the technology and design of locomotives and rolling stock, civil engineering and signalling, have provided a rich vein for the specialist writer and reader. The coming of the railways to cities and towns, and the Victorian architecture of the main terminals and stations, had a major effect on local communities, and the development of transport links affected commerce throughout the country.

It is possible that only in the East India Company could there have been a scale of operations to rival that of the railway companies of the late nineteenth century, having such a profound effect on the societies and economies they touched. The gifted writer on transport, L.T.C. Rolt, described the railway system as 'perhaps the most elaborate . . . feat of organisation ever evolved by man'.

The identification, survey and acquisition of land provided the foundation for the railways and also established, following after the construction of the canals, the surveying profession. Land was required not just for the trackbed but also for stations, locomotive and carriage sheds and works, goods yards, hotels, offices, ports, houses for employees, quarries, steel and gas works. All needed management and maintenance and, over the years, its rationalisation and redevelopment.

It is a complex story, beginning with the Industrial Revolution in Britain, and continuing through the vicissitudes of around 200 years of British history and the development of the surveying profession generally in Britain. Yet in all the books about railways, it is a story that has not been previously told.

I am sure that *The Railway Surveyors* will fill this particular gap and will be of interest to the profession, the railway enthusiast, the historian and the general reader alike. It has been written at a time when the railway, as part of the infrastructure of Britain, is entering an age of renewed importance and vigour, and when property activity is playing a vital role in its development.

As Chairman of the British Rail Property Board, the successor body in this long history of the railway surveyor, I am sure it will provide an interesting and enjoyable insight into the management and role of railway property and the work of its people in the shaping of Britain's railways.

Preface

Railways have had a greater effect on land patterns and the landscape in Britain than in any other country, forming part of the evolutionary changes that have taken place throughout our history. Such a high impact is hardly surprising when one of the world's densest rail networks — at its height only Belgium's was greater, and that but slightly — is imposed on relatively hilly terrain. In rural areas, helped by time, the visual effect has been kind; in towns and cities it has been much less so, although by no means entirely detrimental. Railways have made some notable contributions to our townscapes.

For the first century the railways' impact was positive, in that new physical features were created. In the fifty years that followed, however, leading to our own time, the opposite happened as closures brought about a diminution of the system. Now, with the Channel Tunnel bringing a need for new high-speed rail links, the reality (at last) of urban Light Rapid Transit schemes, and increasingly closer relationships with continental Europe where these things are no longer considered new, there is the prospect of further changes, all of which will require land, both new and the reuse of old. It seems, therefore, an appropriate time to record how the railway in Britain acquired its land, the purposes to which it was put and the effect it had; something about the men who did it; and why, because of our historic and complex system of tenure, all these facets of history profoundly affect the railway still, and undoubtedly will continue to do so.

When I was asked if I would like to think about writing a history of railway property management and the work of the surveyors, my professional interest was immediately aroused. As a transport historian as well, the prospect of researching something new gave added appeal. But my enthusiasm was tempered by uncertainty about available material. I was well aware of a large body of printed sources on the promotion of railways and the strife between the companies, landowners and Parliament, a certain amount of scattered biographical detail, and a growing volume of work on the effect of railways on the country and its economy. But the number of relevant original sources in national and local records, particularly those of the railways themselves, was an unknown quantity. Was there enough to make a balanced account, let alone a whole book?

The incomparable Ottley provided enough on printed sources to justify a synopsis. Insufficient praise is given to George Ottley's *Bibliography of British Railway History*, and the *Supplement* that by good fortune appeared when I was half way through my research; over 12,000 entries on every book that has been written on railways from 1535 to the end of 1980. As it turned out, I had no worries about primary material either. Record offices and libraries around the country provided more than I could use, with additions from friends and acquaintances and, not least, British Rail Property Board's working records, for all of which I am indebted and have acknowledged at the end of this book. Any errors and omissions are entirely mine, of course, and expressions of opinion are personal, in no way reflecting official views or those of the publishers. I have tried to provide an even spread in geographical, historical and railway terms, but any imbalance reflects the amount and type of material available. Some railways simply kept more records, or destroyed less, than others.

The question of text references — how many and where — is always thorny, particularly in a book which it is hoped will have a general as well as a more specialised appeal. I have compromised by restricting references mainly to original sources, quotations, magazine articles and lesser-known or locally produced books and pamphlets. All other books, including standard works, are in a full bibliography. Where no reference is otherwise evident, information has come from Property Board records or, in a few cases, Ordnance Survey maps and plans.

I make no apology for using imperial measurements. That is how they appear in the records, and it would make a nonsense of them to convert to metric. Instead, a table of the relevant metric equivalents has been provided on p7.

For the same reason I have retained pounds, shillings and pence, but have sufficiently unbent to include the decimal equivalents in brackets. Money appears more frequently, my publishers like it that way, and in any case I believe that to some extent they add a little more meaning for readers who have known only decimal currency. What is really needed to make sense of historic costs is a table of indices at, say, ten-year intervals over the last two centuries. Perhaps one day someone will do historians a service and compile one.

To provide an up-to-date account of two important and related schemes in which British Rail Property Board is prominently involved — the Channel Tunnel high-speed link and the development of the King's Cross surplus lands — has proved particularly difficult, such has been the speed of changing events in the first six months of 1990. That is why certain textual references made 'at the time of writing' bear different dates, and why I have resorted to a postscript to the final chapter, for both of which I am grateful to my publisher for his forbearance. It would, perhaps, have been more satisfactory had I been able to be more conclusive but, like time, history never ends.

Gordon Biddle
July 1990

Chapter 1

Antecedents

The First Surveyors

On 29 September 1613, the Lord Mayor of London attended a ceremony in Clerkenwell, close to where Sadler's Wells Theatre now stands, to witness the opening of the New River, an artificial channel bringing water from springs in Hertfordshire to London along a winding course of 38¾ miles. The idea was promoted by Edmund Colthurst of Bath, but after abandonment of preliminary work it was taken over by Sir Hugh Myddelton, a city alderman and jeweller to James I, who was responsible for bringing it to completion.

The route along the 100ft contour required several wooden aqueducts and may have been selected partly by trial and error, although the suggestion has been made that the payment of £20 to Edward Wright for three surveys may have been for checking and rechecking, as well as for the original survey, to avoid the possibility of errors in the levels. At all events, with a fall of only 18ft along the entire length, or 5½in per mile, it represented a remarkable achievement in accurate levelling. Before this, Bishop Morton had constructed Morton's Leam in 1478-90, a straight 40ft-wide drainage and navigation channel bypassing the River Nene between Peterborough and Wisbech, and in 1598 Ralph Agas had measured the fall of Fenland rivers for drainage purposes. Apart from these exceptions, at that period one has to look at the work of European canal builders and drainage schemes in the Low Countries to find surveying ability embodying any degree of precision.[1] In Britain, the New River represented the first, isolated revival of an art that virtually had been lost since the time of the Romans.

Before them, surveying and levelling over long distances had been practised with skill in ancient China, India and the civilisations of the Middle East. The Egyptians were adept at irrigation and the Babylonians built canals more than 2,000 years before Christianity. Sennacherib's stone canal of around 750 BC took water to Ninevah along a 50-mile channel on a falling gradient of 1 in 80 that included an aqueduct of 300yd, while Herodotus considered the aqueduct of Samos, built in the sixth century BC, to be one of the greatest Greek engineering achievements. Two-thirds of it was in tunnel.

Second in extent to the Romans' roads in requiring accurate levels were their spectacular arched aqueducts. It has been said that the Romans 'were as naturally builders of aqueducts as Victorian Britain was of the railway viaducts which so often resemble them.'[2] At least twelve eventually supplied Rome with water and many more were built in the Empire, of which the best-known survivors are the spectacular three-tiered Pont du Gard in southern France and the ½-mile Segovia aqueduct in Spain that still carries water. The Romans also constructed canals, mainly for drainage but some for navigation, while the 3½-mile-long tunnel through the Apennines to drain Lake Fucinus was not surpassed in length with the same precision until the eighteenth-century canal era in Europe. Even remote outposts like Britain saw the construction of water channels, like Foss Dyke and Car Dyke in the Fens and one in Carmarthenshire which ran for 8 miles to a gold mine washery.

Some of the surveying methods used in ancient times are known. The Chinese and the Egyptians used the measuring chain and the bubble level, and the Greeks and Romans developed instruments for measuring angles and distances; but there is uncertainty about how they laid out some of their alignments. That the Romans were well able to measure land accurately is also known, and indeed they held examinations for land measurers.[3] It is from the measuring and recording of land and property that the term 'surveyor' derives, a word of Norman French origin. Edward I appointed a Surveyor to the King's Works to look after his castles and other property, a title that with minor variations continued to apply to those responsible for royal and public buildings until the advent of the more prosaic Minister of Works in modern times. Along the way the post was occupied by men of such eminence in architecture as Sir Christopher Wren and Inigo Jones.

Architecture was one of a number of disciplines embraced by the surveyor. John Fitzherbert's *Book of Husbandry and Book of Surveying* of 1523, the first printed book to use the word, indicated a broad function that included ability to act as land agent, land surveyor and quantity surveyor as well. Such diversity remains today, although surveyors' disciplines in all their branches still stem from the overlooking of property in some form or other. Henry VIII's enactment of 1535, containing the first statutory reference 'concerning the General Surveyors of our Sovereign Lord the King', laid down their duties in administering church estates sequestered by the Crown and clearly showed the surveyor's role to be an adviser on land and property management.[4]

Every civilisation, therefore, had its surveyors, using measuring methods ranging in exactitude from the precision of the ancients to the rough and ready work of the Viking land measurers and their successors in Europe, where accurate measurement did not reappear until the Italian Renaissance. In Britain the re-emergence came later, such expertise as there was being exercised by monks in surveying monastic lands, until a gradual awakening after the Reformation. The developments that followed were due in part to a new ability in making more precise instruments, to a growing sea-borne trade that needed more reliable charts and navigational aids, and to an increasing interest in travel and scientific enquiry; but above all, they were prompted by the need, created by the dissolution of the monasteries and the division of their properties into numerous small estates and landholdings, for more accurate definition and recording of boundaries. They marked the beginning of the great landed estates of the eighteenth and nineteenth centuries that created the position of steward or land agent engaged in estate management, a powerful and multi-disciplinary role that, in addition to embracing commercial, legal and

A surveyor using a plane table, with cherubs carrying Gunter's chain, from The Compleat Surveyor *by William Leybourn, 1674.* (RIBA)

agricultural activities, often required a knowledge of surveying and engineering.

In 1550 the land measurer relied on the medieval measuring rod or staff, and line, which could vary in length according to its age, the climate and, not least, local custom. He might also use a waywiser, a clumsy measuring wheel attached to a carriage, and a pace-counter which was as accurate as the human paces it recorded. Although books on surveying material started to appear from 1571 onwards, there was much error due to lack of knowledge by many who professed to be land surveyors but were, in fact, simply cashing in on the demand. Additionally, there was rivalry with lawyers, who regarded estate management as one of their functions.

During the course of the seventeenth century, the surveyor became much better qualified and equipped: Gunter's chain, inelastic and of standard length, divided into 100 links, was first used about 1620, enabling surface measurement to be calculated in statute acres; the waywiser was giving way to the hand-held measuring wheel, introduced about 1675 and providing greater accuracy; while the surveyor's improved knowledge of geometry and triangulation enabled him to calculate angles with the aid of his chain and a set of scales. He now had the plane table, the circumferentor and, probably the most far-reaching development, a form of theodolite.[5]

15

Thus the middle of the century saw the beginnings of a new professionalism, but without changing the multi-disciplinary role, although by the end of the century the extra demand created by the new enclosures began to encourage more specialisation in land surveying and estate management. Two further consequences, dating from the time of Inigo Jones, were the gradual divergence of architecture into a separate profession and the beginnings of civil engineering — although not known as such for more than another century — as increasing trade led to calls for improved harbours, new docks, and bridges to replace medieval structures, fords and ferries. But like 'surveyor' and 'architect', the term 'engineer', derived from military use, was employed quite freely. Fine bridges were built by men using any or all of the three descriptions and, outside land management, there was indeed little distinction. The profusion of new constructional skills called for by the Industrial Revolution as it gathered pace was a long way from the intense specialisation of the twentieth century.

There were, of course, those who were less creditable, not least the parish Surveyor of Highways, originating with the 1555 Highways Act, who was elected annually. He could be the village butcher, baker or candlestick maker, but rarely was he qualified in any way for supervising the annual six days' labour on the roads extracted from his fellow parishioners. Later, the Turnpike Acts — the first one was in 1663 — empowered the appointment of full-time surveyors, some of whom were of high calibre. It all depended on the outlook of the trustees and the money available, although the competence of surveyors slowly increased, culminating in great road builders like Thomas Telford, who was appointed Surveyor of Public Works for Shropshire in 1786 and went on to build 37 bridges in that county alone, and John Loudon McAdam who became General Surveyor of the Bristol District of Roads in 1817. Again, in present-day terms they were engineers.

So the profession entered a period when the different strands of surveying moved forward, each at its own speed, twisting and untwisting as they went, through a century and a half of advancing technology. Two strands in particular led more directly than any others to the era of the railway. One, concerned with the development of the wooden wagonway and its successors, the iron tramroad and plateway, led to a permanent way designed to carry locomotives; the other, the canal system, produced the confidence and skill that went on to build the railways. A third strand, road building, required a different outlook and to some extent was less exacting in that, given proper drainage and a good surface, steep gradients could be tolerated, although some of the early railway engineers began in road work. But all three strands depended on reliable surveyors.

Wagonways and Tramroads

In the sense that it employed flanged wheels running on rails, albeit both of wood, the railway in the form of the primitive wagonway, with its crude horse-drawn trucks, preceded the canal system in Britain — not, as popularly supposed, the other way round.[6] Huntingdon Beaumont built a 2-mile wagonway sometime between

Above:
An early railway tunnel, built in 1802 to take the Ticknall Tramroad beneath the drive to Calke Abbey, Derbyshire, now a property of the National Trust. (Author)

Below:
The Haytor Granite Tramway in Devon was unusual in having track made up of granite blocks. Built in 1820, it was derelict by 1858, but much of it remains intact. (Anthony J. Lambert)

1603 and 1605, to carry coal from his pits at Wollaton and Strelley to the nearest road, where it could be transferred into carts for Nottingham and the Trent. He was active in Northumberland, too, where he seems to have built a line from Bedlington to the River Blyth in 1608, and later two more. Thereafter wooden wagonways, later overlaid with iron plates to reduce friction and wear, steadily became part of the coal industry of north-east England, providing vastly improved transport to ships and barges lying in the Tyne, the Wear and along the coast. Lines were also built in West Cumberland, West Yorkshire and Fife.

Similar developments occurred in the East Shropshire coalfield. Because many of the mines there were drifts, narrower gauge lines with smaller wagons than those in the north east enabled coal to be carried direct from the coal-face to waiting trows on the Severn. The Shropshire system created its own sphere of influence as it was steadily adopted in South Wales, probably in Lancashire and in parts of Scotland. In fact, it may be possible that a Shropshire line preceded Beaumont's, if only by a year or two, as in 1606 and again in 1608 lawsuits concerning wayleave disputes on lines from Broseley to the Severn were heard before the Star Chamber. One of these lines was operating in 1605 and the others may conceivably have been earlier.

Although, in the eyes of a Denbigh surveyor writing in 1824, these wooden railways were 'but crude and imperfect models of human ingenuity',[7] they represented a big advance from the horses and carts, pack-horses and poor local roads that had constituted land transport before.

The wayleave system was invariably used to gain passage for a wagonway across other people's land. It was a constant cause of friction between freeholders, leaseholders and wagonway owners who were either the coal-owners themselves or their lessees. It was not unknown for a dispute to lead to rails being torn up, although more often this resulted from quarrels and rivalry between owners. Arguments over wayleaves covering the criss-crossing network of wagonways on Tyneside, coupled with intense competition, led larger owners to combine into powerful groups. In some instances the Court of Chancery had to decide whether wayleaves originally granted for carts would be held to apply to wagonways that replaced them, and by 1696 many wayleave rents in the north east were so excessive that petitions were presented to Parliament in endeavours to gain relief. So common were disputes that the terms 'wayleave' and 'wagonway' became virtually synonymous.

In 1828, for example, Matthias Dunn, John Wood and Nicholas Wood advised on terms for wayleaves to be granted by the trustees of the Earl of Strathmore to Martin Pitt for just under 2 miles of wagonway from his Tanfield Moor collieries across their estate at Marley Hill, County Durham. They recommended a rent of £225 a year for the first 1,000 tons of coal, and 4s 6d (22½p) for each additional ton; colliery materials, and lime and manure for both parties' farms, should be allowed free. The lessee was to maintain gates and fences, and make no alteration to the line without the consent of the landlords, although they were to be at liberty not only to grant other wayleaves but to allow others to use Pitt's wagonway provided that he was compensated to a figure to be decided on by two independent adjudicators. At the end of the lease the land was to be restored, except for cuttings and embankments greater than 2ft.[8]

Then there were the negative wayleaves, whereby a landowner agreed to refrain from granting a wayleave to anyone other than the coal-owner paying him, which sounds little different from bribery. Wayleaves covered not only the land required for laying rails, but for drainage, bridges, earthworks and access for construction. Although Shropshire also had its disputes, the situation there was less acute: lines did not cross or encroach on others' territory; there were fewer lines anyway; and wayleaves tended to be included with mining rights that are now often difficult to distinguish.

It was Charles Brandling who, in 1758, gained parliamentary ratification of his wayleaves in 'An Act for Establishing Agreements made between Charles Brandling Esquire, and other Persons, Proprietors of Lands, for laying down a Waggonway' from his pits at Middleton to Leeds. Although it is claimed to be the first railway Act, it did not actually authorise construction, but it is interesting for the way it gave protection not only to landowners by permitting them to 'stop all waggons' if their rents were not paid within 40 days of the due date, but to the coal buyers as well by making Brandling's right of way conditional on his continuing to supply not less than the equivalent of 22,500 tons a year for 60 years at 4¾d (2p) a corf (210lb), which is about 21p per ton in modern currency.[9] Acts on other matters from time to time referred to wagonways, usually protecting existing rights, such as certain Tyneside turnpike Acts that prohibited obstruction of wagonways at level crossings, and also empowered the laying of new wagonways alongside or across them.

The ideal wagonway alignment fell gradually on an even gradient from colliery to staith or wharf, which, of course, was rarely possible without earthworks. Northern lines were usually double track, and it was not uncommon for the downward or 'loaded' way to take a separate course from the uphill or 'empty' way. Downhill, steep gradients or 'runs' were not considered obstacles; the horse was unhitched and allowed to follow the wagon which ran down by gravity under the control of the brakesman, a proceeding not without a generous crop of disasters. Uphill, a gradient easy enough for a horse to haul an empty wagon was necessary, and its route might actually cross the downhill way. Shropshire wagonways were the first to use self-acting inclines, on which the weight of a descending loaded wagon pulled the empty one up on a rope and pulley. It was not until the early nineteenth century that they became common in the north east, when many earlier lines were realigned.

The first use of wholly iron rails laid on stone blocks in the early 1790s spread in two forms: the edge-rail, forerunner of the modern rail, on which flanged wheels ran — generally called tramroads; and the L-section plate-rail used on plateways — also sometimes called tramroads — which accepted flat-tyred wagons or, in theory, ordinary carts provided the gauge was right. The widespread adoption of the plateway, particularly in South Wales and the Midlands, was almost entirely due to Benjamin Outram, a canal engineer. However, it eventually proved to be a dead-end technology and fell into disuse after the opening of the Stockton & Darlington Railway in 1825, which used edge-rails. Even so, plateways in Shropshire were still being extended in the mid-nineteenth century, and the last working one elsewhere, serving the Peak Forest Canal at Buxworth, was not abandoned until 1925. The edge-railed tramroad prevailed in the north east and Cumberland as the wooden wagonways were replaced.

Little appears to have been recorded about the laying out of the early wagonways. The first English textbook on railways appeared in 1797. John Curr, in his *Coal Viewer's and Engine Builder's Practical Companion*, describes and illustrates the setting out of curves, which he calls 'turns', but otherwise makes no allusion to surveying the line. By this time, of course, wagonways were common in the coalfields and iron rails were coming into use. Experience in more accurate surveying had been gained in the first phase of canal construction, so doubtless Curr took it for granted that there was no need for further explanation, and no doubt Benjamin Outram did the same when he wrote his *Minutes to be observed in the Construction of Railways*, first publicly produced in 1801.

Nearly twenty-five years later Nicholas Wood's *Practical Treatise on Rail Roads*, first published in 1825, despite a lament for 'The want of practical information, on the subject of Railroads', is equally silent on the same subject. Wood's book was the first really comprehensive work detailing the construction and operation of railways and locomotives, including a history of railways up to that time. He is, however, critical of the early wagonway builders for what he avers was lack of care in levelling

Primitive wagons standing on iron plate rails laid on stone sleeper blocks on the Little Eaton Gangway, a 6-mile wagonway which ran from Little Eaton on the Derby Canal, seen in the background, to collieries and works at Denby from 1795 to 1908.
(National Railway Museum)

the surface. Casual undulations were levelled, he says, but the 'general line does not appear to have been laid out, with a view to obtaining the best gradients for the road which the country afforded.' As time went on, awkward alignments and steep gradients were eased. By 1750 in the north east a falling gradient of 1 in 10 was considered to be the maximum permissible for laden wagons, and 1 in 30 for the returning empties.[10] The wagonway from the Caldon Low limestone quarries in north Staffordshire down to the branch of the Trent & Mersey Canal at Froghall was rebuilt twice. Authorised in a canal Act of 1776, it was not satisfactory, being described as 'set out, before the true principles of this branch of Engineery was well understood, and was very crooked, steep and uneven . . .'[11] A new line was authorised in 1783 and built by Hugh Henshall, brother-in-law of the canal pioneer James Brindley, but was little better, and it was left to John Rennie in 1803 to lay out an iron plateway with five self-acting inclines. It worked until 1849 when the North Staffordshire Railway, which had bought the canal, replaced it for the fourth time with a narrow gauge railway with cable-operated inclines which remained in use until 1920.[12]

Wood goes on to comment that 'the disposition of the general line of the road, into proper or uniform degrees of inclination, seems then to have been of little moment', but to some extent qualifies his remarks by saying that 'In some deep ravines, mounds of earth were thrown up, and some sudden and abrupt acclivities partially levelled; but trifling undulations do not appear to have been noticed.' About 1819, George Hill and George Stephenson reported on the Garesfield wagonway, which was still of wood — and continued to be until at least 1843 — winding its way over 4½ miles down to the Tyne at Derwenthaugh, 'dipping sharply in some places and gently in others'. 'After taking an accurate survey of the line of way and ascertaining with precision all the various levels with which it abounds', they recommended inclined planes at the two steepest places. The rest of it down to about 2 miles from the river was 'too crooked and irregular' to make improvement an economic proposition, but the final section had a gradient of only 1/50th of an inch per yard (1 in 1,800) — evidence of their accurate levelling — and, significantly, was 'well adapted for a Locomotive Engine'.[13]

Despite such deficiences, some of the earlier wagonways do appear to have been somewhat better surveyed and engineered than Wood suggests. A number of Tyneside lines had substantial embankments and cuttings, most had minor earthworks up to 3ft high or deep, and some employed a form of timber trestle to cross ravines. The Tanfield wagonway of 1725, one of the longest which eventually extended for more than 8 miles from the Tyne across the watershed and into County Durham, included the greatest earthworks. Near Beamish a massive embankment, nearly 100ft high, led to the celebrated Causey Arch, completed probably in 1726 and the oldest surviving railway bridge in the world, which at 105ft had for 30 years the longest single span. As one would expect, the coming of the canals, with their more sophisticated constructional requirements, led to engineering works becoming more common on their feeder tramroads and plateways, including bridges and several short tunnels. The 24-mile-long Sirhowy Tramroad in South Wales, one of the longest in an area noted for lengthy lines running down the valleys, had a 36-arch viaduct 40-50ft high at Risca.

The Canal Men

The canals needed much greater precision in surveying and levelling, although the promoters did not always get it and many a canal surveyor was blamed for having 'lost his level' when things went wrong, while some were downright careless. However, in the frantic scramble to deposit parliamentary Bills in time during the two big canal booms, it was hardly surprising that some surveying was inadequate; this failing was to be repeated in the later railway manias. Geology was one of the greatest problems; the most careful survey and trial borings could still miss faults, pockets of loose material, unsuspected rock or springs of water that played havoc with costs when they delayed construction, particularly in excavating and tunnelling. Surveyors also found themselves checking the works of colleagues and rivals, commonly when arguments arose among proprietors over the best route to be followed. In 1796, for instance, Robert Whitworth, then Brindley's assistant, found an error of as much as 35ft in levels taken by two Lancashire surveyors employed by a group of dissident investors in the Leeds & Liverpool Canal.[14]

How were surveys carried out? Following William Roy's triangulation of south-east England, which was linked to one made by the French on the other side of the Channel, the first one-inch Ordnance Survey map, covering Kent, was published privately in 1801, but the whole country was not covered until 1852. Before then there were some fairly accurate maps, like the work of Henry Beighton, a land surveyor from Nuneaton, who produced a one-inch map of Warwickshire in 1720, and Thomas Martyn's of Cornwall in 1748. But they were not more generally available until later in the century, and then by no means uniformly or comprehensively. The scale was rarely larger than one inch to the mile, and the topographical detail was at best sketchy, so they could act only as a rough guide and there were still large areas of the country that were not properly mapped at all. Consequently, we are left with Brindley's 'ochiler servey or a recconitoring' from which to picture our surveyor setting off on horseback to seek out a possible route, moving back and forth to confirm an initial impression or resolve uncertain features before committing a preliminary line to paper. Such expeditions required above all a good eye for country. Once the line's feasibility was established, Brindley and his fellows then left the detailed surveys to assistants, usually established land surveyors and perhaps local men who had assisted with preliminary information. When in 1800 William Jessop was appointed engineer to the Surrey Iron Railway, which despite its name was a plateway, John Foakes and George Wildgoose were appointed land surveyors to carry out detailed surveys and assist in giving parliamentary evidence.[15]

Because canals were far more permanent and built on a much larger scale than the wagonways, the old system of negotiating wayleaves clearly was no longer a practicable means of gaining right of way. The land needed had to be purchased outright, compulsorily if need be, powers for which could be gained only by Act of Parliament. Canal building was therefore preceded by the floating of a company statutorily authorised to raise capital and purchase land, establishing a pattern that, as we shall see in chapters 2 and 4, became standard practice for railway companies. It was not until 1774 that Parliament required deposited plans to accompany Bills; before then less detailed drawings sufficed.

Once an Act was obtained and agreements to purchase land concluded, the line of the canal could be staked out and cutting commenced. Tunnelling created some of the most difficult problems, for which miners were employed. The course was staked out over the hill and shafts dug at intervals of approximately 150yd. From a string across the top of the shaft in line with the direction of the canal, two plumb bobs were lowered to the level of the tunnel and there connected by a string parallel with the one on the surface, thereby indicating the direction below ground. The required depth from the surface was marked on the wall at the foot of the shaft. While headings sometimes failed to meet exactly, on the whole the method worked well. In building Strood Tunnel on the Thames & Medway Canal, later converted into a railway tunnel and still in use, an astronomer's transit telescope was used, probably for the first time in Britain, mounted in an observatory from which the whole of the tunnel's 3,931yd length could be viewed overland.[16]

The men who surveyed and built the wagonways, the tramroads and the canals had backgrounds as varied as the promoters who employed them. Of the seventeenth-century wagonway builders we know least, beyond that usually they were colliery engineers, or 'viewers' as they were called. In the north east it was customary for the larger coal-owners to employ a 'master waggonway wright' who would build lines as cheaply as possible consistent with economical operation. In other cases, tenders would be sought from wrights at a price per yard or for an overall sum. The coal-owner would decide on the general route and negotiate wayleaves, after which the wright would make a sufficiently detailed survey to be able to stake out the line. Three such men were Francis Baker, Ralph Fetherston and Albany Baker, wagonway wrights employed by prominent coal-owners in the north east who also did work elsewhere and acted as consultants.[17]

The first iron tramroads and plateways were regarded as adjuncts to canals, less expensive and quicker to construct than a branch waterway, and the canal engineers laid them out. It was the canal era that led to the profession of civil engineering, as distinct from military engineering, becoming formally recognised when the Society of Civil Engineers first met under John Smeaton's chairmanship in 1771. The original membership was broadly based and included names already well known, like John Rennie, James Watt and William Jessop, alongside lesser known local men who were employed by canal companies as resident engineers, surveyors and consultants. Smeaton himself, the most eminent engineer of his day, was concerned with a number of river improvement schemes to aid navigation. Several of the early members were established surveyors: John Grundy and John Watté, for instance, called themselves land surveyors and were prominently engaged in fen drainage;

Joseph Hodskinson, who by 1767 was one of the best land surveyors in England, graduated to civil engineering on harbour and coastal works; and George Young twice surveyed the River Severn.[18] Other land surveyors and valuers were employed by canal companies for the purchase of land, as on parts of the Kennet & Avon Canal under Rennie. George Brown of Elgin carried out all the valuations and negotiations for the Caledonian Canal.[19]

James Watt, popularly associated with the steam engine, was a mathematical instrument maker who took up surveying and supervised the construction of canals in Scotland. He made the first survey for the Caledonian Canal and planned a wooden wagonway from the Monkland Canal to Glasgow, although it was not built. Robert Stevenson, grandfather of the novelist Robert Louis Stevenson, laid out extensive tramroads and, later, railways in Scotland. The greatest of the canal engineers, William Jessop, who also laid out many miles of tramroad and plateway, was a pupil of Smeaton and a son of a foreman shipwright. Other eminent engineers came from similar backgrounds of practical craftsmanship, like Telford, who was a stonemason, and Rennie who was apprenticed to a millwright, a craft followed by Joseph Nickolls, who became General Surveyor to the River Thames Commissioners, and by the so-called 'Father of the Canal System', James Brindley.[20]

The millwright's occupation covered all the skills needed in designing and building water-powered mills, including not only the ability to work in wood, brick, stone and iron, but to plot artificial watercourses, which included taking accurate levels and constructing earthworks. The popular conception of Brindley as untutored and virtually illiterate has been disproved by the examples of his notes, plans and calculations in C.T.G. Boucher's *James Brindley, Engineer, 1716-1772*, published in 1968, which clearly show that Brindley was a skilled surveyor. Certainly no unlettered journeyman could have conceived and built the ingenious Wet Earth Colliery water-power system near Manchester in 1752. Conversely, it has been shown that Brindley's role in building the pioneer Bridgewater Canal was more as consultant and as an advocate in Parliament, for he was a persuasive orator. The survey and construction work was mostly supervised by the Duke of Bridgewater's land agent, John Gilbert, while overall supervision was in the hands of the duke himself.[21].

The canal boom produced many such men. Brindley's pupil, Robert Whitworth, was referred to after his death as 'one of the most able engineers in England',[22] and there were many more. In 1794 John Longbotham, who had surveyed and supervised the initial construction of the Leeds & Liverpool Canal, advertised himself for canal survey work at three guineas per day, plus expenses. 'He has men, good surveyors and levellers, very capable of taking the survey of canals, which he charges as common surveyors, and staff holders, exclusive of expenses.'[23] So we can see that many surveyors used their skills to move into the increasingly important world of civil engineering where they shaped its destiny for the next century; others preferred to remain land surveyors, some in independent practice where they

Laigh Milton Viaduct is thought to be the oldest surviving railway viaduct in the world. Seen here in 1987, it carried the Kilmarnock & Troon Railway, a wagonway opened in 1812, across the River Irvine. Scotland's first passenger line, it was converted to a locomotive railway in 1846 and the line diverted, since when the viaduct has been disused. (Author)

engaged in lucrative valuation work for canal companies, others content to stick to their chains and staffs and take employment under their more exalted brethren. One man had a career of such extraordinary diversity in canals, tramroads and railways that it puts him apart from the rest. William James, lawyer, land surveyor, engineer, promoter and, above all, visionary, will be considered in chapter 3.

A good number of the wagonways and tramroads were forerunners of the railways in the literal sense, being acquired later by railway companies for conversion or, in the case of colliery lines, modernised by their owners, although the original courses frequently required modification. Sharp curves and steep gradients had to be eased to take full-sized track capable of being used by locomotives, leaving isolated fragments of the original formation to return to nature. By tracing these courses the work of their builders can be appreciated, identified perhaps by a footpath curving along the contour of a hillside in true canal fashion, a tell-tale shallow embankment or cutting, the line of a double hedge that seemingly has no purpose, the course of a grassy incline running straight up a steep slope, or perhaps by a bridge. A row of half-buried stone sleeper blocks provides even more tangible evidence, together with more monumental structures like the Causey Arch that is now restored and protected, and the two bridges on the Penydarren Tramroad in South Wales, or in need of restoration like the four-arched Laigh Milton Viaduct on the Kilmarnock & Troon Railway, probably the oldest surviving railway viaduct in the world and dating from 1812. The southern portal of the Peak Forest Tramroad's 100yd tunnel can still be seen near Chapel-en-le-Frith in north Derbyshire, as can the whole of the shorter one made to keep the Ticknall Tramroad out of sight where it crossed the drive to Calke Abbey in the south of the same county. Here and there a name is perpetuated. Tram Inn was a station on the Great Western Railway between Hereford and Abergavenny, a line partly built on the site of an earlier plateway and still recorded by the name of a signal-box. There is a Tramway Path in Mitcham marking the course of the Surrey Iron Railway, and an Old Tram Bridge at Preston which, although rebuilt, is on the site of a bridge that carried a plateway connecting the two portions of the Lancaster Canal. Not far away is Outram Close, a misnomer because it was not he but Jessop who was consulted on the line; the latter's name is properly perpetuated in Jessop Place, also at Mitcham. Wherever they are found, these early remains are memorials to the foresight, skill and resolution of the men who laid them out and, in so doing, founded the principles for building the modern railway.

The substantial remains of a tramroad that ran from the Leeds & Liverpool Canal at Skipton, North Yorkshire, to Haw Bank quarry, passing through this cutting and short tunnel alongside the Harrogate road. Seen here in 1968, it has since been filled in for road widening. (Author)

Chapter 2

Promoting a Railway

The System Grows

Two events, five years apart, marked the transition from tramroads to railways. The first was the opening of the Stockton & Darlington Railway in 1825, on which locomotives were first used to operate regular public services, albeit not throughout and, for some years, only for freight. Nevertheless, the Stockton & Darlington proved the reliability of the steam engine in everyday use. The opening of the Liverpool & Manchester Railway in 1830 was an even more important landmark, not in a particularly innovative way but for its combination of four characteristics that, above all others, introduced the age of the railway: mechanical traction on all trains; more elaborate and massive civil engineering works than any before, that have required remarkably little modification to this day; complete control of traction and traffic; and an objective common to all three — speed. The Liverpool & Manchester's double track connected two great trading centres with the prime intention of providing cheaper, faster and more reliable transport than the canals. In short, it was the first main line. Its success was immediate. Moreover, it sparked off railway promotion that by 1844 had provided Great Britain with over 2,000 miles of route, a figure that in 1852 had risen to 7,500 and by the end of the century was some 22,000 miles, by which time there were few countries in the world without railways.

Within 15 years of the Liverpool & Manchester's opening, lines radiated from London to Exeter, Lancaster, Gateshead, Leeds, Nottingham, Great Yarmouth, Colchester, Dover, Brighton and Southampton, while Derby was linked to Birmingham and Bristol, Liverpool and Manchester with Leeds, Sheffield and Hull, and Newcastle with Carlisle. They were built piecemeal. Only five British railway companies authorised by individual Acts of Parliament built 100 miles or more of continuous line: the London & Birmingham incorporated in 1833, the Great Western in 1835, the South Wales Railway of 1845, the Great Northern, 1846, and the Inverness & Perth Junction Railway between Dunkeld and Forres, authorised in 1861. The West Highland of 1889, from Craigendoran to Fort William pier, was just 8 chains short of 100 miles. But far-sighted men visualised a national network and, eventually, through a process of amalgamation, the great trunk routes emerged. Even so, when it came to forming four large groups under the 1921 Transport Act, there were still over 140 separate railway companies, out of which only 19 had more than 100 miles of route. Of the others, about 70 were leased or operated by larger companies as part of their own systems, and when the Act came into force on 1 January 1923 some two dozen minor railways were still left out.

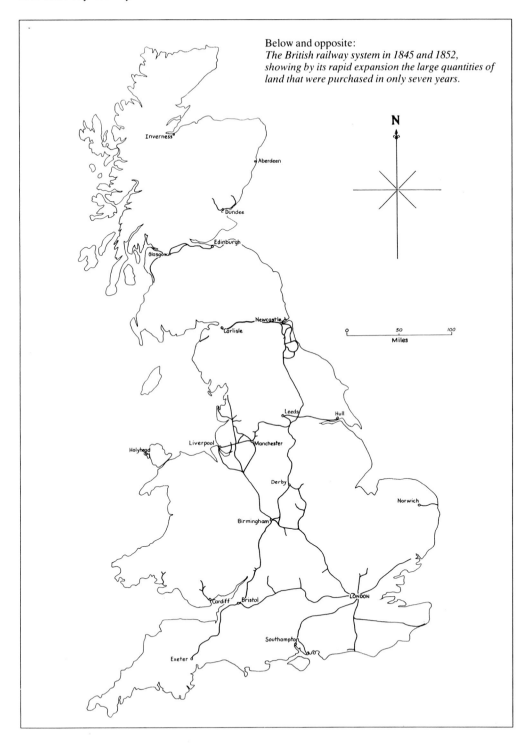

Below and opposite:
*The British railway system in 1845 and 1852,
showing by its rapid expansion the large quantities of
land that were purchased in only seven years.*

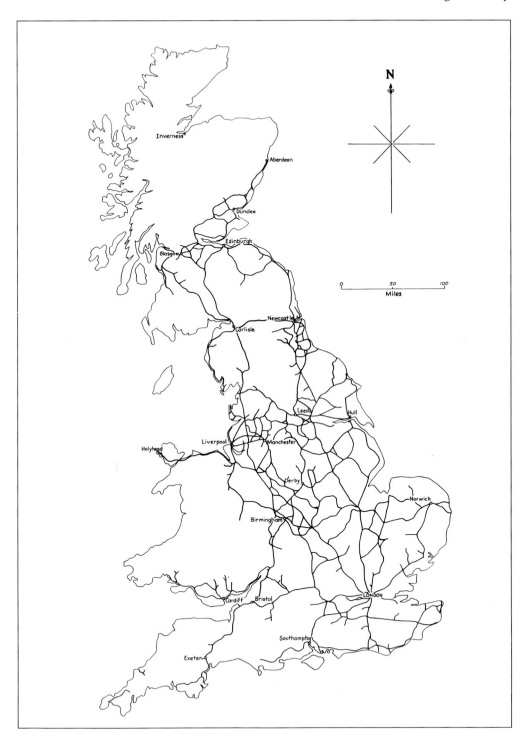

The initial boom in railway promotion was over by 1837, followed by a period of relative calm until 1844 when the Railway Mania gripped the country, a great surge of reckless speculation, much of it in spurious 'paper' companies intended to create nothing more than a quick profit, that ended with the financial crisis of October 1847. A third but smaller boom occurred in 1864-6, by which time most of the trunk lines were established. Thereafter, with some important exceptions, new construction was devoted to infilling lines and to opening up the remoter parts of Scotland and Wales.

The Promoters

Who promoted the railways, seeing a need, putting up money and persuading others to do likewise? No single category of people was responsible, although some, through position, wealth or technical expertise, played leading roles. The first, short lines were promoted by local businessmen anxious to secure improved transport to the nearest market or port, like the Stockton & Darlington promoters led by the Quaker Edward Pease, a Darlington merchant and banker, or the Leicestershire coal-owner William Stenson who, having observed the Stockton & Darlington's success, saw a railway to Leicester as the means of developing his new colliery at Whitwick. With two Leicester surveyors, Samuel Smith Harris and John Whetstone, a suitable route was found. The three then approached John Ellis, a prominent landowner who, after consulting George Stephenson, then working on the Liverpool & Manchester, realised the opportunities and chaired a meeting of local manufacturers, merchants and bankers at which it was decided to promote a railway. Thus was the Leicester & Swannington Railway formed in 1829. A company was incorporated in the following year.

A large proportion of the Stockton & Darlington's capital came from London, as it did for other railways. Liverpool men far outnumbered Mancunians in promoting the Liverpool & Manchester, and went on to play a dominant role in the financial affairs of the Grand Junction Railway, the London & Birmingham and many others; even the little Leicester & Swannington obtained about a third of its capital from the 'Liverpool Party'. Prosperous Norwich, too, provided a frequent source of railway capital. But as a network began to take shape, railways increasingly were regarded as a profitable speculation by a growing part of the investing public. The amalgamations and consolidation that followed the 1844-7 Mania created larger companies, each with a territory it regarded as its own, to be jealously guarded against predatory competitors after a share of the traffic. By the end of the 1840s the railways were very big business indeed.

As well as local men and the London and provincial business communities, a growing number of large landowners saw the advantages that railways conferred on their estates. Not all were by any means as bitterly opposed to railways as has been popularly supposed. A smaller but important category of promoter was the railway contractor. Having assembled a large work-force during the boom periods, he was anxious to keep it together, and when the great initial period of construction was

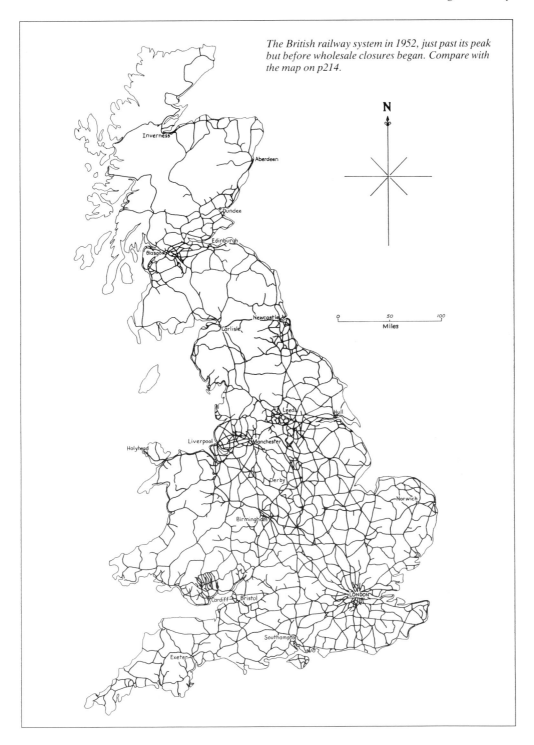

The British railway system in 1952, just past its peak but before wholesale closures began. Compare with the map on p214.

N

0   50   100
Miles

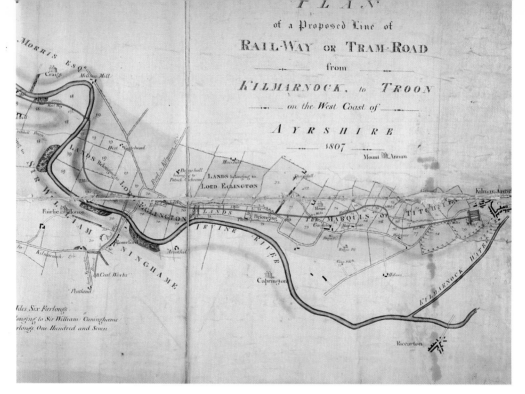

Above:

One of the earliest railways to be constructed under an Act of Parliament was the Kilmarnock & Troon, authorised in 1808 and in essence a horse tramroad. Here a portion of the deposited parliamentary plan of 1807 shows on the left the site of Laigh Milton Viaduct where the line crosses the River Irvine (see p17). (BR Property Board)

Below:

The Caledonian Railway's land plan of Newtonhill station, on the East Coast main line where it runs close to the sea between Montrose and Aberdeen, is a fine example of the Victorians' attention to detail, even where it does not affect the railway. (BR Property Board)

over, particularly in the 1860s, railway promotion was a means of securing work. Using a local company as a front, the great contractor Thomas Brassey bought the land, provided the materials and paid the men who built the Portsmouth Railway, a more direct line from London than the competing routes of the London & South Western and the London, Brighton & South Coast companies, between which it ran. Knowing that he could sell it to one or the other when it was finished — or even to the rival South Eastern, which neither of them would want to happen — after wheeling and dealing Brassey leased the line to the South Western, immediately setting off a bitter quarrel with the Brighton which was finally settled by legal action. David Davies and Thomas Savin promoted and built much of the railway system of central Wales and the border country, providing capital that was not otherwise available in such thinly populated areas. Contractors frequently provided resources for lines that were under-financed or unable to raise money in any other way, like the London, Tilbury & Southend which the partnership of Peto, Brassey & Betts not only built but operated under lease for the first 21 years. Contractors also accepted payment in shares rather than lose a job; much of the London, Chatham & Dover Railway was built by this method.

The engineers themselves promoted lines, too, not necessarily directly but by influencing business interests, at first by advocating a railway instead of a canal, as George Stephenson did with the Stockton & Darlington provisional committee, William Chapman on the Newcastle & Carlisle and Josias Jessop, younger son of William, on the Cromford & High Peak Railway. As railways gained acceptance, the engineers actively promoted routes they had surveyed with parties whom they felt were receptive to their ideas. Engineers were equally partisan with regard to the question of gauge: the Stephensons, father and son, in foreseeing that eventually there would be a country-wide network, ceaselessly campaigned for a uniform gauge — their own, of 4ft 8½in, which eventually became standard. I.K. Brunel had ambitions for his 7ft broad gauge railway into the West Country and South Wales, far beyond the Great Western's original terminus at Bristol. He succeeded, although at the heavy cost of later conversion.

Joseph Locke envisaged a grand trunk line from London to Glasgow, Edinburgh and Aberdeen and, northwards from Birmingham, surveyed and built most of it with his partner John Errington. In the Scottish Highlands the great visionary was Joseph Mitchell. The lines north from Perth to Inverness and beyond, and eastward to Keith, owed their construction to him. He planned their routes, gathered support and supervised much of the work. He also promoted the Scottish Central, south of Perth, and so confident was he that he offered to survey for nothing, provided he was appointed the engineer if a Bill was passed. It was, but unfortunately for him the job went to Locke.

Lastly, existing railway companies promoted extensions and branches, either directly or through quasi-independent companies. An example of this method was the London & Birmingham's branch from Bletchley to Bedford, promoted under the name of the Bedford Railway. Its Act of 1845 included provisions for the London &

Birmingham to buy the land, build the line and then vest it in the larger company when it was finished. More generally, however, a smaller company would go through the procedure of independent promotion and obtain an Act containing provisions to sell or lease its line to a larger company when construction was complete. The latter would contribute considerable legal and engineering expertise and, as often as not, a slice of the capital. Conversely, a number of branch lines were promoted purely on local initiative with the express intention of eventually persuading a larger neighbour to either buy or lease the undertaking or, at worst, assume responsibility for working it in exchange for a percentage of the receipts. If there was a competitor in the neighbourhood, so much the better. One could be played off against the other.

The Prospectus

While preliminary meetings and discussions were taking place, a surveyor or engineer was engaged to establish a feasible route for the proposed line. His report outlined a possible course and pointed out the physical characteristics or, if there were alternatives, stated the advantages and disadvantages of each. This preliminary survey was often somewhat cursory, made by plotting a line on a map and exploring it on horseback and on foot, sometimes accompanied by one or more of the promoters. An experienced man with a good eye could gain enough information in this way to produce a fairly comprehensive report, including a provisional estimate of cost and, often, useful data on potential traffic. Some railway engineers, after experience, preferred to act as consultants, sometimes to more than one railway at a time, following the practice of men like Rennie and Telford in the canal era; others wanted full responsibility without interference from elsewhere. Brunel, characteristically, refused anything but sole control. Robert Stephenson, on the other hand, in 1847 was consultant to six companies.

Once the decision was reached to go ahead and seek wider support, a public meeting was called, a provisional committee formed and subscription lists opened to defray the considerable costs of establishing traffic estimates, making detailed surveys, canvassing property owners and undertaking the legal work entailed in making an application to Parliament. At the same time a prospectus was issued setting out the promoters' case.

Promoters of the earlier railways went to considerable trouble to obtain information for their estimates of revenue. Anticipation of goods traffic came from the tonnages carried by canal and the numbers of carts on local roads, and the proportions that could be expected to transfer to rail, together with consignments promised by merchants and mineral owners who would benefit from improved transport. Passenger volume was based on the numbers travelling by road, broken down between stage-coach traffic and users of posting carriages, gigs, carts, vans and horseback, but ignoring those on foot who, presumably, were considered to be either making only short journeys or too poor to travel by any other means. Passenger estimates produced to support the first Great Western Railway Bill of

THE

North Midland Railway,

UNITING

LONDON WITH SHEFFIELD, LEEDS,

AND THE

MANUFACTURING DISTRICTS OF YORKSHIRE.

Capital, £1,250,000, in Shares of £100 each.—Deposit, £5 per Share.

LONDON PROVISIONAL COMMITTEE.

RALPH FENWICK, ESQ.	FREDERICK HUTH, ESQ.
THOMAS FRENCH, ESQ.	WILLIAM LEAF, ESQ.
GEORGE CARR GLYN, ESQ.	WILLIAM LITTLE, ESQ.
KIRKMAN HODGSON, ESQ.	JAMES MORRISON, ESQ., M.P.
WILLIAM HOOD, ESQ.	JOHN PICKERSGILL, ESQ.

Bankers.

LONDON........ MESSRS. GLYN, HALLIFAX, MILLS AND CO.
LEEDS ....MESSRS. BECKETT, BLAYDS & CO.

Solicitors.

MESSRS. SWAIN, STEVENS, AND CO., *No. 6, Fredericks Place, Old Jewry, London.*
CHARLES PARKER, ESQ., *No. 39, Bedford Row, London.*

Engineer.

GEORGE STEPHENSON, ESQ.

SINCE the superiority of Railways over every other means of communication has been fully established, and recognized by the Legislature in the adoption of the London and Birmingham, the Grand Junction, the Great Western, and other long lines of Railway, the advisability of extending to the North of England the benefits anticipated from those undertakings has been universally felt and acknowledged.

A Company having already been established for the purpose of constructing a Railway, from the London and Birmingham Railway, at or near Rugby, to Derby, it is the object of the present Company to extend that Line from the latter place as far as Leeds, passing through a most populous and highly important manufacturing district, and either touching upon, or approaching within, an easy distance of the towns of Chesterfield, Rotherham, Sheffield, Barnsley, Wakefield, Huddersfield, Halifax, Bradford, and Leeds, comprehending a population not inferior to the manufacturing districts of Lancashire.

It will be apparent to any one who examines the Map of England, that this line, in combination with the Midland and London and Birmingham Railways, must form the main channel for the traffic of the North to London :

Prospectus for the North Midland Railway, authorised in 1836 to construct the line from Derby to Leeds.
(Courtesy R. Dean)

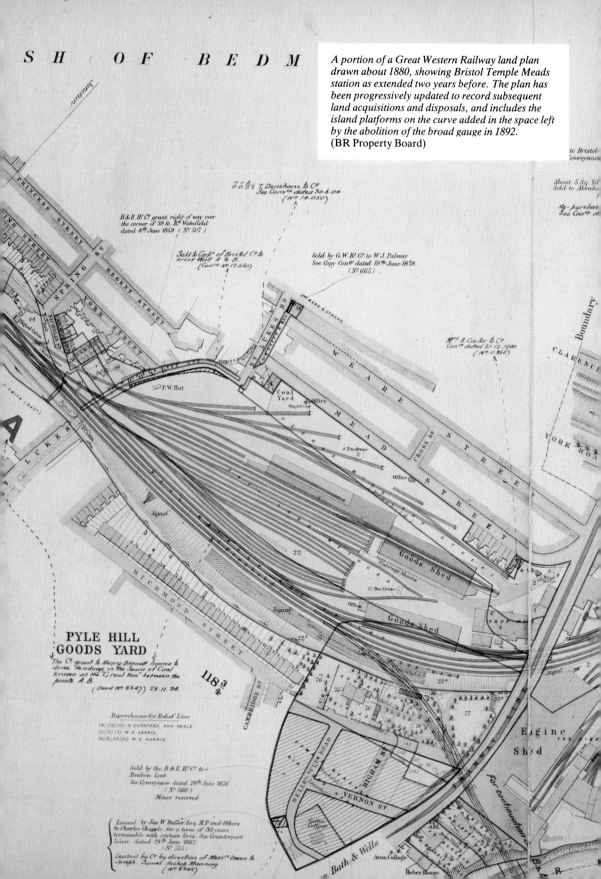

S H   O F   B E D M

A portion of a Great Western Railway land plan drawn about 1880, showing Bristol Temple Meads station as extended two years before. The plan has been progressively updated to record subsequent land acquisitions and disposals, and includes the island platforms on the curve added in the space left by the abolition of the broad gauge in 1892.
(BR Property Board)

PYLE HILL
GOODS YARD

PARISH OF TEMPLE
OR HOLY CROSS

From Bathurst Basin

Sold by G.W.R? C? to the
Mayor, Aldermen and Burgesses of Bristol
See Conveyance dated 14th May 1878
(4781)
7sh of J.C.Wall with right of way over
land coloured Red. (N? 11.312)

M?s E. Day & C?
See Con?s dated 9.10.01
(N? 12.275)

M?s E.M. Wooles & or?s
(N? 11.947)

RIDER LANE

FORTESQUE AND OTHERS
(Leasehold)

Goods Shed

BATH PARADE

APPROACH ROAD

MIDLAND DEPARTURE PLATFORM

G.W.R
General Offices

Booking
Hall
etc.

Refreshment
Rooms

Fish

HARBOUR

PARISH OF ST. PHILLIP & JACOB WITHOUT

118 Miles

To London

APPROACH ROAD

CATTLE MARKET

Cab Shed

Hotel

Bristol
Cattle Market

FLOATING

Smithy

Pumping
House

a.r.p
0.2.25 Sold by the G.W.R? C? to
Cattle Market Trustees April 13th 1839
and repurchased by B & E.R? C? in 1861
a portion being again Sold in June '76
(Deed N? 9004)

G.W.R C? grant to the Bedminster
Right to work All the Vein or Seam
known as the "Great Vein" under
Yellow.   0.2.32
See Licence dated 21.4.18
(N? 10.265)

B

Works

118½

NEW LOCK

Boundary

Land given up by the B & E.R? to the
Cattle Market Trustees in exchange for
land taken for Road from B to A
See Con?e dated 24th June 1876
626?

PARISH OF ST. PHILLIP

6 Sq.yds Conveyed to G.W.R. from
Mess?s S.V.Hare & C.B.Hare reserving
right of access to Spring by means of
Culvert formed by C? under land hatched
Blue.   (Con?e N? 8945)

See new Survey Vol

1834 gave figures of posting to Bath, Swindon, Slough and West Drayton as well as between London and Bristol, aggregating 544,352 miles of travel per week, accompanied by a similar breakdown of merchandise and cattle shipped by road, river, canal and sea that the railway expected to abstract.[1]

John Higgins, surveyor and land agent of Alford, in 1846 provided a comprehensive report on prospective agricultural traffic for the East Lincolnshire Railway. He divided the county into three districts and based his figures on seven principal categories of goods: wheat, spring corn, sheep, fat beasts, wool, bones and oil cake, with the addition of lime and chalk from the southern district. He set out the acreage and population of every parish, but does not appear to have hazarded a figure for passenger traffic which, in a predominantly agricultural area, perhaps was prudent.[2]

The promoters of the Kendal & Windermere Railway stated that in the twelve months from November 1843, 5,934 people travelled between Kendal and Bowness or Ambleside in posting vehicles or on horseback, 3,375 in private carriages and 3,755 by the Whitehaven Mail and *Mazeppa* stage-coaches. Nearly 50 carts a day, excluding coal, lime and public carriers, used the road during one week in November 1844, the worst part of the year, all of which were considered to be potential customers for the railway.[3] Some promoters felt they could justifiably enhance the figures to allow for extra traffic generated by the railway once it was open, like the Birmingham & Gloucester that first doubled its passenger estimates and then tripled them, which proved riskily over-optimistic.[4] The Clitheroe Junction Railway's figures, taken around 1845, were remarkably detailed, contained in a leather-bound, embossed volume with printed headings, as many as 39 routes being observed in a relatively small area.[5] Even the little Bridport Railway employed persons in February 1855 to check traffic through gates on three roads leading into the town and goods imported through the harbour,[6] and the promoters of the Helston Railway in Cornwall produced some quite elaborate calculations to support their conclusion that existing traffic by road would, on a railway, give a 5 per cent return on capital, after expenses.[7]

Not all estimates were so carefully based, particularly during the Mania. The prospectus of the highly improbable Dorking, Brighton & Arundel Atmospheric Railway, while admitting that so far it had no idea of revenue, was quite confident that from an estimate of existing traffic 'a very large income' would be realised.[8] It was typical Mania phraseology, yet the financial collapse that ended it did not crush speculative ardour for long. In 1853 the flamboyantly named North & South Wales Railway thought it perfectly adequate merely to say that 'The promoters are in possession of accurate statistics as to the traffic, and after a very careful estimate it may be fairly stated that . . . a remunerative dividend will be secured', which was just as well for a prospectus that, on examination, turned out to be for a line from Llanidloes, Montgomeryshire, across the Cambrian Mountains to Lampeter in remotest Cardigan.[9] There were hundreds of other equally valueless prospectuses issued for schemes that in many cases got no further.

Extracts from the survey report were written into the more reputable prospectuses, although, as the Mania gained hold and wildcat schemes proliferated, survey information, too, became increasingly sketchy. 'No particular engineering difficulties are anticipated' was a stock phrase that glossed over many an impracticable route. Surveys for the most unlikely of railways often comprised little more than a line drawn on a map, or at best a quick scurry over the country. Indeed, there is evidence that when competition was particularly intense plans were somehow 'leaked' to rivals who copied them, maybe added or deleted a few minor details, and passed them off as their own. Similarly, plans rejected a year or two earlier were resurrected and presented as up-to-date surveys.[10] In such times of frantic activity, with large sums at stake and scruples easily subverted, deception was not difficult.

The Parliamentary Process
Once the decision had been taken to secure an Act of Parliament, the embryonic railway turned into something more substantial. As was the case in canal building, the need for a Private Act, with the heavy expense of obtaining it, arose primarily from the necessity to acquire powers of compulsory purchase. Private agreements with landowners were impossibly difficult on other than the very shortest of lines, and even then were rare, generally limited to a line built by a landowner for his own purposes, such as J.T. Treffry's of Fowey to develop the mineral resources of his large Cornish estate, which included the remarkable ten-arch viaduct, 98ft high, across the Luxulyan valley, finished in 1842 and still standing. The negotiation of wayleaves was an equally unsatisfactory method, giving little security and by now outmoded outside north-east England. To safeguard fully a railway's operations and the subscribers' capital, it was essential to own the freehold of the land on which the railway was to run (although there were a few instances of leases), and an Act was the only way to gain it. Canal, turnpike, dock, water and other public undertakings had long needed statutory authority in order to operate successfully, and it was the same with railways.

In return for the power to purchase, Parliament demanded a measure of control, by setting tolls and charges, giving protection to landowners and occupiers, laying down the method of settling disputes and, as time went on, assembling rules for the conduct of railway finances and management.

Once the prospectus was published and subscriptions started coming in, parliamentary procedure took control, following the same course as that for canals. In fact, the Commons Committee on Standing Orders in 1830 ruled that railway Bills should be treated as canal Bills. Parliament, ever jealous of its privileges, insisted that its intricate procedure should be followed to the letter. Normally a railway Bill was introduced into the House of Commons rather than the Lords. A petition couched in accepted parliamentary form was presented, usually by a local MP, seeking leave to deposit a Bill. Here lay the first of four hurdles to be overcome by the promoters: satisfying the House that its standing orders were being fully observed. Commons standing orders, in the words of a contemporary handbook, threw 'a protecting shield around the property and rights of every individual which the compulsory powers of the Bill may assail . . . to enable Parliament to adjudicate on its public utility'.[11] This 'shield' was designed to ensure that the public had been informed of the promoters' intentions by inserting notices in the *London Gazette* or the *Edinburgh Gazette* and local newspapers in August, September and October or November immediately preceding the Parliamentary session. A copy of the Bill, with plans and sections of the line to a scale of 3in to the mile had, by 30 November, to be deposited with the Clerks of the Peace of all counties and boroughs through which it was to pass, or in Scotland with the principal sheriff-clerk of each county. Plans had to be accompanied by a list of every owner, leaseholder and occupier through or alongside whose property it was proposed to pass, called a book of reference. A similar deposit was required at the Private Bill Office at the House, together with an estimate of the cost of construction, the numbers of owners or occupiers assenting, dissenting or 'neuter' to the proposal, and a list of subscribers to the undertaking.

The Bill was first referred to a Select Committee on Standing Orders, usually in early February, whose duty was to ensure that standing orders were complied with and, if not, whether violations might be overlooked or whether they were serious enough to warrant the Bill's rejection. Here was an opportunity for the Bill's opposers to strangle it at birth if they could prove failure to comply, usually on some technicality. The Committee's decision depended to a large extent on the strength of the opposition. Because the Cromford & High Peak Railway Bill of 1824 was unopposed, the Lords relaxed their standing orders to allow Josias Jessop more time to complete his survey, which had been hampered by bad weather and 'the mountainous district'.[12] Twenty years later, their response would have been very different.

Once past this hurdle, the Bill was presented to the House and given its first and second readings. After the second, the Bill was referred to a Committee on Bills — the second hurdle. At least ten days before the committee met, the promoters were required to deposit a further copy of the Bill and plans with the clerk of every parish on the line of route, or, in Scotland, with the schoolmaster; moreover, evidence had to be provided that half the capital had been subscribed. The committee received objectors' petitions, and proceedings were conducted like a court of law, with both sides represented by counsel and with power to summon witnesses for cross-examination. A great deal rested on the preamble to the Bill, which set out the objects of the railway and why it was desirable. If the opposition could convince the committee that the preamble was inaccurate or that the advantages to the public were overstated, the Bill could be judged 'not proved' and thrown out. Alternatively, the committee could accept the Bill as it stood, particularly if it was unopposed, or alter it to satisfy interested parties by inserting protective clauses or other amendments, subject to the agreement of both sides, before returning it to the floor of the House, where there was opportunity for further amendment.

Once all objections were satisfied, the Bill was given its third reading and then passed to the Lords where it went through a similar process. Examination by committee was conducted in exactly the same manner as in the Commons, except that the Standing Orders Committee confined itself to orders specific to the Lords, those common to both Houses being taken as read. Objectors who had been unsuccessful in the other place now had two more chances. Once these third and fourth hurdles were successfully overcome, the Bill became law by receiving the Royal Assent, usually in July or August, whereby the undertaking became an incorporated company. The whole process of promotion, from initial survey to obtaining an Act, therefore occupied at least a year, assuming an Act was obtained first time — which many were not — with most of the parliamentary proceedings crammed into the second half. More often the best part of two years was needed, and if the first application was unsuccessful it could be three or more.

In an attempt to give more time for preparatory work, Parliament from 1837 changed its Standing Orders. Fully detailed surveys were, of course, necessary in order to prepare the plans and sections. To avoid damaging crops, hitherto they had generally been undertaken from mid-September onwards, after the harvest, when unskilled labour was more readily available for work like staff-holding and chaining. At best, this allowed only two and a half months to make the survey, prepare drawings and have them engraved and printed before the 30 November deadline. Simultaneously, notices of assent had to be sent out and returned, the book of reference compiled, and final drafting of the Bill completed. Otherwise, the promoters had to wait another year. Only too often the result was hasty work in the field and in the office, resulting in a high rate of rejection. The revised procedure required deposits with counties and boroughs by 1 March instead of 30 November prior to the parliamentary session, and with parishes and Parliament within one month thereafter. Half the capital had to be subscribed before presentation of the petition, and three-quarters by the committee stage. Notices in the press were also required earlier, in February and March, as well as in the autumn. After the first deposit, deviations of up to a mile could be made in the line of route, provided that revised plans were deposited by 30 November, which remained the final deadline. In an attempt to deter speculators, a cash deposit of 10 per cent of the share capital had to be made. A year later the standing orders of both Houses were brought into line.

As well as being designed to allow promoters more time, the new arrangements were intended to give greater publicity to schemes and extend the opportunities of interested parties to examine Bills and plans. Parliamentary committees also could see plans earlier and take competing schemes into account, instead of considering each one in isolation. But it did not work out like that.

If undesirable bad-weather surveying was to be avoided, it was still best to survey after the harvest, which meant doing it a year earlier, which was even more undesirable. Otherwise, winter weather was just as likely to result in crude, hastily surveyed plans as was the autumn rush under the old system, with the further disadvantage of adding an extra year to the whole process. Furthermore, the 10 per

ANNO TERTIO

GULIELMI IV. REGIS.

****

Cap.xxxiv.

An Act for making a Railway from the *Warrington* and *Newton* Railway at *Warrington* in the County of *Lancaster* to *Birmingham* in the County of *Warwick*, to be called the Grand Junction Railway. [6th *May* 1833.]

WHEREAS a Railway has been formed from *Liverpool* to *Manchester* ; and another Railway has been formed from the said last-mentioned Railway, at *Newton* (which is nearly equidistant between *Liverpool* and *Manchester*), to *Warrington*; and both the said Railways are now open to the Public : And whereas a Railway Communication between the Towns of *Liverpool, Manchester*, and *Birmingham* would be of great public Advantage : And whereas, with a view to effect such Railway Communication between the said Towns of *Liverpool, Manchester*, and *Birmingham*, the several Persons herein-after named are willing, at their own Expence, to make and maintain a Railway from the said *Warrington* and *Newton* Railway at *Warrington* aforesaid to *Birmingham* aforesaid : And whereas the King's most Excellent Majesty, in right of his Duchy of *Lancaster*, is entitled to certain Lands upon the Line of the proposed Railway : And whereas the beneficial Object herein-before mentioned cannot be effected without the Authority of Parliament : May it therefore please Your Majesty that it may be enacted ; and be it enacted by the King's most Excellent Majesty, by and with the Advice and Consent of the Lords Spiritual and Temporal, and Commons, in Parliament assembled, and by the Authority of the same, That *John Moss, Robert Glad-*

[*Local.*]   6 S   *stone,*

Title page from the Act of Parliament incorporating the Grand Junction Railway in 1833, authorising construction of the line from Birmingham through Stafford and Crewe to Warrington, where it connected with the Warrington & Newton Railway, leading to the Liverpool & Manchester. The Latin heading refers to the 3rd year in the reign of William IV.
(BR Property Board)

cent deposit did little to deter speculators; it was simply added to the figure that had to be subscribed to cover promotion expenses and, in any case, it was not uncommon for promoters to circumvent standing orders by borrowing the money.

Consequently, in 1842 Parliament bowed to pressure and reverted to its old rules, although two years later the Commons did reform its select committee system. Previously the members of a committee generally comprised MPs having an interest in the scheme, one way or the other, which was hardly likely to ensure an impartial hearing. Moreover, attendance was not compulsory and members often voted without having heard the evidence, so that those who had could find themselves outnumbered. Lobbying was rife, and once again Bills were being considered in isolation with no attention paid to others which might be similar. So from 1844, committees were smaller, with more impartial members. Attendance was compulsory and Bills for comparable schemes were placed in groups. The deposit was halved. Supporters and antagonists, however, continued to be well organised, sending out circulars to MPs likely to support their cause. As a result, committees tended to regard themselves more as umpires, instead of guardians of the public interest.

The pressure on Parliament was enormous. In 1836, 29 railway Acts were passed and in 1844 there were about 50, but with the onslaught of the Mania the number leaped to 217 Bills in 1845, no less than 435 in 1846 and 257 in 1847. In an attempt to save parliamentary time a Railway Department was set up in 1844 under the President of the Board of Trade, Lord Dalhousie, to sift railway Bills and weed out the more obvious rejects. Although it did useful work, pressure from influential promoters and lobbyists ensured its demise after 12 months.

All was not quite lost, however. As an alternative, the Board of Trade secured authority to have copies of Bills and plans deposited with it so that it might advise Parliament of features which, in its opinion, merited special attention. Although it was no substitute for Dalhousie's department, it was better than nothing. In the following year, 1846, the work of Dalhousie was to some extent vindicated by the establishment of Railway Commissioners at the Board of Trade, whose duty it was to advise Parliament on new railways. Like Dalhousie, the Commissioners were soon under attack, not all of it from aggrieved promoters. A. Doull, a civil engineer, made a scathing criticism of the lack of technical knowledge displayed in the Board's reports, and of parliamentary procedure generally.[13] As an example, he cited the specimen plan accompanying the standing order on deposited plans which, he pointed out, contained contradictions. The 1846 edition showed a datum level 65ft below the top water of a canal, whereas a Bill had recently been thrown out for that very reason, on the sensible grounds that canals could rise and fall, rendering the datum inaccurate. Despite the committee reforms of 1844, the examiners' technical ignorance could easily be exploited by trained witnesses. Doull contended that committees should have professional assistance to counter well-drilled witnesses brought in by opposing parties with all expenses paid. Even the examination of unopposed Bills would benefit, where collusion to cover up errors often went unnoticed.

Government Control

A measure of government control of railways did, however, begin at this time, with successive Regulation of Railways Acts of 1840, 1842 and 1844, the last, Gladstone's Act, being best known for its provisions for guaranteed cheap, daily trains for the poorer travellers — an early example of consumer-protection legislation. Acts for new railways were simplified by three general measures of 1845, the Companies, Lands and Railways Clauses Consolidation Acts, which did away with the need for repetitive recitation of standard clauses in Private Acts by allowing the use of a single clause referring to the appropriate Consolidation Act or Acts.

The Companies Clauses Act dealt with legal and fiscal affairs of no further concern here. The Lands Clauses Act consolidated clauses setting out procedure for purchase — compulsory and by agreement — security of title, the exercising of rights of entry, sale of surplus land, owners' pre-emption rights and other related matters which will be considered in chapter 4. The Railways Clauses Act, as the title implies, related solely to railways and included further important provisions relating to land and the protection of owners and occupiers, and, to a certain extent, public safety. For the promoter there was greater tolerance of omissions and errors in deposited plans and books of reference, provided that two justices certified that they were genuine mistakes and that corrections were lodged with the county and parish authorities. The total effect of these measures was a reduction in the length of Private Bills and Acts and, consequently, a saving in parliamentary time. That they were sorely needed there can be no doubt when one contemplates one of the longest railway Acts, the Chester & Holyhead of 1844, which ran to 424 clauses. And there were plenty of runners-up.

Once it was incorporated, a railway company was in theory obliged by law to build the line in accordance with its Act. There was no recognition of possible failure to do so, from whatever cause. Very few railways had sufficient capital and estimates of construction costs were almost invariably exceeded, in which case Parliament had to be asked to pass another Act authorising an increase. But if, in the event, insufficient could be raised or for some other reason the scheme fell through, in whole or in part, there was no recourse but to seek an Act of abandonment. What Parliament had decreed only Parliament could rescind, which, in such ultimate circumstances, for the proprietors meant throwing good money after bad. To release companies from obligations they could not fulfil, the Abandonment of Railways Act was passed in 1850, vesting in the Railway Commissioners power to authorise abandonment and providing for compensation to landowners who had entered into contracts to sell or agreements for accommodation works and who considered they would suffer financially if the railway were not built — akin to present-day 'planning blight'. Other clauses gave directions on disposal of bridges and other works already constructed and land already purchased. From 1845 to 1847, 8,590 miles of railway were authorised; under this Act 1,560 miles were abandoned. The Railway Companies Act, 1867, gave further protection to landowners, and a second Abandonment Act of 1869 clarified the position of creditors seeking to wind up a railway company, although neither made any reference to railways that ceased to operate. Before looking in more detail at the field and office work that had to be done to satisfy Parliament, it is worth examining some of the effects of this general legislation on the physical features of the railway.

Always anxious to protect property and the public, Parliament insisted that the responsibility for securely fencing a railway was placed squarely on the company. All Private Acts contained this stipulation, the 1842 Regulation Act reinforced it, and the subsequent Railways Clauses Act of 1845 spelt it out in detail, not only to prevent animals from straying on to the line but to prevent trespass from it on to adjoining land. All gates on accommodation crossings had to open outwards from the railway, and the onus of closing them was placed on the user. The once-familiar exhortation, 'Shut and Fasten Gate. Penalty 40 shillings', stems directly from the Act.

The protection of level crossings on public roads was also well to the forefront, stemming from the Highways Act of 1835 which required crossings to have gates attended by 'good and proper persons to attend to the opening and shutting of such gates, so that the persons, carts, or carriages passing along such road shall not be exposed to any danger by the passing of any carriages or engines along the said railroad'. Private Acts generally decreed that level-crossing gates should be kept closed across the road and opened only for traffic, which the 1845 Act reinforced, but went on to recognise circumstances in which it might be better the other way round, as later became usual with the growth of road traffic. The Board of Trade could authorise exceptions if it considered public safety would be better served. Where a turnpike was crossed, the trustees could ask the Board of Trade to order screens to be erected if it was thought that horses might be frightened by trains. The Railways Clauses Act of 1863 strengthened the Board's hand by empowering it to demand a bridge where it considered public safety required one.

Road bridges figured prominently in the 1845 Clauses Act, which laid down minimum widths, headrooms and heights of arch springings, according to the class of road. Bridges over a railway were similarly subject to minimum widths, parapet and fencing heights and gradients. In all cases the Board of Trade had power to approve modifications where there was difficulty, and to arbitrate in disputes. It was a measure of Parliament's concern for public safety that default by a railway carried heavy penalties.

To the company the same Act gave powers to execute temporary works and occupy land in connection with construction, to divert streams and unnavigable rivers, to lay drains, erect buildings and carry out 'all other acts necessary for making, maintaining, altering or repairing, and using the railway', subject to the payment of compensation for damage.

Some latitude in deposited plans and sections was also allowed, with standard horizontal and vertical tolerances. The Act codified the customary 100yd limit of deviation from the centre line on the plan, or 10yd in built-up areas. Proposals to build a railway alongside tidal water below high-water mark required the consent of the Crown, in the shape of the Commissioners of Woods and Forests, and of the Admiralty. The 1863 Act went further and required access to the shore, and gave protection to navigation. A lengthy clause in the 1845 Act set out the extent of accommodation works for land adjoining the railway and safeguarded mineral rights beneath it.

Deposited Plans
In order to promote a Bill it was necessary to engage a parliamentary agent, whose duty it was to guide it through the elaborate labyrinth of Standing Orders, engage counsel and generally do everything possible to ensure success. Agents and others were not slow to publish instructions and advice to potential clients. Bulmer & Gillan's *Practical Instructions* have already been referred to,[14] in which the great importance of ensuring that standing orders were strictly adhered to, particularly respecting plans and estimates, received the strongest emphasis. The surveyor was enjoined to take his levels with the greatest care, otherwise his calculations of earthworks, gradients and costs would be wrong. 'Accuracy of levels has settled the fate of several Bills.' Numerous textbooks on railway surveying and construction practice were published in the 1840s. H.J. Fuller, a civil engineer, in 1897 devoted a book to the parliamentary aspect in *The Preparation of Parliamentary Plans for Railways*, in which he drew on his considerable experience to give sound practical advice. His book throws interesting light on surveying practice of the time. When traversing the country to establish the line, he recommended his readers to note deposits of gravel that could form ballast, rock and other materials that not only gave an indication of the ground but might later be useful for the estimates, urging them to develop 'powers of intelligent observation, a quality which adds to the market value of brains'. Each evening the centre line of route should be marked on the Ordnance Map, together with any corrections, and not left to the following levelling party, which would only waste their time and cause delay. Most engineers expected surveyors to cover about 3 miles a day when levelling 'in country far from being the easiest possible'. He himself had covered hundreds of miles in all weathers over all kinds of country at 3¼ to 3½ miles a day. He advocated, where possible, two parties, the second checking the main sections to pick up any error made by the first, which otherwise would magnify with distance and be difficult to correct later. The results should be plotted on paper regularly during the survey, usually in the evenings, instead of being left until the end when memory would be less likely to assist.

Grading required great skill, a job not to be left to a junior. The ideal objective was to get over and under roads by easy gradients and a minimum of cut-and-fill, without disturbing their levels. Rarely possible in practice, it faced the surveyor with a conflict: severe gradients with correspondingly light earthworks but heavy running costs when the line was finished, or easy grades needing minimum engine power but increasing the expense of construction. Here a good knowledge of local geology literally paid dividends, enabling cuttings to be made at the cheapest places and

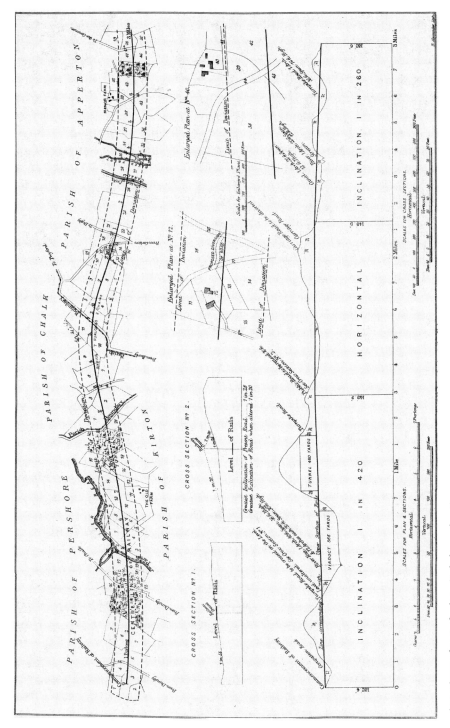

*A specimen of part of a deposited plan and section,
taken from G. C. André's Draughtsman's
Handbook of Plan and Map Drawing, 1874,
specially drawn as an example to show as many
different features as possible. (Courtesy R. Dean)*

steeper gradients where hard rock made cutting more expensive. Level crossings were to be avoided. The continuing cost of a crossing with gates, road metalling, guard rails, signals, a house and an attendant went a long way towards the capital cost of a bridge. Fuller went on to give sound, practical advice on tracing plans and sections, checking proofs and preparing estimates, where he noted that severance of property, fields or estates, which could quickly run up the price, could often be mitigated by laying out a line as close to an existing boundary as possible.

Preparing the book of reference, strictly speaking, was the duty of the solicitor but, as Fuller somewhat ruefully acknowledged, was frequently left to the surveyor, requiring great care, diligence and perception if some of the ruses used by opponents were to be detected. He pointed out that it was not unknown for an opponent to suggest to residents that they give inaccurate information that could be challenged in Parliament, instancing an occasion where some 70 names were incorrectly given, hinting at bribery. At other times an occupancy could change when an occupier realised that a railway was planned, so that what the surveyor had correctly described as waste land could later be found to contain a building or growing crops, enhancing its value.

Wilkinson & Cobbold of Lincoln's Inn recommended in their *Instructions for the Preparation of the Book of Reference* (1845) that those undertaking this important task should stay overnight at an inn located in advance of each day's work so that they walked towards it. 'Be on the ground at 7am every morning', they advised, interviewing occupiers until 4pm, after which there would be time, if needed, to ride off to see a landlord or agent to secure more information. A second booklet, undated, gave advice on tactics: *Instructions as to the Manner of obtaining the necessary Information for preparing the Book of Reference* suggested the engagement of 'some laboring man on the spot, who will generally, for a small gratuity, go over the ground, and supply the names of the several tenants and their residences, and other useful information. There are, in most parishes, some old intelligent laboring men, who know every field . . .' Each day's allocated work should be completed in the day and not put off, otherwise the whole parliamentary schedule could be jeopardised and accuracy imperilled. Every fifth or sixth day should be set aside for visiting more distant owners. Evenings should be occupied in copying out field book notes while the memory was fresh, written in a fair hand for possible future use as evidence. Like the survey, it was not easy work and could be done only on foot.

Once the book was complete, notices had to be sent out requiring owners or occupiers to indicate their assent or dissent to the proposed railway, or whether they

Right and overleaf:
Title and inside pages from the Book of Reference for the projected Alford Valley Railway in Aberdeenshire, 1855. The numbers in the left-hand column relate to plots of land shown on the deposited plan; the other columns give description, owners, lessees and occupiers. (Scottish Record Office)

ALFORD VALLEY RAILWAY.

BOOK OF REFERENCE

TO

THE PLANS

OF

THE PROPOSED RAILWAY

FROM THE

GREAT NORTH OF SCOTLAND RAILWAY

AT

KINTORE TO ALFORD.

CONTAINING—

The Names of the Owners, or Reputed Owners, Lessees, or Reputed Lessees, and Occupiers of the Lands, Houses, and other Heritages, in or through which the said Railway is to be made and maintained, or through which every communication to or from the same is to be, or may be made.

ABERDEEN:

Printed by GEO. CORNWALL, Victoria Court, 51, Castle Street.

1855.

COUNTY OF ABERDEEN—Continued.
PARISH OF KINTORE.

Number on Plans.	Description.	Names of Owners, or Reputed Owners.	Names of Lessees, or Reputed Lessees.	Occupiers.
1	Arable	Duncan Forbes Mitchell	Arthur Smith	Arthur Smith
2	Ditto	The Right Honourable the Earl of Kintore	William Fraser	William Fraser
3	Ditch	Ditto, and Duncan Forbes Mitchell	Ditto, and Arthur Smith	Ditto, and Arthur Smith
4	Great North of Scotland Railway	The Great North of Scotland Railway Company; Sir James Dalrymple Horn Elphinstone, Baronet, Chairman; Robert Milne, Secretary		The Great North of Scotland Railway Company; Sir James Dalrymple Horn Elphinstone, Baronet, Chairman; Robert Milne, Secretary
5	Arable	Duncan Forbes Mitchell	Arthur Smith	Arthur Smith
6	Ditto	Ditto	Ditto	Ditto
7	Saw-mill and Wood-yard	The Right Honourable the Earl of Kintore	Mitchell and Japp; David Mitchell & Francis Japp, the individual partners of said firm	Mitchell and Japp; David Mitchell and Francis Japp, the individual partners of said firm
8	Burn or Strype	Ditto	Ditto and William Fraser	Ditto and William Fraser
9	Arable	Ditto	William Fraser	William Fraser
10	Ditto	Ditto	Ditto	Ditto
11	Ditto	Ditto	Ditto	Ditto
12	Ditto	Duncan Forbes Mitchell	Arthur Smith	Arthur Smith
13	Ditto	Ditto	Ditto	Ditto
14	Ditto	Ditto	Ditto	Ditto
15	Garden	The Trustees appointed under an Act for more effectually maintaining and repairing certain Roads in the Counties of Aberdeen, Banff, and Kincardine, and for making certain New Roads in the said Counties or some of them; Newell Burnett, clerk. The Trustees of the Inverury Turnpike Road; Newell Burnett, clerk		The Trustees appointed under an Act for more effectually maintaining and repairing certain Roads in the Counties of Aberdeen, Banff, and Kincardine, and for making certain New Roads in the said Counties, or some of them; Newell Burnett, clerk. The Trustees of the Inverury Turnpike Road; Newell Burnett, clerk. Alexander Fraser
16	Toll House	Ditto		Ditto
17	Dung Pit	Duncan Forbes Mitchell	Arthur Smith	Alexander Fraser
18	Arable	Ditto	Ditto	Arthur Smith
19	Solum of Old Aberdeenshire Canal	Ditto		Duncan Forbes Mitchell
20	Garden	Ditto	The Trustees of the Free Church Congregation of Kintore; James Milne, treasurer	Reverend Robert Simpson
21	Free Manse, Garden, and Offices	Ditto	Ditto	Ditto
22	Arable	Ditto	Arthur Smith	Arthur Smith
23	Ditto	The Right Honourable the Earl of Kintore	William Fraser	William Fraser
24	Ditto	Duncan Forbes Mitchell	Ditto	Ditto
25	Ditto	Ditto	Ditto	Ditto
26	Turnpike Road	The Trustees appointed under an Act for more effectually Maintaining and Repairing certain Roads in the Counties of Aberdeen, Banff, and Kincardine, and for making certain New Roads in the said Counties, or some of them; Newell Burnett, clerk. The Trustees of the Inverury Turnpike Road; Newell Burnett, clerk		The Public
27	Farm and Accommodation Road	Duncan Forbes Mitchell	Arthur Smith and Andrew Bruce	Arthur Smith & Andrew Bruce

I.

were 'neuter'. Once more, great care was required to ensure accurate returns. Notices had, as far as possible, to be delivered personally, a considerable undertaking on a line of any length, and a record kept of delivery. On the 10½ miles of the Ashburton, Newton & South Devon Railway of 1846, for instance, 474 separate owners, lessees or occupiers had to be seen, and a list prepared for Parliament. Assents covered 6 miles 58 chains of line, a none too comfortable majority; there were 64 'neuters' and 95 people failed to reply. But there were only 15 dissents, and the Bill got through.[15]

Mania Madness

The frantic scramble to place Bills before Parliament during the Railway Mania reached its climax in 1845. On 30 November the offices of Clerks of the Peace in hitherto peaceful county towns were besieged by last-minute depositors carrying bulky bundles of plans. Worcester was crowded with more coaches-and-four than were seen on race days, and at Preston the clerk's office was invaded by an angry crowd of promoters when they learned that he considered the order to open on Sunday referred only to the Board of Trade in London. At the Board's office in Whitehall things were relatively orderly until the hour before midnight, when near pandemonium broke out. Railways promoting new lines or sympathetic to others provided special trains to London, but refused them to competitors, and one promoter was reputed to have outwitted a hostile company by hiring a special for what was ostensibly a funeral party, with the plans and documents carried in the coffin.

Among the hundreds of Bills deposited, five were for lines through Wiltshire, Somerset and Dorset, arising directly from the bitter hostility between the Great Western, determined to push the broad gauge westward, and the standard gauge London & South Western Railway, equally determined to block it. The South Western at this time had reached Salisbury, but its goal was Exeter — and beyond — via Yeovil. The Great Western was intent on the same thing by building connections to and from the Wilts, Somerset & Weymouth Railway, authorised two years previously but still far from complete, over which it had barely concealed control. I.K. Brunel was the engineer. To add a second string to the Great Western bow, the Wilts, Somerset & Weymouth was persuaded to apply for a line that was almost parallel to the South Western's. Either way the Great Western would secure the coveted direct line to Exeter, avoiding the long way round through Bristol. The Bristol & Exeter Railway, as a result, stood to lose considerable traffic which, despite its being leased to the Great Western, it was in no mind to do without a fight. For some time the company had been trying to free itself of Great Western domination, and it now demonstrated its desire for independence by promoting its own Bill for a line from the Wilts, Somerset & Weymouth to a junction with its main line just north of Taunton, thereby also providing a direct line to Exeter. For good measure the Bill contained a branch through Glastonbury and Cheddar to another junction at Bleadon, nearer Bristol. Not to be outdone, the Wilts, Somerset &

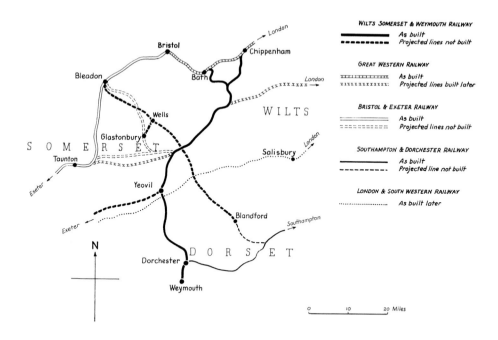

WILTS SOMERSET & WEYMOUTH RAILWAY

▬▬▬▬▬ As built
▪▪▪▪▪▪▪▪▪ Projected lines not built

GREAT WESTERN RAILWAY

ɪɪɪɪɪɪɪɪɪɪɪɪ As built
ɪɪɪɪɪɪɪɪɪɪɪɪ: Projected lines built later

BRISTOL & EXETER RAILWAY

═══════ As built
═ ═ ═ ═ ═ ═ ═ ═ Projected lines not built

SOUTHAMPTON & DORCHESTER RAILWAY

▬▬▬▬▬ As built
▬ ▬ ▬ ▬ ▬ ▬ Projected line not built

LONDON & SOUTH WESTERN RAILWAY

·················· As built later

*Railway projects in Somerset, 1847, showing the
proposed branch to Glastonbury from Wells.*

Weymouth thereupon retaliated with a line from Blandford, connecting with the Southampton & Dorchester Railway, to Bleadon through Wells, where a branch would be made to Glastonbury.

In the midst of this smoking hotbed of railway politics the firm of Davies & Foster, solicitors of Wells, was trying to prepare the Wilts, Somerset & Weymouth's Glastonbury Branch Bill for the 1847 session. Their remarkably detailed accounts provide a vivid picture of how a small-town firm grappled with the complexities and deadlines of the parliamentary timetable at the height of the Mania.[16] Their primary interest was purely parochial — getting a railway for Wells; the political battle between giants in which they became involved was of no real concern. They were simply swept into it, like it or not. It is a story that was being repeated country-wide.

Most of the outdoor work on the Glastonbury Branch Bill seems to have been done by Davies, aided by several clerks. They spent six days compiling the book of reference while Foster and a clerk occupied five days with Maddox, the senior surveyor, pointing out defects and alterations in his plans. Then, late on 29 November 1846, the night before the final date for local deposits, Davies discovered that part of the line was missing from his advance copy of the plans.

Neither of the surveyors responsible for that section could give an explanation. So far as they knew their drawings had gone to London for engraving and printing with the others. The final sets of plans for deposit were due to arrive at any time. There was no alternative but for Davies to hasten to London and see Brunel. The nearest station for London was Bath, 20 miles away, whither he set off in a hastily hired post-chaise to catch the night mail. The train was delayed by an accident and, by fortunate coincidence while he was waiting, the London parliamentary agents' clerks arrived on the down mail with the rest of the plans. A hasty comparison on the platform revealed that theirs were complete; obviously Davies's set had a sheet missing and there were no spares. He arrived at Paddington at 7.30am and, pausing only to knock up his agent, he went straight to Brunel's office in Duke Street. With profuse apologies the missing sheet was supplied and Davies caught the next fast train back, arriving in Wells just in time to make the deposit. For this night and day of travelling he charged 10 guineas plus expenses.

The next job was to serve 449 statutory notices, which in some cases meant giving affidavits in front of magistrates, and preparing the list of assents. The following January Davies attended the first hearings by the Standing Orders Committee, where he discovered that the Bristol & Exeter and the South Western were challenging his Bill, inasmuch as seven cottages in Wells had been missed off the plans, book of reference and list of assents. In fact, no notices had been sent. He immediately rushed back to Somerset to explain the situation to the occupiers and try to gain their assent and persuade them to waive their objections. He was successful, only to find on his return to London three days later that his opponents had filed further objections, this time by two landowners on the grounds that details of their properties were incorrect. Davies despatched his clerk down to Somerset — again overnight — with instructions. 'At first they positively refused to sign the Counter Petition but after much persuasion and argument he [the clerk] prevailed and procured their assent and returned to London by the Express Train the next day . . .'

Davies's troubles were still not over. A day later another opposition petition was received, from the Rev Joseph Pratt of Paston, near Peterborough. His name was not in the book of reference in respect of a field he owned at Loxton, near Wells, and he had not received a statutory notice. So Davies set out on another overnight train journey, from Euston to Peterborough via Northampton 'and thence at daybreak to Paston and a long conference with Mr Pratt but he refused all terms before he consulted his Agent Mr Harwood of Bristol and afterwards his friend Mr Woolley an Assistant Tithe Commissioner . . .' There was no time for all this, as the Committee's examination was due to start two days later, so 'after much persuasion we prevailed on him to waive Mr Harwood's interference and allow us to submit the proposal to Mr Woolley who was stated to be at Somerset House'. But Woolley was not there; he had gone to Cambridge, whence poor Davies had perforce to catch the evening train from the Eastern Counties Railway terminus at Shoreditch. It took him until two o'clock the next morning to talk Woolley round, and then only subject to Pratt's agreement. Although it was less than 40 miles to Peterborough by road, at that hour it was quicker to take the first train back to Shoreditch and then out again from Euston. It now being Sunday, the Rev Pratt at first refused to talk, 'but that difficulty being overcome it appeared that Mr Pratt had already made very advantageous terms for disposal of his land to the Bristol & Exeter Company which we were not before aware of . . .' Now that all was revealed, Davies must have been exasperated beyond measure, but his patience and powers of persuasion, doubtless aided by his client's purse, enabled him to get Pratt's signature to a counter-petition withdrawing his opposition. Then it was back to London, again by the night train, just in time for the Committee on the Monday morning. 'This was rather an important, delicate and fatiguing business. Extra charge for three nights Travelling, £15.15.0d.' Surely an understatement.

Exhausted though he was, Davies now had to face examination by the Committee, where his relentless opponents alleged that the plans incorrectly showed a public road at Coxley as a parish one and should, therefore, indicate how the railway was to cross it. The agents advised calling a parish vestry meeting in an attempt to obtain a petition from the inhabitants asking for the objection to be dismissed. As the Committee was also examining the other Bills put forward by the warring companies, its hearings were likely to be protracted, so there could just be time if Davies acted quickly. By now he must have been cursing the surveyors. It was 20 January and a vestry meeting required statutory notice, which meant it could not be convened until the 28th, which was the last day for presenting petitions.

The parishioners were unaware of the workings of Parliament, much less the technical infringement of standing orders, so eight days were little enough time for all the explaining and persuasion to be done. Further, it was vital that the meeting should proceed smoothly. There must be no question of discussion, for that would cause delay, making it impossible for Davies to get back to London in time. He first saw the two waywardens and the parish overseer of roads, none of whom lived in Coxley, and obtained their formal agreement to a meeting, following which notices were posted on the doors of the church, the chapel and the Coxley Pound Inn where the meeting was to be held. He then set about canvassing the principal inhabitants, starting with the squire. If their consent could be obtained, he suspected the rest would follow. It worked. There was unanimous approval and the petition was signed. Davies paid the innkeeper and shot off to Bath for the train, reaching the House in time for the precious petition to be accepted.

With so many other Bills presented in the session, parliamentary proceedings obviously would be extended, so Davies spent the time between committee hearings in strengthening his case. During February he spent 11 days canvassing for assents from those who had not returned their notices. Then at the end of the month the agents asked for a petition of support from the citizens of Wells, which meant four more days getting signatures and a separate petition from the city council and the MP. Davies then learned that the South Western company and the Duke of Buckingham were organising a counter-petition 'and making specious representations of a better line . . . . Both ourselves and all our Clerks engaged at raising a hue and cry against them forewarning and cautioning all persons signing any opposing Petition, when the Majority of the persons on whom we called promised not to sign it, and the efforts of our Opponents as to the Petition were effectually thwarted.' Although it took longer, he charged only for one day.

Throughout March there was still more work to do as agents and counsel devised first one and then another stratagem to counter the opposition's moves. To persuade the owners of Wookey Paper Mills to oppose the Bristol & Exeter, a deviation further away from their mill was agreed on, involving taking one of the owners to London to sort it out with Brunel, who was also called on to assure the Wells Turnpike Commissioners that he would 'obviate all difficulties about the drainings and other obstructions or disfiguration of the Town'. A stocking and brush manufacturer employing 300 people agreed to supply written evidence in support, and one of the partners in Stuckey's Banking Company of Wells was taken to London to give evidence in person. Simultaneously, the Bristol & Exeter's Bill had to be opposed, in much the same way. When a signature was required from one of the partners in Wookey Paper Mills who lived in Abersychan, Monmouthshire, a clerk was despatched at midnight to catch the 5am Newport packet from Bristol to obtain it.

For their ten months' work from October 1846 to July 1847, Davies & Foster submitted to the Wilts, Somerset & Weymouth a bill amounting to £2,738 4s 11d (£2,738.24½), something over £50,000 in present-day terms. Although at the time surveyors and lawyers were strongly criticised for profiteering from railway work, particularly highly paid counsel specialising in parliamentary representation, Davies & Foster would certainly appear to have earned their fee. It must have been a sad conclusion to their efforts when, after 53 days in committee, their Bill was rejected. The Bristol & Exeter and South Western Bills went on to the Lords, where it was now so late in the session that hearings were suspended until 1848, when both were passed. It was a hollow victory; the financial crash towards the end of 1847 had already seen to that. The London & South Western did not enter Exeter until 1860, while the Great Western simply sat back and did nothing more towards a direct line until the end of the century, the final link not being opened until 1906. The Bristol & Exeter reached Glastonbury and Wells in 1859, and in 1876 was absorbed by the Great Western.

Ancient and Modern
With the exception of a relatively small number of branch lines built under the Light Railways Act, 1896, virtually the entire British railway network was created by this system, thankfully with less frenetic activity once the Mania had subsided, although it was rare for there to be no opposition from competing lines. The same parliamentary process has to be observed today. The timetable is similar, extending over at the very least twelve months and often longer. Because the British Railways Board is a statutory undertaking with powers deriving from the hundreds of

individual Acts obtained by the old companies, a Private Bill has to be promoted whenever land is required for new works or alterations to existing railways, highways or navigable or tidal water not already provided for in existing powers. Under the 1962 Transport Act the consent of the Secretary of State is required first. In practice, the Board promotes at least one Private Bill each year, seeking powers for its various requirements during the forthcoming year. They can range from the acquisition of a small parcel of land for a bridge to replace a level crossing, to a larger quantity for a new line. The deviation line and new tunnel at Harecastle, near Stoke-on-Trent, for example, needed in connection with electrification, was included in the British Transport Commission Act of 1962. The more recent Selby diversion on the East Coast main line was authorised by a separate Special Act in 1979.

Many of British Rail's annual Bills have been concerned with small, possibly innocuous works to which no one would object, but necessary purely because execution would infringe the provisions of a railway Act passed a century or more ago, there being no other way to vary them. The ancient principle that only Parliament can vary that which Parliament has enacted, however long ago, still holds good. In seeking to alter a highway or a footpath, though, the railway does have an alternative to legislation, if the highway authority is prepared to make an Order under the Highways Act or the Town & Country Planning Acts. As a local authority is invariably involved, either as highway authority or agent for the Department of Transport, this procedure is often used, which speeds up the process. Compensation disputes are now dealt with under the Land Compensation Acts, 1961 and 1973, and the ultimate court of appeal is the Lands Tribunal.

In 1988, however, the parliamentary Bill process gained prominent attention when BR published the optional routes for the Channel Tunnel high-speed link through Kent and south London to King's Cross. Until then there had been virtually no public awareness of the archaic procedure British Rail has to adopt when it needs to acquire land, however large or small the amount, for the simple reason that no new railway on that scale has been built since the Great Western's new Birmingham line from Princes Risborough to Aynho, near Banbury, was completed in 1906-10.

At this point it is worth looking at the procedure for building a new road which, although similar powers are needed, is quite different. In the case of trunk roads and motorways, which are the responsibility of the Department of Transport, the Government makes an Order under the Highways Act, 1980, setting out the proposed route. Other, local authority roads can be planned under the 'deemed planning consent' procedure whereby the authority grants itself planning permission. In both cases land is purchased by Compulsory Purchase Order under the Acquisition of Land Act, 1981, which sets out procedures, the ultimate arbiter in cases of dispute being the Lands Tribunal, although its offices are seldom required. Negotiations are undertaken by the District Valuer or the local authority's land agent as the case may be, using widely recognised rules.

Advance publication of Draft Orders, over a statutory period, allows time for objections to be lodged which, if they cannot otherwise be resolved, are presented at a public enquiry before an independent inspector appointed by the Minister. The Government is not bound to accept his recommendations, but in most cases does so. Authorities, central and local, usually engage in some form of public consultation and publicity exercise before Draft Orders are published, to give the scheme an airing before the statutory procedure starts. At the end, when an Order has been confirmed, aggrieved parties can still challenge it in the High Court if they consider there has been some technical infringement. It is not uncommon to find this right exercised in an attempt to get a judicial review of the whole scheme, which can create further delay. Consequently, highway engineers find that the time taken from the feasibility study to the start of construction of a government-owned road can be as much as seven years, or even more.

Hitherto, BR's policy has been to consult the main interested parties before going to Parliament, in an endeavour to be as accommodating as possible and to agree prices and compensation. It had the additional merit for both sides of avoiding expensive and time-consuming parliamentary opposition, and for the size of the works involved, including the Selby Diversion, in general it has worked well for all parties. But the Channel Tunnel link is very different, in time as well as scale. So while it may be tempting to suggest that BR and its overlords at the Department of Transport might have tried to adapt the road men's methods of public participation to the parliamentary system, there is no disputing that there simply was not time. Add to the tight timescale the inflexible political directive from the government that it was not prepared to change the system, even for a project of a magnitude unprecedented in the present century, and that finance must come from private or BR's own resources, and it is clear that the railway's options were nil. It could, no doubt, have publicly compared the levels of noise and environmental disturbance created by a railway and a six-lane motorway, but beyond broad observations like that the railway's scope for public consultation and reassurance was extremely limited. At the time of writing (March 1990) the affair is still history-in-the-making that has yet to fully unfold, and further comment would be inappropriate here beyond saying that any rational assessment must conclude that, to provide the public with the degree of consultation it so obviously wants, and to restore confidence, the rules for building new railways need changing.

The Channel Tunnel Bill was among the first of a number introduced into Parliament, to the extent that at the end of the 1988-9 session at least seven railway Bills, including three urban Light Rapid Transit schemes, were caught up in a procedural log-jam and had to be carried forward to the 1989-90 session. Two more Private Bills for a metro system for Bristol were added in the same session, and with more from BR and the Passenger Transport Executives in the offing for future sessions the position is likely to worsen before it improves. With the nation's transport system increasingly choked up, there is clearly an urgent need to overhaul the entire procedure and devise one that is simultaneously less time-consuming and more democratic. Without it, we shall be overtaken by events.

Chapter 3

Preparing the Route

The First Railway Surveyors

The slow separation of the broadly intermingled and diversely practised disciplines of surveying, engineering and architecture that began in the canal age was greatly speeded up by the demands of the railways. By the end of the Mania period not only was the process virtually complete, but the emerged surveying and engineering professions themselves were beginning to divide, the engineers into civil and mechanical. The surveyors were splitting up less tidily into three categories: land surveying, which, as we shall see shortly, was effectively taken over by the Ordnance Survey or simply became a branch of civil engineering; land and property valuation, which blossomed; and a new discipline in quantity surveying. Like later branches, the last need not concern us here beyond noting that Sir Henry Arthur Hunt, who pioneered it and produced, single-handed, accurately detailed quantities for Barry's new Houses of Parliament in 1835-6, became Consulting Surveyor to the Office of Works and also worked for several railways.

The most likely source from which the early railway promoters might seek the expertise they needed, the canal men, did not feature to anything like the extent that could be expected. True, they had developed the necessary technology, but for several reasons comparatively few moved into railway work on any scale; perhaps surprisingly, considering that the demise of canal construction and the growth of railways were relatively gradual and overlapped.

The great names were either dead or were becoming old. William Jessop died in 1814 when canals were near their zenith, and his son, Josias, who laid out the Cromford & High Peak Railway and probably would have gone forward to do more, died at the age of 45 in 1826. Outram also died young in 1805. Though Telford, the greatest of them, lived to see the beginning of the railway age, he was too old to take an active part and in any case acknowledged the new transport mode only with reluctance. In 1821 the elder Rennie died and of his sons only two followed their father. George, the eldest, tended to concentrate more on running the Blackfriars machinery and engineering business, and assisting his famous brother John Jr, later Sir John, in civil engineering, mainly in a secondary capacity. They surveyed the final route of the Liverpool & Manchester Railway but, because their terms were unacceptable to the committee, the post of engineer in charge of construction went to George Stephenson. John Rennie also surveyed a route for the London & Birmingham Railway, which was not chosen, and one for the London & Brighton which to a large extent was, but again he built neither. Thereafter most of his railway work was done in Europe.

A contemporary of the Rennies and former pupil of their father, Francis Giles, perhaps more than any other encompassed canals and railways, but despite making a name for himself he was not a very competent organiser and attempted too much, so that few of his many schemes came to fruition. He was associated with the younger John Rennie's earlier Brighton schemes and produced one of his own for the London & Birmingham. He started building the Newcastle & Carlisle and London & Southampton railways, both major projects, but was forced to relinquish them to others to complete. In Scotland, Robert Stevenson was equally unfortunate with his many canal, tramroad and railway projects, not from shortage of ability, for he was a far-sighted and able engineer, but from lack of financial support, although he was successful in other fields of engineering.

The main body of railway planners and builders came from the new civil engineering profession, established on a formal basis when the Institution of Civil Engineers was inaugurated in 1818. Their backgrounds were varied, although the most famous, George Stephenson, was never a member. Untutored but brilliantly practical, and astute into the bargain, he developed his skills and belief in railways from the collieries and wagonways of north-eastern England. Between 1825 and 1835 he and his associates virtually cornered the market, and he trained his son Robert and other pupils like Joseph Locke, who by their mid-twenties were making their own claims to fame. I.K. Brunel also learned from his father, Marc, builder of the first Thames tunnel; Joseph Mitchell, surveyor and builder of so many railways in the Scottish Highlands, was a pupil of Telford before succeeding his father as surveyor of Highland roads and bridges; Charles Fox, whose name survives in the well-known firm of Freeman Fox & Partners, was articled to John Ericsson who designed a locomotive for the Rainhill trials, and then worked for Robert Stephenson on the London & Birmingham before becoming a leading designer of iron structures and bridges as well as building railways around the world.

Several engineers and surveyors embarked on railway work from the army when their military careers were terminated by the end of the Napoleonic Wars. Charles Blacker Vignoles, a captain of infantry, had a taste for engineering and mathematics which he put to good use in North America before starting a career in railways under the Rennies. Part brilliant, part unfortunate, ultimately he was honoured as an engineer. William Scarth Moorsom learned surveying as an army captain. His elder brother, Admiral C.S. Moorsom, like other ex-officers, chose the administrative side of railways in which to use his talents. He became a director of the London & Birmingham and found William a job, in which he impressed Robert Stephenson. But he lacked the capabilities of his brother and only one of the many schemes for which he became engineer actually got through Parliament, while the constructional work he did was seldom entirely satisfactory and he could not be called a successful engineer.

A considerable body of the railway builders started as surveyors. One of the foremost Victorian engineers, James Brunlees, commenced as a landscape gardener and then learned surveying on road works. Thomas Grainger, too, was originally a surveyor of roads who built railways in Scotland and the north of England; Frederick Thomas Turner, who had been articled to a London surveyor, built most of the London, Chatham & Dover Railway and much else at home and abroad, while the man whose name more than any other became associated with railways in central Wales and the border country, including Barmouth Viaduct, Benjamin Piercy, trained as a surveyor and valuer under his father. Similar backgrounds respectively led William Parsons, county surveyor for Leicestershire, into architecture, including railway stations between Leicester and Peterborough, and Thomas Brassey into becoming the greatest of the nineteenth-century railway contractors.

Although many engineers of the period supervised everything, they usually required the help of surveyors in establishing a feasible line and laying it out. This point was made at an early meeting of the Surveyors' Institution in 1869,[1] although they were not often recorded on plan or prospectus. The plan accompanying Robert Stevenson's 1818 report on the projected Edinburgh & Dalkeith Railway also bears J. Steedman's name as surveyor,[2] but between 1810 and the end of 1835 only 8 out of 65 Scottish railway plans show the name of a surveyor as well as an engineer. Thereafter they dwindle right away.[3] The Stephensons' plans of the Leicester & Swannington Railway of 1829-30 carry the name of Thomas Miles, surveyor,[4] while Nicholas Cundy was joined by John Willy, surveyor, on the London & Brighton Railroad scheme of 1836.[5] One suspects some local men may have lent their names to help gain support for a project in areas where they were better known than the engineer, for an appropriate fee; certainly they were in demand for their local knowledge and helped to gain access to land. Colonel George Landmann, who built the first railway in London, the London & Greenwich, in 1836 used Charles Dean of Exeter for his London, Salisbury, Exeter, Plymouth & Falmouth Railway, or so the prospectus said.[6] Whether a survey was done for so ambitious a scheme, other than on a map, is conjectural, because the prospectus seems to have been both beginning and end of the project.

Engineers took on work in their own names; there were few partnerships. Notable exceptions were Joseph Locke and John Edward Errington who worked together on a number of lines, particularly those which made up much of the trunk route from Birmingham to Aberdeen. The only instance of a specialist firm formed to carry out railway surveys and promotions was George Stephenson & Son (not to be confused with Robert Stephenson & Co) in 1824, an attempt by George and his backers to gain a monopoly. With so many other ambitious men now entering the field, many of them trained by Stephenson, it was bound to fail.

William James, Visionary

A remarkable man of the old school who, with some justification, considered that he, not Stephenson, should have been called 'Father of Railways', was William James. Had he tempered his remarkable vision and enthusiasm with more delegation and less insistence on detail, he might have been so. Born in Henley-in-Arden, Warwickshire, in 1771, the son of a solicitor, James received legal training in

London. As was customary, this included estate management, in which he set up in business, first in Henley and then in Warwick where he became agent to the Earl of Warwick and Deputy Recorder of the town. He surveyed the Warwick to London turnpike, and later opened a London office and surveyed the levels for drainage works on Lambeth Marsh, designed a bridge across the Thames and steadily built up a large practice that in 1824 was said to be the largest in the kingdom, with several provincial offices. He bought or invested in a number of collieries in the Black Country, Warwickshire and Derbyshire, and purchased two large estates in Warwickshire and South Wales. By 1812 he was said by his daughter, Mrs E.M.S. Paine, to be earning £10,000 a year and to be worth £150,000, which in present-day terms would make him several times a millionaire although, as that statement was part of a later attempt in vindication, it must be treated with reserve.

James was keenly interested in canals and, after work stopped on the Stratford-on-Avon Canal in 1797 for lack of cash, he carried out a re-survey and three years later bought shares. In 1812 he undertook to complete it and also became superintendent. A year later he purchased the Upper Avon Navigation with which the Stratford Canal connected when it was finished in 1816. For some time now James had been enthusiastic about railways and three years later he surveyed and actively promoted a Central Junction Railway from Stratford through Moreton-in-Marsh to Oxford, Thame and London, seeing Stratford, with its waterways connections to the Midlands and the north, as a great transhipment centre. He

William James, 1771-1837; surveyor, engineer and railway promoter extraordinary.
(Science Museum)

returned from seeing Stephenson's locomotive at work in Northumberland convinced that steam power was the traction of the future; he also made out a case for malleable iron rails instead of cast iron, on the grounds of greater strength and lower cost, suggesting that they could be welded together for several miles, thereby anticipating modern continuous-welded rail. But his ideas were before their time; in severely emasculated form his railway ended as a horse tramroad from Stratford to Moreton.

James's very first railway survey was for a line in Somerset in 1799-1800, and the next twenty years saw him planning lines in counties from Cornwall to North Wales and Lancashire. His vision was as unbounded as his energy. Unlike Stephenson, he foresaw railways carrying passengers as well as goods. For his General Railroad Company he envisaged a capital of £1 million, and in 1823 he presented an address to George IV advocating railways linking London and Chatham with Brighton and Portsmouth, over which the entire requirements of the navy could be conveyed in one day.[7] To help agriculture and the depressed economy he recommended large-scale land reclamation, using convict labour and steam railways, going on to suggest a new harbour at Chatham 'where the entire Royal Navy could be afloat', overlooked by a new city on government land which, if sold for building, would fetch high prices — anticipating, it could be said, present-day privatisation. Among his many schemes were railways from London to Birmingham via Oxford, Bristol to Southampton and Birmingham to Manchester. He surveyed them all at his own expense.

It was in 1821, on one of his frequent business trips to Lancashire, that James was introduced to Joseph Sandars, a prominent Liverpool businessman closely concerned with attempts to improve communication between Liverpool and Manchester over which canal and river interests held a stranglehold. James offered to survey a railway, which he commenced in the following year, while Sandars secured support and formed a provisional committee. James's team comprised his brother-in-law, Paul Padley, a professional, as principal surveyor who was also responsible for preparing the plans, George Hamilton, Hugh Greenshields and, significantly, Robert Stephenson, who later became a good friend and whose inclusion was indicative of James's close relationship with George. From his preliminary survey James was able to say that a railway was feasible and to recommend a route. The committee decided to lose no time in presenting a Bill and a detailed survey was begun with the intention of going to Parliament in the 1823 session. Meanwhile, on the strength of James's report, the promoters went public.

It was the beginning of his downfall. The survey was delayed by intense hostility from landowners, James himself was ill, and to make matters worse his railway activities had caused him so to neglect his other business interests that early in 1823 he was declared bankrupt. Between November 1822 and August 1824 he was unfortunate enough to spend three spells in a debtors' prison, and to the committee's consternation the 1823 session was, of course, missed. Whether the survey was fully completed is not clear; James insisted that it was, but the committee could not afford to dally and appointed George Stephenson as engineer with instructions to make a new survey. It was James who had introduced Stephenson to the committee, probably as a supplier of engines and plant.

Stephenson's first step was to engage Padley, Hamilton and Greenshields, which suggests that he thereby secured James's plans. James always insisted that this was so, but whatever the truth may be Stephenson certainly gained the three men's experience and knowledge of the route, which to a large extent he followed. Despite his tribulations, James still tried, unsuccessfully, to maintain some connection with the Liverpool & Manchester, which he regarded as his own creation, and kept up a lively interest in railway affairs, although to no financial advantage. In 1826 he was dismissed from the Stratford & Moreton with £200 — he was owed £163 10s 10d (£163.54) in any case — and he retired to Bodmin in Cornwall where he resumed his land agency business in a small way, still trying to retrieve his reputation. He died in 1837, a poor man. James's family took up the fight for recognition, and in 1861 his daughter attempted to vindicate her father in her biography *The Two James and the Two Stephensons*. Despite these efforts, James's achievements continued to be undervalued until modern historians, notably L.T.C. Rolt in his biography of the Stephensons, made impartial assessments. James had enormous drive and foresight, which led him to attempt too much, too quickly; in many ways he was a man before his time. In 1840 his sister, Elizabeth Mudie, petitioned the Great Western Railway,[8] and possibly other companies; apparently her brother had intended to bequeath her £10,000, but his bankruptcy had left her destitute and the sad little

William James's monument: the viaduct across the Avon at Stratford, built to carry his Stratford & Moreton Railway in 1826. The building at the far end was the toll collector's house. The structure is now a public footpath, photographed here in 1989.
(Author)

document asks for financial help, in recognition of James' work. In 1846 his eldest son, William Henry, got up a testimonial to his father which was signed by Robert Stephenson and nearly all the foremost engineers of the day — except George Stephenson. According to Mrs Paine, he succeeded in suppressing it, furious at his son's response, although Robert is stated to have made a contribution in memory of his old friend and freely testified to his pioneering achievements. But George never acknowledged the worth of James's work, much less its contribution to his own success. Yet James has his monument: the long tramway bridge across the Avon at Stratford, with a preserved wagon at the end of it. Although he probably did not design the bridge, it is an impressive tribute to his vision.

Surveying the Route
In the year following James's death one could travel by rail from London to Birmingham, Liverpool and Manchester, by the end of 1840 to Southampton and to York, and in 1841 to Bristol and Brighton. The momentum of railway promotion grew rapidly, railway investment became a craze and in 1844 the Railway Mania hit the country. Surveyors were at a premium and any man having a passing acquaintance with land measurement or building work could become a railway expert overnight. One who witnessed it all, John Francis, writing in his *History of the English Railway* in 1851, recalled how a few years before 'Artists and artisans reaped a golden harvest. Professional men were tempted from abroad, trusting that they had the necessary information. Youths not out of their servitude were employed on works which demanded mature judgement . . . As long as the survey was made and the sections lodged in time, the directors were satisfied, and whether they were correct was of small importance in a majority of cases. The pay was in proportion to the urgency, and many men received for a week's work more than they could have honestly earned in a year's labour.' Hitherto, for at least 20 years the normal fee charged by a railway surveyor had been two guineas (£2.10) a day plus expenses, and one guinea (£1.05) or 10s 6d (52½p) for his assistants, according to experience, which was the scale used by John Turner on the Stockton & Darlington in 1826.[9] Alternatively, three guineas (£3.15) a day inclusive of expenses was also common, as charged by John Dymond on the South Devon Railway in 1844,[10] but the Mania changed it all.

A civil engineer, F.H. Grundy, told a similar story in his *Pictures of the Past, Memories of the Men I have Met and Places I Have Seen*, published in 1879. He recalled that promoters were prepared to pay any price, and how at the age of 21 he was offered £20 a mile to prepare parliamentary sections which he could have done at the rate of five miles a day, whereas the Stephensons paid him six guineas (£6.30) for an eight-hour day and double time on Sundays. Unqualified men, such as schoolmasters, clerks and clergymen, set up as engineers and surveyors. Grundy had met men who were unable to set up a levelling instrument, and one even wanted to know the meaning of a gradient and another a sleeper. Sixty men left the Ordnance Survey for better paid railway work, where they shamelessly presented their old credentials to gain entry to land. George Godwin, the outspoken proprietor and editor of *The Builder*, blasted the scores of 'pseudo surveyors . . . utterly incompetent and yet are paid immense salaries . . . youngsters, hardly able to tell the right end of a theodolite, who are receiving two, three and four guineas a day and their expenses'.[11] Newspaper advertisers offered to teach surveying in a week for three guineas (£3.15), and one charlatan ran off to America with his advance payments before uttering a word to his gullible students. Captain Francis Yolland, later an inspector of railways at the Board of Trade, stated in evidence that unscrupulous surveyors would obtain copies of Ordnance Survey maps at 10s (50p) a mile and charge their employers between 30s and 80s a mile (£1.50 and £4.00).[12] An indication of the demand is shown by the spate of textbooks. In the ten years between 1840 and 1850 twenty-odd books on railway surveying and estimating appeared, ten of them in 1847 alone, while eight dealt specifically with setting out curves, which novices found particularly tricky. There was plenty of plagiarism, about which Thomas Baker in particular complained bitterly in his *Railway Engineering, or Field Work Preparatory to the Construction of Railways* of 1848.

In his *Autobiography* (1904), Herbert Spencer, the political economist, remembered from his days as a railway engineer those opportunists who, during the Mania, 'needed but to take a map of Great Britain and look out for a comparatively blank space where there was a town of some size, run a pencil-mark through a string of them; gather together some known local names headed, if possible, by one with a title; issue flaming advertisements; and people rushed to take shares.' An engineer called William B. Prichard was one who engaged Spencer to assist in a survey for a line across country from Northampton to Worcester. Spencer formed a low opinion of the promoters, who he considered were motivated only by greed, but he found the work pleasant enough, with days spent taking levels followed by a good dinner at an inn and half an hour reducing them ready for drawing, after which his evening was free. It all changed when Prichard put him in charge of his London office to supervise the work on the parliamentary plans for his schemes, most of which were 'more or less wild', and in the final week of November some twenty extra staff were drafted in for the last rush before the 30th, during which he did not see his bed for four days. As Spencer expected, none of the Bills passed. The work was too hurried and imperfect.

John Brunton, by contrast, found railway surveying a rough life. He surveyed and levelled the London & Birmingham from Kilsby Tunnel to a point near Brandon, between Rugby and Coventry, working from daylight until dark and with no Ordnance Survey to help him. In those days curves were set out by making offsets every chain-length, calculated according to the required radius, a long, tedious business before theodolites were used for the purpose. An empty pub in St John's Wood was rented as a drawing office where twenty draughtsmen worked day and night to prepare the plans. Even lithographers broke down under the pressure, and when Brunton took a set of plans to deposit at Birmingham he slept throughout the 11½-hour coach journey.[13]

Spencer and Brunton, and many more, were experienced surveyors of integrity who could be relied on to do a competent job. Like William James earlier, they often combined a variety of talents and were not afraid to advance bold ideas. One such local man was Job Bintley of Kendal. In 1838, what was to become the West Coast main line had reached Preston and work was progressing on extending it north to Lancaster. Further on, various schemes were being examined to penetrate Cumbria in order to reach Carlisle and thence into Scotland. George Stephenson had surveyed a roundabout but virtually level route along the coast, which was rejected, while Joseph Locke favoured a line up the Lune Valley and over Shap Fells, much shorter but steeply graded, which found more favour. An influential body of promoters from Kendal, alarmed that Locke's route would bypass their town, engaged Bintley to make an independent survey in 1837.

Bintley was described as a land surveyor and woollen draper, although it would probably be more accurate to call him a 'merchant'. Kendal had a considerable trade in woollen goods so, after the fashion of the times, it would not be regarded as inconsistent with his surveying activities. He had a considerable local reputation and, so it proved, no mean talent. He later acted as valuer for enclosure awards, became borough surveyor, engineer to the Ulverston Waterworks Company and, in 1840, surveyed a railway from Dalton-in-Furness to Barrow that foreshadowed the Furness Railway. His son Joseph expanded into architecture and became the first county surveyor for Westmorland.

To enable his route to pass through Kendal, Bintley took a more westerly course up Longsleddale and through a 2¼-mile tunnel to join Locke's route south of Penrith. But it was no wildcat scheme. In giving evidence to the Royal Commission appointed to decide on the merits of an east- or west-coast route to Scotland, it was clear that he had made detailed surveys, costings and calculations, particularly with regard to the tunnel which he estimated would need three shafts, the deepest 824ft, and take six years to complete. Moreover, he was not afraid to stand up to Locke, who by now was a national figure, pointing out, when questioned, that Locke was at the time building the Woodhead Tunnel on the Manchester–Sheffield line that was 3 miles long, with its deepest shaft 582ft. His gradients did not exceed 1 in 100, whereas the railway that Locke eventually built over Shap rises at 1 in 75 for four miles. When Locke was building the Lancaster & Preston Railway in 1838, Bintley advised him to put the terminus on the west side of Lancaster, whence it could easily be continued northward, which he was sure would not be long delayed; but Locke stuck to his plan for a terminus overlooking the town, with the result that when the Lancaster & Carlisle Railway was built a new station was necessary and the sharp curve off the old line still slows trains through Lancaster today. Locke, of course, at that time saw the Lune Valley as the ideal route — which it was — while Bintley was for Kendal. In the event, the chosen route was a compromise, but Bintley had the satisfaction of seeing the adoption of the greater part of his route between Lancaster and Kendal.

In 1845 Bintley was busy surveying the projected York & Carlisle Railway, one of a multitude of competing schemes for a line across northern England. His account book gives an insight into work of a railway surveyor at that time.[14] As the route lay mainly across pasture and high moorland, there was no harvesting to wait for, so Bintley and his nine assistants worked during the spring and summer. The proposal was for a line from Northallerton to Tebay and Penrith, linking the East and West Coast main lines which, in the end, had both been recommended by the Royal Commission. On the East Coast route London was already connected by rail with the Tyne, and work was in progress on the Lancaster & Carlisle in the west. In March Bintley spent a week viewing the country from Tebay and Penrith through Kirkby Stephen and across Stainmore to Barnard Castle and Bishop Auckland, establishing a provisional route. Four days later he sent a party to survey and take levels at the western end, and in early April a second group started work in the east. Several alternatives were explored over the high Pennines, and by September the field work was done, parliamentary plans and sections drawn ready for lithographing, and Bintley presented his bill, all in good time for the end of November. It must have been one of the few railway surveys in the Mania period that was not a race against the clock. Moreover, Bintley charged only the normal two guineas (£2.10) a day for himself, scaled down for his assistants, plus expenses, although doubtless at this time he could have earned considerably more. His bill totalled £948 2s 4d (£948.11½). Parliament in its wisdom decided that the York & Carlisle should be merged with a similar scheme and called the Northern Counties Union Railway, but like so many at the time the company subsequently collapsed. However, Bintley's route eventually formed much of the Stockton, Darlington & Lancashire Union Railway, opened in 1861.

Once the Mania had subsided, the work of planning routes for major lines passed increasingly to established engineers as the large company groupings took shape, creating powerful spheres of influence, leaving only connecting lines and branches to local men, some of whom were still jacks of all trades. David Jones, surveyor, in 1846 prepared a comprehensive estimate for the Aberdare Railway in South Wales that included way and works, station, warehouses, two locomotives, four coaches, 100 coal wagons, survey, Act and, if successful, 'superintending formation of line and Directory' (ie management) as well.[15]

Once they had obtained an Act, railway companies extensively employed local surveyors to set out the line ready for the contractors. R.G. Bolam of Newcastle was engaged by the York, Newcastle & Berwick Railway in 1847 to survey land and calculate quantities in Boulmer and Alnwick, and for a proposed Gateshead–Durham line along the Team Valley which was eventually built in 1862. Bolam had considerable difficulty in finding a practicable route through the built-up area around Chester-le-Street, and had to contend with wagonways and other railways intersecting his route. But from the number of doodles and sketches that enliven his field book, he does not seem to have been overworked.[16]

Thomas Frederick Hebblethwaite of Hull performed a very thorough and comprehensive job for the Hull & Holderness Railway in 1853-4, seeing it through from the first meeting of promoters.[17] Although Thomas Cabry of York was the engineer, he seems to have acted in a fairly nominal capacity and to have left Hebblethwaite to work out a route with the directors, solicit support, negotiate with landowners, survey and level the line and design stations. Hebblethwaite organised the printing and depositing of the parliamentary documents, gave evidence in committee and travelled far and wide agreeing values. An Act was obtained with little trouble, after which he completed land purchases and drew up bills of quantities in readiness for the contractors, occupying in all 207½ days for which he charged £496 17s 2d (£496.86).

The pressures of the Mania brought work for the surveyor from both sides — railway and landowner — particularly in areas that became battlegrounds for competing schemes. The disruption this work could cause in the comfortable life of a country surveyor is revealed in the diaries of John Martin of Evershot in Dorset, who in the first part of 1845 found himself copying plans and preparing opposition for the Duke of Cleveland and Lord Ilchester, owners of large estates in the area, in between beagling, attending Weymouth races and practising with a new theodolite which he found somewhat difficult to master. In the autumn things warmed up when, from 1 October to 14 November, he was more or less continuously engaged in surveying for the Exeter, Yeovil & Dorchester Railway in the race to get plans deposited by the end of November. Even so, he still found time to gather his apples and perform his duties with the Dorset Yeomanry.[18]

Not all surveyors gave satisfaction. Hugh Steel and Elijah Galloway Jr were in George Stephenson's survey team for the first Liverpool & Manchester Bill of 1825, the defeat of which was partly due to Stephenson's poor showing in committee. Their survey of the eastern end of the line, including Chat Moss, contained serious errors which Stephenson either had not checked or had failed to detect, but which his opponents did. In a letter of May 1825 to Henry Booth, who became the company's treasurer, Galloway blamed 'mismanagement of the instrument' in 'another department of the survey than mine', declaring somewhat virtuously that 'it is a frequent misfortune in Society that an innocent individual is so united with others as to be unable to free himself from an equal share in censures those only deserve'.[19] An accompanying note headed 'Galloway', which indicates that he assisted Steel, suggests that he was regarded as the junior of the two, even though in the previous year Steel was still only an apprentice to Stephenson, and it seems that Galloway was blaming one or the other. Not long before, Stephenson had named both of them chief assistants, with Joseph Locke, in his ambitious attempt to form George Stephenson & Son, so it seems unlikely that Galloway would risk impugning his chief. As for poor Steel, in 1827 he incurred Stephenson's wrath for changing the route during construction of the neighbouring Bolton & Leigh Railway, and committed suicide.

When I.K. Brunel was made engineer to the Great Western in March 1833, William H. Townsend was appointed his assistant surveyor. For a preliminary survey they were paid £500 between them. Townsend was a local land surveyor and valuer who had surveyed the Bristol & Gloucestershire Railway — a tramroad — and was supervising its construction. His was among three names put forward with Brunel's as possible surveyor and engineer for the whole line, probably because of his reputation as the builder of Bristol's first railway, but that he lacked the stature for such an undertaking is perhaps demonstrated by his willingness to act under Brunel, then only 26, who somewhat ungraciously accepted him. Three days later they set out from Bristol. Townsend 'as usual' was late. When in September the detailed survey was commenced, Townsend was given the western end but continued to irritate Brunel. On 24 September he recorded in his diary 'Met Mr Townsend. Breakfasted and started in his phaeton. Went as far as Keynsham; got out and walked over the line. Arrived at the valley at Brislington found the staffs up — all to double the curve agreed on. Could not make him understand the theory or rational[e].'[20]

Others fared worse. When Rice Hopkins' survey of the Llanidloes & Newtown Railway was examined in the Lords committee in 1853, his levels at one point were found to be 18ft below the River Severn. Not surprisingly, the Bill was lost. Richard Asquith of Carlisle surveyed land required for the Silloth Railway & Dock, but when he gave evidence in the Commons committee in 1854 his anticipated low-water level in the dock, which he had obtained by taking soundings, was proved wrong by an Admiralty surveyor.[21] As recently as 1924, Balfour Beatty's survey team working on the British Aluminium Company's Lochaber narrow gauge railway near Fort William were 100ft out in their levels and had to steepen the ruling gradient from 1 in 30 to 1 in 25.

Working under these engineers was no financial sinecure, either. They were responsible for checking the surveyors' accounts and authorising payment, and as the final cost invariably exceeded their original estimates (with the notable exception of Locke's) they had a vested interest in reducing expenditure.

Simultaneously with Townsend in the west, Brunel had Thomas Hughes at the London end of the Great Western, surveying the route towards Bristol. He seems to have been doing a conscientious job at good speed, but it was not fast enough to satisfy the impatient Brunel who questioned the surveyor's expenses, which he suggested could be reduced if Hughes sent his field books into the London office for plotting. Hughes stoutly defended himself, implying that such a course could only result in skimped work which he refused to countenance: 'I beg however to submit to you that it is not usual for a Surveyor to do the laborious work in the Field and afterwards give up his Section Book to be plotted at a cheap rate by another person, neither do I think without my assistance such plotting and locating of places could be depended upon . . . I have even done ten miles in one day — but be assured such Levels cannot be depended upon when done so very hurriedly, it would be almost Miraculous if errors did not creep in. I came in here [Wantage] last night dripping wet having stood in the rain two or three Hours, to work after I get home to catch up.' He concluded by asking for £5 to pay his inn bills, as long absence from home had exhausted his ready cash. Brunel sent it three days later.[22]

The old-established Sheffield firm of surveyors, Fairbanks, working on the London & Birmingham Railway in 1830, had occasion to clash with Robert Stephenson over their rendered accounts.[23] Josiah Fairbank wrote to Stephenson: 'We had scarcely commenced the survey before circumstances arose which rendered it impossible for us to be paid in the manner agreed upon', going on to point out the long distance from home compared with other surveyors, and the 'extraordinary exertions required to complete it on time'. Evidently Stephenson had questioned their expenses, at which Fairbank reminded him that his original response had been 'only get on and the Committee will not be nice' (ie over-particular). Apparently Stephenson argued that the Fairbanks had been engaged for surveying and levelling, whereas in fact they had prepared plans, drawn up books of references and notices, and had carried out a variety of other work for between 12 and 18 hours a day, and on occasions 24. The party had to pay high prices for accommodation, which no doubt was true; one can imagine the innkeepers of Leighton Buzzard and Daventry making the most of the opportunity before their coaching trade disappeared to the railway. Stephenson refused to back down, but eventually the London & Birmingham paid up, twelve months late.

This kind of thing was not unusual. Railway committees faced with a continuous outflow of cash and no prospect of revenue until at least part of the line was finished, perhaps several years off, were in no great hurry to pay for services rendered. Francis Giles had to instruct solicitors to get his bill paid by the London & Birmingham, and then only after a compromise.[24]

John Gibson suffered even more when he worked on the Pannal section of the Leeds & Thirsk Railway under Thomas Grainger, who reduced his final account of £317 18s 7d (£317.98) by £57 8s 0d (£57.40) without reason and refused to budge. One suspects some personal animosity, for a subsequent board enquiry established that Gibson had submitted his time sheets regularly and had worked a lot of overtime, including two Christmas Days. His salary and expenses had not been queried until after his contract was finished. He, too, had to instruct solicitors, who extracted his money, five years late, plus an extra £93 16s 4d (£93.86½) interest.[25]

The effectiveness of a railway survey depended on the manner in which it was organised. On the Stockton & Darlington, George Stephenson was accompanied by Robert and John Dixon, together with two staff-holders and two chain-men. Later on, surveyors sought ex-soldiers as chain-men and general factotums, preferably non-commissioned officers. The end of the French wars had put many on the labour market and their disciplined attitude made them ideal. Staff-holders were usually farm labourers armed with billhooks to clear a way through hedges and undergrowth. For his Liverpool & Manchester survey Stephenson divided the route into sections, but one of his failings was to delegate too much, with results that we have seen. His reputation was growing rapidly and he was busily occupied with installing stationary engines and boilers, as well as with railway work. Consequently his knowledge and experience were not as freely available as they would have been had he exercised closer control. Robert Stephenson, Locke and Brunel were careful not to make the same mistake.

Locke, Robert Stephenson, Brunel and Vignoles were among the first of that breed of engineers who combined technical skill and competence with organising ability and, above all, the enormous physical and mental endurance that was needed to build the great trunk railways which only youth could provide. It was one of the reasons why the older generation, like Telford, the Rennies, the canal men and George Stephenson himself, dropped behind. In 1837 it was the main factor which gained Robert, at the age of 27, first the commission for the London & Birmingham parliamentary survey and, three years later, the post of engineer-in-chief, against established figures like the Rennies and Francis Giles. Another was the reputation of the Stephenson name among the influential Liverpool financiers who provided a large part of the cash. Robert's chief assistant was Thomas Gooch, a fellow ex-pupil of George's, and they in turn, on behalf of the promoters, engaged other surveyors, to whom sections of the route were allocated. The same system was employed when

Very few illustrations of early railway construction show surveyors at work, but J.C. Bourne's print of the stationary engine house being built at Camden on the London & Birmingham Railway, published in 1839, includes a levelling party at the bottom left.
(National Railway Museum)

construction started. Stephenson split the line into four districts, each under an Assistant or Resident Engineer, with three sub-assistants.

One of Stephenson's pupils was Charles Fox, who was subsequently made Resident Engineer for the London to Tring section. In conjunction with Stephenson he designed the iron roof for Euston station, which set him on the path of structural engineering for which he became well-known. Near the end of 1837, when the line was open as far as Tring, Fox took on Herbert Spencer as a sub-engineer. Among his first tasks was to measure spoil heaps left by the contractors for disposal or making embankments, which he did in pouring rain, blackened water dripping from his hat on to his notebook. Within a year Fox secured him a job as a draughtsman under W.S. Moorsom, engineer to the Birmingham & Gloucester Railway, where he met another autobiographer, F.R. Conder, an ex-pupil of Fox's.[26] The two men's books provide a picture of life on railway survey work in the late 1830s.

As the experience necessary for supervision lay in older men, so the younger ones were in great demand for the field work, and engineers quite freely lent their pupils to one another, or arranged temporary transfers under suitable financial arrangements. Consequently a young trainee could find himself frequently moving about the country. Indeed, young men who could handle a level and chain suddenly found themselves important and, as Spencer put it, there was plenty of work, with good pay and good fun. In the years before the Mania, for a man prepared to travel there was a good, healthy, pleasant living to be made from railway surveying. Conder stressed the importance of taking the right clothes for four to six weeks' field work: two outdoor suits, one for indoors, a greatcoat, a travelling rug and a waterproof cape. He does not mention footwear, but presumably two or three stout pairs of boots were also advisable.

About this time the steadily advancing Ordnance Survey started to make work easier for those prepared to use the maps intelligently, forming an excellent guide for the railway projector. But according to Conder, in his time few engineers used them, preferring to prepare their own. He hints that professional pride may have been behind their reluctance to buy ready-made maps, although shareholders might have raised eyebrows had they known how their money was being spent on needless detail.

Moorsom presided over the Birmingham & Gloucester office at Worcester, where hours were 9am to 5pm, with an hour for lunch and Saturday afternoons free — an unusual advantage at that time. According to Spencer, the sub-assistants were all 'young bloods', younger sons of the gentry, many of them ex-army officers with corresponding tastes and habits, although Spencer seems to have found their company congenial and remarks that most of them made good. Compared with the tight schedules of parliamentary surveys, the more detailed work that preceded construction was relatively leisurely. Moorsom ran a club for his assistants at which technical papers were presented, a sort of mutual improvement class for which he deserves credit, despite his faults as an engineer and manager. In 1840 Spencer was appointed Moorsom's technical secretary, when he learned surveying and geology.

The Parliamentary Deadline

In 1844 the Birmingham & Gloucester proposed to make a branch from Droitwich to Wolverhampton. The Mania was gathering force, and the company was looking to protect its flank against rivals. Spencer was put on survey work, and the dramatic transition from the easy life as Moorsom's secretary, accompanying him around the pleasant Worcestershire and Gloucestershire countryside, to that of surveying to a tight schedule in the industrial Black Country, with the dreaded 30 November only weeks away, was a test of his qualities. He found the country something of a nightmare, 'a jumble of coal pits, iron works, cinder heaps, tramways, canals, lanes, streets, ground which has subsided and houses which were cracked in consequence of the abstraction of coal from beneath; and that the levels had to be taken in the midst of wind and rain and more or less smoke.' Measuring spoil heaps in the rain must have been child's play by comparison. There were only ten days left at the end of November in which to prepare the plans, which he did with four others at The Swan in Birmingham.

Conder and other writers described in detail the intense activity in drawing the plans and sections for Parliament. There was never sufficient time, so the work in the last few days continued day and night. Last-minute corrections added to the rush of plotting sections, copying plans, and numbering and copying the references. Plotting the lines was done by pricking the survey points on paper and joining them up — close, eye-straining work needing sustained concentration. Printing had to be clear and there were no short cuts for fear of infringing standing orders. Conder cites an occasion of pressure in 1836 when a local surveyor was called in to help. 'A man of mature age and quiet manner, he was at once one of the most industrious, and one of the best draughtsmen of his day. He had published one or two local maps of great precision and beauty . . . and all his work resembled copper-plate engraving.' To save time he had invented some instruments of his own, to divide instantly a line into three, draw two lines simultaneously and various patterns of broken lines. This paragon seemed to be able to work for three or four weeks with hardly any food and rest, for which he would charge no more than his rate for a seven-hour day.

The completed plans had to be taken to lithographers, who sometimes broke down under the strain. One office hit on the idea of reproducing plans by pricking through a dozen sheets at once, which meant that slight errors appeared on the lower ones when the holes were joined together; these might not be noticeable to a parish clerk or county surveyor, but were pounced on by skilled opponents in committee. The engineer airily attributed the discrepancies to unequal expansion of the paper.

Once the plans were safely deposited, everyone could relax, the surveyors and assistants awaiting summonses to London to give evidence. The Palace of Westminster was being rebuilt following the fire of 1834, so committee hearings were held in temporary wooden buildings where there was much hanging about awaiting the call. Their role was usually confined to giving factual evidence, leaving their superiors to undergo cross-examination.

Forth Bridge surveyors and their assistants line up with their instruments for an official photograph in December 1885. A bundled chain, tape measures and a spirit level lie on the ground in front. The bridge was opened 100 years before the year of publication of this book. (Scottish Record Office)

The Fairbanks of Sheffield organised large-scale surveys on a subcontract basis.[27] Established by William Fairbank I around 1739, this family firm undertook estate work, first in Yorkshire and Derbyshire and, as time went by, further afield. William Fairbank II was a surveyor of considerable standing, whose sons William III and Josiah I undertook canal surveys in south Yorkshire, including work for the important River Don Navigation. In 1815-16 Josiah surveyed a route for a proposed tramroad from limestone deposits on Mam Tor in the Peak District to kilns to be built on the River Derwent, including a tunnel; in 1820 he made estimates of excavations for the Carlisle Canal; and in 1824 surveyed a Sheffield & Manchester Canal project for Telford. With the advent of railways Josiah and his eldest son, oddly named William Fairbank Fairbank, rapidly expanded the business.

They surveyed many lines in Yorkshire and surrounding areas on their own account, and between 1830 and 1841, as survey subcontractors to leading engineers on trunk lines that included John Rennie's London & Brighton Direct, the Bletchley–Rugby and Coventry sections of the London & Birmingham, the first Great Northern Railway and the London & York. They also did work for George Stephenson on the North Midland. They appear to have devised a system of carrying out a preliminary survey with the engineer and preparing outline tracings, following which they engaged a team of other surveyors and assistants to do the levelling and plotting and, where necessary, to mark out the line. The teams fed in their data to a central office where it was transferred to paper and lithographed copies prepared for deposit. The whole programme required a high degree of organisation and was totally reliant on the Post Office for next day deliveries, which seem invariably to have taken place, providing an interesting commentary on present-day reliability. The Fairbanks were constant recipients of aggressively insistent instructions and curt requests from engineers, solicitors and parliamentary agents demanding plans and answers to queries, and they communicated with their own men in similar vein.

It was not always easy to recruit. On the London & Brighton job in 1836 the Fairbanks tried as far afield as Lancaster and Manchester, from where William Johnson replied that he had twenty full-time surveyors working for him and was fully occupied for the rest of the year. To add to their difficulties, there were peremptory letters from Rennie. On 28 November 1836 he ticked off Josiah at Godstone: 'How could you be so foolish as to take away your Section of the main Brighton line with you — I am compelled to send the bearer Mr Lowe for it. It is too bad to give us so much trouble, you ought to have known that we cannot get on without it. Pray therefore let Mr Lowe have it at once or tell him where to get it. Let me know the levels of the branch you are about to get on — come to the town afterwards.'

For the Gainsborough, Sheffield & Doncaster project of the same year, Martin Durham agreed to work for Fairbanks, levelling between Sheffield and Gainsborough at £3 a day, Fairbanks to provide a tracing of the course and mark it out on the ground 'so that the line may be seen'. Again that year, they undertook to survey the Gainsborough, Sheffield & Chesterfield Railway, employing Henry Sanderson of Stamford, William Bull of Sheffield and George E. Hamilton, 'civil engineer and architect', of Wolverhampton. The last may well have been the same George Hamilton who worked for William James on the Liverpool & Manchester. He was a prolific and wordy correspondent, sending almost daily letters to Sheffield giving immensely detailed reports on his progress, or lack of it. He was also a moaner. Near Dronfield in March he found Brierley Wood 'a most awful obstacle . . . I never was in such a tangle of briars, binds and underwood.' It was also raining, which reduced his survey to 1 mile that day.

Later in the year Hamilton was working on 'the Boston line' — probably the first, unsuccessful, Great Northern scheme — out in the Lincolnshire fens, and it was still raining. On 6 November he wrote: 'To level amid the rain, as you know, is impossible, for the Glasses [of the instrument] become so dimmed, so as to be useless — all we can do is watch the weather and take advantage of any cessation of rain — for it has been little else since I have been here . . . the Dykes all filling fast, every ditch becoming a Dyke, and every Dyke a river, would it be advisable to put some person at Peterboro' and commence levelling to meet me? — for if such weather as we now have continues, where shall we be even a fortnight hence?' He fears that his assistant, White from Newcastle, is sickening with the 'Fens fever':

'This morning he ate nothing and complained of feeling ill . . . if he knocks up, which I have great apprehension of, for he certainly is very far from well, where shall I be?' Seven days later another rain-soaked letter reached Sheffield from Spalding. 'What a Contract. What weather. This country is only fit for Ducks and Geese and human Amphibia. In fact we are all amphibious here.' He occupied his time constructing a portable wooden bridge for crossing dykes, at a cost of 17s (£0.85), which could be carried by two men.

Frederick Wood (see also chapter 7, p.175), who was despatched from Peterborough with three men, was made of sterner stuff. 'The wind has been so very boisterous nearly to blow one away from the Instrument . . . but I have broken in the Men . . .' Even he was deterred at Peakirk, whence he had to return through knee-high floods 'which I have had to walk through'. They managed to meet up at Market Deeping with only days to spare for preparing the plans.

Back at the centre of operations in Sheffield, the Fairbanks were under even greater strain, despite their highly organised methods. With a number of projects under way at the same time their health was undermined, and in 1844 Josiah died aged 66, overwhelmed by railway work. A year later, after the Mania had crashed, William was taken ill with 'nervous excitement' and was forced to convalesce at Clifton, 'caused by the improper conduct of some of the promoters [of the London & York] . . . respecting the evidence . . . I doubt whether I shall be ever able to attend to any business again.' There were difficulties in getting accounts settled, too, particularly in a case where three successive subcontracts were concerned and William Cubitt, engineer to the London & York, was asked to intervene. William Fairbank's gloomy prognosis was only too well-founded. While in London on parliamentary business in 1846 he had a stroke which partly paralysed him. He struggled on with what office work he could manage, but in 1848 he died of a further seizure, aged 43. With his death the firm that four generations had built up into a prosperous and respected country-wide practice came to an end.

Meeting Opposition

The vigorous, at times violent, hostility encountered by railway surveyors from landowners has become part of the folklore of early railways, and despite the embellishments some of the stories have acquired there is little doubt that initially the majority of the landed interest was bitterly opposed to the invasion of property. As the years went by, the realisation that railways could enhance values, and pockets too, changed entrenched attitudes even in the most diehard proprietors, although in many cases it took a long time; but for the surveyors of the first main lines there were few friendly faces as they chained their way across England.

To gain access, the surveyor had to rely either on the owner's or occupier's goodwill, which frequently was denied him, or his own good sense and ingenuity, of which he developed a large store. Even the legal right of access granted by an Act, once it was obtained, often did little to help where the most obdurate landlords were concerned, although in the last resort the surveyor could always invoke the law.

Conder recalls how the surveyor would carry with him a copy of the Act as evidence of his authority, and brandish it before threatening farmers, who would later retaliate by accidentally ploughing up survey pegs, obliterating the route.

There were others, sensitive to threats to the landscape, who opposed railways which they thought would despoil sacred places, the equivalent of environmentalists in our own day, although they would not have recognised the term. Wordsworth and Ruskin are the best remembered. Twenty years before the 1845 Mania, there occurred a minor boom in railway speculation, prompted by the successful construction of the Stockton & Darlington, then nearing completion and opened in September 1825, and the intense interest in the Liverpool & Manchester Bill. John Clare, the Northamptonshire poet, recorded in his journal an encounter near Helpston, taken here from *The Prose of John Clare*, edited by J.W. and A. Tibble (1951):

Saw 3 fellows at the end of Royce Wood who I found were laying out the plan for an 'Iron Railway' from Manchester to London it is to cross over Round Oak Spring by Royce Wood Corner for Woodcroft Castle I little thought that fresh intrusions would interrupt & spoil my solitudes after the Enclosure they will despoil a boggy place that is famous for Orchises at Royce Wood end.

Thomas Bowles of Evesham was taking no chances when he had this notice printed in 1865, prohibiting railway surveyors from entering his garden before gaining the consent of the local justices.
(BR Property Board)

To the Evesham and Redditch Railway Company, their Secretary, Servants, and others it may concern.

I hereby give you Notice

NOT TO ENTER INTO OR UPON THE GARDEN GROUND now in my occupation, in the Borough of Evesham, in the County of Worcester, the subject of enquiry before the Justices at Evesham aforesaid this day. And that if you the said Railway Company, or your Servants enter upon the said Garden Ground and Land, you and each and every of you will be deemed to be WILFUL TRESPASSERS, and be PROCEEDED AGAINST ACCORDINGLY.

Dated this 13th Day of May, 1865.   *Thomas Bowles*

J. Pearce, Printer, &c., Bridge-street, Evesham.

The line was possibly for the Northern Railroad Company, which was projecting a railway from London to Manchester via Cambridge and thence north westward to link up with the Cromford & High Peak Railway in Derbyshire. The Rennies were planning it and had surveyed as far as Cambridge before the scheme fell through. Maybe Clare's three fellows were reconnoitring beyond.

William James's team on the 1822 Liverpool & Manchester survey met organised opposition from tenants and employees of landowners, delaying their work. They were stoned, a mob of miners near St Helens threatened to throw them down the pit, and a prize fighter hired to guard the theodolite attracted the most extreme attentions. In September Robert Stephenson wrote to James at Newton-le-Willows: 'I was so unfortunate as to have my level kicked over just as I was finishing tonight, will you be so good as to bring Mr Hamilton's level and legs with you in the morning.'[28]

Three years later George Stephenson met the same response, as Rolt records, quoting a letter written to Stephenson's old friend Edward Pease:

We have sad work with Lord Derby, Lord Sefton and Bradshaw the great Canal Proprietor whose grounds we go through with the projected railway. Their ground is blockaded on every side to prevent us getting on with the survey. Bradshaw fires guns through his ground in the course of the night to prevent the surveyors coming in the dark. We are to have a grand field day next week. The Liverpool Rly Co are determined to force a survey through if possible. Lord Sefton says he will have 100 men to stop us. The Company thinks these great men have no right to stop our survey. It is the Farmers only who have right to complain and by charging damages for trespass is all they can do.

Bradshaw was managing trustee of the Bridgewater estate and determined to protect the canal at all costs. Stephenson himself was threatened with a ducking in a pond, and was twice turned off by Bradshaw's men who promised to carry him off to Worsley Hall if he did not retreat. The company enjoined the surveyors to work as unobtrusively as possible and at all costs to avoid damaging crops, hedges and fences. T.S. Brandreth, a director, wrote to Henry Booth to say that after complaints from Lord Sefton 'our own surveyors were cautioned and were told they would not be supported if they behaved improperly; that by setting the landowners against us they would do us more injury than their services would ever be worth.'[29]. Surveyors in a hurry were not always particular, as the Trent Valley Railway discovered when Sir George Chetwynd of Grendon Hall, near Atherstone, presented it with a bill for £27 14s 10½d (£27.74) for trees 'unfortunately cut down by the surveyors' before he could stop them.[30]

Robert Stephenson encountered even greater hostility on the London & Birmingham, which met with more concerted opposition from landowners than any other railway. The surveyors had to resort to working while the landowner and his family were at dinner; in the case of a landowning parson, while he was at church; or as a last resort, at night, using shaded lanterns. Owners set their men to watch and to

LONDON AND BIRMINGHAM RAILWAY.

OFFICE, 69, CORNHILL,
4th *Jan* 1834

THE London Committee of Directors have requested me, as their Chairman, to inform·you, that the Company's Engineers, in the performance of their duties, and in pursuance of the provisions of the Act of Parliament, have entered upon your land for the purpose of staking out the Line, and taking the levels and surveys by which the quantity of ground required by the Company must be determined. The Engineers are instructed, on all occasions, to consult the convenience of Proprietors and Occupiers to the fullest extent which may be consistent with the due execution of their work; and the Committee are anxious, in any case of damage, to afford a fair compensation for it, by amicable arrangement.

I am requested to add, that as soon as the Engineer in Chief, shall have reported to the Committee the portion of your property, which will be wanted for the construction of the Railway, they are desirous of treating for the purchase upon the principle which may appear best adapted to ensure a prompt and equitable adjustment of the respective interests of the Proprietor and the Company.

The Committee trust that under these circumstances, the Company's Engineers may be allowed to hope for your friendly countenance and assistance in their operations.

I have the honor to be,

Your obedient Servant,

I. SOLLY, *Chairman.*

A London & Birmingham Railway Notice to Enter of 1834. Despite the courteous phraseology, the notice makes it clear that the company has statutory authority to enter land; there is no question of asking for permission. (Buckinghamshire Record Office) patrol their boundaries, and tenants and locals were told to report any unusual activity when railway surveyors were known to be about. In retaliation, the surveyors sent out decoys. Francis Fox, in his memoirs *River, Road and Rail* (1904), recalled how three gamekeepers were sent to patrol outside the hotel where he and his colleagues were staying, and each time an attempt was made to enter the estate they were warned off. So they hit on the idea of sending out three parties to widely separated parts of the estate where they tried to look busy without actually entering it. Each party was, of course, followed, leaving the coast clear for the real survey team to depart in the right direction and complete its task.

On occasions there was violence. *The Builder* recorded several cases.[31] A well-known hunting celebrity, Assheton Smith of South Tidworth, Hampshire, threatened to call out the Andover Yeomanry to protect his coverts. A survey party on the Bletchley–Oxford line insisted on crossing land at Bicester, resulting in bloodshed and the reading of the Riot Act, while at nearby Islip the villagers forced the surveyors to turn back. Keepers employed by Mr Foljambe of Osberton, near Worksop, saw lights at night which they took to be poachers, but were surveyors 'armed, not with sickle, dragnet, or air gun, but with brass tubes, long poles and chains, the lights proceeding from divers bull's-eye lanterns. Each party prepared for action, the game-watchers levelling their guns and the intruders their long poles with a flag at one end and pointed with iron at the other, like so many foot lancers.' The keepers were in a minority and retreated.

Court cases frequently ensued. Railway surveyors involved in a fracas at Adlington, Cheshire, were fined 5s (£0.25) each and 15s (£0.75) costs, although those who struggled with Sir W. Milner's servants at Appleton, near York, and were charged with assault, fared better. They were bound over to keep the peace for six months which, their job completed, they were happy to accept. In the Scottish Highlands, on at least one occasion clan warfare broke out between rival groups of promoters. The Scottish Grand Junction Railway, headed by the Marquis of Breadalbane, was one of a number of Mania schemes hoping to open up the western Highlands, aiming to connect Stirling and Callander with Oban via Crianlarich, whence a 'branch' would run down Glen Falloch through the Trossachs to Glasgow. A rival project using much the same route from Glasgow, the Caledonian Northern Direct, had as its provisional chairman the Duke of Montrose. Glen Falloch was Breadalbane territory, so it was more or less natural that, when a Caledonian Northern survey party was seen at work in the glen, Breadalbane supporters should organise a raid of lead-miners from Tyndrum who threw the surveyors and their theodolites into a ditch. Montrose gained an interdict restraining the opposition from interference and his surveyors prudently kept to the road as far as possible. When a solitary surveyor and his man were spotted, Breadalbane's miners went into action again, this time non-violently, contenting themselves with holding their plaids in front of the theodolite. The bursting of the Mania 'bubble' saw the end of both projects, and the others, and the West Highlands had to wait over thirty years for railways.

The most celebrated case of harassment became known as 'The Battle of Saxby'.[32] In 1845 the Midland Railway planned to take its Leicester–Peterborough line through Stapleford Park, the seat of Lord Harborough who, having spent £80,000 on improving his estate, adamantly refused the company access. The surveyors, therefore, decided to conduct their survey from the towing path of the Oakham Canal, which passed through the park, unknowing that in return for his lordship's having reconstructed it, the canal company (illegally, so it transpired) had surrendered to him their rights over that section of the towing path. Drama quickly followed. According to the *Leicester Advertiser*,[33] the surveyors were stopped by a group of Lord Harborough's men led by a keeper named Biddle (to whom the author, as far as he is aware, is not related) who, on being threatened with a pistol, doughtily retorted 'Shoot away'. After some argument the surveyors withdrew, but Biddle applied for a warrant against the pistolier, a surveyor called Charles Frowe of Thorpe, near Lincoln. Frowe was arrested and spent the weekend in Leicester jail.

Two days later the Midland men tried again at Saxby Bridge, this time supported by a gang of navvies. A scrimmage took place as the railway party tried to force its way on to the towing path, although the presence of several policemen prevented it developing into a fight and, after some surveyors had been chased along the canal bank and a chain was broken, both sides agreed to submit to the decision of the magistrates on the following Tuesday. But it was mid-November, and if a Bill was to be placed before the 1846 Parliament the plans had to be ready and deposited by the 30th. So it was decided to ignore the agreement and mount a dawn raid on the Saturday. The railway company assembled some 80-100 men, but Lord Harborough's steward got wind of it and brought out a party of estate workers to meet them. While the two sides faced each other, the distraction actually enabled the surveyors to do some work, but as reinforcements for Lord Harborough arrived a fight broke out in which staves, cudgels and sticks were freely used and at least one man was threatened with a billhook. Lord Harborough's men won, and six from the railway party subsequently appeared before Lord Chief Justice Tyndall at Leicester assizes in March 1846, where they were convicted of assault, fined 1s (5p) each and sentenced to a month's first-class imprisonment. That meant that they were confined in relative comfort, and they were reported to be quite enjoying it. Meanwhile, the survey had been finished in time, so the Midland paid for their defence and compensated them for their incarceration.

Not all railways were so bitterly opposed. J.K. Fowler of Aylesbury, in his *Recollections of Old Country Life* (1894), told how, when Stephenson's original route for the London & Birmingham through Uxbridge, Amersham and Aylesbury was opposed by every landowner, the engineer was sent for by the Countess of Bridgewater at Ashridge and asked why he did not follow the line of the Grand Junction Canal through her lands at Berkhamstead and Tring 'already gashed by the canal'. As it already divided her property she suggested that there might be less severance to pay for, her consent would disarm the opposition and the locks would provide a guide to the levels. Fowler said that Stephenson took her advice.

The Profession Changes

After the parochial and tithe surveys were finished in the 1840s, the profession of land surveyor started to wane. The surge in demand by the railways arrested it for a few years, but after the Mania railway surveying increasingly became a branch of civil engineering, aided by the steady spread of the Ordnance Survey which eventually rendered the detailed surveying of new lines largely superfluous. The excesses of the Mania did nothing to help land surveyors; so many charged exhorbitant fees and others without experience passed themselves off as qualified that they brought general discredit on the profession. The social reformer Edwin Chadwick in 1842 condemned surveyors as a whole as expensive and inefficient compared with the Ordnance Survey,[34] which was not entirely fair. While there was no excuse for the charlatans, the pressures imposed by avaricious or simply anxious promoters, and a totally unrealistic parliamentary timetable, transmitted through ambitious engineers to the surveyors in the field, at times forced the most competent and conscientious men to take short cuts. The engineers themselves were not entirely blameless. Capable of sustained mental and physical effort that would leave many present-day 'workaholics' standing, they expected no less of those working for them and were not minded to accept even the most justifiable excuse if delay might endanger a programme, and thereby a reputation. Deadlines had to be met regardless; if there was a risk of missing the deposit of a Bill almost anything was acceptable rather than wait another year. Inaccuracies, in any case, might possibly be overlooked, or argued away by skilful advocacy, so if a choice had to be made the engineers and promoters were always prepared to chance a few errors. Consequently, surveyors who worked as furiously as men like Hughes, Gibson and the Fairbanks could hardly be blamed for charging the highest fees they could get.

The primary blame lay, of course, with Parliament, as contemporary writers so often stressed, echoed by the Midland's defending counsel over the Saxby affray in the court at Leicester. If Parliament required fully detailed surveys, Parliament should provide adequate time and legal authority to perform them. None the less, there is no doubt that the old-style land surveyor, overtaken by new methods and contributing to his own decline, was on the way out, and by 1870 he was virtually extinct.

On the other hand, those surveyors who developed their valuation skills prospered. Good valuers and negotiators were in as great demand by the railways as those who manipulated theodolite and level, and continued to be so throughout the railway age. It has been suggested that by 1870 the 13,000-odd miles of railway then open had taken perhaps 2 million acres of land at a very rough average estimate, all of which required the services of valuers, in most cases employed by both sides — railway and vendor — bringing in an estimated £½ million in fees.[35] The top men, in addition, were in demand as umpires and arbitrators, work which, on major schemes after the Lands Clauses Consolidation Act of 1845, increasingly fell to a small group of firms and made their reputations.

Chapter 4

Land for the Line

The Landed Interest

George and Robert Stephenson were not being entirely practical when they said that the ideal railway should follow the lowest possible relief in order to economise on locomotive fuel, consistent with a route that was the least expensive to build, even if it was not the most direct, which should avoid wherever possible the parks and pleasure grounds of country seats.[1] The first two principles were rarely compatible, but the third was soundly based on their personal experience.

Historians have long been exercised by landowners' attitudes to railways and their effect on routes. Wholesale condemnation by contemporary writers like J. Francis, echoed by F.S. Williams in *Our Iron Roads* (1883), has been widely accepted until fairly recently, when objective investigation has produced more balanced judgements.[2] Abuses such as those they exposed were certainly commonplace. The evidence is there. Powerful landowners undoubtedly cost the railways a lot of money by forcing changes of route, demanding excessive prices for land in exhange for support, exacting tribute in the form of elaborate works and structures, gaining concessionary travel, or combinations of all four.

Speaking to the Institution of Surveyors in 1874, F.A. Philbrick put two opposing arguments.[3] Should an owner who has sunk his money in his property, or perhaps simply likes it as it is and does not want it changed, be forced to sell against his will? And if the law compels him to do so, is he therefore not entitled to as much as he can get? Conversely, Parliament only grants compulsory purchase powers when it considers there is an overriding public interest, as in the case of public utilities like gas, water and railways. Why then, should a right of compensation be granted in addition, when other lawful buying and selling is based solely on market price with no inbuilt protection against loss?

For all the scandals it created, the Railway Mania brought home to opponents the fact that railways were there to stay, causing them to change their attitudes as the base of the economy changed from agriculture to industry and commerce. Michael Robbins made perhaps the wisest comment in *The Railway Age* (1962), when he pointed out that of the £50 million spent building 27 main railways between 1825 and 1850, land purchase accounted for about 13.9 per cent, and promotional and parliamentary costs generally less than 5 per cent; 'not intolerable proportions' which, when viewed against the total of £1,100 million invested in Britain's railways, were really rather insignificant. That some landlords received excessive payments does not mean to say that they were characteristic, and we shall later look at the other side of the coin. Like so much in our own day, events that made news were not necessarily typical.

Nevertheless, it is important to examine the effect of landed interests, and more so to appreciate the attitudes that influenced them. There is no doubt that in 1830 landowners as a class were, in the main and in varying degree, opposed to railways, with certain clear exceptions we shall come to later. Railways in the countryside were seen as a gross intrusion on centuries-old privacy, destroying the enjoyment of estates on many of which large sums of money had been spent during the previous half century, and which, it was believed, would suffer a fall in value. It had been bad enough to have canals carving up the land by compulsory purchase, but the railways were much worse — noisy, dirty, more prominent and less flexible in their ability to change route. The oft-quoted anxiety about the effect of trains on grazing livestock was very real, too. Worst of all, to the aristocracy railways represented the ascendancy of commerce which, by banding together, they endeavoured to defeat. As an example, although fears of ruined hunting may today seem somewhat quaint, to the squire of 1839 it was important, ranking high in his priorities. Henry Fellowes, master of The Vyne Hunt, warned the Duke of Wellington that the London & Southampton Railway would destory hunting in their best country and advised him to withdraw his support.[4]

In the cities, landowners were less united. The Duke of Bedford steadfastly refused to allow railways through Bloomsbury, determined to maintain its exclusiveness and therefore its value, but small property owners were more amenable if more rapacious in their claims. On the whole, in large towns railways found it easier and cheaper to deal with a few big landowners than a large number of small ones.

The Effect on Routes

The rejection of the London & Birmingham Railway's first parliamentary Bill is a classic example of defeat at the hands of the landed property interest. Near Watford the Earl of Essex at Cassiobury Park and the Earl of Clarendon at Grove Park drew on their earlier experience with the Grand Junction Canal. Eton College, owners of land at Weedon, Thomas Reeve Thornton of nearby Brockhall, Lidlingstone at Elmdon near Birmingham, and Kensal Green Cemetery Company — all were obstructive, along with other lesser landowners and, understandably, canal companies, turnpike trusts and the coaching trade. Lord Brownlow, of Ashridge, successfully opposed the third reading in the Lords, claiming 'that the directors had not made out a case which would warrant a forcing of the proposed railway through the lands and properties of so great a proportion of distinguished landowners and proprietors'.

To succeed, the London & Birmingham had to spend close on £73,000 in buying off the opposition, and building Watford Tunnel, 1 mile 75yd long, to avoid Cassiobury and Grove parks. It promised a sharp curve to avoid Weedon and a tunnel at Brockhall, and avoided Elmdon entirely. In the event it was able to ease the Weedon curve, while Thornton settled for a deep cutting, but Kensal Green Cemetery held out, forcing the railway to tunnel under a corner of their ground.[5]

Towns which wanted railways could find themselves at loggerheads with landowners. Lord Exeter has been blamed for the Great Northern Railway avoiding Stamford in preference for Peterborough, although it appears that he only wanted a minor deviation further away from Burghley House. It seemed that originally Earl Fitzwilliam had also played a part in changing the Great Northern's route as some recompense to Peterborough for his opposition to the London & Birmingham's branch from Blisworth, a tactic which, it was suggested, Lord Exeter might copy when the Midland projected its Leicester–Peterborough line through Stamford. But he wanted the Midland no more than the Great Northern and commissioned Francis Giles to survey a line further away, to the anger of Stamford townsfolk. It also in turn upset Sir John Trollope of Casewick Hall, who found himself likely to be sandwiched between two railways, so he asked Earl Fitzwilliam to intercede with the Midland on his behalf to ensure that the line passed through Stamford — which it does, safely screened from the town and from Burghley Park in a cutting and a tunnel.[6]

Further west on the same line, Lord Harborough continued to be troublesome. In its Act the railway sought peace by securing the authorisation of two alternative routes, south of Stapleford Park through a tunnel or north along the line of the Oakham Canal which the Midland bought out. However, when the contractor set

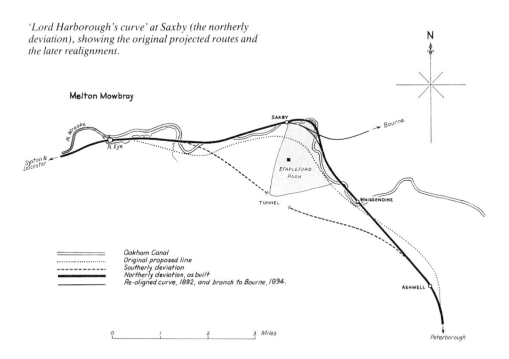

'Lord Harborough's curve' at Saxby (the northerly deviation), showing the original projected routes and the later realignment.

N

Melton Mowbray

SAXBY

Bourne

R. Wreake

R. Eye

Syston &
Leicester

STAPLEFORD
PARK

WHISSENDINE

TUNNEL

Oakham Canal
Original proposed line
Southerly deviation
Northerly deviation, as built
Re-aligned curve, 1892, and branch to Bourne, 1894.

ASHWELL

0   1   2   3 Miles

Peterborough

about cutting through the hill to make the tunnel on the southerly route, in contravention of the Act which said it must be bored without surface disturbance, Lord Harborough got an injunction stopping him, so there was no recourse but to use the canal, involving a sharp curve. In 1892 the line was realigned to permit faster running but the site of Lord Harborough's Curve is still visible today.[7]

Smaller proprietors could be equally awkward at strategic points. Ann and James Taylor secured a clause in the Manchester & Leeds Act of 1836 preventing the line from being built closer to Todmorden Hall than 70yd unless it was in a tunnel — and even then it had to be no closer than 30yd — while the 1867 Act for the Furness Railway's branch from Arnside to Hincaster Junction stipulated that part must be on arches, 'In order that the view from Dallam Tower Estate may be obstucted as little as possible', resulting in the necessary bridge over the River Bela becoming an unnecessary viaduct. Mrs Ann Owen did not allow her shareholding in the Oswestry & Newtown Railway to distract her from refusing passage through her property at Glansevern on the west bank of the Severn near Berriew. Consequently the river had to be bridged and the line taken over higher ground with a 2-mile climb at 1 in 110-195 to Forden.

Nearly 25 per cent of Scottish land was owned by only 12 people, and 50 per cent was owned by 70, with one owner possessing over 1.3 million acres. Fewer assents were needed than in England and in many instances they were easier to get. A number of the great estates were in straitened circumstances, and as railway development in Scotland occurred later the advantages were starting to be perceived. Even so, there were difficult men, particularly the Duke of Atholl who objected to most railways in the Highlands and successfully opposed the Perth & Dunkeld Bill of 1837, determined to keep his tolls over Dunkeld bridge, although when the Highland Railway was planned through Blair Atholl, Joseph Mitchell seems to have done much to win the Duke over through sheer force of personality. Every route towards Edinburgh and Glasgow from Carlisle was blocked by the Duke of Buccleuch's huge estate. When a railway was eventually built up Nithsdale in 1845 it had to be on a route over 1½ miles from Drumlanrig Castle that included a ¾-mile-long tunnel. North of the Moray Firth the Dingwall & Skye Railway was delayed for two years in the 1860s by landowners around Strathpeffer who forced the line on to a deviation with a 4-mile climb at 1 in 50 to Raven Rock which still hampers train working today, leaving Strathpeffer to be served by a branch, to its eventual detriment. Likewise the busy little port of Garlieston in the south west had to be content with a branch owing to Lord Galloway's opposition to the Wigtownshire Railway crossing his estate, even though his son was chairman. If the West Highland Railway in 1894 had not been thwarted by landowners in its intention of extending from Fort William to the coast at Rushven, instead of going to Mallaig seven years later, it would have saved 15 miles and have served the finest natural harbour on the west coast. But the pattern was reversed when, after initial objections, Lord Seafield supported the routing of the Highland Railway's first main line to Inverness through Grantown and Forres instead of by the shorter route through Carr Bridge and Nairn, in order to transport his timber.

To a considerable extent commercial motives also dictated the route of the Newcastle & Carlisle Railway in 1839. The natural route between Haltwhistle and Carlisle lay down the River Irthing to the Eden, but Lord Carlisle was not prepared to accept a branch line to join his mineral railway at Brampton so the main line went that way instead, avoiding Sir Hew Ross's estate at Hayton in the process. The company saved £10,000 on the Brampton branch and £8,000 compensation to Sir Hew, which can have no more than dented the extra cost of three viaducts, high embankments and deep cuttings, including a mile at Cowran Hills up to 110ft deep.

Crown Property

Government agencies were no more amenable. The Commissioners of Woods and Forests, jealous guardians of Crown lands, had wide powers by means of which, commented A. Doull (see p43), they extorted the most arbitrary conditions and were as bad as private landlords. They certainly used their powers to the full when the Great Western and the London & South Western wanted to build branches to Windsor, demanding £25,000 from one and £60,000 from the other in circumstances that looked suspiciously like double-dealing. The Commissioners were hard bargainers with the Southampton & Dorchester over its line through the New Forest, which they would have forced on to a coastal route had one been practicable. Instead, they decreed that it should take a winding course through Brockenhurst to

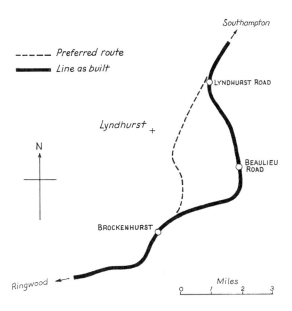

The Southampton & Dorchester Railway's preferred route through the New Forest, and the more circuitous line that was built at the insistence of the Commissioners of Woods & Forests, today forms part of Network SouthEast's main line to Bournemouth.

Ringwood instead of direct through Lyndhurst, a town which thereafter has had to be content with Lyndhurst Road station 2 miles away.

Lines projected along the coast below high water mark attracted the interest of the Commissioners or the Admiralty, although the Hull & Selby Railway had obtained its Act in 1836 and started to buy land along the Humber foreshore at Hull before the Commissioners woke up and claimed that it was Crown property. The adjoining landowners, considering that they had good title, held out and the case went to court, taking two years to resolve and delaying the opening of the line. The Commissioners won and generously let the land go for a modest figure,[8] unlike the Admiralty at Rye which got £10,000 from the Brighton, Lewes & Hastings Railway for harbour improvements and their consent to a bridge. Brunel's line below the cliffs at Dawlish on the South Devon Railway had to be taken further inshore than he wanted, and a footpath made along the new sea wall to compensate for restricted access to the beach. On the Whitehaven Junction Railway the Admiralty claimed jurisdiction as far as 100yd above high water mark, and the Chester & Holyhead's Act contained quite detailed provisions for an embankment across the head of the beach near Flint, the sea wall at Abergele and the use of Stanley embankment near Holyhead. The whole question of the Commissioners' and Admiralty consent was codified in the Railways Clauses Act of 1845.

When it seemed that railways might compromise defence works, the War Office flexed its muscles. The South Eastern was compelled to curve inland from the coast at Dover instead of cutting through or under Archcliff Fort to reach the pier, while at Portsmouth only a branch line to the naval dockyard was allowed to pierce the inner defences until the Harbour station was opened in 1876.

Fighting the Landowners
The year 1833 can be said to have been a turning point in the development of the railway system when, on the same day, the first two trunk lines were authorised, the London & Birmingham and the Grand Junction railways. Although the latter was completed first, it was the progress of the London & Birmingham which attracted the greater interest. Having been defeated in Parliament once, its success in avoiding hostile territory or, where that was not possible, in buying off the opposition notwithstanding the enormous expense, was duly noted by other promoters. They followed suit, and during the next four years most Bills for important railways succeeded at the first attempt — the London & Southampton in 1834 and a whole clutch of lines in 1836, including the South Eastern, Manchester & Leeds, York & North Midland and the three lines that shortly amalgamated to form the Midland Railway. The London & Brighton also got through first time, in 1837, although the landed interest concerned Parliament rather less than the task of choosing between six competing schemes. The Great Western was the only important casualty through failure sufficiently to placate landed opposition in 1834, which it was careful to rectify when it introduced a second, successful Bill in the following year. After 1837 money became tighter and the capital that was available for investment earlier in the

decade dried up, but even so the success of so many important schemes in five years proved the railway protagonists right and set the stage for the future.

The particular significance of the London & Birmingham was its clear demonstration of a railway company's resources to pay vastly inflated prices for land and to absorb large increases in construction costs arising from unforeseen engineering difficulties like Kilsby Tunnel, yet still be able to complete 112 miles of line in less than five and a half years. The magnitude of this physical, organisational and financial performance was not lost on landowners. More than anything else it impressed on them that railways were unstoppable. They might be delayed, they might be diverted from their preferred route, and they could certainly be made to pay, but in the end they would take the land they wanted. So landowners bargained, and bargained hard, on all fronts.

In laying down methods of settling disputes over compulsory purchase, early railway legislation followed a modified form of the procedure in the canal Acts. If there was failure to agree, a jury would be summoned of twelve 'sufficient and indifferent men' qualified to act in court, which meant that they had to be enfranchised and therefore were citizens of some substance. Repetition in individual Acts was cut out and parliamentary time reduced in 1845 with the passing of the Lands Clauses Consolidation Act, under which disputes were settled by an arbitrator or, if there was disagreement over a single appointment, two, with an umpire to decide on points of difference; as time went on a considerable body of case law on the interpretation of the Act was established.[9] There was still the option of a jury, and there is little doubt that the Act as a whole favoured the landowners. In the canal days the market price of land was generally adjudged a reasonable basis of settlement, but the Lands Clauses Act enshrined the principle of separate awards for the value of the land and for compensation for loss of amenity. The Caledonian Railway shareholders' committee investigating the company's finances in 1849 was in no doubt: land estimated to be worth £173,000 had cost £389,979, an increase mainly due to the arbitration clauses that had been invoked in nearly all instances, including some by directors. Only the chairman, J.J. Hope Johnstone, to his credit, had accepted the valuer's figure.[10]

The decision on when to open negotiations for land could cause something of a dilemma. Support from large landowners, or at least their consent not to oppose, was essential for the success of a Bill. Yet negotiations before an Act, when there were no rules, left the promoters at landowners' mercy and invariably ended in a legally binding agreement to whatever terms he might extract that was subject only to an Act being obtained. The alternative was to chance overcoming powerful opposition in Parliament and obtaining the limited protection of the Lands Clauses Act, a risk few railways were prepared to take.

John Duncan, solicitor to the Eastern Counties Railway, expressed forthright views on this point before the House of Lords Select Committee on compensation in 1845. Questioned on the favouring of landowning MPs to gain their support for a Bill, he frankly admitted that in such cases 'we are not very nice about the Price that we pay; and also where we feel that we can save expense by stopping opposition, we likewise settle on that ground more frequently. It is the same thing to us whether we spend the Money in the one Shape or the other.' He said that in the 1830s it was more usual to agree a price before a Bill, whereas now it was more frequently done afterwards, and John Clutton, land agent to the South Eastern, said that his company thought they now achieved a better deal that way. He stated that as a rule large owners were dealt with before the Act and smaller ones, who were unlikely to have the resources to oppose the Bill, afterwards, from which he thought they benefited. On the other hand, John Cramp, a land agent from Margate, considered that small men suffered most. Even so, one small man, William Welsh of Inverness, a noted local crank, cost the Inverness & Nairn Railway extra time and expense when he changed his mind about supporting it and opposed the Bill right through to the House of Lords, to the anger of townsfolk. Welsh's Bridge signal-box perpetuated his memory.

Compensation was claimed for every conceivable injury, real or imaginary. Apart from damaged amenities to the parks of the aristocracy and gentry, the unity of farms that had lately been created under the enclosure awards was threatened by railways cutting across them. Fields only recently made were arbitrarily divided, leaving small, odd-shaped plots, for which upset yeomen and tenant farmers averred accommodation bridges and crossings were a poor recompense. Owners and occupiers demanded that whole fields should be taken, sometimes farms and buildings, when the railway required only a small portion, and in doing so the companies acquired all manner of odd properties which they were not always able to sell later.

Opposition was well organised. In 1830 Sir William Wake took the chair at a meeting of Northamptonshire landowners and farmers opposing the London & Birmingham, and a petition was drawn up. Notices were placed in local newspapers and copies of the proceedings were sent to neighbouring counties urging them to do the same. The unanimity of the opposition was not always quite as solid as it seemed, though, as a letter from Thomas Thornton of Daventry to P.D.P. Duncombe of Brickhill, Buckinghamshire, showed a year later when he was drumming up opposition to the second Bill: 'I have taken care to call such persons *only* together who will oppose the Railway.'[11]

'A body of Wiltshire Landowners' in 1845 solicited support through the *Hampshire Advertiser* against the Southampton & Salisbury Junction Railway, whose prospectus aroused particular ire by claiming substantial local support and stating that the land required was of little value. 'We trust, with the help of our Hampshire neighbours, that, by setting our shoulders to the wheel, we shall cast off the smoking engine from that "valueless land", which is nevertheless of "high price".'[12] The Duke of Cleveland's opposition to the Northern Counties Union Railway was more subtle. In return for his assent he secured agreement to a figure of £35,000 over and above the price of his land, knowing that it could well bankrupt the company before construction began, which it did, thereby keeping railways out of

Barnard Castle for over ten years. Both sides quickly learned how to take tactical advantage. Richard Creed, joint secretary of the London & Birmingham, commenting on the extension from Camden to Euston in 1834, said that as the terms agreed with Lord Southampton would influence the Duke of Bedford, 'it is desirable to deal with the least grasping proprietor first'.[13] When it was contemplating its extension to London, the Midland Railway quietly started buying land in north London through its agents Cluttons, thereby acquiring it much cheaper. Landowners, for their part, adopted delaying tactics like failing to keep appointments with surveyors and quibbling over minor points of compensation. George Coates of Norton-on-Tees tried four times to meet Sir William Chaytor of Witton Park to agree formally values for the Bishop Auckland & Wearmouth Railway, finally managing it on a Sunday. His survey accounts are typical, revealing many fruitless journeys.[14] The Ramsden trustees, who owned most of Huddersfield, took particular advantage of their strong tactical and geographical position in obtaining an arbitration award of £40,500 for land for which the Huddersfield & Manchester Railway had offered £10,000, and used the money to consolidate their position by buying more land that increased in value after the railway was built. To be fair, there was also a degree of public spirit, in that as a result, the railway did little physical damage to the town itself, while the money it generated went into developing a new central area of considerable architectural quality, focussed on one of Britain's most outstandingly handsome stations. Without railway money and the Ramsdens, Huddersfield would have been the poorer. In return the railway received the Ramsdens' powerful support and had only one party to deal with, although when the tunnel and viaduct which had been imposed on it came to be widened later, the cost must have outweighed any earlier benefit.[15]

Sir John Kennaway, who owned the Escot estate in east Devon, carefully hedged his bets when competing schemes aimed to cross his land in the drawn-out battle between the standard and broad gauge interests over a direct route to Exeter. Although he was a member of the provisional committee representing the standard gauge camp, he refused full support unless it built a viaduct, two tunnels and a station, which were grudgingly agreed to. Simultaneously he was extracting a similar agreement from Brunel who, Kennaway's solicitor warned him, should be treated with caution in case he tried 'whittling it down'.[16] When the South Western main line was eventually made, it missed Escot entirely, looping away to the north to avoid high ground — and, doubtless, the tunnels and viaduct — and a station was built at Feniton.

Nor was it unknown for landowners to try to play one another off. John Hales Calcraft of Rempstone Hall, Dorset, Lord of the Manor of Wareham, in 1863 objected to the route proposed by the Isle of Purbeck Railway, which he thought would damage Wareham and Corfe Castle, as well as his property. He petitioned Parliament that 'the aforesaid line to the East of Corfe Castle instead of to the west is not for the benefit of the public, or in any respect is it a better line, but simply and solely because the Promoters of the Bill know your Petitioner to be possessed of small means and therefore a weak antagonist, and that if they take the better, easier and more commodious line to the West of the said Town, they might have to contend against all the resources of a large estate and a heavy purse.'[17] He meant the Earl of Eldon at Encombe and won his case for Wareham, but not for himself. A railway was not built until 1885, however, when it avoided the centre of Wareham altogether.

Sir Thomas Maryon Wilson in 1866 owned much of Hampstead and found himself in the fortunate position of being a monopoly supplier of sand and gravel to the Midland Railway, which had some 7½ miles of line through north London that were isolated between the unfinished Belsize and Elstree tunnels, making it difficult to supply materials. Sir Thomas sold the company a quarter of an acre for £1,500, or 1s 6d (7½p) a yard, a high price, and the deposits were dug out on both sides of what is now Spaniards Road, giving it the appearance of running along an embankment.[18]

The railways often regarded commons as land that could easily be acquired because Lords of the Manor and copyholders saw sale to them as the only way of getting money for their holdings, ignoring the wishes of local inhabitants who might not find out until it was too late. One of the Commons Preservation Society's first successes was to secure a change in standing orders in 1877 making public companies announce their intentions.[19]

The Petre Affair
Case law contains a number of decisions on the validity of contracts to purchase entered into by railways before obtaining an Act. It was established that when a railway entered into an absolute and unqualified agreement, it was subsequently obliged to honour it even though the land might no longer be required. Lord Howden obtained £5,000 from the York & North Midland in this manner, even though the route had been changed so that none of his land was needed and he suffered no damage.

The most celebrated case concerned Lord Petre and the Eastern Counties Railway, which proposed to pass through the grounds of Thorndon and Ingatestone halls near Brentwood. Lord Petre suggested an alternative route, still across his land but further away from the two houses. Otherwise the price of withdrawing his opposition in Parliament was the staggering total of £120,000 for 8 miles of line, comprising £20,000 for the land and £100,000 compensation, plus a covenant prohibiting stations. The Eastern Counties committee agreed to pay and executed a formal agreement. It was by far the largest single payment to a landowner, in present-day terms coming to close on £2½ million, and attracted widespread criticism, especially from the Eastern Counties shareholders when they found out. The Bill was passed in 1836, whereupon the newly incorporated company refused to ratify the agreement, seeking instead to summon a jury.

Lord Petre dug his heels in. He obtained an injunction restraining the company from calling a jury and from entering his land; the railway appealed and lost. These legal processes now having used up most of the two years allowed by the Act for the purchase of land, the Eastern Counties tried to promote a second Bill seeking powers for extra time, which Lord Petre successfully blocked. The company was cornered. Its finances exhausted — the Bill also sought to raise more capital — it went cap in hand to Lord Petre who magnanimously agreed to accept £20,000 down and the balance in instalments over five years, in return for a long list of more restrictive covenants. On these terms the Bill was allowed to proceed and was passed in 1838. When the company wanted to make a deviation three years later, the price was a further £3,750 for additional severance, £550 for permission to build a specially designed station at Ingatestone (which previously he had refused at any price), and £600 for 3 acres of land to build it on, making a total of £4,800.[20]

Lord Petre's neighbour, Peter Labouchere of Hylands, near Chelmsford, also extracted harsh tribute, claiming £35,000 for his land. As his son Henry was a Privy Councillor and Vice-President of the Board of Trade, his support was vital.

Two questions arise. There is no doubt that Lord Petre's and Labouchere's claims were excessive, and when the company tried to reopen negotiations in 1836 it engaged seven surveyors to give an independent opinion, led by Charles Comyns Parker who recorded the proceedings in his diaries.[21] He and his colleagues were instructed to make a detailed examination of both claims and produce realistic figures 'taking a large and liberal view', which sounds extremely fair. They reported that Lord Petre was incorrect in saying that the railway would be visible from Thorndon Hall, where he spent nine months of the year — it was in a cutting over a

Ingatestone station, Essex, built with Tudor-styled embellishments to meet the wishes of Lord Petre, before recent restoration with substantial financial support from the Railway Heritage Trust.
(D. Thompson)

mile away — and that the place where he objected to it crossing his approach road was not, in fact, on his property. Their verdict on the prices was startling: £3,600 for Lord Petre's land and £16,400 compensation, and £4,000 for Labouchere. They were unable to put figures on severance without knowing something of the tenancy arrangements, but considered that the amenities of neither gentleman would be adversely affected.

One immediately suspects a put-up job, but the fact of there being seven surveyors who, presumably, on occasions were in competition, hardly bears this out. Parker himself on occasions acted severally for the Eastern Counties and for its opponents, and enjoyed high professional standing locally and as a member of the Surveyors' Club, forerunner of the Institution. He was mayor of Maldon, chairman of the guardians and Deputy Lieutenant of Essex — not a man, one would think, who could easily be swayed. But why did the Eastern Counties agree to pay in the first place?

By the time the agreement was signed, 28 April 1836, the committee was getting desperate as the Bill was well on its way through Parliament and it was now imperative that Lord Petre's opposition should be withdrawn. True, they were not aware of the land's real value, but one of their signatories must have been — William Tite, a noted architect, director of several railways including the Great Western, successful businessman and, above all, an experienced valuer who was later in demand as an arbitrator. It is inconceivable that he did not have at least a shrewd idea. So one can only conclude that from the outset the committee had no intention of paying up but deliberately assumed, erroneously as it turned out, that the arbitration clauses in their Bill would override the agreement once it became law. It would be charitable to say, also, that they were thinking of their shareholders.

The second question is why, on losing its case in 1838, the company did not then accept Lord Petre's alternative route, which was still on offer. The engineers Joseph Locke and John Leather appear to have vouched for its practicability.[22] The answer may lie in the company's utter disarray, with a divided board, shareholders refusing to pay calls and shares 50 per cent below par. Construction work was behind and there was no immediate prospect of any revenue. To avoid Thorndon would mean another Act and it was too late to amend the Bill already before Parliament which, to succeed, again needed Lord Petre's agreement.

As for Lord Petre's undoubtedly stubborn and outrageous attitude, he was, as Jack Simmons has said,[23] simply insisting on the performance of a perfectly legal and binding contract. He did not want the railway at all and, like his contemporaries, saw no reason why it should be forced on him. After all, his grandfather had put £¼ million into building Thorndon and he felt entitled to enjoy his inheritance. Initially his demand for £120,000 may well have been intended to coerce the Eastern Counties into accepting his alternative route, but positions became entrenched and he was not prepared to make sacrifices, however imaginary they may have been.

On later occasions railways encountered reverse attitudes when authorised lines were not built, as happened when the Midland tried to back out of its statutory obligation to build the Settle & Carlisle line. Landowners *en masse* signed a petition against the proposed abandonment Bill on the grounds that they would suffer loss from thwarted development or improvements, some of whom had entered into contracts with the railway.[24] It was akin to present-day 'planning blight'. Similarly the Muswell Hill Estates Company and the Alexandra Palace were in danger of losing a large part of their £650,000 investment when an abandonment Bill was proposed for a branch railway after the local company was taken over by the Great Northern, which was eventually persuaded to continue with construction.

Privileged Treatment
An entire book could be filled with the special conditions imposed on railways by landowners. The Acts of incorporation, agreements and conveyances are thick with them, applying restrictions on the uses to which the land could be put, providing benefits for the vendor or his tenants, and safeguarding a bewildering variety of rights from access to fishing to provision of roads; even, in one instance, the replacement of thatch with slates in case engines set it on fire. A flat roof was demanded, and obtained, on a new signal-box at Ponsandane, near Penzance, in order to minimise damage to the view for the Bolitho family of Chyandour House.[25]

Several instances of unnecessary tunnels to keep the railway out of sight have already been noted. Marley Tunnel on the South Devon Railway was built to appease Sir Walter Carew; Gisburn, on the Lancashire & Yorkshire in north

Ponsandane signal-box, alongside the shore of Mount's Bay near Penzance, was a standard Great Western design introduced in 1896, except for the flat roof which was specially provided to reduce obstruction of the Bolitho family's view from Chyandour House. The photograph was taken in 1950, and the box has since been demolished. (Author)

Gisburn Tunnel, on the Blackburn–Hellifield line, is one of a number around the country built solely to preserve a landowner's amenities, in this case to hide the railway from the drive to Gisburne Park, seat of Lord Ribblesdale. The ornamental portals were also part of the price that was paid for land. Photographed in 1989. (Author)

Lancashire, was made to conceal it from the drive to Gisburne Park, complete with crenellated parapets; Cane Hill, on the London, Brighton & South Coast Railway in Surrey was considered necessary by the London County Council to hide the line from their asylum. The Eastern Counties was compelled by its Act to construct no less than three tunnels, of specified lengths, through Lord Braybrooke's estate at Wendon and Littlebury, in addition to which he also got an ornamental *porte cochère* to keep him dry when he used the station at Audley End. Local interests prevailed at Aberdovey, forcing the Aberystwyth & Welsh Coast Railway to go behind the town to avoid the harbour, requiring four tunnels and a 1 in 98 gradient.

Ornamental bridges were favourites, some carrying the landowner's armorial bearings. There are two within 5 miles on the Coventry–Leamington line. The first, bearing the arms of the Gregory family of Styvichall Manor, is prominent over a public road, but arms on the second, Lord Leigh's of Stoneleigh Abbey, look down on the line from an accommodation bridge joining two fields and are seen only from a train. One of the most elaborate bridges carries the Trent Valley Railway across the Lichfield Drive to Shugborough Hall in Staffordshire, designed for the Earl of Lichfield, together with the portals of the nearby tunnel, each one different. The Act authorising the London & South Western's branch to Windsor required the Thames bridge at Richmond to have three 100ft spans, no more and no less, and the Acts for the extension of the London & North Western into New Street station at Birmingham specified 15ft high parapets on bridges over the line to prevent horses from seeing the trains. The station itself had to be entirely roofed over, goods trains were not permitted and engines were prohibited from standing in the station any longer than necessary; these were requirements of street commissioners as a condition of acceptance. The first two provisions were strictly observed, but the third one was interpreted very liberally.

When they realised the advantages the railways brought, landlords turned from prohibiting stations to requiring them, and a considerable number were built as part of a land deal, usually within a specified time and some to be kept open 'for ever'. Four widely separated examples were St Leonards in Sussex, North Kilworth in Leicestershire, Houston near Glasgow and Doldowlod on the Mid Wales line. On the neighbouring Central Wales line the conveyance of land covenanted that a station would be built which 'shall be called and designated Cynghordy station'. Following a pre-Act agreement between Sir William Fowke Fowke Middleton of Shrubland Hall, Coddenham, Suffolk, and the Eastern Union Railway, stations were built at Needham Market and 'the crossing of the Claydon and Blakenham turnpike' (Claydon), but none was permitted on his estate. No bridges were to be built of iron, gatekeepers whom Sir William adjudged guilty of misconduct were to be sacked, and the company was to facilitate any desired exchange of land with Lord Ashburnham.[26] The local justices were enjoined by the Warrington & Altrincham Junction's Act to decide whether Warrington station should be built on the left or right bank of the Mersey under a clause, like those for Birmingham New Street,

One of the most elaborate bridges built to meet the demands of a landowner crosses Lichfield Drive in Shugborough Park, Staffordshire, home of the Earls of Lichfield and now a National Trust property. The embellishments include the family arms supported by a lion and a sea horse, coronets and the motto 'Nil Desperandum'. Built in 1847, the bridge carries the busy West Coast main line unaltered, a tribute to its builders. Photographed in 1989. (Author)

intended to ensure facilities for the ratepayers. Local industry was catered for at Strines, on the Hayfield branch in north Derbyshire, where a station was required near the print works for 'luggage trains'. Passengers were not mentioned. The Commissioners of Woods and Forests felt a need for a station at Beaulieu Road on the edge of the New Forest; the South Western did not, although it had to provide one. A year later it complained that the takings barely paid the staff's wages.

Lord Petre was not the only landowner to insist upon a specially designed station. Usually the wording in Act or deed was 'designed to the satisfaction of . . .', leaving the owner and the railway to thrash out the details between them. Ingatestone was in Tudor style; Brocklesby in Lincolnshire, for Lord Yarborough, and Sandon, near Stoke-on-Trent, for Lord Harrowby, were Jacobean; both peers were railway directors. On the Bedford–Bletchley line a complete series of half-timbered cottage-style stations was built to a design approved by the Duke of Bedford at Woburn. The pseudo-French turret adorning the elaborate station at Box Hill in Surrey was among the demands of Thomas Grissell who owned Norbury Park. He had made his money from railway contracting so he knew all the tricks in the book and made sure that his agreement with the railway safeguarded him against every single one.

Although less common, there was a surprising number of private stations opened for the personal convenience of landowners, accompanied by agreements allowing them to stop trains on demand.[27] West Moor between Hereford and Hay, Watchingwell on the Freshwater, Yarmouth & Newport Railway on the Isle of Wight, two on the little Maryport & Carlisle, Crofton and Dearham, and Crathes on the Deeside line, were examples, while the wooden station provided at Boreham in Essex during the lifetime of Sir John Tyssen Tyrell was promptly demolished on the day after his funeral. Some private stations eventually became public. Where a

Redmile station, Leicestershire, served Belvoir Castle, seat of the Dukes of Rutland, who had a private waiting room containing an elaborate oak fireplace. The ducal arms were displayed in this finely carved and moulded brickwork on one of the gables. The station was closed in 1953, unfortunately before the days of preservation, and the photograph was taken early in 1954 before it was demolished. (National Railway Museum)

station could not be secured, a private waiting room might be negotiated. The specially elaborate station at Redmile, for Belvoir Castle, possessed a sumptuous room for the Duke of Rutland, the Earl of Kintour had one at Inverurie, and successive stations at Berkhamsted contained a private room for the Earls Brownlow, a privilege that existed until 1929. By then it had not been exercised for twelve years so the London, Midland & Scottish Railway paid £225 for the right to be extinguished.[28]

Less exacting, or perhaps less influential, landowners might gain the right to stop trains at their nearest station as the price of their co-operation, many such agreements lasting into modern times. In 1893 the North Eastern had 26 obligations of this kind, and although it tried to get rid of them when opportunities arose only two had gone by 1905.[29] Usually, notice had to be given to the stationmaster or the guard, although it might be as little as half an hour before the train's arrival. In some cases all the owner of the privilege had to do was to turn up at the station and ask for the signals to be set against the train. An agreement might specify certain trains, or the right could apply to any train. In 1901 Lord Leconfield initiated a chancery suit against the North Eastern because it refused to stop its new Harrogate expresses for him at Collingham Bridge, arguing that as the agreement referred to 'trains between Leeds and Wetherby' it did not apply to the new service which stopped at neither. The company compromised by stopping one Harrogate express a day and by putting

Tallington station, on the East Coast main line, where the Earl of Lindsey was fond of exercising his right to stop trains — usually the 'Flying Scotsman' — to the intense annoyance of the Great Northern Railway. The station closed in 1959 and has since been demolished. (D. Thompson)

on an additional morning and evening train to Leeds, from which the local populace no doubt benefited also.[30] To the Great Northern, the Earl of Lindsey's perpetual right to stop trains at half-an-hour's notice at Tallington, on the main line between Peterborough and Grantham, was a continual irritant because of his habit of stopping the crack train of the day, the 10am Scotch Express from King's Cross, the 'Flying Scotsman'. Though it might be full, as it usually was in summer, the Earl steadfastly refused to use the following relief train and still expected his reserved first-class compartment. Periodic exchanges of letters with his solicitors seemed to be part of the exasperated Superintendent of the Line's way of life.[31] Unfortunately for the Great Northern the agreement extended to 'future owners or occupants . . . at Uffington House', so it was unable to extinguish the right, which was not done until the British Transport Commission Act of 1959, thereby allowing the station to be closed. At this period a number of contractual obligations prevented station closures without specific clauses in the railway's annual Private Acts, until the passing of the British Railways Act, 1963, which extinguished all such remaining rights.

Assent to a railway occasionally gained the neighbourhood a new piece of road, particularly where an existing one had to be diverted, when the parish would ensure that the new one was wider and better made than the old. An entirely new thoroughfare was more rare. The Great Western's Act required the provision of a 30ft-wide street on Earl Manvers' land at Bath, across which the Earl was empowered to erect barriers to prevent its being used other than for access to the station. Two hundred yards long, it made a handsome approach to the station and was appropriately named Manvers Street. The same company had to ensure that 'approaches and avenues' at Leamington Spa were the same width as the neighbouring streets, which at the time were being laid out particularly spaciously, and screens were required to shield bridges and the station, again 'for ever'. Because the station at Giggleswick in north Yorkshire served Settle, just over a mile away, the 'Little' North Western Railway Act of 1849 laid down that a new road must be made into the town, not directly from the station but from a point on the existing road ¼ mile away, in order to provide a shorter route.

Wayleaves, Feus and Leases
In north-east England the old wagonway system of wayleave agreements persisted well into the present century. The North Eastern Railway inherited large numbers from absorbed companies, all carefully documented in printed registers.[32] One of the largest sets came from the Brandling Junction Railway, which ran for more than 26 miles on wayleaved land. Even part of the Great North of England Railway, which formed a section of the East Coast main line, was originally built by wayleave. The wayleave rents paid on ecclesiastical land owned by the Bishop or the Dean and Chapter of Durham were notoriously excessive. Payment of £280-300 per mile on part of the Stanhope & Tyne Railroad, which crossed 17 miles of ecclesiastical land, was a major contributor to the company's financial trouble that led to its closure and sale in 1841, and the Hetton Colliery Railway paid around £300 a mile over 9 miles of

line. When, under the terms of its Act, the Clarence Railway approached the Dean and Chapter for land for the Byers Green branch in 1836, the church tried to cling to the old system by claiming high compensation based on the notional rents it would have obtained from wayleaves, which a jury sensibly rejected. The railways fought the wayleave system for a century or more, regarding it as expensively archaic and one more example of grasping landowners profiting from railway enterprise. Parliament was sympathetic and insisted on normal compulsory purchase clauses in Acts for new lines, relenting in one case, in 1853, on condition that the Duke of Northumberland gave a 1,000-year lease to the Blyth & Tyne Railway, which at least safeguarded it against periodic increases under the old short-term system. Even then subsequent alterations and additions complicated the arrangement so much that in 1913 a new lease was drawn up, simplifying it. Parliament did nothing towards the abolition of existing wayleaves and their renewal, which is what the railways really wanted, and in 1929 the London & North Eastern sought a different solution by gaining authority in its General Powers Act to purchase wayleaves, although it was only partially successful in using it. Wayleaves were also granted on some early Scottish railways, although where land was not sold outright it was more usual to subject it to an annual feu duty, a type of perpetual lease. Feuing on railways was common and is still quite widespread today. The Caledonian Railway, for instance, in 1875 had a long list of feus, including twelve on the main line inherited from the Scottish Central and Scottish North Eastern companies.[33] A typical example is the agreement between the Dunblane, Doune & Callander Railway and the Earl of Moray, dated 1856, in which the annual feu duty was based on twice the value put on the land by two valuators, redeemable by the railway at two and a half years' purchase, a figure usually based on annual sources of revenue and often other factors. The railway was relieved of claims from tenants although it had to pay the Earl £750 for damages, provide a station (which does not seem to have been built), replace interrupted water supplies and take over the £3,000 debt of the Doune & Callander Turnpike.

Leasehold railway land in England and Wales was not common, other than in the north east, and usually related to ancient custom. The unique Haytor Granite Railway on southern Dartmoor leased a right of way in Lower Down and Bovey Heathfield in 1825 at £5 5s 0d (£5.25) a year for 45 years,[34] while land in the Forest of Dean was held on annual rental from the Crown. Mining and other industrial activities, including tramroads, were permitted only under licence from the Comissioner of Woods and Forests, who granted leases of up to 31 years to tramroads, and railways that replaced them. Licences were also required authorising construction.

In 1835 the narrow gauge Festiniog Railway leased 150 acres at Moelwyn 'for the purpose of making a tunnel and Building Cottages' for 60 years,[35] and part of the West Cornwall Railway ran on leasehold land as a means of avoiding the capital cost of buying it. But only in north-eastern England was the practice at all widespread, and today a number of examples still remain. On the 7 miles of the North Tyneside coast line between Tynemouth and Benton — now part of Tyne & Wear Metro — for instance, there are six sizeable lengths built on land subject to 1,000-year leases, including Backworth station and junctions, part of Whitley Bay station, the whole of Cullercoats and half of Tynemouth. In general, however, leasing only applied to private or industrial railways, like the Duke of Buckingham's Wotton Tramway that eventually became London Transport's Brill branch, where it crossed a mile of his neighbours' land on a 31-year lease to reach his estate from the main line at Quainton Road station.[36]

Railways and Land Values
The beneficial effect of railways on land values depended on several factors. In country areas, improved access to markets and faster, more frequent deliveries of supplies made for a marked increase, varying, of course, with the proximity of a station. The value of land near stations rose faster than on more distant property, which is one of the reasons for landowners' progressive conversion to railways where there were none. It was estimated that on average the selling price of rural property increased by 10 per cent, or three years' purchase, some farms by 25 per cent and residential estates by 20 per cent.[37] Land actually bordering a railway rapidly rose in value. A farmer with 200 acres near Leighton Buzzard reckoned that the London & Birmingham quickly raised the value of his land by 30 per cent.[38] Another on the same line, who had already received generous compensation, asked an even higher price when the railway wanted more land later, arguing that the railway had increased its value. John Clutton, in his evidence to the 1845 Lords Select Committee, cited an owner on the London, Brighton & South Coast who received handsome compensation because of the proximity of the railway to his house, which immediately gained in value when the opening of the railway reduced traffic on the road which ran even closer. One wonders whether history could repeat itself if the Channel Tunnel high-speed link opens. It was always a sore point with railway managements that their lines nearly always conferred measurable benefits on landowners, whom they had paid for the privilege.

Increases in Scottish land values were much less marked. The valuation rolls of the agricultural counties of Midlothian, East Lothian, Peebles, Selkirk and Roxburgh, for instance, show an average rent increase of 30 per cent between 1862 and 1877, in an area served almost exclusively by the North British Railway. While the figure is relatively low compared with England, it still contrasts with the company's average dividend of 1 per cent over the same period.[39] In the Highlands, increases in values after railways were opened were slower still, and railways were viewed essentially as a long-term benefit.

The effect of railways on urban land was more diverse. John R. Kellett, who has examined the subject in great depth in *The Impact of Railways on Victorian Cities* (1965), concludes that loose generalisations are not possible. In central business districts, values tended to rise rapidly by the 1840s, the fastest near to stations while, later on, railway routes within a mile or so of city centres created marked deterioration, particularly in parts alongside viaducts or criss-crossed by a complex of lines and junctions, to the point of dereliction. Land in suburbs and on urban fringes which the railways made ripe for development increased in value, and there were numerous instances of owners hastily drawing up plans to show building plots, perhaps accompanied by a few digging operations, in order to enhance compensation claims. Many were bogus and cattle continued to graze. The projected extension of the Metropolitan & St John's Wood Railway through Hampstead prompted a developer, David Nicoll, who was a director of the railway, to lay out quickly new roads and building plots along West End Lane so that he could inflate his claim against his own company.

Kellett quotes general increases in the 1860s within 30 miles of London of up to 35 per cent within a mile of a station on level roads, 25 per cent up to 2 miles, and a still perceptible rise up to 6 miles. He notes the effect on prices per acre in nascent commuter towns as well. Between 1839 and 1867-9 they rose by 13 times in Caterham, 14 in Redhill and 200 in Weybridge. Land values in Hastings rose from £300 per acre in 1849 to between £2,000 and £10,000 20 years later. The pattern of train services was significant. Property values in Soho, Handsworth and Perry Barr, Birmingham, quadrupled over 12 years after the London & North Western Railway introduced a half-hourly circular suburban service in 1872. But, as we shall see in chapter 5, with certain exceptions the railways in the nineteenth century were not particularly disposed to promote suburban services by building new lines and stations unless they were sure of an immediate financial return. Precluded by statute from acting as developers themselves, they saw landowners as profiting from all stages of railway development at their expense. Hence, without a strong incentive or a statutory obligation like that imposed by the Cheap Trains Act of 1883, they were reluctant to encourage suburban growth by offering cheap fares when they were unable to share fully in the fruits — not an entirely logical attitude, with hindsight. What really mattered was the net value of the traffic.

Valuations and Arbitration

With the steady accumulation of experience, the arbitration procedures under the Lands Clauses Act settled into a pattern. At first there was no guidance or rules on prices, and the Act was in fact criticised for omitting to give any. John Duncan told the 1845 Committee that 30-35 years' purchase, based on actual or hypothetical rent, was used as a basis for prices of farm land, or 20-26 years' for house property in towns, excluding compensation. Edward Driver agreed. He had bought land for the first 20 miles of the Great Western from London, and the whole of the London & Brighton's land, and as a general principle had worked on 33 years' purchase to which he added 25 per cent for compulsory purchase and 10½ per cent as compensation for severance, the equivalent of a total of 58 years, which, with minor additions, he would round off at 60. Kellett suggests that around 10 per cent was added for compulsory purchase in towns, but could be as high as 50 per cent in the country. John Swift, solicitor to the Grand Junction Railway, said that in the mid-1830s their surveyor also started at 30-35 years' purchase and that the rest was compensation. He had paid 66 years' purchase, which at the time he thought was high, but said that since then expectations had risen and instanced the Lancaster & Carlisle, then being built, where they were higher still.

Juries generally were called only by the large landowners. Railways tried to avoid them, considering they tended to favour claimants. They were expensive and tiresomely protracted, delaying the works. Swift admitted that the Grand Junction would pay well over the anticipated jury award just to have a purchase agreed quickly and expedite construction, although he was speaking of the first flush of railways before the money market tightened. On the 34 miles of the South Eastern's Dartford Loop and Tonbridge line via Sevenoaks, in 1865-8, 397 purchases were by agreement, 26 went to arbitration and only 8 to juries.[40] As might be expected, all the Committee's expert witnesses agreed that it was virtually impossible to generalise beyond adopting broadly comparable methods of valuation. Kellett considers that as a whole railways commonly paid twice the current value.

The Committee had been set up to try to establish some principle of compensation. It concluded that it was impossible to establish a fixed rate and, hardly surprisingly considering its composition, suggested that compensation in some cases was too low. A few minor recommendations were made and, as we have seen, the Lands Clauses Act ignored the issue.[41]

Accommodation works were among the most contentious matters and, again, the large landowners scored. One was awarded 14 level crossings in 3¼ miles. The Maryport & Carlisle Railway tried to ease the problem by adopting a policy of purchasing small plots of severed land,[42] and all railways sought alternatives to providing crossings and bridges if they could. The Cheshire Lines Committee offered Lord Derby two road diversions and four bridges on its Aintree line in 1875, and purchased some severed land to avoid a fifth and to be able to abolish two more on its main line near the junction. On the same line Clutton, as umpire, reduced a £12,000 claim to £1,415.[43] The land agreement books of railway companies are full of such awards, and solicitors' papers fill in the detail, showing the extraordinary lengths taken by some owners to try to outwit railway companies.[44]

Co-operative Landowners

It has already been said that by no means all landowners were antagonistic. Some supported railways from the outset, particularly those with mineral interests which railways would promote, and in Scotland coal-owners invested heavily in the Edinburgh & Dalkeith in 1826, local landowners helped to promote the Dundee & Newtyle in 1825 and rescued it from a financial crisis in 1839, Lord Panmure provided two-thirds of the Dundee & Arbroath's land for a nominal feu in 1835, and on the Wishaw & Coltness and Slammannan railways land was given free. There were many others.

J.T. Ward's study *West Riding Landowners and the Railways*[45] details the attitudes of Yorkshire owners, many of whom bought shares, provided cheap land

and became leading figures on railway boards. The Duke of Devonshire let the Cromford & High Peak Railway pass through his land without charge, and in 1871 Sir Thomas Acland gave land to the Devon & Somerset Railway for nothing; 'being assured that the value of a large portion of his lands in North Devon will be greatly enhanced by the said railway' he not only saw his action as an expression of 'the good will he bears the undertaking', but had it recorded in the conveyance. In the same county Sir John St Aubyn gave land at Devonport for the London & South Western's new line.

Highland landowners supported railways in the hope that they would open up the country, particularly the Duke of Sutherland, though his support for the line north of Invergordon was conditional on its going inland. He built 17 miles at his own expense between Golspie and Helmsdale, while Sir J.G.T. Sinclair offered land free around Thurso. Landowners and tenants in the north east supported the Formartine & Buchan Railway in 1859 with offers of cheap land or low feus, and the buying of shares, in order to open up the district.[46] Only the Earl of Aberdeen objected, and when his son later realised it had been a mistake and tried to build a branch to Methlick at his own expense, he found the cost prohibitive.

A few owners made amends for earlier avarice. When Lord Taunton, formerly Henry Labouchere, realised that his estate had not suffered to the extent anticipated, he returned £15,000 from the £35,000 his father had received in the Petre case.[47] Generously minded landowners desirous of a station did more than insist on a clause in an Act or deed; they gave land as well, like Sir John Rogers in 1848 who promised the South Devon a free approach road at Ivybridge.[48] Sir Thomas Hesketh gave the West Lancashire land for Hundred End station in 1894.[49] On the London & Birmingham Lord Grafton sold the company 3 acres for the price of the topsoil, £600, to expose the bed of clay for brickmaking, which he gave as an inducement to build Blisworth station and thereby increase the value of his land. Although generosity was seldom entirely altruistic, it none the less helped the railways' cause and was considerably more widespread than has been suggested. Sometimes municipalities helped if they thought railways would benefit their towns. Carlisle sold land to the railways, including that for Citadel station, as Derby also did, although only on the understanding that the three companies concerned would all use one station.

Tunnels

In the first years of railways, and for several decades afterwards, it was considered essential that they should buy the land over a tunnel, and it was customary to acquire a narrow strip no wider than necessary except at shafts, where extra was taken for tipping spoil. Primrose Hill Tunnel on the approaches to Euston was an early exception. It was built because the London & Birmingham's Act of 1833 required it, to satisfy Eton College whose estate lay over it. An open cutting would otherwise have sufficed. The college had laid out Adelaide Road in 1830 to attract developers, a timely move that enabled it to claim extra compensation. The Act required the tunnel to be bored, rather than made by cut-and-cover, and the land remained college property. The tunnel had to be strong enough to support houses where the soil was 15ft deep or more, and at the London end the mouth was required to have 'a substantial and ornamental Facing of Brickwork or Masonry to the satisfaction of the Surveyor or Architect of the said Provost and College, so as effectually to prevent the soil immediately above or around the said Mouth from giving way or slipping down'. In the event the tunnel lay under the back gardens of houses that were built in Adelaide Road. When the second tunnel was cut in 1879 it, too, was squeezed under gardens except for six houses which had to be demolished, but the two single-line tunnels made in 1921-2 were more expensive as demolitions were unavoidable. The Great Northern Act of 1846 and the Hampstead Junction of 1853 had similar provisions for Copenhagen and Hampstead tunnels respectively.[50]

In later years tunnel land was not always purchased, except around shafts, and access was gained by easements. Land over Linslade Tunnel near Leighton Buzzard was sold in exchange for an easement over the second tunnel constructed in 1857, and the third was made by an easement agreement in 1871. At the 1845 Select Committee, Clutton agreed that land over tunnels should be valued in the same manner as any other required by the railway, as it was nearly always used for spoil and caused disruption. Interestingly, it was held that the limits of deviation prescribed in the Railways Clauses Act, 1845, did not apply to tunnels, which had to be built on the exact line shown on the deposited plan, other than by agreement with the landowner. This ruling was modified by the 1863 Railways Clauses Act, which allowed the Board of Trade to permit deviations.

Because railways were under a legal obligation to purchase buildings on the line of a tunnel, Scotland Street Tunnel in Edinburgh was built below the streets of the New Town in 1842, which fortunately were straight. The city council charged the Edinburgh, Leith & Newhaven Railway 1s (5p) for 'the right of Tunnelage'. The same requirement later led directly to the London underground railways being built beneath streets where they could. Even so, the sub-surface lines of the pioneer Metropolitan and Metropolitan District railways caused substantial disruption and large sums were paid in compensation. A few hundred yards of road would be closed at a time and buildings immediately adjacent to the excavation shored up, although even the greatest care could not always avoid collapse. Similar problems had beset the London & North Western in 1847-9 when it was penetrating central Birmingham using cut-and-cover methods. Because the authorities ordered the demolition of buildings showing signs of collapse, the railway was forced to purchase them. Fear of a similar catastrophe caused the owners of industrial premises in Horsley Field, Wolverhampton, to obtain a court order requiring the Oxford, Worcester & Wolverhampton Railway to strengthen the cut-and-cover tunnel it proposed building beneath, and, just to make sure, a cross-section was included in the deed of agreement.

To avoid the prohibitive cost of buying surface buildings, the London deep-level tube lines ran beneath the streets, resulting in sharp curves, particularly on the

Bakerloo line. North of Trafalgar Square trains squeal round a curve of under five chains radius, and in one or two places under narrow streets the twin tunnels are above each other instead of side-by-side. A Joint Select Committee, meeting in 1892 to advise on underground railway proposals, recommended that they should be enabled to purchase wayleaves under property instead of the freeholds, with free wayleaves under public streets in return for cheap fares, arguing that at so great a depth there was no risk of disturbance or vibration. Property owners were less sure and wanted compensation. Parliament decided to do nothing and the Acts made no requirements.[51]

Following a paper at the Institution of Surveyors it was stated that some promoters issued unnecessary notices to treat, in order to persuade owners to make claims, when it could be demonstrated that no damage would occur. The claimants then settled for a low figure, thereby precluding any future claims for vibration damage. Most owners did not rise to the bait, although the Lord Chief Justice, who was present, suggested that the promoters were merely being prudent where they anticipated an awkward or litigious owner. It was remarked that very little friction had in fact occurred during the construction of the early tubes.[52] The Victoria line, opened in 1969, was the first to be constructed by tunnelling rights not following streets. Main line tunnels are now built under the same procedure, wherever possible.

Surplus Land

The Lands Clauses Act compelled railways to sell surplus land within ten years of the time specified for completion of the works, except in towns and built-up land. The original owner or his heirs had absolute right of pre-emption, followed by adjoining owners. A lot of surplus land came from purchases the railways had been compelled to make in order to secure agreement but, when it came to selling, seldom realised much increase in value because purchasers were reluctant to pay more than agricultural prices, supported by arbitrators. During the statutory ten years, the companies were supposed to be barred from selling to anyone else, and from developing the land in any meaningful way. Only the Metropolitan Railway eventually overcame this disability by legal means, to be mentioned in chapter 5. The companies' returns, therefore, were well below those of other lineside landowners.

The courts were fairly indulgent towards the railways when it came to deciding what was meant by surplus, although the Great Western failed to convince the court that land at Basingstoke bought for dumping soil and subsequently turned into allotments was not surplus, and it reverted to the plaintiff.[53] The courts also held that land on top of tunnels was not surplus within the terms of the Act.

It has been suggested that railways hoarded land, which is not entirely correct. In the face of such rapid and unforeseen expansion it was natural that the companies were cautious about disposing of land they might need in the future, although as time went on it did, without doubt, tend to become a habit. However, from time to time some of them set up surplus land committees to investigate what could be sold. The Great Western did so in 1881-4, for instance[54] and the Caledonian in 1902;[55] their activities will be considered in chapter 6. The land plans of the London & North Western's line from London to Birmingham show continuous disposals from 1840 to 1863 and after, including some large plots. Not all surplus land was easily saleable in any case; it might be an awkward shape, of poor quality, or low-lying, marshy and subject to flooding, for which the original owner had been glad to find a buyer.

The Great Central found itself in some difficulty in 1902 over land and houses it had been compelled to buy over St John's Wood Tunnel. There had been enormous trouble in passing beneath Lord's cricket ground, and further on cut-and-cover construction had caused disruption and some dereliction. The company's London Extension Act precluded building over the tunnel and on any part of plots under which it passed and, as there was a special pre-emption section favouring the Portman and Eyre estates, any lease could only be on an uneconomic short-term basis. The problem was only solved by obtaining another Act increasing the statutory 10 years to 30 and giving powers to lease or sell land over the tunnel.[56]

Railways and the Profession

By bringing surveyors together on field work, in courtrooms and at parliamentary committees, railways played a leading part in the formation of, first, the Land Surveyors' Club in 1834, and then the Institution of Surveyors in 1868, predecessor of the present Royal Institution of Chartered Surveyors. Of the 20 founder members, 15 were prominent in railway work.[57] Many of the well-known present-day firms owe their growth to surveying and valuing for railways. We have already encountered John Clutton and Edward Driver. Also in London, Francis and Robert Vigers worked for the London, Chatham & Dover and the Metropolitan. In the provinces the Sturges of Bristol acted for the Great Western, Bristol & Exeter and other West Country and South Wales railways; Jeremiah Matthews of Birmingham for the London & Birmingham and various Black Country railways; and in Glasgow Thomas Binnie purchased much of the land for the West Coast main line in Scotland, while Thomas Smellie became a leading Scottish railway valuer and established recognised principles of valuation. J.F. Rolleston of Leicester prepared the Great Central's estimates of land for its London Extension and was knighted in 1897. Many made names for themselves as arbitrators and umpires.

In the earlier years the leading surveyors faced accusations of operating a clique on behalf of landowners, but by the 1860s the opposite was being said when they were charged with being in the railways' pockets. It was vigorously denied, and the evidence shows that landowners were still being handsomely compensated. What really happened was the creation of a group of leaders in the profession who, through railway work, became well known to one another. Civilian land surveying as it had been known had gone, and the new men were far more professional and commercial.

A commercial attitude meant more competition, although rivalry was not unknown in the early days. Henry Smith, land surveyor of Bath, was not slow to cast doubts on the ability of H.E. Goodridge's estimates in the Lords Committee on the first Great Western Bill, and the committee rooms saw many a disparagement. Thomas Nash of Royston, Hertfordshire, shows through his letters how a small but astute country surveyor could win business from a leading railway company and oust a well-known professional figure.[58] Nash had been in business for only a few years when in January 1847 he asked the Great Northern for an appointment as land purchase negotiator, to be told that W.T. Head of London and T.S. Woolley of Nottingham had already been appointed. Woolley was well known. An Assistant Tithes Commissioner, he became a founder member of the Institution and was one of the first land agents formally to train articled pupils. Nash persisted and in March was given part of Woolley's district, much to the latter's annoyance, particularly when Nash questioned some of the figures he had provisionally agreed. Nash's brash approach upset other notable figures. J. Bailey Denton accused him of sharp practice in taking possession of a client's land without first referring to an umpire; 'never was such an aggression committed', he complained. Nash's methods were a combination of a very low offer, a refusal to budge and various delaying tactics designed to wear down his opponents by sheer attrition. 'I am miserably tired of the business,' wrote one, 'do my dear Sir let us put an end to it.' The Great Northern occasionally intervened if he was unduly holding up the contractors, but seemed sufficiently satisfied with his services to keep him on for ten years.

Surveyors touted both sides for business. In 1836 a bridge on the London & Birmingham collapsed near Cheddington, whereupon William Andrews of Chesham offered to negotiate compensation for inconvenienced farmers.[59] Surveyors, land agents, valuers, call them what one will, throughout the British Isles put their businesses on broader, more secure foundations than they had ever previously known by working for, or against, the railways.

Chapter 5

The Influence of the Railway

Most people's concept of railway property is one of the infrastructure itself — the track, bridges, viaducts, tunnels, stations, traction depots and workshops that are the prominent parts of its operations. They have been well documented, excepting railway warehouses, which still await a detailed study. The railways' property interests, however, were and still are much wider, at one time embracing such varied adjuncts to their business as docks, canals, hotels, golf courses and a very large number of employees' houses, together with an enormous range of other acquisitions gained, willingly or otherwise, through land purchases in the past. They included such diverse properties as toll bridges, ferries, fishing rights and pew rents. The Great Western at one time owned collieries in South Wales. The next two chapters will be concerned with some of these developments, but in order to appreciate the management of such a large and varied estate we must first give brief attention to the influence the railways had on the country at large, its landscapes and townscapes, starting with a short look at the influence of routes.

Routes and Land Patterns
Although a number of factors affected the route of a railway, not least, as have seen in chapter 4, the attitudes of landowners, there is no doubt that the influence of geography was overriding, tempered by engineers' preferences and beliefs.

The Stephensons' early insistence on avoiding steep gradients came from the belief that anything more than 1 in 330, or 16ft per mile, would overtax the locomotives of the day. This meant that Kilsby Tunnel had to be driven for 1 mile 666yd under the narrowest part of the watershed at Watford Gap in Northamptonshire. The cost was enormous and the difficulties delayed completion of the London & Birmingham Railway in 1837 by six months, highlighting the practical impossibility of combining easy grades with minimum expense. The line was certainly direct, though, and beyond Camden is still the best graded 111 miles of main line in Britain. However, other engineers' greater faith in the capabilities of locomotives, which were rapidly becoming more powerful, quickly led Robert Stephenson to modify his ideas.

As far as Kilsby the London & Birmingham broadly follows earlier transport routes — the Roman Watling Street, Telford's Holyhead Road and the Grand Junction Canal. Likewise, over the 156 miles from London to Doncaster, only at Peterborough is the Great Northern Railway more than 5 miles from the old Great North Road, while for 92 miles across the Grampians the Highland Railway between Dunkeld and Daviot follows Telford's road, now the A9, built in the early 1800s which, as far as Dalwhinnie, follows a military highway built some 70 years before that by General Wade. Telford's road from Fort William to Arisaig similarly is followed by the West Highland Railway.

In hilly districts particularly, natural routes used by earlier engineers were usually the first choice. The Manchester & Leeds and Huddersfield & Manchester railways across the Pennines closely hug river, road and canal most of the way, as did the lines taking coal down the narrow, parallel South Wales valleys, often cheek-by-jowl with another, competing railway. The three lines that crossed the valleys laterally all required extensive earthworks, viaducts and tunnels. The Edinburgh & Glasgow Railway, across the waist of Scotland, also is never far from first the Edinburgh & Glasgow Union Canal and then the Forth & Clyde. In planning the Great Western from London to Bristol, Brunel followed the Thames to Reading, but then eschewed the Kennet & Avon Canal to Bath, avoiding the sharp curves that beset the Berks and Hants line which took that route later, at the expense of a slightly longer course to the north on which he would maintain easier gradients and simultaneously gain commercial advantage from the places served.

Vignoles' contrasting route for the Sheffield, Ashton & Manchester boldly took the most direct one that was practicable. Originally suggested by a Sheffield surveyor and completed by Locke, the line climbed up steep river valleys on each side of the high watershed before tunnelling through it for 3 miles at Woodhead. Even where relief is relatively low, a direct line across the grain of the country could entail heavy

The valley of the River Tame in Greater Manchester is an example of a natural route for the climb out of Stalybridge, chosen first for a canal and then by successive railway engineers. Seen here in 1979, the river is on the left. The canal was completed in 1811, and was paralleled first by the Huddersfield & Manchester Railway in 1849 (out of sight on the far left) and then in 1885 by the Micklehurst loop on the embankment alongside the right-hand bank of the canal, forming a duplicate route that was closed in 1964. (Author)

engineering if excessively steep gradients were to be avoided. The London & Brighton Railway, sweeping due south from the capital, followed the Brighton road and deviated only at Haywards Heath, requiring tunnels through the Weald and the North and South Downs. The route was deliberately chosen for its directness, in preference to five easier but circuitous alternatives. In some ways the glaciated through valleys of the Scottish Highlands made planning easier for the engineers, enabling railways to make gradual though longer and more devious ascents without tunnelling, which is why in Scotland there are only eight tunnels more than ½ mile long (other than the underground lines beneath the centre of Glasgow) and only a few that are less.

In achieving direct routes or easy gradients, many of the earlier main lines missed important traffic centres. Between Stafford and Warrington Locke's Grand Junction Railway passed through nowhere of importance (Crewe did not then exist) and completely missed the Potteries, while the London & Birmingham, in avoiding the Nene Valley, bypassed Northampton by less than 4 miles. Sheffield, Halifax, Bradford, Worcester and St Helens were among other important towns that had the mortification of seeing a railway pass them by, leaving them to be served afterwards by a branch line or a loop. On the other hand, the Scottish Midland Junction portion of the Perth–Aberdeen main line deliberately left the natural route along Strathmore, forsaking the road, in order to serve Forfar and Montrose, rejoining the strath further on at the expense of 8 extra miles. When, later in the century, competing lines were built, the best routes were usually occupied, resulting in expensive engineering for the newcomers. The Great Northern lines in part of West Yorkshire and through Derbyshire, and the Great Central's London Extension, suffered in this way.

Engineers and surveyors everywhere took maximum advantage of the contours, particularly on secondary and branch lines where cost was paramount and the speed of trains of little consequence, producing some remarkably serpentine routes. The line from Meldon Junction to Holsworthy in north Devon was a good example, delicately wriggling for 16 miles along a narrow, winding spur of land between rivers before dropping down to the coast at Bude. There is equal but different finesse in the way in which the long, sweeping curves of the Settle & Carlisle line were engineered with supreme skill, picking up a contour at the head of one valley and then another in order to obtain 7 miles of almost level line between Blea Moor and Garsdale at a height of over 1,110ft, no mean achievement. It was at the expense of two large viaducts and two tunnels, including Blea Moor itself, nearly 1½ miles long, but on this line speed was important. In hilly or mountainous districts the coast often afforded the best route along low-lying margins or at the base of cliffs, although where there was restricted space expensive sea walls and tunnels through headlands were required. Coastal lines of both kinds form parts of the Chester & Holyhead, South Devon, Cambrian coast and west Cumbria lines, while between Folkestone and Dover the line runs along and through the cliffs. Selecting a route, therefore, was a continuous balancing act between terrain and cost. The South Wales Railway provided two directly contrasting but complementary examples. The company's Act of 1846 authorised a deviation inland between Bridgend and Port Talbot to avoid shifting sands along the coast, needing steep gradients but saving 3 miles. Further on, between Kidwelly and Carmarthen, the opposite happened when a heavily graded inland route with a tunnel was discarded in favour of one along the coast and Tywi estuary, 3 miles longer but virtually level.

The coast could also form a barrier. Joseph Mitchell surveyed 204 miles in Sutherland and Caithness in an unsuccessful search for a direct coastal route to Wick and Thurso that would best satisfy local people, but was forced a long way inland, first by Dornoch Firth and then by the rocky and precipitous coastline north of Helmsdale, although it has recently been suggested that a coastal line would not have been impossible and the inland route was chosen to open up the country. Such a line would certainly have been expensive, and an attempt at a cost-effective exercise would prove interesting.

However, although the impact of railways on the landscape depended so heavily on the terrain, it was less than that of a modern main road and much less than a motorway. A double-track railway is considerably narrower than a trunk road; the grey or brown ballast, steeply sloped embankments and cuttings, and brick or stone bridges blend easily into the landscape compared with concrete-edged tarmac and concrete bridges. In hugging the slopes of valleys railways were often less visually intrusive in hill country than in flatter areas. Because so many viaducts, until later years, were built in local stone or brick, they were quickly assimilated into the landscape and became accepted features, nowadays to the extent of generating demands for their retention where they have become redundant. Only in the flat fenlands of eastern England were railways at all obtrusively prominent, and then mainly from the air, as they cut straight as a die across the grids of roads and watercourses, ignoring field and drainage patterns, only rising up to cross the great drains and levels. Just three lines followed water to any extent, the longest one in Lincolnshire where the Great Northern's original main line between Boston and Lincoln for much of its 31 miles ran virtually along the bank of the River Witham, resulting in several sharp curves. In the north of the county the Axholme Joint Railway for 3 miles between Haxey Town and Epworth, opened in 1904, cut clean across land still farmed on the medieval strip system. Each strip was freehold, so an extraordinarily large number of transactions was necessary for such a short length of railway line.

Lines along the coast caused changes, altering beaches, straightening shore lines and, at times, giving opportunities to reclaim land, although seldom extensively. Embanked estuaries changed tidal patterns, lines that bridged them even more so, creating new channels, sandbanks and marsh. The viaducts across the Loughor and the Mawddach in Wales, Little Petherick creek on the Camel in Cornwall, the Leven estuary in south Cumbria and the mouth of the remarkable Montrose Basin on the Angus coast, for instance, altered age-old conditions in the local ecology, in fishing or, in some cases, in the life of small ports. However, this was not always the case:

113

The Isle of Axholme Light Railway is shown in this aerial photograph passing from left to right across the centre, bisecting the medieval field strip system that survives in this area of north Lincolnshire. The view is looking west and Haxey Town station is on the far left. The line closed in 1956.
(Courtesy C.W. & M.A. Atkin)

the railway's sea wall on the south Devon coast, for example, had only a minor effect on the long sand spit known as Dawlish Warren.[1]

William Madocks' reclamation of the Glaslyn estuary and the creation of Porthmadog in north Wales pre-dated the railway which, when it arrived in the shape of the narrow gauge Festiniog Railway in 1836, used his embankment. Later, his work also allowed two other narrow gauge lines, the Welsh Highland and the Croesor Tramway, to penetrate much further inland on straight and level routes than would otherwise have been possible. When the Cambrian brought the standard gauge to Porthmadog it built a separate embankment across reclaimed marshes to the north, and nearby at Penrhyndeudraeth built a toll road along its embankment and bridge over the Dwyryd estuary. Towards the end of the century the Dornoch Light Railway was built across The Mound, Telford's embankment across the head of Loch Fleet that was intended to encourage reclamation, connecting the county town of Sutherland with the railway system. Near Llanelli the Llanelly Railway & Dock Company and the Great Western both built lines across reclaimed land enclosed by the Berwick Embankment, built under an award of 1810, and had to contribute to its maintenance.[2]

The railway was directly associated with land reclamation on the Isle of Wight, where in 1882 the Brading Harbour & Improvement Company opened a branch from Brading to Bembridge, partly behind a new sea wall that enabled extensive marshes to be reclaimed. The construction of the Ulverston & Lancaster Railway —

later part of the Furness — acted both ways, changing the northern shore of Morecambe Bay and the estuary of the River Kent more than any previous human agency. Between its opening in 1857 and the 1870s, well over 1,100 acres of sand and salt-marsh were reclaimed, but above the viaduct at Arnside the opposite took place when it retarded the tidal flow, causing silting and 700 acres of new marsh, some of which was later reclaimed.[3] Also in the north west, the railway to Fleetwood ran along a 2-mile embankment that was intended to reclaim some 5,000 acres of tidal marsh from the River Wyre, but it was used only from 1840 to 1851, when a deviation was built inland and the reclamation never really got under way. Today, the greater part is still marsh. In Norfolk, the Norwich & Yarmouth Railway alignment of 1844 materially assisted land drainage.

Abandonments and Might-have-beens
Former railway routes are now accepted features in the landscape, but the post-Second World War large-scale abandonments were by no means the first. Between 1827 and 1947 well over 500 stretches of line were closed to passenger traffic at one time or another; they are listed by M.D. Greville and Jeoffry Spence in *Closed Passenger Lines of Great Britain* (1974). Most were retained for goods trains, although a surprising number, mainly short connecting curves, were abandoned for good, to which can be added some that never saw a train. They all required the purchase and eventual disposal of land, and remain overgrown reminders of one-time aspirations or as expensive monuments to railway rivalry. Most are still visible today; a short selection will have to suffice here.

Abandoned curves exist at both ends of the Bletchley–Oxford line. The first south-to-west curve at Wolvercot, north of Oxford, lasted only from 1854 to 1861, but the south-facing Bletchley curve had a more varied history, laid in 1854 to give through running from Euston to Worcester during the Great Western's territorial war with the London & North Western. Ten years later the rails were removed, but were relaid as a siding in 1934 and came back into full use as a strategic wartime connection in 1942. Now the curve has reverted to an overgrown embankment. Two connecting curves on the Somerset & Dorset served different purposes. The connection to the Great Western at Bruton was purely political and never carried a train; the other, north-to-east at Templecombe, was built solely to give contractors access when they were building the line and was abandoned when it was finished, as was the 1¼ mile connection from the Watford–St Albans branch to the Midland's new main line under construction at Napsbury. Some of its course might see reuse if the proposed Colne Valley Transit scheme comes to fruition. In northern Cumbria, the orginal junction between the North Eastern's Eden Valley line and the London & North Western south of Penrith, opened in 1862, faced south at Clifton station. Within a year a more useful north-facing spur was built, to give access to the new Keswick and Workington line, leaving Clifton no longer a junction station and the original line of little value. It was lifted in 1875, but two stone bridges mark it, oddly isolated in fields.

Before Beeching the abandonment of a main line was rare, confined principally to the relegation of a few early sections to secondary status when they were superseded by better routes, like the approach lines to the ferries that preceded the Severn Tunnel and the Forth Bridge, and those that were bypassed by the Great Western's cut-off lines in the late nineteenth and early twentieth centuries. When the Great Western came to rebuild the five timber viaducts between Saltash and St Germans in Cornwall, however, it decided to replace 5 miles of main line by an entirely new one ¼ mile shorter, needing only three viaducts although a tunnel was necessary. It was opened in 1908, but the old line can still be traced. In our own day the replacement of 11 miles of the East Coast main line between Selby and York in 1983 falls in the same category, although for a different purpose, to avoid valuable coal deposits. It was paid for by the National Coal Board.

The Bruton curve was not the only one never to carry traffic. The Oxford & Rugby Railway, promoted by the Great Western, was another tactic in its struggle to take the broad gauge into London & North Western territory. When the line reached Knightcote, north of Fenny Compton, in 1849, however, the Birmingham & Oxford Railway was well under way, taking the GWR much more directly to Birmingham. So the rest of the Oxford & Rugby was abandoned, leaving a few hundred yards of embankment striking off across a field in the direction of Rugby. Meanwhile, a much more monumental memorial to the gauge war was being erected in Birmingham. The Duddeston Viaduct was built to enable the Great Western to enter the city over

The earthworks of the uncompleted Oxford & Rugby Railway of 1845 branch off to the right from the Oxford–Birmingham line near Knightcote, north of Banbury, forming a low embankment before petering out in the middle distance. They were photographed in 1957. (Author)

the LNWR's line, much to the latter's irritation. In 1852 it reached the London & North Western's boundary. That company refused to make a junction, while the Great Western had now lost interest after securing powers for a station of its own at Snow Hill. So neither company wanted the viaduct, which was left unused; some crumbling arches remain, still partly owned by British Rail.

The disused viaduct at Tadcaster over the River Wharfe in West Yorkshire is in a much better state. Built in 1847-9 for a direct line from York to Leeds, the collapse of George Hudson's railway empire stopped further work which was never resumed. The handsome 11-arch viaduct stood disused until a siding to a mill was laid across it in 1883; that was removed in 1959 and the viaduct now carries a footpath.

Derelict earthworks like those at Knightcote are evidence of ambitious schemes that did nothing but lose investors' money. Close to Hurst Green, near Clitheroe in north Lancashire, a shallow cutting runs for 300yd across a field, remains of the Fleetwood, Preston & West Riding Junction Railway. Its grand-sounding title is self-explanatory, but all it did in the late 1840s was build 2½ miles of line at Preston that became part of the Longridge branch, and the isolated earthworks at Hurst Green, which prompt the question, why was work started there? More substantial remains in the valley of the Sussex Ouse mark an attempt by the London, Brighton & South Coast Railway to shorten its route to Hastings in 1864, in competition with the South Eastern. Some 2 miles of embankment with bridge abutments and other fragments were left between Balcombe Viaduct and Uckfield, abandoned in 1869 when the Brighton company got cold feet and concluded a pooling agreement with the South Eastern instead.

Up in the Welsh mountains, the road to Aberystwyth from Llanidloes is accompanied by the obvious remains of a railway for some 3 miles to just beyond Llangurig, all that is left of the eastern end of the Manchester & Milford Railway referred to in chapter 2. This section was built and ready for use by 1864, complete with signals, but saw only contractors' and the odd goods trains. It became derelict and the track was lifted in 1882, victim to ambitions that were unable to appreciate the practical difficulties or to attract finance. A line about the same length in west Leicestershire had a similar existence, connecting the Ashby & Nuneaton Joint line at Stoke Golding with the Nuneaton–Leicester line near Hinckley. Why it was built has never been clearly established; certainly its joint owners, the London & North Western and the Midland, were not always the best of partners. The line was ready for traffic in 1873 but, so far as is known, never carried any revenue-earning trains and in 1889 it was taken up, although it was not legally abandoned until the Midland Railway Act of 1914[4].

Finally, in this selection of railway might-have-beens, the Duddon Viaduct. From the late eighteenth century men have dreamed of an embankment that would reclaim Morecambe Bay or, in recent years, provide tidal power. George Stephenson and John Hague in 1837-8 saw an embankment as a means of taking a railway to Scotland around the Cumbrian coast, as we have seen in chapter 3 (p66), and both men included a second one across the Duddon sands a little further north. Hague's report was much the more detailed, and he calculated that 52,000 acres would be reclaimed, which at £23 an acre would realise £1,196,000, although neither engineer suggested to whom the land thus created might belong. Others thought the Crown would claim half. Then, in 1867, the Furness Railway revived the Duddon Viaduct scheme, or, more accurately, had it thrust upon it by a rival, only to abandon it after starting some minor works and a short cutting near Askam. But they were sufficient to make John Wakefield, the landowner, demand compensation for severance and damage, and for loss of anticipated reclamation and drainage improvements. Job Bintley and Henry Hoggarth arbitrated and awarded him £186 15s 0d (£186.75).[5]

Some schemes never progressed beyond the purchase of land, leaving it to be disposed of, sometimes years later. The Manchester, Sheffield & Lincolnshire Railway's 1884 bid to break the traffic monopoly at Blackpool, despite strong local support, failed to materialise into anything more positive than substantial land purchases in the Fylde and around Wigan, on which £302,000 had been spent when the Blackpool Railway was wound up in 1896. Final disposals were not completed until quite recently. The London, Midland & Scottish Railway kept powers alive for a deviation to avoid the Shap incline, dating from 1898 when the LNWR carried out some preliminary work. They were allowed to lapse in the 1930s.

Several major improvement schemes planned by the Great Western between the wars went the same way. As part of its South Wales rationalisation schemes, it intended completing the Clydach valley line between Cwmgorse and Pontardawe, each end of which had been opened to collieries in 1922 and 1923 but not joined up. Two stations were built but not opened, and although the connecting line was fenced no track was laid. Coal traffic was charged for as though the line had been completed, even though it was sent out by a much more circuitous route. In the West Country the company planned to relocate inland the coast line between Exminster and Newton Abbot, and land was bought, but the war stopped the project. Even more interesting is a grandiose scheme that was planned to replace the tortuous, steeply graded Looe branch with a new line from near St Germans, together with an hotel, superior housing development and a golf course at the terminus. Large quantities of land were purchased near Looe, where massive engineering works were necessary, including two long viaducts, 123ft and 144ft high, and two tunnels, respectively 700yd and 1¼ miles in length. In 1937 it was stated that work had commenced,[6] but only the golf course was completed before war stopped work. The idea was to promote commuter and holiday traffic with a fast line from Plymouth and London, but even if the growing influence of the motor car and the coach are discounted, one wonders how the most optimistic of development prospects could have justified the expenditure of close on £1 million. Looe would have needed to become another Torquay to produce the traffic to pay for it.

An equally ambitious but operationally more rewarding scheme was planned by the North Eastern on Tyneside in 1919 for a direct line east of Newcastle from Heaton to Pelaw and Washington, avoiding the sharp curves and congested junctions around Central station, and including a new high-level bridge across the Tyne at

Projected lines on Tyneside in the 1920s, but not built. All land purchased has now been sold — an instance of Property Board sales that were other than closed lines.

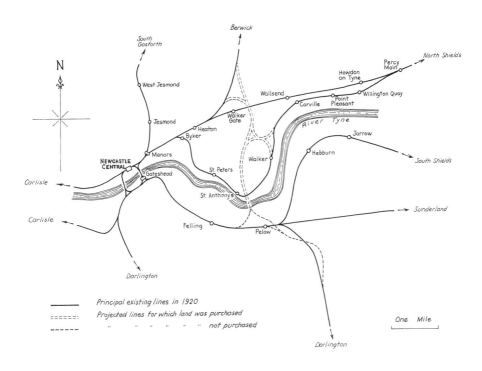

St Anthony's. Although no parliamentary powers were sought, the North Eastern's successor, the LNER, bought all the necessary land north of the river. However, the depression of the 1920s halted the scheme and none was bought on the south side. It was resold in 1931 and 1951, but was not built on until comparatively recently. Post-war maps clearly showed the swathe of empty land that was intended for the new line. In the case of Clydach, Shap and Looe some land still remains in British Rail ownership. The war also prevented the Southern from finishing its new line from Motspur Park to Leatherhead, which stops short at Chessington South, and most of the land onwards has now been sold.

We must turn now to a few examples of the effect of railways on the built environment. A detailed and lucidly comprehensive study is contained in Jack Simmons' *The Railway in Town and Country, 1830-1914*, to which part of the following is indebted.

Railways in Towns

Chapter 4 has shown how, initially, railways increased inner urban land values and then, away from the immediate environs of the main stations, began to drag them down, accompanied by marked physical deterioration. In most large towns the reality of 'the wrong side of the tracks' was only too apparent, with its assorted industries and streets of terraced houses for their employees. One also sees it in smaller towns as different as an industrial one like Worksop from a residential town like Tonbridge.

The station as the focal point of a street pattern or a square, deliberately planned in the European manner, was almost unknown in Britain. It happened at Stoke-on-Trent, not through municipal enterprise but created by the railway itself. The North Staffordshire Railway laid out Winton Square with houses for senior employees on two sides flanking an hotel, all in a style matching the rich neo-Jacobean of the station opposite. It would have been a noble setting for the headquarters of a great trunk railway, much less a small provincial company possessing only 215 miles of closely knit route. Stations deliberately styled to harmonise with their surroundings were not uncommon in the earlier years, but the only other planned station environment, albeit on a small scale, occurred at the Worcestershire spa of Great Malvern where the station approach road, gardens, overbridge and adjacent hotel were designed as an entity by a single architect. As we have seen (p91), co-ordinated planning was imposed on the centre of Huddersfield by the landowner, which included the station. The new station at Harrogate, reached in 1862 by taking the railway across a large open space called The Stray, became the focal point of the town centre, but not in the sense of formal planning.

A few centrally sited stations stand in squares, although none is outstanding. Forster Square in Bradford, which later gave the Midland station its name, was meagre in the extreme. City Square in Leeds was rather better, but did not obviously contain a station; it was hidden behind the company's Queens Hotel, which was just as well, because it had no proper frontage at all. At Hull the original station entrance, which was quite handsome, faced an open space until it was hidden by buildings at the beginning of this century. Meanwhile a new entrance had been built alongside the railway's hotel fronting on to the new Paragon Square. Rather surprisingly, Blackburn station fronts on to a square optimistically named The Boulevard (actually it is a triangle), laid out in 1889-90 following rebuilding of the station three years before. Although the station dominated, neither it nor its companion buildings were of 'square' quality — a brewery, nondescript shops and houses — apart from one side which faced the parish church, later made a cathedral. Neither the town nor the Lancashire & Yorkshire Railway at that time were noted for their architecture, but it was an attempt. Newcastle's magnificent station fully deserved to grace a great square or complete a townscape, but did neither, although Richard Grainger, who laid out new streets in 1835-9, tried. Liverpool fared best. Over a period an enlightened corporation laid out a spacious square, placing St George's Hall in the centre and complementary civic buildings along one side. They paid the railway to erect a classical screen front to Lime Street station along a second, but spoiled the effect by failing to do anything comparable with the other two. The railway also failed when it replaced the screen by a lofty French Renaissance hotel that, in terms of the square, was imposing enough to acknowledge its continuing obligation, but no more. The railway quickly spoiled Euston Square.

A fine new street to a station on the edge of a town was no more common. We have already noted Manvers Street at Bath (p100). It was broad, and Brunel designed an asymmetrical station façade that was central to the street. Important new streets were made at Norwich and at Brighton, along which the towns extended, at Brighton gradually shifting the commercial centre with it. But in some towns the approach to the station was tortuous, as at Chesterfield which waited over 30 years for a decently direct road to the station,[7] and Coventry the same, although the one it got in 1871 was commendably wide and lined with detached villas. Indeed, Coventry was one of the few industrial towns to escape railway blight. The main line passed to the south of the city which, through local peculiarities of land ownership and freemen's ancient rights, was hemmed in so that expansion came late, and when it did, was in the opposite direction.[8]

The prestigious railway hotel seldom did much to encourage developments of a kind to enhance station precincts. At Euston, King's Cross, St Pancras and Paddington the hotel did nothing to halt the downward slide, and it was much the same elsewhere. The emphasis was on convenience and close proximity to the station. Edinburgh and Glasgow fared better than most, and the hotels at Preston and York were among the best, with gardens and a view over the river. The railways also built or acquired hotels at smaller towns that were important junctions, like Derby, Peterborough, Perth and Bletchley. In their heyday they were uniformly good and set high standards, becoming synonymous with quality and service. At the 1923 grouping there were 80 of them, of which 52 had been built by the railways themselves.

The influence of the railway on small towns was much the same, attracting industry and artisans' housing close to the station. At Bedford, for instance, the triangle of lines outside the old town became occupied by a foundry and streets of workers' dwellings, and more were built off the street leading to the Midland station, which was renamed Midland Road.[9] Watford, a declining town, was revitalised by the railway, slowly at first but with increasing impetus between 1850 and 1870 when the area between the station and the town was filled with streets of small houses.[10] Braintree, in Essex, expanded towards the station with new industries, so that by 1860 the face of the town had completely changed,[11] a process repeated many times elsewhere, like Uckfield in Sussex. There, an area called the New Town sprang up around the station after it was opened in 1858, comprising mainly villas. It grew as a residential area but remained separate from the old town, which underwent its own development, massively after the Second World War, but still clearly divided by the railway.[12]

The effect of railways on the growth of suburbia has also received some attention in chapter 4 (p103), where we saw that generally railways did not actively promote development, the spread of towns along railway routes being due more to the fact that they were there. What were village stations became suburban ones. Blackheath, for instance, expanded immediately after the railway opened in 1849; Surbiton, probably the oldest suburb in Europe, if not in the world, owing its existence to a railway, grew around the station for Kingston; and Willesden developed after the station became a junction in 1866. Until the last two decades of the century the railways' role was nearly always passive. There were exceptions: the Manchester, South Junction & Altrincham Railway was opened as a suburban line in 1849, the Sutton Coldfield branch from Birmingham in 1862, and in the same city the West Suburban and Harborne lines in the early 1870s. Other specifically suburban lines which were not primarily parts of through routes or connecting links did not appear until the 1880s, when lines like the Edinburgh South Side, the Cathcart Circle in Glasgow, the Mersey Railway between Liverpool and Birkenhead, and a number in London, started a slow and somewhat patchy development that was halted by the electric tram. Indeed, only London and Glasgow had what could be called a suburban network. North of the Tyne the circular route from Newcastle to the coast, which came to carry a heavy suburban traffic, was not designed as such but was made up of separate lines that were joined together. Some suburban lines were failures, like the Nottingham Suburban Railway and the Great Eastern's Fairlop loop, built in anticipation of development which failed to materialise. In the London area, developers sponsored lines or stations by giving land or cash subsidies, or by guaranteeing a minimum level of revenue, particularly between the wars on the Southern and the Metropolitan.

The provision of season tickets, however, helped the growth of suburbs and satellite towns by encouraging commuting. Some companies even issued free first-class passes to builders of houses, to go to the first owner as a way of stimulating passenger traffic. The pass could usually be transferred to a new owner or tenant. In

1846 the London & North Western issued them from Alderley Edge to Manchester for the extraordinarily long period of 21 years, which stimulated growth, but when it did the same in 1853 to Euston from stations between Harrow and Tring, for new houses of £50 rateable value or more, the story was different. The poor train service did not encourage commuting and, as P.G. Scott has pointed out in *Harrow Station, 1837-1987* (*British Railway Journal*, Special London & Birmingham Railway Edition, 1989), the line capacity probably precluded much improvement, so that by 1867 when the facility was discontinued, a total of only 208 passes had been issued in respect of all 8 stations, hardly a success. In 1855 the East Lancashire Railway did the same at Aintree, Maghull, Town Green, Ormskirk and Burscough, for periods that increased with the distance from Liverpool: 7 years at Aintree, up to 18 at Burscough. Other railways tried to promote the growth of coastal resorts in the same way (p131).

To a considerable degree the extension of London's underground system kept pace with development, but seldom was in front, although the Hampstead Tube's extension to green fields at Golders Green was quickly justified. Land values rose six or seven fold in the first three years but, of course, the railway was unable to share in the bonanza. Only the Metropolitan Railway circumvented this statutory disability and came to occupy a unique position among British railways, as fully explained by Alan A. Jackson in *London's Metropolitan Railway* (1986).

In 1870 the Metropolitan found itself with a considerable amount of surplus land that it had managed to retain by means of special provisions in its successive Acts, thereby overriding the Lands Clauses Act, which Parliament either had not noticed or had ignored, including powers to lease. A Land Committee was formed to carry out a policy of positive estate management, followed in 1885 and 1887 by Acts setting up a separate development undertaking with a capital of £2.64 million, based on the value of the surplus estate, but still firmly under railway control. Starting with Willesden Park in 1880-1, estates were laid out at Harrow, Pinner and Wembley Park, where in 1900 land was also leased to the newly arrived Great Central Railway. Wembley Park was initially intended as pleasure gardens with a rival to the Eiffel Tower, 175ft higher but in the event reaching only 200ft before work stopped. The undeveloped part of the park was sold in 1922 for the British Empire Exhibition. The well-known publicity slogan 'Metro-Land' appears to have first been used in 1915.

To accelerate development, Metropolitan Country Estates Ltd was set up in 1919 at the suggestion of the company's energetic general manager, R.H. Selbie, to operate side-by-side with the Surplus Lands Committee but with emphasis on buying land expressly for housing. To avoid questions in Parliament the new company was ostensibly quite separate, though all but one of the directors were Metropolitan directors, together with Selbie, and some services were provided by Metropolitan staff. As Jackson says, 'it was a cosy arrangement which enabled the railway to direct all investment and development to where it would best serve the railway's interests, whilst the company benefited from the close association with the railway's respectable image.' Selbie himself explained how the railway could hardly lose by carrying all the building materials, household goods and coal, as well as, he estimated, selling at least one season ticket per household. The railway connection minimised the speculative element; if railways were only given direct statutory powers, he went on (surely tongue-in-cheek), that element would entirely disappear.[13] Estates were developed at Chorley Wood, Wembley, Kingsbury, Harrow and neighbouring areas, and as far out as Amersham. By 1933 the company had ten estates totalling over 1,200 acres.

Displaced Persons

Railway construction in towns inevitably meant demolition of houses and displacement of the occupants. It was large-scale, relatively ruthless and, until the

THE NORTH EASTERN RAILWAY ACT, 1898.

NEWCASTLE-UPON-TYNE

SCHEME FOR NEW DWELLINGS FOR PERSONS OF THE LABOURING CLASS.

WHEREAS under the powers of the North Eastern Railway Act, 1898, the North Eastern Railway Company propose to purchase or acquire in the City of Newcastle-upon-Tyne ten or more houses, which, on the 15th day of December, 1897, were, or have since that date been occupied either wholly or partially by persons belonging to the labouring class as tenants or lodgers:

AND WHEREAS the said Railway Company have, in pursuance of section 31 of the said Act, submitted for the approval of the Local Government Board a Scheme for providing new dwellings for such number of persons as were residing in such houses on the said date, or for such number of persons as the Local Government Board shall, after inquiry, deem necessary, having regard to the number of persons on or after that date residing in such houses and working within one mile therefrom, and to the amount of vacant suitable accommodation in the immediate neighbourhood of such houses, or to the place of employment of such persons, and to all the circumstances of the case :

NOW THEREFORE WE, the Local Government Board, have deemed it necessary that a Local Inquiry shall be held by one of our Inspectors in relation to the said Scheme, and for giving effect to the provisions of the said section, and We have accordingly directed R. H. Bicknell, Esquire, M.Inst.C.E., to hold the said Inquiry at the TOWN HALL, NEWCASTLE-UPON-TYNE, on THURSDAY, the SIXTH day of JULY, 1899, at SIX o'clock in the Evening.

AND WE HEREBY GIVE NOTICE that any persons interested in the matter of the said Inquiry may attend and give evidence before the Inspector at the time and place aforesaid.

S. B. PROVIS,

Local Government Board,   *Secretary.*
22nd June, 1899.

Printed by A. T. ROBERTS, SON & Co., LTD., 5, Hackney Road, London.   9302—220—6-99

An example of a statutory notice under which the railway was required to rehouse occupiers of 'the labouring class' if ten or more houses were to be compulsorily purchased for railway works, subject to the approval of the Local Government Board which, in this case, elected to hold a public enquiry. (Author's collection) end of the nineteenth century, carried no obligation to rehouse. In that, the railways were no different from other public works, like docks and new streets, but they had a much greater impact. London, because of its size, felt the effect first. Numerous tenants were evicted by the London & Greenwich Railway in 1834; two years later the London & Blackwall demolished 3,000 houses, and in *Dombey and Son* Dickens described the scene at Camden Town on the London & Birmingham. Much of the property consisted of slums which, because they were easier and cheaper to acquire, influenced the railways' selection of routes wherever possible. The Charing Cross Railway displaced over 4,500 people in the small area between Waterloo Road and the river.[14] St Pancras station swallowed up some 4,000 houses, and the land taken next to it for Somers Town goods station housed 10,000 people.[15] At least until 1885, railway clearances frequently aggravated the slum problem. Provision of workmen's cheap fares, although designed to solve it, enabled only skilled workers to move further out, leaving the lower paid semi- and unskilled with no alternative but to cram into already overcrowded areas nearby.

In a weak attempt to exercise some sort of control, the House of Lords' standing orders were amended in 1853 to require all private Bills involving demolition of more than 30 houses in any one parish to include a return of the number of persons to be displaced, but as there was no means of checking these Demolition Statements, they were valueless. Some were vague estimates, others deliberately misleading. The North London Railway admitted counting only the heads of households for its Broad Street station Bill, producing 25 per cent of the true figure.[16] Between 1854 and 1902, statements accompanying London railway Bills amounted to 72,000 persons, but Kellett estimates that the real figure was over 120,000. The story was the same in Manchester, Liverpool, Glasgow and Leeds, and in smaller places. In 1871-8 the Great Northern demolished 260 houses in its passage through Derby, displacing 1,500 people. At West Hartlepool in 1872, 24 fishermen petitioned the North Eastern to provide them with new homes close to the shore or, pathetically, to give them more time to try to find 'any local capitalist or builder who might feel like erecting houses' for them.[17]

The South Eastern Railway's Act of 1872 authorised a short curve in Southwark which cut through a densely populated area. It stipulated that before taking 15 houses or more, public notices were to be displayed 'within a reasonable distance', not less than eight weeks in advance and to the satisfaction of the local justices, but all it did was prevent summary evictions.

In 1875 the Commons tried to tighten control by requiring Bills to include provisions for alternative accommodation, which the railways either ignored or avoided, followed by a further attempt after the Royal Commission on Housing of the Working Classes reported in 1885. Before then, the only replacement housing provided was that which might have been required as part of a bargain with a landlord or occupier, or for commercial purposes like the 50 houses built by the Manchester, Sheffield & Lincolnshire and Great Northern companies for fishermen at Grimsby, in order to promote fish traffic. After 1885, limited provision was made in Acts by restricting the number of 'houses of the labouring classes' that might be taken, usually to 10, without the consent of the local authority, which had power to require approved replacements. The 1887 Act for the enlargement of Liverpool Street station required the Great Eastern to rehouse 600 people (although 737 were in fact dispossessed),[18] for whom 10 four-storey tenements were built at Spitalfields, Whitechapel and Bethnal Green. Five more were built about the same time in connection with the Fenchurch Street–Stepney widening.[19] The London & North Eastern Railway sold them in 1933, together with blocks at Stratford.[20]

The Great Central — or the Manchester, Sheffield & Lincolnshire as it then was — probably had the best record in rehousing, but only because its extension to London was the last main line to cut across heavily populated towns and was built when pressure for reform was mounting. The company's Act of 1893 stipulated that before houses were demolished, new ones approved by the local authority had to be provided, although at Loughborough the company tried to do it the other way round until the town clerk stopped it.[21] Rehousing cost the Great Central around £500,000, for which it had not made provision in its authorised capital; half of that figure was needed in London alone, where 507 houses with 3,073 occupants had to be replaced. So a separate company was formed, called the Wharncliffe Dwellings Company after the chairman, to build six blocks of five-storey tenements.[22] In 1900 the board was concerned that 69 houses bought in St John's Wood, but not demolished, were still empty and deteriorating, losing around £5,400 a year in rents. They were gradually made habitable again. By the time the line was finished in 1899, 315 houses had been built at Nottingham, 300 at Leicester on two estates, 26 at Loughborough and, in connection with new works at Ardwick, 100 in Manchester.[23] The company agreed to provide venetian blinds for the ground-floor front windows to give a 'genteel and uniform appearance . . . so much better than with every variety of blinds the tenants will put up'.[24] Despite this refinement, the Leicester Borough Engineer thought the tenants deserved better houses than those that were submitted for his approval.[25] They were all sold in the early 1930s along with the Great Eastern tenements. At that time the LNER owned 746 houses and 325 tenements that had been erected for rehousing.[26] The London & South Western was similarly compelled to build 10 blocks of tenements to rehouse displaced tenants in 1901-4, when land was taken for the rebuilding of Waterloo station and widening the line out to Clapham Junction, and the South Eastern and London, Brighton & South Coast companies similarly for the last of their successive widenings out from London Bridge. The South Western also built a block at Fratton, Portsmouth, so that after the Grouping the Southern Railway inherited a total of 1,523 tenement dwellings.[27]

Despite legislation, however, there were still evasions. The Caledonian bought land for rehousing when the Glasgow Central Railway was authorised in 1888, and did in fact provide some alternative accommodation, but not the proposed £40,000 scheme for new houses. The land was still vacant in 1902.[28] In the nineteenth century the railways never willingly accepted any liability, moral or statutory, and when action came it was too late. By the time serious steps were taken to force railways to rehouse, expansion was nearly at an end, and in the present century changed social attitudes, mercifully, dictated different actions. In 1936 the London, Midland & Scottish Railway acquired land at Euston for its new station project, and paid £86,000 for 584 tenants to be rehoused in flats built by the St Pancras House Improvement Society on the company's land at Kentish Town. The chairman laid the foundation stone and when they were finished in 1938 the land was leased to the Society.[29]

Villages and Country Junctions
The effect the railway had on a village depended on the location of the station. Where it was close, the change was sometimes a smaller version of what happened in the towns, with artisans' houses and small country industries springing up. Alternatively, there might be very little change, even shrinkage when the railway took people away to work in the towns. Other villages grew into small towns, although the railway was not necessarily the sole influence. Proximity to a town, the nature of local agriculture and the development of industry or mineral extraction all played a part. But usually the railway was the catalyst.

A year after the Colne Valley Railway was opened in Essex, in 1860, the local newspaper noted improvements under way in the village of Earl's Colne. A new village hall doubled up as a mechanics' institute, a new chapel had opened and there was talk of providing gas.[30] A small engineering works developed and in 1903 the owner gave land to enlarge the station. When a corn exchange was established at nearby Halstead in 1865, it was built near the station, as were agricultural businesses elsewhere, like maltings, grain warehouses, saw mills, small country foundries and cattle markets. Auction marts quite commonly were established close to stations, like Gisburn in Lancashire, Ferryhill in County Durham — which had two — and Appleby after the opening of the Settle & Carlisle line. At Lazonby station on the same line, the market was moved there from Kirkoswald, a mile or so away. However, although these were not untypical, the overall picture is more complex, so here we shall look at some fairly straightforward examples: places that were changed by the railway, some that hardly changed at all and new settlements brought into being as a result of the railway, but not by it. Those will be considered in chapter 6.

A station on the edge of a village encouraged expansion on that side. If further away, a separate settlement might spring up, perhaps a few houses as at Hartlebury in Worcestershire and Cheddington in Buckinghamshire where the stations were quite close, or with an inn or hotel, as at Tring, Hertfordshire, where it was further away, or, indeed, a small village in its own right, often taking the station's name, including 'Station'. Thornhill Station is a group of houses beside the railway a mile from the Dumfriesshire village. The station closed in 1965, two years before Ferryhill where the area next to the site is still called Ferryhill Station, like Welton Station in Northamptonshire and a number of other places. At Udny Station in Aberdeenshire, the railway has gone entirely, closed in 1979; Udny itself ceased to be a station in 1966. The environs of Beaworthy station in north Devon started to develop when it became Halwill Junction in 1879, renamed after a village 1½ miles away, and by 1907 the name had been adopted by the new settlement, which now had an hotel and a cottage hospital. Despite closure of the station in 1966 and its disappearance beneath new development, the name remains and all signposts still seem to lead to it. When the railway arrived at St Boswells, in the Borders, in 1849, the station was built at Newtown, a small mill hamlet a mile away where a few more houses and the Railway Hotel sprang up. By 1899 there was much more development, with an auction mart and the 'County Rooms', which marked its beginning as the administrative centre for Roxburghshire. It is now called Newtown St Boswells.

Development took a different pattern at Kenilworth, Warwickshire, where the station was ½ mile or more from the village. Sir Walter Scott's novel sparked off a little residential growth before the railway arrived in 1844, blocking expansion to the east of it. Thereafter, scattered development westward was enough to start a small town, with infilling as the century proceeded, but there was no 'railway district' around the station, despite a new road. Artisans' dwellings were concentrated in a separate quarter where there were some small industries, principally brickworks and the gasworks, near the railway but away from the station. Housing did not appear close to the station until the end of the century, and was of a decent kind. Kenilworth's conversion from a village to a town remained predominantly residential.

The suffix 'Road' was a favourite device used by railway companies to indicate that a station was for a place, rather than at it, much used by the Great Western in particular. There was a number in Cornwall. St Columb Road, 2 miles from St Columb Major, had only one house — probably the station-master's — in 1888, no doubt due to its close proximity to the villages of Indian Queens and Fraddon; but by 1907 there was a brickworks and a group of houses there, the station had given them its name, and the place continued to grow. Grampound Road, 2 miles from the ancient borough of Grampound in the south of the county, had some houses, two hotels, a chapel and a school by 1908, and has continued to expand so that it is now as large as Grampound itself. Like Halwill Junction, the name from the long-closed station is perpetuated. Conversely, Bodmin Road attracted nothing when it became a junction in 1887, and today, renamed Bodmin Parkway, has no sort of settlement, while in 1907 Port Isaac Road on the London & South Western's North Cornwall line had one solitary house. Even now it has only one or two more, still quite isolated, but, with the railway gone, is unremembered by the Ordnance Survey.

Berkeley Road in Gloucestershire and Clarbeston Road in Pembrokeshire were small settlements that have retained their railway names, the latter its station as well, and at least two telephone exchanges are named after stations (1989) which have not existed for many years: Otterham Station in north Cornwall, which comprises a row of ex-railway cottages, two houses, a farm and a caravan site, and Horam Road in Sussex. The latter is one of the many curiosities in station nomenclature. It started as Horeham Road for Waldron in 1890, when Horeham Manor was the only house nearby. By 1910 a residential settlement also called Horeham Road was growing around the station, and today it is a sizeable late-Victorian and twentieth-century village. Meanwhile the station name has been changed three times, finally becoming Horam, like the village. The station closed in 1965, but British Telecom still clings to the 'Road'.

In industrial areas, station settlements tended to become joined on to their parents. Station Town, County Durham, in 1898 comprised six streets of terraced houses next to Wingate station; by the early part of this century it was linked to the village. At Horbury Junction in West Yorkshire, a somewhat inaccessible station was opened in 1850 and gave its name to an industrial colony comprising an ironworks, Charles Roberts' well-known carriage and wagon works, and a small woollen mill. In 1894 there were three terraces of houses, an hotel, a school, a chapel and a mission hall, which in 14 years expanded with more houses. By 1930 Charles Roberts had taken over nearly the whole site, which was now joined by houses to Horbury, which itself had grown into a small town. The junction station was closed three years before and a new one, Millfield Road, opened in a much more convenient location, but the area is still called Horbury Junction. Bedlington Station in Northumberland was situated at West Sleekburn and became a sizeable place which, by 1924, was joined to Bedlington by a long road of terraced houses. In 1938 it had doubled again, and the area between the two places has now been fully infilled. But, oddly, West Sleekburn was not called Bedlington Station until some time during the Second World War. It is now the official name, despite the station having closed in 1964.

In parts of Scotland a number of planned villages were created, three of them in the north east, around stations. Two were close to each other. At Newtyle, terminus of the Dundee & Newtyle Railway, Lord Wharncliffe, a strong supporter, started feuing land for a new village next to the station in 1833, ¼ mile from the old village. George Kinloch, principal promoter of the railway's extension, the Newtyle & Coupar Angus, in 1835 did the same a few miles further on. He called his village Washington. It was the larger of the two, but after a few years failed to develop and subsequently took the name of Ardler, little more than ¼ mile away but in the next county, where there was also a station. Washington station was closed in 1847.[31] Dyce was commenced on the Muir of Dyce near the station by the local laird in 1865, and by 1901 had developed on a rectilinear plan, with a mission hall and a school. It has now become a suburb of Aberdeen, its development influenced by the airport.

Country junctions could spark off the growth of a village where otherwise there might have been none. Often the railway development was a recognisable offshoot of an existing village that sooner or later absorbed it, and by so doing retained its own identity. Tebay in Cumbria and Hellifield, North Yorkshire, were two examples; Barnetby in Lincolnshire another. Ladybank, in Fife, became established with the railway in 1847, growing into a small town and eventually a burgh, and Strathyre likewise developed from nothing when the Callender & Oban Railway opened in 1870.

Maud, junction for the Buchan line in Aberdeenshire, until 1865 was called Brucklay. By 1873 it still had only a post office, a school and a large poor-house, but by 1902 streets had been laid out, together with the Victoria Hall and an auction mart, all attributable to the presence of the railway. Craven Arms in Shropshire and Llandudno Junction developed similarly around junctions, the first named after an inn that was the only building there when the railway came, and which grew into a large village with a cattle market. There was nothing at all at Llandudno Junction when the station opened in 1858, but the same thing happened, and even though the railway predominated it was by no means the sole provider.

Now two villages that grew into small towns, where the railway was highly significant but not sufficiently so to prevent them from retaining their identity by attracting other growth: Normanton and Didcot. The first, in West Yorkshire, possessing a sixteenth-century grammar school and a market, saw its population double after the railway junction opened in 1840. Although the station's fortunes rose and fell several times, the junction was always important as a freight interchange point. The railway built five terraces of houses but did not dominate the town that grew up; it shared its importance with coal. Didcot, a Berkshire (now Oxfordshire) junction, was also an ancient village which managed to stay to one side of the small new town that grew after the railway came in 1844. Development at both was uninspiring, but neither place became a typical company town, and at Didcot both old and new have now been swallowed up in post-Second World War development.

Finally, some country junctions that did not develop at all, but were purely passenger interchanges. There was a clutch in Wales: Bala Junction and Dovey Junction were approached only by footpaths across fields; Moat Lane, Afon Wen, Morfa Mawddach and Three Cocks junctions had roads to them, made by the railway, but no more. Three Cocks also had an inn after which it was named, and at nearby Talyllyn Junction a few scattered houses appeared. Roudham Junction in Norfolk, Killin Junction in the Highlands and Georgemas Junction in the far north of Scotland were similar examples.

The Seaside

Again, it is impossible to generalise. There were no resorts that the railway did not assist sooner or later, even though some, like Weston-super-Mare, Cromer and Bournemouth, at first discouraged it, but one can say little more than that. Others, like Brighton, already well established in 1841, Blackpool and Eastbourne, found a place on the railway map fairly early. Blackpool at first grew slowly after the coming of the railway in 1846, but mushroomed from the 'sixties, completely reliant on the railway to feed it with customers. Eastbourne was put on the railway through the foresight of the Duke of Devonshire, the principal landowner, who knew how railways had assisted his Furness mineral interests. Blackpool, the Kent coast resorts, those in Ayrshire and others near industrial areas benefited also from the crowds of day trippers the railways brought in.

Railways made positive contributions in a number of ways. After Samuel Morton Peto, one of the great railway contractors, promoted the Lowestoft Railway & Harbour Company, he proceeded to add a resort to the port by developing an area south of the town. The railway from Norwich was opened in 1847 and a second from Ipswich in 1859, again with Peto's backing, and Simmons judges that he can be considered as the founder of modern Lowestoft. Peto played similar roles at Southend through the construction and operation of the London, Tilbury & Southend Railway, together with Thomas Brassey and Edward L. Betts; and as chairman of the Chester & Holyhead which actively encouraged the emergence of the North Wales coast resorts. Peto was concerned with development at Abergele, where in 1857 the railway offered cheap fares to new householders and which in three years grew into a small town. Rhyl, Colwyn Bay and Llandudno also developed as a consequence of the opening of the railway.

Thomas Savin, builder of so many Welsh railways, had ambitions to create a string of resorts along the line he was building up the Cambrian coast from Aberystwyth to Porth Dynllaen on the Lleyn peninsula, with big hotels at Aberystwyth, Borth and Aberdovey for which combined rail and hotel tickets would be available. His row of boarding houses next to the station formed the nucleus of Borth, and he converted a mansion at Aberystwyth into the Castle Hotel — it is now part of the university college — while the Aberystwyth & Welsh Coast Railway itself in 1864 put forward a scheme for hotel building, but Parliament rejected it. Its successor, the Cambrian Railways, bought land for hotels at Abererch in 1883, but a year later went bankrupt. Even so, the railway was instrumental in opening up Cardigan Bay, and completely changed the pattern and character of Aberystwyth.[32] It was still trying hard in 1905, when its May–June Tourist Arrangements booklet advertised 'House Passes' to encourage the building of houses on the coast as summer residences.

ISSUE OF HOUSE PASSES.

The Company, with a view of encouraging the building of houses as summer residences at the Watering-Places on the Railway, have arranged to issue a Free Pass for five years to the head of a family who may build and occupy a house of not less than £50 annual rental, the plans to be submitted to and approved by the Company's Engineer.

Further particulars may be obtained from the Secretary, Cambrian Railways Company, Oswestry.

The Cambrian Railways' advert in their 1905 tourist booklet offering free passes to seaside house builders, with the object of promoting traffic. (Courtesy R. Christiansen)

The main agent of change at Skegness was Lord Scarbrough, the principal landowner. When he saw the anticipated traffic on the railway that opened in 1873 rapidly become reality, he quickly laid out a town, and other developers followed. The railway, operated by the Great Northern for a small local company, provided the initial impetus and, unusually, built a station large enough to meet future requirements, which was quickly justified. At Hunstanton there was, again, close collaboration between landowner and local railway. Promotion and construction went on side-by-side with laying out a new resort. Land was given to the railway, which was opened in 1862, and the successful partnership fully met expectations. Another small company, the Hull & Holderness, opened in 1854, was less successful in encouraging development at Withernsea. Free tickets were offered to 'Parties Building New Houses'. An estimated annual rental value of £10-20 entitled the householder to a free third-class pass to Hull for five years, £20-25 a first-class pass, and £30-50 a first-class pass for 10 years. Building workers were offered cheap fares as well, but they were to little avail. In four years only 70-odd houses, a gas works and the Queens Hotel had been built and four new streets remained empty.[33] The planned pier did not materialise and, like Hornsea just up the coast, Withernsea never gained significance as a watering place but became something of a dormitory for Hull. Further north the Scarborough & Whitby Railway was involved with development companies at Robin Hood's Bay and Ravenscar, through its directors, and the company's offices were used for dealing with enquiries. The Ravenscar scheme was quite extensive, but did not succeed.

Direct promotion by the railway was less common, but happened in two ways at Saltburn and Cleethorpes, and differently again on the Cumbrian coast at Seascale and Silloth. Saltburn was developed by the Stockton & Darlington Railway through a group which, if not nominees, was effectively so. The company's secretary and solicitor acted for it and the railway's architect designed the Zetland Hotel. The branch railway opened in 1858 and, as Simmons says, the group's activities were indistinguishable from the railway's, which built some speculative houses on its own account. In the early 1880s the Manchester, Sheffield & Lincolnshire built the promenade at Cleethorpes to protect the cliff, at the same time rebuilding the station, laying out gardens and constructing an exhibition hall, museum, aquarium, amusement park and baths, all administered by the company's estate department. Dining and refreshment rooms were operated by the hotels department.[34] Prince Albert Victor performed the opening ceremony. The company took a lease of the pier, extended the sea wall and by 1900 owned all the foreshore through to Grimsby, having spent £106,000. For 20-odd years it was a good investment but by 1925 the direct return was down to 1.6 per cent. The LNER sold out to the district council in 1936 for £27,500, after making an average loss of £670 over the previous five years.[35]

Seascale was virtually a non-starter. Following the satisfactory experience at Grange-over-Sands, where a group of Furness Railway directors promoted the Grange Hotel and a gas and water company, the railway sought to repeat it by developing surplus land at Seascale. It planned an hotel, avenues of detached and semi-detached houses and a promenade in 1879, but over ten years barely a dozen houses were built. By the end of the century there were a few more, the railway had provided gas and water, and a golf course had been opened, but Seascale never really took off.[36] Further north on the Solway, the Carlisle & Silloth Bay Railway's activities were much more successful although equally illegal. The company's Act allowed the purchase of 15 acres for 'extraordinary purposes', of which property development was not one, yet it steadily bought more land in the 1850s and '60s amounting to 210 acres, and commissioned an architect to lay out all the appurtenances of a resort: streets, gardens, hotel, gas works, baths, all of which the company duly provided, together with a policeman and bathing machines. The building plots were leased out and strict control was exercised over every aspect of development. The railway owned everything, even the sewage system, and when it was dissatisfied with the standard of house design it built a terrace itself. The Bishop of Carlisle enthusiastically described Silloth as 'the Torquay of the North'. Unfortunately the heavy expenditure landed the small company in financial difficulties, but as Silloth was also a port the North British Railway stepped in and leased it in 1862 and, for a time, maintained standards. When money was required for maintenance of the town's services, however, the North British was reluctant to spend it and the town stagnated. Although Silloth retained its popularity and did not decline, and eventually the local authority took control, expansion did not reach

An aerial view of Cleethorpes sea front in 1960, showing the promenade and sea defences built alongside the line by the Manchester, Sheffield & Lincolnshire Railway from beyond the station and pier (top right) to the big dipper (bottom left) as part of its plan to develop the resort. The company also owned the foreshore as far as Grimsby. (Grimsby Evening Telegraph)

early expectations. But the port prospered.[37] Rather differently the Southern Railway in 1929 tried to promote Allhallows-on-Sea as a resort in north Kent, in conjunction with developers who gave land for a branch line and contributed towards its cost. Development completely failed, and the line was closed in 1961.

The railways saw ownership of seaside hotels as a way of attracting passengers, and several examples have already been noted. Country-house style hotels, however, whether on the coast or inland, were a much later development with which the railways did no more than flirt. The Furness Railway's conversion of the partly twelfth-century manor house next to the station at Furness Abbey as early as 1847 was the only venture in this field until 1878, when the Great Western took up the idea and bought Tregenna Castle at St Ives. In the meantime Peto had dabbled unsuccessfully. He persuaded the Chester & Holyhead to take shares in an hotel project at Rhyl in 1857, which came to nothing, and to participate in an ambitious scheme for a large hotel set in 25 acres of park on railway land near Menai Bridge. Sir Joseph Paxton and a Liverpool architect produced designs, and more surplus land was earmarked for housing which it was hoped would be the beginnings of a small town. The railway offered leases at peppercorn rents, 25 per cent commission on railway tickets for hotel guests, and a new station, but response was poor and Britannia Park got no further than a prospectus plan. Otherwise, the railways preferred to stick to running holiday hotels at resorts, at which they were successful, and country-house hotels had to wait for the motor car, when access from a station no longer mattered. The Great Western did not repeat its experiment until 1927 when it bought the Manor House at Moretonhampstead in Devon, followed by the LMS with the Welcombe Hotel at Stratford-upon-Avon in 1931 and, in 1939, the one and only railway holiday camp at Prestatyn, which remained in railway ownership until 1952. Five Scottish railway country hotels thrived on golf: the Cruden Bay Hotel of 1899, to which the Great North of Scotland Railway built an electric tramway from the station; Dornoch and Strathpeffer by the Highland Railway in 1904 and 1911; Turnberry on the Ayrshire coast, served by a light railway built by the Glasgow & South Western principally to serve the course it acquired and the hotel it built in 1906; and the world-famous Gleneagles, completed in 1924, where the Caledonian had laid out two championship courses.

Ports and Docks

Port development, like canals and railways, accompanied the Industrial Revolution. In the last century and the greater part of this, railway connections were essential and there was barely one port, even among the smallest, that did not have one. The great dock systems of Liverpool and London operated their own private railways, as did the Manchester Ship Canal, while other large mercantile ports like Cardiff, Hull and those on the Tyne, Clyde and Forth, relied on the main line railways to provide services over dock and harbour lines. At many ports there were competing railways, while more than a few were monopolised by a single company and some ports were bought or built by the railways themselves. Collectively, the railways were the largest dock owners in the country. More than that, all the large railway companies were shipowners, providing services to the Continent, Ireland and within Great Britain. Maritime property, therefore, formed a substantial and important part of the railway estate, usually with its own management.

The earliest railway-owned dock appears to have been at Llanelli, which was bought by the Carmarthenshire Railway, a 16-mile tramroad, in 1802, although the line to it was not completed until 1806. Later there followed a number of combined railway and dock companies in South Wales, designed to handle coal, among them the Llanelly Railway & Dock Company of 1835 with over 36 miles of route, the Port Talbot Railway & Dock of 1894 with 33 miles, and the Alexandra (Newport & South Wales) Docks & Railway of 1865, the longest named but with the shortest mileage — 9. The largest and most successful was the Barry Railway that, from 1884, built the Barry Docks system, operated 68 miles of railway and in terms of tonnage became the leading port in South Wales. Probably the most remarkable railway-and-dock undertaking was established in Suffolk opposite Harwich, where a local landowner formed the Felixstowe Railway & Pier Company in 1875. Renamed the Felixstowe Railway & Dock Company, it built a dock in 1884 but did not develop much further until the 1960s, since when it has expanded enormously and become one of the leading east coast ports.

A combined development with a different outcome took place at Fleetwood. There, Sir Peter Hesketh Fleetwood started to build a new resort and port on a virgin site in 1836, which he named after himself. He founded the Preston & Wyre Railway Dock & Harbour Company and the railway opened in 1840, but the port grew only slowly. It was left to the Lancashire & Yorkshire Railway, which became joint owner of the line with the London & North Western, to finish the dock in 1878. A second one was opened in 1909 and for a time Fleetwood became the third largest fishing port in Britain. Fish was also the trade of Grimsby Docks under railway ownership, vigorously promoted by the Manchester, Sheffield & Lincolnshire which bought the dock company in 1845 and immediately set about large-scale expansion. Two other main east coast fishing ports were railway-owned, Lowestoft and Hull, but not Great Yarmouth, although the Great Eastern invested heavily there. Hull Docks came late into railway ownership. For a long time the North Eastern Railway monopolised access to Hull which was, of course, much more of a general port. The NER bought the dock company in 1893, but before then the Hull & Barnsley — another combined railway-and-dock company formed specifically to break the North Eastern's monopoly — had opened the Alexandra Dock in 1885. Later the two companies sank their differences and built the George V Dock in 1904-14. So Hull became a railway-owned port, but split between two companies. The North Eastern also owned Hartlepool Docks and was prominently concerned with others in the north east.

The docks at Goole were owned by the Aire & Calder Navigation Company, forming a canal-owned port, although they were a stronghold of the North Eastern and Lancashire & Yorkshire railways as well. The same happened at Grangemouth on the Firth of Forth, where the Forth & Clyde Canal built docks, but which in this case came into railway ownership when the Caledonian bought the canal in 1867, principally to get hold of the docks. The railway set out on an expansionist course that turned Grangemouth into an important Scottish port. On the opposite shore the North British acquired the ports of Alloa, Methil and Leven, and at Burntisland it appointed half of the harbour commissioners and lent money for development. At Immingham, although the Great Central was not the legal owner of the dock, it financed the Humber Railway & Dock Company, whose Act provided for a 999-year lease to the railway as soon as it was completed. Opened in 1912 on a virgin site, it was to all intents and purposes a railway-owned port.

The greatest railway port was Southampton, purchased by the London & South Western in 1892. The company invested £5 million to create a docks system designed to capture the lion's share of the ocean liner trade, in which it was eminently successful, rivalling Liverpool and, in post-war years, overtaking it. For a few years Southampton had a rival of sorts for the transatlantic trade in Fishguard, a venture undertaken jointly by the Great Western and the Great Southern & Western Railway of Ireland; opened in 1906, its primary function, however, was as a packet station for Rosslare. Capital of £3 million had to be raised to pay for the works on both sides of St George's Channel and for ships.

Railway investment in packet stations had a history going back to the purchase of Folkestone by the South Eastern in 1844. Although the Admiralty owned Dover, Harwich and Holyhead, the railways had substantial stakes in them, particularly at Holyhead where the London & North Western owned the inner harbour and most of the land, and provided all the services. When Harwich became too small the Great Eastern built new berths, a station and an hotel at Parkeston Quay, 2 miles away, in 1882, complementing work by the Dutch at the Hook of Holland. On the southern shore of Morecambe Bay, Heysham Harbour was developed by the Midland Railway, opening in 1904 to compete with Fleetwood as a packet station for Belfast. It had deep-water accommodation that its predecessor, Morecambe, could not possibly provide and Morecambe was abandoned as a railway port, despite significant investment after it was created by the railway in 1848, leaving the town to continue to develop as a resort. Barrow will be considered in the next chapter as a railway town.

The most northerly Irish Sea packet station, Stranraer, struggled from 1874 until a consortium of two Scottish and two English railways took it over in 1885. They set about improving the service to Larne. The Harbour station was built on the east pier, which the railways owned. On the same coast the harbours at Ayr, Troon and Largs were purchased by the Glasgow & South Western Railway between 1899 and 1919, and the Caledonian owned piers at Gourock and Wemyss Bay, from which they engaged in highly competitive Clyde steamer services. In England, passenger trains ran on to piers at New Holland for the ferry across the Humber to Hull, at Ryde, Isle of Wight and, for a time, at Portishead, all owned by railways which built stations on them, as did the Highland Railway at Kyle of Lochalsh.

Chapter 6

Railway Communities

In this chapter we look at some of the communities of railway families and those who served them, in settlements built by the railways themselves and by private developers who perceived a demand.

Railway Towns

The rapid expansion of railways quickly outgrew the capacity of early locomotive builders to supply engines. The railways had to build their own, which meant building factories. Where these were away from centres of population, work-forces had to be brought together and houses provided, either from scratch on a green-field site or superimposed on to an exisiting settlement which in a number of cases the railway came to dominate. Later, this dominance tended to recede at all but a few, where it continued well into the twentieth century, but none the less at all of them it made a lasting impact.

The first railway town was created by the Stockton & Darlington Railway in 1826 at Shildon, a tiny settlement in the east Durham colliery district. By the early 1830s the small works and the houses erected on land owned by the railway or its directors were growing and the population was already 900.[1] In 1871 the North Eastern Railway made Shildon its principal wagon works, a role that continued through LNER and British Rail ownership, when all wagon building was concentrated there. By 1902 the town had nearly 2,500 people and by the mid-1970s over 15,000, due almost entirely to progressive enlargement of the works. Shildon remained a single-industry town right up to BR ending wagon building and the sale of the works in 1984.

The early street layout was haphazard, unlike Wolverton where, from the outset, the London & Birmingham laid out streets in a formal pattern. The company chose this small Buckinghamshire village, which in 1821 had only 335 people, because it lay half way between the termini and was well placed for the delivery of materials by canal. The works was opened a short distance away in 1838 and by 1844 there were some 200 dwellings. In 1851, when 2,070 lived there, they comprised 'a series of uniform brick houses in rectangular streets . . . for the benefit of this population the Directors have built a church, schools for boys, for girls and for infants, which are not the least remarkable or interesting parts of this curious town.'[2] An offshoot settlement was built at New Bradwell, and in 1863 the London & North Western Railway, as the London & Birmingham had now become, transferred all locomotive building to Crewe and carriage building to Wolverton, which became the largest works of its kind in Britain. Four streets contained company houses, and by 1897 there were eight more containing houses built on land laid out and sold for the purpose by the railway. In 1914 New Bradwell had 202 railway houses lining three streets.[3] With railway encouragement McCorquodales, who did much railway printing, set up a factory on land sold to them in 1882, when the population was 3,600, but otherwise Wolverton remained a railway town with a population that by 1906 was twice that figure. In 1931 it was 13,000, but in post-war years Wolverton has been swallowed up in Milton Keynes New Town and the works are now much reduced in capacity.[4]

The Great Western followed the same policy, but less successfully, at Swindon in 1841, where it bought land near the small Wiltshire market town to build a works and a new town. As the junction for the Gloucester line and the point where it was desirable to change engines for the steeper gradients towards Bristol, and again on a canal which could bring in supplies, it was a convenient place. Brunel designed the layout and it has been suggested that Matthew Digby Wyatt, who later worked with him on Paddington station, may have assisted with architectural detailing. However, as he was only 20 at the time it is unlikely; more probably, if anyone, it was Francis Thompson, a little-known architect responsible for some of Britain's most sensitively designed stations, with whom Brunel corresponded on this subject following some design work Thompson did for the Swindon refreshment rooms.[5] To save the capital outlay, the houses were built by one of the railway's contractors, for whom the company collected the rents and to whom, also, the station refreshment rooms were let as part of the agreement. As the contract required all trains to make a refreshments stop, it was a lucrative arrangement for the lessees which the Great Western came to regret. So it could be said that New Swindon was built on the profits from Bath buns and coffee.

The houses were built in neat streets and, for their day, were to a high structural standard for artisans' dwellings, although for some years conditions were poor, with an inadequate water supply. The customary cess-pit drainage did not help, and a typhus epidemic in 1853 put a stop to building which the company did not resume. Moreover, the Great Western's future policy of not building houses anywhere unless circumstances absolutely forced it to, a failing that continued until the 1920s, at Swindon caused endemic overcrowding. In 1851, when the population had risen to 4,800, it was severe, and was still bad in 1914. A lodging house nicknamed The Barracks was built in the mid-1850s but was not popular. The company built a school, library, market house and mechanics' institute, donated substantially to a church and paid the vicar's stipend.[6] For a long time the New Town stayed separate from old Swindon, which also grew but was not physically joined to it until 1890. They were incorporated as a single borough in 1900, when New Swindon was already an Urban District in its own right. In 1931 the combined population was 62,700 and in the mid-1970s 90,000, by which time new industries were well established. Now it is the core of the new district of Thamesdown and a centre for high-tech industry. The railway works has closed and a large part has been demolished, overtaken by late twentieth-century technology.

Crewe ranks with Swindon as the best-known railway town. Roughly contemporary, because its creators pursued a more sustained and vigorous housing policy, it suffered fewer problems. Joseph Locke laid it out for the Grand Junction Railway, aided by the Liverpool architect John Cunningham, on a rural Cheshire site at the junction of the Liverpool, Manchester and Chester lines. In 1843 the new town was populated almost overnight when 800 inhabitants were transferred from the company's outgrown works at Edge Hill, Liverpool. It seems that everything was ready for them, or nearly so. Certainly by the end of the year there were schools, an assembly room, a magistrates' court and a temporary church. Building went on apace and by 1848 there were 520 company houses (by now the property of the London & North Western) and 300 private. The railway houses were seemly in appearance and for the times were well designed and built. The population was approaching 4,500 and eventually the railway owned over 900 houses in Crewe. After Locke's initial layout was completed, development was less orderly and the company took little interest in planning, although it gave to the town four churches, a hospital, eight schools, a market house, baths, mechanics' institute and Queen's Park, together with provision of gas and water. Administratively Crewe came within the parish of Monks Coppenhall, which set up a Local Board in 1859 and changed its name to Crewe in 1869, but the LNWR and its chief officers at the works effectively governed the town until 1890. The works expanded enormously, becoming the most self-sufficient railway establishment in the world, including the smelting and rolling of steel rails and the manufacture of bricks. The population in 1911 was 45,000, but the inter-war years were difficult and it was only 1,000 more in 1931. Then, in 1938, Rolls-Royce came and Crewe ceased to be purely a railway town. Its mid-1970s population was 50,500 and, although there is still a locomotive works, in size it is greatly diminished.[7]

Our fourth town is somewhat different in that not only did the railway build it for its own immediate purposes, but introduced docks and other major industries as well, either directly or through its directors. Barrow-in-Furness in the early nineteenth century was a mere hamlet, but close to deep water, which made it more attractive to the local slate industry than the established port of Ulverston. The discovery of rich haematite iron ore led to the promotion of the Furness Railway in 1844, but it was 1857 before the line was connected to the main railway to the south. Meanwhile, shipping services started and Barrow became a port for the coastal trade and, later, for the Isle of Man and Belfast. The creation of the town can be attributed to a partnership between James Ramsden, the visionary general manager of the railway, and his chairman, the 7th Duke of Devonshire, who was one of the two principal landowners. In 1854 the company bought the Hindpool estate and Ramsden drew up plans for a new town with wide streets and extensive quays. Barrow became known as 'the Chicago of the north', perhaps extravagantly, with Ramsden as its 'father', but these appellations give an indication of how its extraordinary growth was regarded. The Furness invested in an ironworks, steelworks, rolling mills, jute factory and a shipyard, and by the early 1860s the railway was synonymous with Barrow, providing a church, the town hall, a market, gas works, waterworks, schools and a gridiron of housing. For a time the new civic corporation met in the company's offices. That in doing all this the company repeatedly exceeded its statutory powers was freely admitted. By 1861 some 3,000 people lived there; four years later there were over 8,000 and, with Middlesbrough, which was railway-inspired but not railway-developed, it was the most remarkable example of an industrial boom town in nineteenth-century Britain. In 1863 the railway took over the harbour, built two large docks and acquired Barrow Island. One end of the channel was closed off to reclaim land and in 1872 two more docks were built so that by the end of the 1880s the total enclosed water space was 294 acres, exceeded only by London and Liverpool, on which the Furness had spent £2.1 million. Towards the end of the century the local iron ore started to run out, without which the new port was too far away from other industrial centres to succeed. Barrow started to decline and the railway began to dispose of its industrial assets. When Vickers bought the shipyard in 1896 Barrow changed from a short-lived railway-dominated community to a shipbuilding town, which it largely remains.[8]

Lastly, Eastleigh in Hampshire. The railway arrived at Bishopstoke in 1840 when there were just a few scattered houses. It was a fairly important junction, but the village grew little until 1891 when the London & South Western Railway moved its carriage shops there from Nine Elms in London, and the place was renamed Eastleigh. The population jumped from 600 to 3,500, but the railway left it to speculative builders to provide housing, which they did scandalously badly, to the extent of provoking a public enquiry. Planned extensions to the works were delayed by lack of workers' accommodation and at length in 1903 the company built 54 houses, and 100 more in 1910 when it moved its locomotive works there. A year later the population was 15,200, but beyond providing employment, contributing £500 towards enlarging the church and building the LSWR Institute, the company had done little to assist.[9] Eastleigh became an Urban District in 1894 and continued as a railway town, growing slowly to a population of 18,300 in 1931. Post-war growth has been rapid, with 46,000 in the mid-1970s, and although the railway works is still significant the town is now virtually an outlier of the Southampton/Portsmouth conurbation.

Railway Enclaves

Railway works built in or close to existing towns did not necessarily change their essential function and character. When the railways arrived at Derby in 1839-40, for example, it was an old-established county town and regional centre with its own industries. The Midland Railway's station, works and headquarters were concentrated to one side of the town, together with some company housing, which was not extensive, and a considerable area of private housing occupied by railway workers. The railway soon became the largest industry, but its enclave, which covered a large area, remained separate and, after Rolls-Royce moved to Derby in 1907, the town expanded past it. Although up to the Second World War Derby was a railway town in the sense that the Midland and its successor, the LMS, was among the three largest employers, outside the enclave the railway left little mark.[10]

A railway colony of over 220 houses was built by the Great Northern Railway in the 1850s close to its locomotive sheds and repair shops north of Peterborough. Called New England, it had a company gas works and school, and the company made a major contribution to a church. The settlement steadily expanded with private houses, eventually becoming a large suburb which now forms a substantial extension of Peterborough.[11]

When the Great Northern moved its works from Boston to Doncaster in 1852, much the same happened as at Derby except that the railway installation was split. The works was close to the station on the west side of the town, and the locomotive sheds and yards were to the south. Some 2,500 people were added to the population, for whom the company built a few houses, but existing accommodation and speculative building provided for the majority. The company spent £1,000 on schools, but the shareholders jibbed at a church, which was funded by subscription, the railway providing the land and free carriage of Ancaster stone. Doncaster continued to grow, with the railway as the largest employer, but the essential fabric of the town itself was not affected by it.

At Gateshead the North Eastern Railway transferred its small works to a larger site between the town centre and the Tyne in 1852-4. Although the works was very much part of the town and the railway, again, was the largest employer, there was no company-housed community. By 1910 the works was too small and new locomotive building was transferred to Darlington, where the Stockton & Darlington had transferred locomotive building from Shildon in 1863. The new works in North Road became the North Eastern's mechanical engineering headquarters, but as the town was already a heavy engineering centre the railway works, despite being the largest, did not dominate it; nor was the housing owned by the company, mainly in Whessoe Road, extensive for a work-force of 3,500 which in 1911 amounted to some 17 per cent of employed males.[12] The works closed in 1966. At Brighton the London, Brighton & South Coast Railway in 1901-3 chose Preston Park as a site for 125 houses, as well as others elsewhere in the town, for its works employees.

Both Manchester and Glasgow had railway colonies that were a mixture of railway company and private locomotive works. The Manchester, Sheffield & Lincolnshire railway started building locomotives at Gorton, Manchester, in 1846, and built 140 cottages, followed by a school, institute and library. The works expanded, eventually swallowing up the houses which were not replaced. Meanwhile Beyer Peacock's works next door made Gorton a railway colony in a double sense, but it was not distinctive as it became absorbed in the rapid urbanisation of eastern Manchester. At Springburn, Glasgow, the story was different. There, the St Rollox works of the Caledonian Railway, Cowlairs works of the North British, and the private Atlas and Hyde Park locomotive works were all close together. The Caledonian saw no great need to build dwellings for its men, but the predecessor of the North British, the Edinburgh & Glasgow, held a competition for a model village in 1863. It was won by

'The Blocks' at Cowlairs, Glasgow; tenements built
by the Edinburgh & Glasgow Railway for its
employees in 1863 as the first part of a model village
which was never completed. Housing management
was an important part of the railway estate
department's work. (Springburn Museum)

Andrew Heiton of Perth, a well-known Scottish architect who had already done
work for the company, with a design for tenement blocks in four different styles
forming terraces and crescents on the hillside above the works. A large square
contained shops and a fountain, there was a Tudor-styled school and library, and a
spacious recreation ground. The cost was estimated at £30,000, which proved to be
too much for the company so that work on this railway Elyseum stopped after four
terraces were finished. The North British added to them later, and in 1865 had 21
other houses around the works. The original terraces were known as 'The Blocks'
and they remained a prominent landmark until they were demolished in 1967.[13]

On the south side of the city the Glasgow & South Western built a complete model
village next to its new Corkerhill locomotive depot, opened in 1897. There were 132
dwellings in 10 two-storey tenement blocks that cost £70,000. The village was
self-contained, with mains services provided by the railway, together with a large
institute incorporating a church, school meeting hall, reading room, library, baths,
recreation room and shop. Community affairs were managed by a committee of 31
tenants which levied rates and administered services, including a fire brigade.[14]

Railway tenements were also built in London. The Great Northern had its
somewhat infamous Culross Buildings, 40 flats built at King's Cross about 1890, and
the Midland the larger Polygon Buildings in four blocks alongside the Somers Town
goods station at St Pancras. Each block contained 72 flats, and they were demolished
in the 1970s. Of other railway enclaves in London, the earliest was at Stratford, to

where the Eastern Counties Railway moved its works in 1848 and built 300 houses, forming a distinct colony then on the edge of the metropolis and known as the New Town. After the Second World War they were replaced by local authority housing. In the 1880s and '90s the Midland Railway built extensive locomotive and carriage sheds and marshalling yards at Cricklewood. Sixteen terraces of houses in five streets were built off what is now Cricklewood Broadway and named after the company and four of its senior officers, while on the other side of the line a further nine rows formed Midland Brent Terrace. Near its Willesden engine sheds the London & North Western built 177 houses from 1857 onwards, and there were two other enclaves at Neasden, where in 1882 the Metropolitan Railway established first locomotive and carriage shops and then a power station. During this time 142 houses were built, with shops, a school and a church, and in 1924-7 a further 202. Four of the streets were named after stations in Buckinghamshire. When the Great Central Railway entered London on parallel tracks in 1899 it, too, built 156 cottages and villas near its engine shed and workshops on the opposite side of the line from the Metropolitan's estate, including a wooden church.[15] The company did not retain them, however, but leased them to the House & Shop Company. South of the river the London, Brighton & South Coast built eight blocks of railwaymen's tenements at Bermondsey in the 1890s, named after coastal resorts which earned them the nickname 'Seaside Buildings'. The London & South Western's Granby Buildings at Vauxhall comprised five terraces of houses, and Coronation Buildings formed four

Culross Buildings, near King's Cross, comprised 40
tenements built by the Great Northern Railway in
1890, together with a railway mission. Refurbished,
they now form flats for single people, and the mission
hall is a residents' community centre.
(BR Property Board)

tenement blocks hard against the viaduct. At New Cross and Slade Green the South Eastern built small estates.

The communities considered so far were all in large towns or cities; a number of smaller places were also affected, such as Ashford, a Kentish market town that was selected by the South Eastern Railway for the transfer of its works from New Cross in south London in 1847. By 1851 some 600 workers were housed in 72 dwellings on an estate east of the town, designed by Samuel Beazley who had built some distinguished stations for the company and was known for his architectural work on theatres and country houses. They were in blocks of four around a large green, some being two-storey flats built back-to-back, together with a bath house, mechanics' institute, chapel, school (designed by William Tress, another station architect), shop and pub. The works provided gas. The South Eastern named it Alfred Town but to most people it was New Town, and still is. Sixty more houses were built in 1850, and others about 1900; gates were erected at the two entrances and all vehicles entering had to have a company pass.[16] The estate was sold in 1971 and now only the lofty bath house, school, church, pub (still the Alfred Arms) and shop remain, together with the 1900s houses, the earlier ones having given way to a modern development, although still centred on the green and quite separate from Ashford itself.

A not dissimilar, but less attractive, development took place when the London & North Western established a community opposite its wagon works near the ancient borough of Newton-le-Willows, Lancashire, in 1853. Named Earlestown after a director, 200 'first class' cottages were erected at £138 5s 0d (£138.25) each, and a superindendent's house for £650.[17] Eventually there were 340 railway houses. A further railway association lay in the Vulcan Foundry, which made railway equipment, and the combination attracted several other industries. The railway estate was enlarged by private housing and, unlike Ashford, became physically joined to Newton. But Earlestown kept its name, and in railway and engineering circles was much the better known place.

Moving on to the present century, the Great North of Scotland Railway built a small estate of tenements in four streets at Inverurie when it moved its works there from Kittybrewster, Aberdeen, in 1901-5. They were erected alongside the works on the edge of the ancient royal burgh, a town that had grown under the influence first of the Aberdeenshire Canal and then the railway, and now received a further fillip from over 500 men and their families. The estate was lit by electricity from the works, and a park and allotments were laid out. Inverurie easily assimilated them, more easily than the closure of the works in the late 1960s.

By no means all railway communities lived in company houses. By and large the railways provided dwellings only where no others were available, and then often only under pressure, usually the need to attract and keep skilled labour. Many places that were host to an important railway installation expanded at the hands of speculative builders. Take, for instance, the area of north London between Kentish Town and Gospel Oak stations which, after the opening of the Midland and associated lines in 1868, became a railwaymen's quarter put up by speculative builders around the yards, junctions and engine sheds. Examples at the other extreme include Bletchley, a very small Buckinghamshire village that grew into a town after it became a railway junction in 1846, which had only a few railway houses;[18] Bromsgrove, a Worcestershire market town chosen by the Birmingham & Gloucester Railway for its works in 1840, where the company built a dozen cottages and two detached houses but nothing more, despite its becoming one of the Midland's principal carriage and wagon repair shops, employing 600 men; and Oswestry, near the Welsh border in Shropshire. There the Cambrian Railways built a works and headquarters but provided no accommodation beyond one or two houses near the station, and the Railway Institute, despite doubling the population in the fifty years following 1861. Equally, Redhill in Surrey, a town resulting from the junction of the South Eastern and Brighton railways in 1841, was composed largely of private houses, although many were built on Brighton Railway land; the South Eastern successively built three small groups of houses near the station but they amounted to only 48 in total. Yet from the outset and for many years the majority of the inhabitants were railway families. In Cambridgeshire in 1889, March, with four marshalling yards and a quarter of the male population in railway employment, had only 41 railway houses. The rest were private. When the yards were extended at Whitemoor by the LNER in 1933, no more were built; instead the company encouraged the men to build their own houses by offering them surplus land at £50 a plot.

Boston in Lincolnshire is an example of a small, old-established town that had a distinct railway enclave of private houses. Between 1848 and 1852-3 the Great

A street of new tenements on the Great North of Scotland Railway's estate at Inverurie, built when the company moved its works from Aberdeen in 1901-5. They still exist, in 7 blocks, and have spacious gardens, outhouses and access roads at the rear. (Scottish Record Office)

Northern had its locomotive works there before, as we have seen, transferring it to Doncaster. This short period was sufficient to generate a work-force of around 700, representing nearly a 19 per cent increase in population for which speculative builders laid out six streets of houses between the railway and the river, later extending beyond.[19] After the exodus the works carried on with repair work, and more houses were built when the railway took over the sleeper creosoting works in 1877, so that by 1912 the largest employer was the Great Northern, with 900 men, mostly living in the area which, separated from the town by the railway, remained quite distinct. None of it comprised railway-owned housing.[20]

Against these places must be viewed small communities where the railway virtually took over. Horwich was an insignificant Lancashire textile town, little more than a village, before the Lancashire & Yorkshire Railway moved its works there in 1884-6. It was the right moment, as a trade slump provided some 400 empty houses in the area and there was ample spare company land for more. Nineteen streets were set out alongside the works, named after famous engineers, and building plots were sold at a profit handsome enough to cover the cost of the entire 300 acres the company had bought and a lot of the workshops as well. The houses could be mistaken for railway housing, but they were not, although the LYR provided a large, well-appointed mechanics' institute and an hotel, and the directors paid for a sports ground with a bandstand, and a cottage hospital. By 1891 Horwich had tripled its population. The town continued to grow slowly, attracting other industries, so that by the 1930s the railway that had brought the place to life, although still the largest employer and a significant power, had a diminishing influence. Now it has gone; the works that once employed 4,000 was progressively sold off from 1983, while the branch line passenger service went well before that, in 1965.

Two small rural communities in Norfolk and Northamptonshire underwent strikingly similar transformations. In 1882 the parish of Melton Constable, noted for its fine seventeenth-century hall but with very little else, was rudely shaken when the Lynn & Fakenham Railway opened workshops there. Through the influence of the hall's occupant, Lord Hastings, a strong supporter on whose land most of the railway was built, Melton became the junction of four lines, although the site on one of the highest points around was hardly the most suitable, entailing steep gradients on all sides. It became the headquarters first of the Eastern & Midlands Railway and then, after the railway was rescued from bankruptcy in 1893, the Midland & Great Northern Joint Railway, coming to be called 'the Crewe of North Norfolk'. Melton was a very small Crewe, comprising at first only one terrace of houses with no community facilities. After the joint companies took over, there was some expansion.[21] The population of 118 in 1881 rose to 1,157 in 1911, gas and water were supplied, sewerage installed, a railway institute opened and schools set up. Melton Constable became as synonymous with the M&GN as Swindon was with the GWR, although it never grew enough to become a town, even though it was called as much. Locomotive work ceased in 1936 and the railway closed entirely in 1964; the population sank to 650, the works were converted for small industrial uses and

The bus shelter at Melton Constable, Norfolk, is one of the few reminders that the village was once the hub of the Midland & Great Northern Joint Railway, including an important junction and a works. Seen here in 1989, the old station awning brackets contain the monogram of the Central Norfolk Railway, one of the joint line's constituents, while the picture alongside depicts one of the works' products. (Author)

Melton resumed its rural calm. Now, physical traces of the railway are hard to find, although some station ornamental ironwork is incorporated in a bus shelter, the Railway Institute still stands, a half-hidden iron water tank bears the cast letters 'MGN' and — a pleasing touch — the new road into the works is named Marriott Way after a long-serving engineer and general manager.

Woodford Halse and its close neighbour, Hinton, were typical Northamptonshire ironstone villages on which the opening of the East & West Junction Railway on the south side in 1873 made little impact; there was not even a station. When the Great Central came in 1898-9 things were quite different. The new line sliced between the two villages, making first a junction with the older line and then throwing off an important connection to the Great Western at Banbury. An engine shed, wagon shops and sidings were laid out and 170 red-brick terraced houses were erected by private builders and leased to the railway for its employees. There were shops, a gas works and, in 1922, a council housing estate. When the railway closed in 1966 Woodford was again transformed and the former yards are now an industrial estate, entered from Great Central Way.[22] Now, at Woodford and Melton, a group of Victorian urban houses sits incongruously among fields, reminders of 60-70 years of railway dominance.

Another very small early nineteenth-century community, Carnforth on the northern edge of Lancashire, did, however, become a small town and the seat of an Urban District. The village, although it was barely that, found itself on the main London–Carlisle line in 1846, but nothing much happened until 1857 when it became a junction and started to grow. Ten years later it was served by three companies, each with its own engine shed. Later on, two of them built their own terraces of distinctive houses, the London & North Western and the Midland, although the Furness Railway does not seem to have built any. After only nine years railway dominance ended when an ironworks was built, to return in 1929 when the works closed and Carnforth again became predominantly a railway town until the last engine shed closed at the end of steam. The population in 1857 was less than 400, which the railways doubled by the time the ironworks opened and which was doubled again by the time it closed. Although still an important junction, Carnforth's continued growth is no longer attributable to the railway, which has ceased to be a significant employer.[23]

Lastly in this brief review of railway enclaves, an anti-climax. In 1896, when the Lancashire, Derbyshire & East Coast Railway was built, Tuxford in Nottinghamshire would have ranked as no more than a medium-sized village were it not for its market and some historical importance from its position on the Great North Road. The LDECR had big ideas — no less than 170 miles of railway from Warrington to a new port in Lincolnshire. Workshops employing about 130 were built at Tuxford and the little town seemed set to expand with the new railway. But the promoters' optimism exceeded the size of their pockets and in 1907, with only 58 miles built, their grand plan ended when the company sold out to the Great Central. Only 6 railway houses were built, and a private terrace of 17 near the works. Otherwise, so small a work-force was absorbed locally and what little impact railway employment made was hardly noticed.

Railway Villages

Before turning to railway houses themselves, we should look at one more type of settlement: the villages that railways built solely for their own purposes, some in isolated locations where there was nothing else. With the development of road transport a few did eventually attract other development, but others were so remote that they were never other than a railway village.

On the high moors of western Durham at Waskerley, for instance, the Stockton & Darlington in 1849 had two engine sheds, a wagon shop and a store at the top of the cable-worked Nanny Mayor's incline. For the workers there were 24 cottages, a station house and a school,[24] later increased to 30 cottages, several larger houses, allotments, post office, Primitive and Wesleyan Methodist chapels and an institute. They made no formal pattern, but were scattered randomly around the railway layout as it developed. The settlement dated back to the Stanhope & Tyne Railroad, a wagonway of 1834, and the line closed in 1968, when the village on the lonely moor was abandoned. All that is left are three houses and the Wesleyan chapel, while the Primitives' chapel and a goods shed serve as barns.

Remoter still, and perhaps the best known, was Riccarton Junction, high in the Border hills where the Border Counties Railway joined the North British's Waverley Route from Edinburgh to Carlisle. Taking its name from a nearby burn and a farm

2 miles away, the junction came into being in 1862 with an engine shed, carriage shed and six cottages bought from the contractor. As traffic increased, the community grew to comprise 30 houses, a gas lighting plant, school and recreation hall, all provided by the company. Railwaymen opened their own co-operative store on the platform and the post office was in the booking office. There was no road access, so everything went in and out by rail. The line closed in 1969, when all the buildings were razed apart from two cottages, the schoolmaster's house and his schoolroom, and Riccarton went back to moorland and sheep. But in 1984 a new life started. The hills were afforested and work began on digging up and processing some 30ft of furnace slag and ashes that originally were put down to level the site. It is removed by lorry along the trackbed to the nearest road, to make breeze building blocks.

Nearer Carlisle on the same line, Riddings Junction, although nowhere near so isolated and served by a road, was nothing more than a station next to a farm from which it took its name; the few other houses were all railway cottages. But Riccarton had a near-counterpart on the Settle & Carlisle line at Hawes Junction (now Garsdale), opened in 1876, where the Midland built 22 cottages. In an area of high moorland and scattered farms, the station became something of a local community centre. Church services were held in the waiting room which also did duty as a library, and the water-tank house contained seats, a stage and a piano for social occasions and, later on, cinema performances. Although the 'amenities' are no longer needed, Garsdale is still a recognisable railway village. A similar community existed on the Central Wales line at Builth Road where the London & North Western crossed the Cambrian. Each line had its own station, and the London & North Western also had an engineer's depot. It built three terraces of red-brick houses, one opposite the station and two near the depot, forming a curious urban-like street. Apart from a corrugated-iron mission hall, a pair of similarly-built cottages and a detached house for the Cambrian station-master, there was nothing else and, although the Cambrian line has now gone and its station is a pub, the place is much the same today.

The North Eastern Railway built 37 houses in a purely railway village on the edge of the North York Moors at Battersby, over a mile from the village of that name. At first it was completely isolated, with no public road. Despite greatly reduced status, the station remains open because the former junction is still a reversing point for trains from Middlesbrough to Whitby. A smaller settlement, with 12 houses (including the station-master's) existed in a scattered fashion at Pilmoor, once a junction on the East Coast main line north of York, together with a mission chapel. The post office was in the station booking office, a feature still to be found at a few stations today.

The London & South Western in 1840 passed within a mile of the village of Micheldever in Hampshire, but built a station 2½ miles away on the road to Andover. Although the town was 10 miles distant, the station was built to serve it and was called Andover Road, but two years after Andover got its own station on the Salisbury line the name was changed to Micheldever. By 1865 there was still

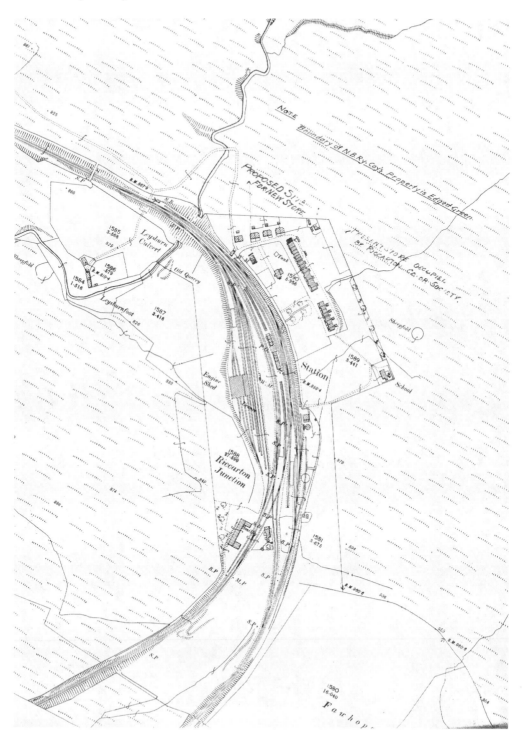

Left:
Plan of Riccarton Junction, Roxburghshire, in 1898, on the Waverley Route from Edinburgh to Carlisle. One of Britain's remotest stations, it was 2 miles from the nearest road and formed a self-contained railway community with workers' houses and a school. (BR Property Board)

Above:
Riccarton Junction photographed in 1961, when it was no longer a junction, the Border Counties branch having closed five years earlier. The engine shed has gone and the sidings are empty, but the school now has a master's house next door; both were still in use in 1989. (G. Sellar)

nothing there but the station and an hotel, but eventually a group of eight railway houses was built, with a school and a few neighbouring estate houses, although even now only a few more houses and bungalows have been added. Further west, Seaton Junction in Devon was almost as isolated, with its own small group of railway houses a mile from the village of Shute. Other than an hotel, a small factory and a few extra houses, there is still nothing else; the station closed in 1966.

Carstairs Junction was one of the most extensive Scottish railway villages, so named to distinguish it from the old village a mile or more away, although the station at the divergence of the Caledonian Railway's Edinburgh and Glasgow lines from the south, opened in 1842, is named simply Carstairs. Later, three more lines were served, engine and carriage sheds were built and the junction became one of the most important in Scotland. By 1884 the railway had built 14 rows of houses and

151

two-storey tenements, a shop, a school and a school house.[25] There was a church, and Carstairs Junction was made a separate ecclesiastical parish. Apart from an hotel, a few villas and the farm that preceded the railway, the Caledonian virtually owned the place until the 1920s, when council houses were built, doubling the village's area. Although it is still an important junction, branch line closures, electrification and rationalisation have severely curtailed Carstairs' other functions and the railway village has disappeared. The land it occupied is now covered by new housing, completely changing the face of Carstairs Junction.

Lines in the Highlands called for small settlements at stations and crossing loops. The North British provided staff houses at the remote Rannoch station, in the middle of the moor. Too small to be called a village, nevertheless its remoteness called for a school which was also used by the children of Gorton, an even lonelier crossing loop 7 miles south. Tiny settlements were necessary at some of the Highland Railway's stations, too, like Altnabreac out in the vast peat mosses of Caithness, and Dalnaspidal near Drumochter summit; stations that were built as much for operating purposes as to fulfil a public need.

Company Housing Policy

The railways were by no means the only industry to provide housing for employees. Company villages were being built around rural factories, mines and mills in the eighteenth century, many forming the nucleus of a new town. Among early railway settlements, Waskerley on the Stanhope & Tyne has already been noted, one of several groups of houses built for the men who worked the cable-hauled inclines and weighing machines on the wagonways and tramroads. The Stockton & Darlington leased some houses at Stockton until it could build its own.[26] The first main line railways similarly provided houses for crossing keepers and station-masters, a practice that grew. In 1850-1 the Newcastle & Carlisle, opened in 1838, had 70 houses and cottages, including station houses,[27] and by the present century about 10 per cent of railwaymen throughout the country lived in company houses. The South Eastern secured specific powers to build employees' houses 'near to any of their stations' in its 1872 Act, although no other railways appear to have thought statutory sanction necessary.

Collectively, therefore, the railways formed one of the largest private house landlords, owning some 27,000 houses occupied by employees, out of a total of 55,700 'not forming part of the Railway or Stations', as the Board of Trade Railway Returns and Annual Reports put it. The balance came from houses acquired with land at various times and let to outside tenants. If houses on stations were included there could well have been 1,500-2,000 more. If we take the 23 companies with over 3,000 employees, excluding joint lines, in 1921 near the end of their independent existence, some interesting figures are revealed when their sizes in terms of employees are compared with the numbers of staff houses. For the purposes of comparison the 'league table' opposite has been compiled showing the theoretical number of employees per dwelling.[28]

1 COMPANY	2 EMPLOYEES		3 STAFF DWELLINGS		4 EMPLOYEES PER DWELLING	
	Number	*Position*	*Number*	*Position*	*Number*	*Position*
London & North Western	101,483	1	4,325	2	23.46	12
Great Western	91,985	2	1,464	6	62.83	21
Midland	81,731	3	2,608	3	31.33	17
North Eastern	65,048	4	4,592	1	14.16	4
Lancashire & Yorkshire	45,388	5	752	13	60.35	19
Great Eastern	44,602	6	1,322	10	33.73	18
Great Northern	38,190	7	1,356	9	28.16	15
Great Central	36,378	8	597	14	60.93	20
North British	31,869	9	1,708	4	18.66	6
London & South Western	31,247	10	1,544	5	20.23	9
Caledonian	29,316	11	1,457	7	20.12	8
South Eastern & Chatham	27,017	12	*1,386	8	19.49	7
London, Brighton & South Coast	18,285	13	809	12	22.60	11
Glasgow & South Western	12,142	14	926	11	13.11	3
North Staffordshire	6,577	15	367	17	17.92	5
Taff Vale	5,600	16	186	18	30.10	16
Barry	4,206	17	163	19	25.80	13
Metropolitan	4,114	18	157	20	26.20	14
Great North of Scotland	3,528	19	459	16	7.68	2
Highland	3,490	20	482	15	7.24	1
Metropolitan District	3,412	21	11	23	310.18	23
Hull & Barnsley	3,338	22	27	22	123.62	22
Furness	3,221	23	154	21	20.91	10

*Comprising South Eastern 1,086; London, Chatham & Dover 126; South Eastern & Chatham 174
Sources: See Note 28

In Column 3 (dwellings occupied by staff), the first three, the North Eastern, London & North Western and Midland are fairly predictable, serving as they did large, densely populated areas containing closely knit networks. Column 4 (employees per dwelling), however, holds some surprises. Top of the league are the two smallest of the Scottish companies, the Highland and the Great North of Scotland, the figures doubtless reflecting the isolated and sparsely populated locations of many of their stations. Other small companies with a creditable showing are the North Staffordshire at fifth place and the little Furness Railway at tenth. The latter had only 138 route miles of line but owned 822 other houses in addition to those in the table, doubtless from the days when the company was so closely involved in the development of Barrow. They included 564 tenements on Barrow Island.[29] The most remarkable position is occupied by the South Eastern & Chatham Managing Committee at seventh place, to which the South Eastern contributed the lion's share, 1,086 houses in little over 400 route miles. The London, Chatham & Dover's contribution was puny by comparison. Neither of these two companies, which in 1899 had concluded a working agreement, was prosperous, nor noted for high standards.

Apart from the North Eastern at fourth place, none of the giants performs particularly well. The London & North Western, which built far more houses than any other company — 50 per cent more than the next highest — is only 12th, and the Midland is down at 17th. The villain of the tables is the Great Western, second in terms of employees (and first in route mileage) but only sixth in Column 3 and almost bottom in Column 4. True, the company served some large rural areas, but even so the figures bear out its long-standing reputation for parsimony in housing its employees. The large gap in Column 4 between the Great Western at 21st and the Hull & Barnsley and Metropolitan District at 22nd and 23rd would, in fact, be filled by seven other railways but for the fact that they all had under 3,000 employees. A number of them performed creditably; the Maryport & Carlisle, for instance, with barely 43 route miles, achieved a house for almost every 12 employees, while the Rhondda & Swansea Bay, with 31 miles, housed employees in houses bought when the line was constructed and also built Rhondda Buildings at Briton Ferry.

Only four companies had no houses of any kind: the Isle of Wight Central with only 28 route miles and well under 300 employees; the Cannock Chase & Wolverhampton, a colliery line; the Snailbeach District, a 3-mile narrow gauge mineral line in Shropshire; and the Stratford-on-Avon & Midland Junction. The first three are not surprising, but the position of the last one, a company with 68 route miles and 317 employees, despite its precarious and impecunious existence, seems rather deplorable. Of its eleven stations, only two, Towcester and Salcey Forest, incorporated a house, so the reason does not lie there. Even small light railways like the Southwold and the Weston, Clevedon & Portishead did better.

The location and concentration of houses owed something to the availability of local accommodation. The London & Birmingham built blocks of houses at Rugby and Coventry because the stations were outside the towns and accommodation was scarce. In Manchester the LNWR built a number of blocks near London Road station and the Lancashire & Yorkshire close to its Thorpe Bridge carriage works, but apart from the Cheshire Lines Committee, which will be mentioned shortly (p162), none of the other lines entering the city built significant numbers.

Rows of houses accompanied many large locomotive depots, like the 41 houses in Midland Terrace at Manningham, Bradford, and the Great Northern's three rows of back-to-backs at Hammerton Street in the same city. The North Eastern built nine terraces at Tyne Dock, and in the 1880s the Caledonian built eight next to its new engine shed at Motherwell. Four of the seven companies that entered Carlisle provided enginemen's houses, including Caledonian Buildings at Kingmoor. In 1867 'enginemen's barracks' were built at Crewe for men working 'lodging turns', and from the 1890s other companies started providing hostels for crews whose duties took them away from home overnight, although the idea of communal living went back at least to 1841 when the London & Birmingham fitted out its new goods warehouse at Camden as temporary lodgings for railwaymen's families displaced when the line was being widened.[30] Most enginemen's hostels were in insalubrious districts close to the sheds, and were usually spartan. Some were dirty, cooking was often poor and consequently the hostels were not popular. An early Great Eastern hostel was in the middle of Stratford locomotive yard with no windows and only roof louvres for ventilation, which let in almost as much soot as air. The large-scale reorganisations that followed the 1923 Grouping created longer runs without crew changes, and more hostels were built. In 1925 the LMS Land and Rating Committee authorised the purchase of the old city workhouse at Carlisle for conversion.[31] The Southern's at Eastleigh was between the ash pits and the coaling stage, and the Great Western pressed old carriages into use,[32] although it did build several new hostels during the Second World War, including one at Didcot, as did the LMS and LNER.

Companies provided houses from mixed motives. They were seen as a means of promoting loyalty among key staff, keeping a work-force together and discouraging conditions likely to lower discipline. To take an example, in 1857 Sir Richard Moon, chairman of the London & North Western, advised his board of the absolute necessity of resuming house building to prevent men becoming demoralised through being forced into poor lodgings, where they came into contact with bad characters. Most country station-masters were given a house, and for higher ranking officers the railways built or purchased superior houses and villas, a policy that continued until recent times. In 1920 the Highland Railway bought two villas in Inverness, for the station-master and for the parcels agent.[33] Many country stations had a house incorporated in the platform buildings or on railway land close by, which was also an aid to security. On the London, Brighton & South Coast Railway in 1871, 27 per cent of station-masters had a house, and 40 per cent on the Great Western in 1890. Housing was also a cheap way of manning level crossings, where a platelayer's wife would attend to the gates in return for a rent-free house alongside. Out of 125 staff taken on when the first section of the Great Northern was opened in 1848, houses were found for 30 gatekeepers and signalmen, and cottages had to be built for platelayers because there was a shortage of lodgings. As time went on, a house on some lines became recognised almost as a condition of service in certain grades. In 1853 the Blyth & Tyne Railway decided to stop providing houses. It owned 32 and rented others for its men, many of whom also had free coal, but it resolved that in future it was preferable to pay increased wages and leave employees to find their own houses and coal.[34]

Although policies varied widely between companies, and within a company altered periodically to reflect changing conditions, overall the proportion of jobs that included a house was fairly small, except for station-masters, and in general houses were provided only where they were considered imperative for the running of the railway. Some companies were more prepared to put resources into providing houses during prosperous periods, when full employment made rented accommodation scarce, than during slumps when there were more empty houses yet wages were low and rents were high, which added to employees' difficulties. During a depression in 1873, when prices were rising fast and landlords were putting up rents, 387 signatories, perhaps more, petitioned the North Eastern board to the effect that they were finding it 'almost impossible to get the common necessities of life as regards Food and Raiment', asking the company to 'build a certain number of Cottages suitable for their Workmen, so as to disannul the tyranny of our present landlords'.[35] We have already noted that the Great Western stopped building houses at Swindon in 1853, despite continuing heavy demand and, with the exception of houses for station-masters, crossing keepers and in isolated locations, built very few elsewhere until 1907 when over 100 cottages were erected at Goodwick for the new port of Fishguard, forming a cliff-top village.

Compared with the generality of industrial and agricultural worker's housing, purpose-built railway houses were usually superior, although some of the smaller companies had poor records; not all railways were concerned to carry out improvements and repairs, and some employees were housed in acquired houses that were near-slums. The North Eastern's Estate Department carried out a very detailed survey of its houses in 1862, mainly acquired from the smaller lines that by a series of amalgamations had formed the company eight years previously. It sheds interesting light on the living conditions of railway families in north-east England. Seven people occupied a four-roomed house at Tyne Dock, for example, an engine driver and his family sleeping in one bedroom and his mother-in-law and a lodger in the other. Yet the only comment was that the house ought to be fenced off from the railway. Another, at Pelton, which had only a kitchen and two bedrooms, accommodated a family of eight, and at Starbeck a gateman, his wife and six children lived in a two-roomed cottage, sleeping 'in both rooms' and evincing the comment that another should be provided. At Yarm a family of seven slept in three beds in a room 'without division or screen' in a house 'in very bad condition', while at Sprouston a three-roomed cottage housed a platelayer, his wife and four daughters, with two drivers and two firemen as lodgers, 'sleeping in all three rooms'. The only comment was 'Difficult supply of water; wants the cottage papering and the area repairing', which suggests that the night-time arrangements were accepted as normal. The other extreme was represented by an inspector, his wife and two teenage children occupying a four-bedroomed house.[36]

Ten 'room and kitchen' houses taken over from the small Portpatrick Railway by the Glasgow & South Western in 1892 were described as 'in wretched condition', while two years later the Midland & Great Northern Joint Committee received a letter from the station-master at Weston, a small station in Lincolnshire, complaining that he was still awaiting improvements promised by the Eastern & Midlands before it went bankrupt. His kitchen was 9ft 6in by 8ft 6in, the 10ft square living-room was made from old sleepers that let in the wind and rain, and the two bedrooms, 11ft 9in by 10ft 9in and 10ft 3in by 8ft , had to accommodate himself, his wife and their eight children. Well-water was contaminated from the cesspit. Yet his station had 6,000 passengers a year and on occasions ladies had to be accommodated in a bedroom, presumably because there was nowhere else. The new owners doubled his accommodation and built a new booking office, ladies' room and 'gents' at an estimated cost of £360.[37]

Some of the large companies established in earlier years, such as the Midland and the London & North Western, had fairly consistent good records. The latter, for instance, continued a policy of housing that stemmed from the London & Birmingham and the Grand Junction and, with some intervals, went on building houses up to the 1923 Grouping. Some of the other larger companies slowed down, but only the Midland's stock was appreciably reduced after 1913, when it fell by over 700 up to 1921. Some local authorities had started building houses to rent before the 1919 Housing Act laid a duty on them to do so, and were providing facilities such as baths and water closets considerably in advance of what was otherwise available, and at low rents. In 1914 the London & South Western's housing committee set out its policy of provision under six heads: station-masters; traffic and permanent way men or other grades where accommodation was scarce or some distance away; gatemen; special cases where there was an acknowledged need; Eastleigh works; and dormitories for engine crews away from home. The committee noted that 337 cottages had been built since 1890, but was now finding that staff could get equivalent housing elsewhere at lower rents. Moreover, not all wanted to live alongside their workmates, while wives often preferred to live nearer shops and schools, to do which their husbands would cycle to work.[38] It was a sign of the times; long-standing customs and attitudes were beginning to change.

House Design

It has been suggested that in railway houses the emphasis was on cheapness, and in some cases this was true. The house at Weston was, after all, at the most 35 years old when its tenant complained so bitterly, while many of those that showed up so badly in the North Eastern's survey were a lot younger. But, despite their small size, the houses built by the more prosperous railways were substantially constructed and well appointed by the standard of the day. There may have been cesspit drainage in the first houses at Wolverton and Swindon, but that was the accepted method, while individual back yards, privies and ash pits, not to mention some houses with front gardens and wash houses, made them distinctly superior. Wolverton and Swindon had piped water to communal taps, Crewe at first had large tanks placed at strategic points before water was laid on. Such amenities placed railway houses there well above the average town or country workman's cottage, where earth floors, no water or even elementary drainage and communal facilities were not unusual. The trouble at Swindon was that the Great Western's good intentions came too late and, when the town became established, were not sustained. The works started production before houses and services were ready, and such was the pressure for accommodation that cottages were let when the plaster was barely dry. 'Most of the houses were very damp and containing only two rooms', noted Daniel Gooch. 'Not a cupboard or a shelf . . . and the unfortunate inhabitants obliged to keep the grub in the bedroom. Not a drop of water to be had but what comes from the tenders or out of ditches . . . not fit for a jackass to drink.'[39] Overcrowding continued to be acute for

157

many years, and it was not until the 1850s that some of the facilities originally planned were finally provided.

The railways prepared detailed specifications and carefully supervised building. In the 1820s the Stockton & Darlington specified ashlar stone — a surprisingly superior finish — from its own quarry for houses at the inclines at Brusselton and Etherley, 'the roof to be square (not hipp'd)'.[40] The companies insisted that materials should be carried as far as possible over their own lines, in order to secure the revenue, subject to penalties, although sometimes contractors were allowed reduced rates. Builders were paid monthly on the engineer's certificate.

The first London & Birmingham houses at Wolverton, Rugby and Coventry had a parlour, kitchen and two or three bedrooms, and later on boilers were provided for hot water. At the end of a row there might be a double-fronted four-bedroomed house for a supervisor or foreman, with a front garden. The managerial staff often had detached villas; the Wolverton Works Manager's house in 1886 had a cellar, three reception rooms, study, kitchen, scullery, three bedrooms, dressing-room and a bathroom with WC.[41] The terraced houses were in plain red brick with small multi-light sash windows, although the Crewe and Swindon houses were given Tudor touches, with projecting gables, curly bargeboards and four-centred arch doorways at the former; at Swindon they had splayed window recesses and door hoods, angled chimney clusters and pointed arches to the rear passageways. End houses were three-storeyed, some with a pub on the ground floor.[42]

Chambers' Edinburgh Journal of 31 January 1846 had this to say about Crewe: 'The dwelling houses arrange themselves in four classes: first, the villa-style lodges of the superior officers, next a kind of ornamental Gothic constitutes the houses of the next in authority; the engineers [i.e. mechanics] domiciled in detached mansions, which accommodate four families, with gardens and separate entrances [today they would be called two-storey maisonettes] and last, the labourer delights in neat cottages of four apartments, the entrances within ancient porches. The first, second and third, have all gardens and yards; the fourth also has gardens . . . Each house is supplied with gas; the water is always on at present in the street, but is to be immediately introduced into the houses.' And in 1850: 'The streets are wide and well paved . . . The accommodation is good, and it would be difficult to find such houses at such low rents . . . '[43] As Professor W.H. Chaloner has remarked, the houses at Crewe did not need investigation by the sanitary reformers, although in 1854 required standards had progressed to the extent that improvements had to be made to the ventilation of 40 Wolverton houses 'by means of a pipe inserted in the ceiling', and Rugby Board of Health demanded improvements there that cost £340.[44]

Out along the line, considerable style was introduced into many companies' stations up to the 1860s, before standardisation started to develop, reflected in lineside houses that were built to match. Six *cottage orné* houses were designed for the Southampton & Dorchester Railway at Dorchester in 1847, each with a kitchen, parlour and two bedrooms,[45] and up and down the country crossing houses and stations appeared in a variety of styles from classical to Gothic, expressly designed as an entity. W.J. Livock designed a charming series of Tudor and Jacobean crossing houses to match his stations on the Trent Valley Railway between Rugby and Stafford, and there were Tudor examples on the North Staffordshire south of Stoke, probably by Henry Hunt. The Great North of England Railway built an attractive row of cottages at Pilmoor, bearing plaques engraved with the company's initials and the date, 1843. Elsewhere local vernacular styles were adopted, and in Scotland they continued longer than in England and Wales. On the Callander & Oban Railway west of Tyndrum, for instance, opened in 1880, traditional single-storey cottages with porches were built at Loch Awe, Falls of Cruachan and Taynuilt, whereas by this date standardisation regardless of location was the rule south of the border.

This development was brought about by the railways' own ability to carry materials cheaply and in bulk, thereby ousting local products, and also by the requirements of the public health acts and other reforming legislation. The standard houses were generally plainer than their predecessors, but with larger rooms, higher ceilings and improved services, like the terrace of three designed for the Great Northern & Great Eastern joint line at Misperton and other stations some time after 1879.[46] Consequently railway house styles now started to display their ownership as clearly as if they bore their owner's name. From 1882 the London & North Western built large numbers of uniform, plain red-brick houses with bright red brick banding, from an isolated pair near a country signal-box to long terraces at an important junction. Characteristically, almost everything except the slates and cement came from Crewe. The bricks were from the company's own works, the woodwork, joinery and iron fittings from the workshops, and they were built with the company's own labour for £350-400 a pair.[47] F.W. Webb, the company's Chief Mechanical Engineer, designed them in conjunction with the Estate Surveyor, Charles Hull (knowing Webb, Hull must have played second fiddle), and Webb was instructed to supply 'doors, windows and such material and fittings as can be made at Crewe Works of uniform pattern'.[48] They appeared all over the system from London to Carlisle, Yorkshire to South Wales, standing out uncompromisingly regardless of their surroundings.

The North Eastern's houses were equally uniform but better proportioned with shallower roofs, deeper eaves and paying greater respect to local materials, being found in stone, brick or rendered. Other companies changed their fashions from time to time. The Midland's earlier terraces were plain brick with pointed, polychrome brick window openings, sometimes rendered; later the company adopted a 'Board School' style, with gabled porches, in brick or stone according to locality. After its formation in 1866 the Cheshire Lines Committee started building distinctive rows of cottages with dormer multi-light casement windows, usually in rendered brick. Because they were three-up-and-three-down they were curiously staggered, so that one house had two rooms at the front and one at the back, and the next the other way round. Separate privies and boilers for hot water were provided. About a decade later the style changed to give larger rooms and higher roofs, plainer with eight-light sash windows and banded brickwork, but retaining the staggered

Some railway housing
all photographs except
Hilton Crossing being
taken in 1989.   (Author)

*Restored early London &
North Western houses in
Tollitt Street, Crewe, built
to a Grand Junction
Railway design of pre-1846.
Crewe had more company
houses than any other
railway town.*

*Midland Terrace,
Manningham, Bradford,
where there was a large
locomotive depot.*

*Hilton Crossing house,
Egginton Junction, North
Staffordshire Railway, in
1984.*

Pilmoor Cottages alongside the main line north of York, built by the Great North of England Railway in 1843 and bearing the date and initials on the shields over the doors.

Typical Scottish railway cottages at Loch Awe, Callander & Oban Railway, probably dating from 1880.

Late-Victorian semi-detached houses for higher grades at Redhill, South Eastern Railway.

arrangement.[49] In 1893 the committee bought 88½ acres at Stretford, at £900 an acre, for housing employees at the new large engine shed at Old Trafford nearby. The land was resold at £750 an acre to Nowells, the contractors, who undertook to lay out streets and build 250 houses to be let exclusively to CLC men, but the agreement fell through and the land was sold in plots to other builders on the same basis. The committee lost money, but houses for the men were urgently needed.[50]

Until the 1890s the standard houses of other companies were generally very plain, but with the approach of the next century new houses started to reflect changes in architectural taste and expectations. The London & South Western designed semi-detached houses, of which there are examples at Templecombe and Dorchester, while the Brighton, whose early cottages — like the row of nine at Hassocks — were quite small, later built some quite roomy terraced houses in short rows, with hipped roofs, double-sash front windows and dormers; there was a row of four at Purley. In Scottish cities, traditional tenements and flats comprised the usual railway housing. Glasgow had two main types: 'room-and-kitchen' apartments in large blocks, and two- or three-bedroomed flats near suburban stations, some, in later years, with bathrooms.

Standard houses did not appear on the Great Western until the 1890s, when it was forced to review its policy of not providing houses. A standard house was designed in 1892, of which there are three terraces at Didcot, one of which comprises double-fronted houses, and three detached. Because building was more intermittent and smaller in scale, there was more variety. A standard four-bedroomed house for a 2nd class station-master cost £400 in 1892, a detached three-bedroom for a lower grade was £240, and signalmen's and platelayers' three-bedroomed cottages £195 detached or £175 each in a terrace. In some cases local materials were introduced, such as stone quoins and dressings, and a number were not unattractive, particularly when compared with the standard red- and blue-brick stations they so often accompanied.[51]

In exposed locations, bare brick might be protected with cement rendering, as can be seen on the rows of London & North Western and North Eastern houses at Tebay, sandwiching an earlier, more attractive North Eastern terrace with traditional Lake District slate walling which required no protection. Midland houses at Castleton in the Peak District, and at Meldon Quarry and Dunsland Cross on the London & South Western were slate-hung, the Meldon ones to an elaborate specification designed to withstand Dartmoor weather. The stone walls were first cement rendered, then coated with bitumen and finally slate-hung on wooden battens. Numbers of Lancashire & Yorkshire terraced houses also were rendered, like the long row of 28 at Low Moor which has a three-storey house at each end.

Houses that formed part of a station building were usually two storeys high with the booking office and waiting room in part of the ground floor or in an adjoining single-storey building. If the station was on an embankment the arrangement was occasionally reversed, as at Heighington in County Durham and Launton in Oxfordshire, where the living quarters were on the ground floor and the offices

Station Masters' Houses.

Above:
Living on the job at Dunmow, Essex, where the typical Great Eastern Railway station incorporated the station house in the main platform buildings, a common practice at smaller stations. Where stations are now unstaffed, many houses have been refurbished and sold. (Author's collection)

Below:
Not a country vicarage, but the station house at Warwick (Milverton), once the station for Leamington Spa, possibly dating from the days of the London & Birmingham Railway, photographed in 1952 and, like the station, now demolished. (Late R.E.G. Read/Author)

above at platform level. Joseph Locke designed houses to be built against embankments for the Grand Junction in 1834. A station house, probably for Whitmore, comprised two dwellings, with bedrooms and a waiting room on the first floor. It was a pretty little building, but very cramped.[52] The single-storey tradition was followed at many Scottish country stations, sometimes with dormer bedrooms in the roof, although the twelve intermediate stations on the Scottish Central Railway, with the exception of Forgandenny, had two-storey houses, much better than most of that period.[53] When stations required enlarging or rebuilding later, it was generally the practice to build a separate house nearby. Some were quite handsome. Because many of the early stations were so small, new houses were required after only a few years when stations became outgrown. Very seemly early station houses were built, possibly by the London & Birmingham at Watford and by the Grand Junction at Wednesfield Heath (the station for Wolverhampton) and Winsford, or by the London & North Western shortly after its formation in 1846, while there was a particularly handsome example at Warwick (Milverton) — the station for Leamington Spa — looking like a comfortable country vicarage. Station-masters who enjoyed a detached house like these were very well housed compared with those who lived on the station. The late-Victorian house at Colnbrook, a small station on the Great Western's Staines West branch, was quite massive, with Dutch gables matching those on the station. Like the elaborately Dutch-styled house at Sutton-on-Sea in Lincolnshire, it was built by a small local company from which something more modest might have been expected.

Some railways identified their houses with numbers, as they did bridges. The London & Birmingham fixed an oval cast-iron number-plate bearing the company's initials over each door, a practice followed by the London & North Western with

Means of identification.
Stockton & Darlington Railway ceramic house number at Beechburn, 1973. (Author)

London & Birmingham Railway cast-iron house number plate on one of the railway cottages at Coventry in 1950, now demolished. (Author)

164

circular plates. Others simply gave the street or terrace a name and house numbers in the conventional manner. The Stockton & Darlington used small ceramic plates showing a code letter relating to the stretch of line, as well as a number, a system that as far as is known was unique.[54] The exact purpose is unclear, but probably related to the company's rent roll.

Rents

At first, railway houses frequently were provided rent-free as part of the employee's terms of employment. The Newcastle & Carlisle, London, Brighton & South Coast, London & South Western and South Eastern adopted this policy. Others made housing allowances or paid their employees' rent for private accommodation. The Great Western charged rent from the outset and from the 1840s onward most other companies gradually changed, although the London & North Western's board decision of 1843 was evidently disregarded in some quarters as five years later the General Finance Committee noted that some servants were still living in company houses rent-free, and ordered them to be charged rent in future.[55] Lettings were usually subject to seven days' notice to quit, and rents were deducted from wages (fortnightly on the London & North Western); tenants were required to keep their houses clean, in some cases they were responsible for internal repairs, and the only lodgers permitted were railway servants.

Attempts were made to fix rents to give a return of between 4 and 6 per cent on capital. The Grand Junction tried to obtain 5 per cent at Crewe, plus 1¼ per cent for repairs and depreciation, but the rents caused hardship and in 1843-4 were twice reduced, when the smallest (class 1) houses fetched 2s (10p) a week, class 2 3s (15p) and 3s 3d (16p), class 3 3s 3d (16p) and 3s 6d (17½p), and the most superior ones, class 4, 6s 3d (31p), all including rates, water and gas for lighting. In 1846 the return was 5 per cent, except class 4 which was only 4 per cent, excluding the cost of the land.[56] James Bland, an employee who also rented a grocer's shop from the company at Crewe for £60 a year, was refused a reduction when he complained about loss of trade after the London & North Western opened the cheese market.[57]

Daniel Gooch considered the rents at Swindon to be extortionate: 3s 6d (17½p) for a single and 7s (35p) for a double cottage, 'and won't allow any of the men in their employ to sell anything whatever'.[58] Certainly they were high compared with Wolverton and Crewe, and in the first years conditions were inferior. They were even higher when compared with a cottage let by the Edinburgh & Glasgow to an inspector of the line for £12 a year, excluding repairs which he was to do himself.[59] Indeed, rents in general remained relatively stable for most of the century. At its end London & South Western tenants at Dorchester paid 7s (35p) a week for a two-up-and-two-down, and 5s (25p) at Moreton.[60] In 1901 the Midland board directed that rents should be based on those for comparable private housing, with tenants paying rates and taxes,[61] but in 1914 the South Western was still striving for 6 per cent on new houses while acknowledging the difficulty of building them for less tha £200 to meet this criterion. The company was actually getting only 2 to 3½ per cent on its existing stock;[62] a year later the Caledonian's return was an average of 3.99 per cent,[63] and the Great Western's in 1918 3 per cent.[64] After the war there was resistance to rent increases. When the LNER proposed converting three disused stations at Nottingham into staff houses at £1 a week, the scheme was abandoned after employees refused to pay more than 15s (75p).[65]

Assisted Housing

Immediately after the First World War and during the 1920s the railways experienced considerable difficulty in housing their staff. The North Eastern bought 57 ex-army huts in 1919, some to augment the accommodation at existing houses where there was overcrowding, and others for use as dwellings at Pilmoor.[66] There was a general shortage of houses to rent, accentuated by the economic depression and the numerous transfers that followed the Grouping. In 1920 the London & South Western advanced £30,000 from its locomen's pension fund to Guildford council for the building of 20 houses. In 1923-5 the London, Midland & Scottish spent close on £¼ million in buying over 300 houses for managerial and senior staff.[67] To alleviate the problem at lower grades, only the Southern Railway continued a vigorous policy of house building, for which it established a Cottage Building Fund to finance half the cost, the other half being charged to the capital account, an arrangement that kept rents down to give a return of 4-5 per cent. Over 300 houses were built between 1923 and 1929, including 80 houses and 48 flats started by the London & South Western for the new Feltham marshalling yard in 1922, some with a government subsidy, and a number of redundant station buildings were converted into houses and flats.[68] At Eastbourne, 48 were purchased from developers with the aid of a municipal subsidy.

The other three large companies created by the Grouping adopted different policies. The Great Western and the London & North Eastern formed co-operative housing associations in which the residents had a stake. The Great Western's long-standing opposition to wide-scale housing provision made its problem particularly acute. In 1922 locomotive men from five depots, where overcrowding and high rents were bad, presented petitions asking the company to provide housing, including Old Oak Common in west London where 2,000 were employed. At first the company tried to apply pressure on local authorities to fulfil what it considered to be their obligations under the Housing Act, but most councils were unwilling to incur rate support for municipal houses for railway employees, particularly after the Government cut grants in 1922. So in 1923 a subsidiary company, Great Western Housing Ltd, was set up to make loans, but its effect was marginal because the majority in need either had insufficient capital for a deposit or were subject to frequent moves that made house purchase unattractive.

The Estate Surveyor, F.W. Showers, therefore produced a scheme under which the company would buy land, lay out roads, sewers and services, and then lease it to a staff housing society to build houses to rent. The company provided 90 per cent of the capital, repayable over 50 years, the balance being met from members' subscriptions. A pilot scheme called the Great Western (London) Garden Village Society was instituted in 1923 to lay out estates at Acton and Hayes in which each tenant took a £25 share, payable by instalments if desired, under a committee of tenants with Showers as chairman. Administration was placed in the hands of the Welsh Town Planning and Housing Trust Ltd whose architect, T. Alwyn Lloyd, designed layouts on the garden village principle with a maximum density of 12 houses per acre. Most houses were semi-detached or in blocks of four, in two types, 'parlour' and 'non-parlour', and all had three bedrooms and a bathroom. Hedges and trees were planted and a gardener was employed to look after communal greens and shrubberies. Rents ranged from 15s 6d (77½p) to 19s 6d (97½p) a week.

Instantly the two estates were successful, to the extent that in little more than a year other societies were set up at Caerphilly, Barry, Plymouth, Penzance, Swansea, Truro and Severn Tunnel Junction. Such speed was a measure of the desperate housing situation.[69] Further estates were built at Banbury and Newton Abbot immediately after the Second World War. After the loans were repaid the societies were wound up, and the houses were sold in 1985-6.

The London & North Eastern's three associations provided cheap mortgages in a similar manner. LNER (Gosforth) Garden Village Ltd commenced in 1923, followed by one at York and a third in County Durham that had estates at Durham, Darlington and Tyne Dock. Capital at 4 per cent was provided through the North Eastern Railway Housing Trust which had been set up in 1921 for the purpose. But the company's southern and Scottish areas showed no interest. The associations were wound up between 1954 and 1959 after the final mortgage repayments were made,[70] but the Trust lasted until 1982 when it was merged with the NER Cottage Homes & Benefit Fund to form the independent Railway Housing Association. The Cottage Homes Fund was established in 1919 to provide 930 houses for war-wounded railwaymen or the dependants of those who were killed. A further LNER scheme met with difficulties. When locomotive work was concentrated at Darlington and Gateshead Works was closed, houses proved impossible to obtain, so in 1932 the company agreed that the Workmen's Housing Association should build up to 600 houses on approved sites. The railway would guarantee the rents for 10 years and collect them on 5 per cent commission. But the association was unable to raise sufficient capital so the LNER leased 50 houses then being built near North Road Works and in return granted the builders an option on 17 acres of surplus land, which was subsequently exercised and more houses built.[71]

All four grouped companies had housing loan schemes for salaried staff, the Great Western's through Great Western Housing Ltd, the LNER and the LMS through building societies. The LMS, which had by far the largest housing stock, did build a few houses. In 1924 it abandoned a scheme to erect 500 because government aid was refused,[72] but in 1928-9 an estate of 70 was built at Heysham, close to a street of ex-Midland houses, for workers moved there when the company's Belfast shipping services were concentrated at the port. But, by and large, the LMS geared its housing policy to cheap loans by perpetuating a long-established policy inherited

167

from the London & North Western. In 1892, 1899 and 1900 that company had bought land at Wolverton for sale to works staff as building plots, at no profit after allowing for the cost of laying out roads and services. Many of the men borrowed from the Wolverton Building Society, which had been formed by the management some years before to improve morale at a time of unrest by encouraging house ownership. It was stated that there were few other places where more men owned their own houses. Capital was provided by the Bucks & Oxon Bank — later Lloyds — and when it wanted to reduce its commitment the company took over part on security of the mortgages. Interest at 4 per cent was deliberately set to forestall the Co-operative Wholesale Society from offering cheap mortgages in Wolverton; the LNWR was still intent on keeping ultimate control. Crewe and Earlestown showed little enthusiasm, however. When F.W. Webb tried to form a building society at Crewe there was no support.[73] In fact, there appears to have been only one railway building society, the Railway Permanent Benefit established at the Railway Clearing House in 1850. In 1867 it had only 650 members, not all railwaymen, and it did not grow.[74]

The LNWR's house-purchase scheme started in 1903, through the company's savings bank (a number of railways had one), again at 4 per cent interest. The Estate Department made the valuations, and fees and legal charges were kept low. This was the scheme continued by the LMS until 1934, when it was transferred to the Abbey Road Building Society (now Abbey National) by which time over £2 million had been advanced to 3,908 members. A separate railway account was kept, there was a 5 per cent ceiling on the interest rate, and members had the advantages of automatic tax relief and a continuing mortgage if they left the company. The LMS gained some £1.25 million in liquid assets and saved the cost of administration.[75]

Since nationalisation, railway policy has been to dispose of houses and today most of them have been sold. The national and social emphasis, in any case, has changed, first to local authority housing and now more to private rentals, accompanied by a large increase in owner-occupancy. Many of the older railway houses were condemned after the Second World War, so that most of the early housing in former railway settlements has gone. The New Town at Swindon has survived, however, restored and refurbished as a Conservation Area by the local authority, and a few restored terraces remain at Derby and Crewe, although all the original houses at the latter have disappeared, as at Wolverton. Over the country as a whole, the few remaining railway-owned houses are either on stations or at level crossings, the latter steadily reducing as automatic barriers are installed. But considerable numbers of former railway houses remain in private occupation, many of them altered yet still retaining characteristics that proclaim their original ownership.

The railways provided large numbers of allotments on lineside land; in 1932 the Southern had 13,000. They were popular with employees and, although the rents the companies received were low, they did provide some income from often narrow strips of land that were of little other use. Now, like the houses where their cultivators lived, most of them have gone.

Chapter 7

Railway Property Management, 1830-1946

The Early Committee System

Unlike the canals, where control was usually exercised by a committee of directors equivalent to a present-day board, the railways, because they were larger organisations, tended from the outset to have a main board which delegated various functions to committees. Once a company was incorporated, the most important committee was the one concerned with buying land and constructing the line. Indeed, the London & Birmingham Railway's provisional board established a survey committee nearly three years before it obtained its Act, charged with liaising with the engineer on the choice of route, contacting landowners and advising the board on tactics. The committee quickly took charge of the appointment of surveyors and solicitors, diligently canvassed landowners and requested weekly progress reports from Robert Stephenson, which it did not always receive.

Once the Act was obtained, a subsidiary board was set up in Birmingham, and there and in London a 'Sub-Committee of Compensation and Works' supervised land purchases, contracts, negotiations and all matters concerning construction, including the hiring of staff and payment of accounts.[1]

The minutes of the Grand Junction Railway Committee of Works from 1845 to 1853 give a picture of the variety of subjects discussed.[2] The enlargement of Lime Street station in Liverpool took up much attention until 1851, including its design and the building of the 2-mile Victoria Tunnel from Edge Hill to the docks at Waterloo. But the committee also found time for such multifarious duties as letting refreshment rooms at Lime Street and Manchester Victoria, authorising the purchase of land for widening at Huyton and Rainhill, agreeing to the enlarging of St Helens Junction and Stafford stations, letting an arch alongside the Irwell at Manchester to the Albert Boating Club, approving contracts for houses at Crewe and Earlestown, collecting rents and paying John Gibson £1,620 for his marble statue of George Stephenson that went in St George's Hall, Liverpool. In 1846 the Grand Junction became the Northern Division of the London & North Western by amalgamation, but for many years resisted attempts at overall control from Euston; in 1849 the committee refused to accept the reduced status of 'Northern Section of the General Construction, Works and Estate Committee'.

Geographical division of control gave considerable advantages in negotiating for land. Local directors could often deal better with landowners, many of whom they knew. The Scottish Central in 1845-6 had Land and Works Committees separately for Stirlingshire and Perthshire, each with full powers to 'negotiate with Owners,

Lessees and Occupiers; and transact, arrange, and conclude with them on the most advantageous terms possible'. The town clerk of Stirling was clerk and agent to the Stirlingshire committee, and Andrew Galloway of Glasgow was official valuer whose first, and doubtless tricky, assignment was to estimate the compensation to be offered to the committee's convenor and another director. There was an interesting arbitration over the claim of a brick and tile maker, James McAlpine, who demanded £1,966 12s 0d (£1,966.60) and was paid £1,087 13s 0d (£1,087.65), which dragged on and slowed up construction. The Perthshire land committee's duties, under the chairmanship of the Lord Provost of Perth, were even wider: rails, locomotives and rolling stock were ordered; station sites decided on; fares fixed and tickets printed; and negotiations opened with connecting railways.[3]

On some lines the system was decidedly *ad hoc*. The Edinburgh & Glasgow, for instance, between 1838 and 1864 had a plethora of committees dealing with land, property and related affairs, some, to say the least, somewhat distantly, such as police, which must have confused the officers.[4] The growth of large companies by rapid amalgamations and leases made matters worse, and it was not until the 1860s that some of them were able to start sorting themselves out. By the end of the century a fairly consistent pattern of estate management had emerged. Land and property affairs were controlled by a land or estate agent, or in Scotland a factor, answering to a board committee. Rating was a separate function under a rating surveyor, usually answerable to the company's solicitor or the secretary, but as time went on land and rating were frequently combined in one estate department under a single chief officer.

Estate Surveyors

Chapter 4 concluded by touching on the part played by surveyors and land agents in buying land for railways. These men were, of course, in private practice, counting railway companies among their most valued and lucrative clients. Some became full-time employees. Property management was often divided into two tiers. Valuations, negotiations, purchases, sales and rating were the province of outside professionals on a fee basis; the day-to-day work of collecting rents, supervising property repairs, letting land and buildings and general property supervision was done by a salaried officer.

The London, Brighton & South Coast Railway extensively employed Edward Driver for buying land and, when the main line was finished, disposing of surplus land. In 1845 three more valuers were appointed, each responsible for designated lines and branches, of whom one, Osborne, was only to be engaged if he had not already been taken on by 'the opposition'. Meanwhile Edward Grantham had been engaged as full-time rent collector, with instructions to attend to property repairs and letting.[5] The opposition in this case was the London & Portsmouth, which employed John Clutton to assist Joseph Cubitt on the initial survey and to advise on land values and severance claims, while the actual purchases were made by

Washbourne and Keen of Westminster, who worked for £40 per mile including expenses, with extra for jury cases.[6]

The Manchester, Bury & Rossendale Railway employed John Ashworth & Sons of Manchester to make valuations. After it became the East Lancashire Railway, John Slatter of Bury, land agent to Lord Derby, was employed to negotiate purchases on the Liverpool, Ormskirk & Preston line, the company seemingly seeing nothing untoward in allowing Slatter to fix the price when some of his lordship's land was wanted.[7] In 1846 the Oxford & Rugby was using as many as six valuers at 3 guineas (£3.15) a day in an effort to push the line forward with all speed. They had authority to conclude purchases where they considered it expedient to do so and the agreed price was not much over market value. After a year one of them, J.A. Hornblower of Birmingham, was dismissed for being too slow.[8]

It was lucrative business, establishing many firms of which a number, such as Cluttons and Drivers Jonas, still practise under the names of their founders. Among well-known names William Tite can be singled out as one of the most successful, with a wide diversity of interests. Remembered as the architect who rebuilt the Royal Exchange, opened in 1844, and who designed a number of churches, many other public buildings and numerous railway stations, he was also a prominent valuer in heavy demand by railways for buying land and as an arbitrator. As well as developing an extensive architectural, surveying and valuing practice, he was prominent in other business affairs, was director of two banks, MP for Bath, a heavy investor in railways and chairman of the North Devon Railway & Dock Company from 1857 to 1865. Tite carried out a great deal of land valuation and purchase for the London & Blackwall and Eastern Counties railways, of which he was also a director, and for the London & York with James Beadel. The latter was another surveyor prominent in railways whose son, William James, succeeded Tite as land agent for the Great Eastern and London, Tilbury & Southend railways, and was a founder member and a president of the Surveyors' Institution.

Tite was one of the original Great Western directors named in the 1835 Act of Incorporation, and negotiated the purchase of the company's first offices in London. Thereafter he was prominently involved with the Great Western's great rival, the London & South Western, for which he acted as architect, surveyor and valuer for many years. It has already been suggested (p94) that he played some part in the affair of Lord Petre and the Eastern Counties Railway; in 1863 he was also actively concerned with the London, Tilbury & Southend which was leased to the big contractors, Peto, Brassey & Betts, for whom he also acted as surveyor. It transpired that Tite had tried to use his interlocking responsibilities to gain financial advantage for Petos, who were losing money on the lease, an affair which did him no credit, although it evidently did him no lasting harm as, six years later, he was knighted and 12 months later was made a KCB. He left a large fortune of something under £400,000.

One of the first full-time railway estate surveyors was probably J.R. Wright, appointed as Head Surveyor by the newly formed Lancashire & Yorkshire Railway in 1847 for five years. His contract was not renewed, but subsequently he was engaged to prepare a set of land plans of the line.[9] The practice of employing a full-time surveyor became more prevalent as the rapidly growing system created a need for professional estate management, so let us now look at the career of a man who was pre-eminent.

Edward Ryde and the South Eastern
In 1855 the South Eastern Railway appointed as its surveyor Edward Ryde, at about £267 a year, in succession to William Tress, an architect who had also designed a number of notable stations on the line. Ryde became a leading figure in his profession, a president of the Institution and the author of eight text books. He was an authority on valuation and rating, establishing many principles still observed today, and was in great demand as an arbitrator, umpire and witness whose opinion was rarely disputed.

Ryde's diaries present a detailed account of his personal and business life from 1844 to his death in 1892.[10] He was 32 when a South Eastern board committee interviewed him, with four others. He went away 'impressed with a confident belief that I am the most likely to be successful.' That confidence never left him. He had to provide a surety of £1,000 which he obtained from an insurance company, and he was given an office at London Bridge station, a clerk and a book-keeper. Although he was regarded as one of the chief officers, life with the South Eastern was no sinecure. Shortly after his appointment, what we would call a 'board room revolution' took place, and one of the new board's objectives was the improvement of the company's property. In an economy drive a year later, he recorded: 'My staff is inquired into and very nasty remarks are made as to its expensiveness and extent. Sheppard is ordered to be dismissed. This is a day to be remembered with much dissatisfaction by South Eastern Heads of Departments.' However, neither this setback nor seeing Captain R.H. Barlow, the railway's superintendent, summarily sacked after giving adverse evidence (doubtless truthfully) at a Board of Trade enquiry into an accident near Reading, deterred Ryde from seeking, and getting, a rise of £100.

The South Eastern's new secretary was Samuel Smiles, remembered as the author of *Self-help* and *Lives of the Engineers*, with whom Ryde struck up a friendship, together with C.W. Eborall, the new general manager and superintendent, and Toogood, the company's solicitor. The four were instrumental in promoting the line across the Thames to Charing Cross, although there is no doubt that the idea was Ryde's own, occurring to him when he was surveying the London Bridge–Waterloo extension and publicly acknowledged by Smiles in a speech at the opening-day dinner. The South Eastern approved the scheme but refused to finance it. They agreed that a separate company should be formed to build the bridge, railway and station, with Sir John Hawkshaw as engineer, Smiles as secretary, Toogood as solicitor and, after some argument, Ryde as surveyor. Hawkshaw's fee was £15,000, Toogood's £10,000 and Ryde's, for buying the land and preparing plans, £2,800, which he considered 'the best contract I ever made'. In mid-1858 Ryde prepared a plan for Charing Cross station and in November recorded: 'All my spare time and all my energies are now taxed to the utmost to get Charing Cross plans and reference ready for Deposit.' The Bill passed through Parliament in 1859 only after strenuous opposition from St Thomas's Hospital trustees, who were successful in obtaining a clause requiring the Charing Cross Railway Company to buy the whole of the hospital and its grounds, even though only a small corner of land was wanted. Subsequently this provision involved Ryde prominently in an important arbitration case. The hospital first demanded £750,000 for their land, buildings and compensation, later reduced to £440,000. Ryde valued them at £190,000. The case lasted over two weeks, during which one of the hospital's witnesses, after cross-examination, swore he would never enter a witness box again. 'Hurrah. Oh that a dozen others would say the same', Ryde exclaimed. The arbitrator awarded £296,000, which Ryde noted seemed to satisfy his colleagues. A few days later he proudly took formal possession of the hospital, placing a policeman in charge. 'Thus ends the great case of St Thomas's Hospital and the Charing Cross Railway.' He was at first against the suggestion that the station should include an hotel — 'the proposal is so silly that I will not waste time by recording more about it' — but he came round to the idea and collaborated closely with Edward Middleton Barry, the architect.

Meanwhile, he continued to look after the many and varied property interests of the South Eastern and was asked by a director to take on a friend's son as a pupil, for which he thought of asking a premium of £200-250. But the board objected so Ryde took Smiles' advice and engaged the lad as an office boy at a low salary and trained him that way. In 1860 he felt that his hard work deserved another increase in his salary: 'In consequence of the last week's traffic which amounted upwards of £29,000, the largest they have ever had, and because I think the Company is in a state of great prosperity. If ever I am to get an increase I think this is the time.' He didn't succeed and was displeased with his own performance before the board, which thought that his remuneration from the Charing Cross company should be taken into account. 'I am a bad hand at doing business for myself', he wrote uncharacteristically. He visited the new Victoria station in September 1860, considering that 'the Brighton Company have a very tolerable station tho' much complicated at the entrance. But the Great Western and East Kent [which shared what became the Chatham side of the station] are in very poor quarters for the present.'

In 1863, still without a salary increase, he talked to Smiles who thought he would do much better in private practice than as a salaried officer. During most years he had, in fact, had other work, much of it railway valuations, surveys and estimates for projected lines, but also rating appeals, advising on building an hotel at Cowes, acting as umpire or arbitrator and increasing land agency work which he was keen to develop. In the following year the South Eastern board at length agreed to his engaging in unlimited private practice, which suggests they had hitherto acquiesced in his more limited activities. One of his first appointments was as surveyor to the

London Bridge Land Company, and thereafter he never looked back, undertaking a rapidly increasing variety of work, country-wide. His railway interests grew. In 1862 he had been concerned with Toogood, Hawkshaw and Lucas, the contractor, in promoting a line from King's Cross to Piccadilly, agreeing to share the costs of a Bill equally with them, but now they abandoned the idea in favour of a more ambitious scheme called the North Western & Charing Cross Railway. The London & North Western, Great Northern, Midland, South Eastern and Charing Cross companies sought to link Euston, St Pancras and King's Cross with Charing Cross via Tottenham Court Road, thereby breaking into the Quadrilateral that had existed since 1846. The North Western was in the forefront, and Ryde and Wood, the North Western's surveyor, were asked to value the land required. Ryde's figure was £800,000, Wood's £821,000. 'This we consider very good estimating and we are each much satisfied with it.' It was too much, however; the scheme was dropped and in 1868 Ryde accepted £250 for his services.

In 1871 Ryde concluded a new agreement with the South Eastern whereby he was retained as consulting surveyor at £250 a year, plus £3 3s 0d (£3.15) a day for valuations, which included an annual valuation of all the company's property. He stipulated that he should be used exclusively in compensation disputes, at 1 per cent of the settled figure within the London area and 2½ per cent beyond it. That year, following Tite, he became consulting surveyor to the London & South Western, a position he shared jointly with Virgo Buckland, a fellow-founder of the Institution, from 1882 to 1888. In 1872 he received a similar appointment with the London, Brighton & South Coast and London, Chatham & Dover companies as well. The latter must have made the South Eastern choke — the two companies were bitter rivals — but it is a measure of Ryde's standing that it was accepted. He was indeed doing better in private practice, as Smiles had predicted. His non-railway work was now extensive, particularly among public utilities. He was still keen to drive a railway across central London, however, and was surveyor to the London Central Railway in which he worked closely with the engineer, Sir John Wolfe Barry, brother of Edward. In 1871 an Act was obtained for a line from Euston and St Pancras to Charing Cross via Leicester Square, with a capital of £2 million. Ryde was to get 1¾ per cent of all purchases, up to a maximum commission of £23,000. It would have meant big money for him, but like similar projects it was too ambitious and came to nothing. It was revived in 1884 as the London Central Electric Railway from Charing Cross to the City, but was rejected in Parliament. Ryde's connection with the company appears to have ended two years earlier. His association with the South Eastern ended with his death in 1892 at the age of 70, covering 37 years. His sons carried on the practice, Arthur Lyon Ryde being appointed to the South Eastern in his father's stead, and the firm continued as a leader in the profession.[11]

Edward Ryde was regarded as co-father of the Surveyors' Institution with John Clutton, and was a prime influence in its affairs although, for some reason, when he became aware of a case of corruption in the late 1860s, he took no action beyond giving the culprit a dressing down. Had he acted more positively he might have averted a notable scandal nearly 20 years later. He gave many papers, joined in discussions and devised a widely- and long-used scale of fees for compensation cases. His work output was prodigious, yet he found time to devote to his family, his friends and social and public affairs at Woking where, latterly, he lived. Although he did not consider himself rich he was certainly very well off, building himself a new house in Westminster in 1864 and 12 months later buying Poundfield House, near Woking, to which he continually made improvements and added to the estate. He owned a number of properties in Surrey, including two farms which he managed himself. After his death his financial assets were valued at £11,264, excluding real estate which must have been worth very much more. From his eminent position in his profession he, probably more than any other, established railway land management on a sound basis.

Railway Estate Departments
The administration of the South Eastern was relatively simple when compared with the affairs of the larger railways that expanded by amalgamation. Co-ordination, integration, rationalisation — call it what you will — of diverse systems caused as many headaches then as they do in large growth organisations now. As many wheels turned full circle in endeavours to find cost-effective systems and, because human nature does not change, influence, prejudice and internal politics were just as strong.

In January 1855, Frederick Wood became land agent to the London & North Western Railway, based at Rugby where he lived.[12] Previously he had worked for the Oxford Canal Company, first as resident engineer responsible for straightening Brindley's original route through Warwickshire in 1831-4, then as part-time agent and engineer. In 1836 and 1839 he surveyed the Birmingham & Warwick Junction Canal, and he has been mentioned in chapter 2 (p76) surveying the first Great Northern Railway in Lincolnshire in 1836. The Oxford committee felt they were suffering 'serious inconvenience resulting from his engagement with other parties', and in 1840 his salary was increased to £500 a year on the understanding that 'the whole of his services are henceforth given to the Company'. When he took up his railway appointment he at first worked from his home at Albert House; later he had an office on the station, and for two years continued to attend to canal affairs as well, at £250 a year.[13] The railway company already had divisional estate agents or surveyors who dealt with day-to-day matters, but Wood was primarily concerned with valuing, buying and selling land throughout the system, and was regarded as a senior officer.

In 1860 Charles Hull commenced as Wood's assistant at £175 a year, and in 1864 he was given charge of the Northern Division estate office at Liverpool at £350 a year. Meanwhile rating, which hitherto had been the responsibility of the Stores and Rating Department, was placed under a separate Rates and Taxes Department under H. Edmunds, who by 1878 was earning £850 a year. In 1869 Hull was placed in charge 'generally' of the company's Estate Department, with an assistant in the Southern Division at Euston, but excluding lines north of Preston where estate

175

affairs continued to be looked after by S.B. Worthington, the Northern Division engineer, until 1872. As the northern lines were specifically excluded a month after Hull's promotion, one senses already the rivalry between engineering and estate departments that for a long time characterised railway operations in this field. A month later the North Western's Permanent Way, Works and Estate Committee accepted Hull's recommendation that his department should be divided into six districts under his office at Liverpool, each in charge of a 'Clerk and Collector'. Typical district office staff at Euston in 1870 comprised a clerk, two rent-collectors, two apprentices and a draughtsman, and at Birmingham two to three clerk-collectors and 'an office boy or two'.

Wood continued at Rugby as land agent, where he appears also to have trained staff for Hull, and in 1877 his salary went up to £2,500, with extra fees payable for work on joint lines. After three more years he expressed a wish for partial retirement. He was retained as consultant land agent and arbitrator at £1,000 a year, and Hull was appointed combined land and estate agent at £1,500, rising to £2,000 after twelve months, based at Euston. On their joint recommendation there followed some consolidation of districts.[14] Wood retired to Brighton in 1882-3, where he lived for at least ten years. He was a member of the Surveyors' Institution from its foundation in 1868 (his membership number was 5), becoming a Fellow. His membership ceased in 1892-3,[15] but surprisingly the Institution's *Transactions* contain no obituary.

Hull died in service in 1898 and was succeeded by Edward Mackie until 1917, when J.R. Ball took over, continuing to act as land and estate agent for the LMS after the Grouping. On appointment he got £1,350, and by 1919 was earning £2,000 a year, plus £100 in respect of the North London Railway which was controlled by the North Western,[16] the same salary as Wood's 42 years earlier and Hull's in 1881, which puts their standing into perspective. After the amalgamation with the Lancashire & Yorkshire in 1922, the rating surveyor was A.D. Lomas, and both he and Ball were chief officers reporting direct to the general manager.

Compared with the North Western's highly centralised system from the 1860s, the Great Western's handling of estate matters was less sure. In 1867 Arthur Currey, the company's estate agent, made a report to the chairman on the working of his department. He was earning £500 a year, his surveyor, Thomas Laughton £400, and he had a staff of 12, excluding Edmund Wood who looked after South Wales. Wood had joined the South Wales Railway in 1850 and still managed the estate independently of the Paddington office. It was obviously a sore point with Currey. Since 1854 the Great Western had acquired nearly 580 miles of line from smaller companies and the land records were in a mess. Currey was still trying to extract deeds from local solicitors and his plans were all different, with no uniform scale. A complete resurvey was urgently necessary, during which surplus property could be identified and disposed of.

The board decided to split the department, making Currey registrar of deeds and Laughton the estate surveyor, but leaving South Wales still separate under Wood.[17]

Currey seems to have organised things well and in 1875 was able to give a good account of his eight years' work.[18] The Estate Department was less satisfactory, however, for in 1870, after only three years, a special committee headed by the chairman decided to disband it and gave Laughton and Wood three months' notice. Estate accounts went to the Accountant's Department, property repairs, surveys and plan drawing to the engineer, and a new, smaller Estate Department was set up to deal solely with rents and lettings.[19] Richard Hall & Sons of Westminster were appointed surveyors for buying and selling land. Hall had worked with Brunel and was another founder member of the Surveyors' Institution, and its current president, but it was his son, Richard Jr, who received the actual appointment at £500 a year, with a free pass and an office at Paddington.

The arrangement lasted until 1880, during which time Hall had several disputes with the company over payment. As a consequence the board appointed James Rippoth Bonny as land agent and surveyor at £750 a year, increasing in 1885 to £1,100 with £100 a year travelling expenses, in return for 'all services'. Meanwhile, the Estate Department was still being run separately, with many of its former duties restored, by Abel Lewis Jenkins. He had spent two years as secretary of the South Devon Railway before it was taken over by the Great Western in 1876. When he resigned on health grounds in 1892, the board decided to combine the two departments. Bonny, then 65, wanted the combined job but he was a diabetic and, to his great disappointment, was retired, being retained as consultant on half pay for two years.

Instead, the board approached 22 firms of surveyors, inviting them to tender on a regional basis. Six declined and two did not reply. In the event, W.H. Williams of David Williams & David, of Llandaff near Cardiff, and agents to the Margam Estates, was appointed full-time land agent and surveyor at £800 a year, with a staff of 7 at Paddington and 16 more spread over 8 district offices, a total staff of 23. By 1905 it was up to 41, and he was trying to increase rents, including those on employees' houses, arguing that it was better to pay higher wages in return for fair rents than low wages and low rents. The company received 'little or no credit for letting houses at less than they are worth', he wrote.

In 1913 a board committee carried out a wide-ranging enquiry into the work of Williams' department, during which it looked at the North Eastern Railway's system which it thought was effective, apart from old-fashioned, inefficient office systems. The committee was critical of the lack of co-operation between Great Western divisional engineers and superintendents and the divisional estate agents, instancing £4 10s 0d (£4.50) a week relief and lodging allowances paid for four months to a new station-master at Stogumber while correspondence flowed back and forth about whether to spend £10 on repairs to the station house he was waiting to move into. The committee's report made radical recommendations that included giving the engineers and the operating and locomotive superintendents responsibility for tenancies for their own staff, the use of commission agents, station-masters and goods agents for rent collection, transfer of boundary verification to the engineer, and improved accounting. Some were implemented, with beneficial results, before the First World War intervened. In 1913 Williams staff was 48, with 3 more on detachment responsible for canals, Plymouth Docks and the Bristol Harbour line, which included extensive commercial properties.[20]

The committee resumed in 1920 and made further sweeping changes, reducing costs by streamlining the organisation and centralising more work at Paddington, including the drawing office from which all the district offices had to requisition plans and drawings. But the powerful Engineering Department retained control of tenancies within the permanent-way boundary, and the Locomotive Department kept in its hands the maintenance of property at Swindon, for which it made a 15 per cent establishment charge on top of labour and materials.[21] An interesting statistic was that in 1920, 9,708 pieces of wallpaper were supplied to tenants with which to do their own decorating. Williams retired in 1922, to be succeeded by the former rating agent, Francis William Showers, at £2,500 a year. The office of rating agent had been merged into the Estate Department in 1919, when Showers became assistant surveyor, a post he had previously held with the Great Northern.[22]

The North Eastern Railway's Estate Department under Arthur G. Stevenson had wider responsibilities, with much less involvement by the civil engineer. It had, for instance, taken over house repairs from the Engineering Department, which was too slow and did unnecessary work, and had put it out to contract, cutting expenditure by 50 per cent over 10 years against a rising rent income. District agents had more discretionary powers. New houses, however, were the responsibility of the Architect's Department, which the Great Western did not have.

The Lancashire & Yorkshire also had a full-time architect, Henry Shelmerdine, who was appointed land agent and architect — an unusual combination — in 1882 when aged only 27, at £5,000 a year, twice as much as the chief engineer, William Hunt, was earning, which must have raised some eyebrows. He practised in Liverpool, where he was responsible for a number of buildings, and he designed many of the company's stations, including Liverpool Exchange. He was also in charge of rating and was a Fellow of the Surveyors' Institution from 1890 to 1924 but was not, it seems, a member of the Royal Institute of British Architects. He retired on health grounds in 1920 and died in 1935.[23] For a time the company simultaneously used Elias Dorning, a Manchester mining engineer, for land purchases. He was a well-known arbitrator in the north of England, bought land for the London & North Western as well as the LYR, and for the latter secured the land for Horwich works at a bargain price.

The Midland Railway's Estate Department was centralised at Derby, and in 1921 had a particularly cumbersome system of dealing with repairs. Applications were sent to the Engineering Department for an estimate before being authorised by the estate agent, who then returned it to the engineer who in turn put the job out to contract. Anything over £10 required board approval into the bargain. Estate Department staff did all the survey work, including boundaries, and controlled all property inside as well as outside the permanent-way fence. But they were not responsible for rent collection and rating, which came under the Secretary's Department.[24] The Midland's first full-time estate agent was J. Sherland Gretton who held office from 1861 until 1888 and also acted as secretary to the Ashby & Nuneaton and Swinton & Knottingley joint committees, on which the Midland was a partner with the London & North Western and North Eastern respectively. On Gretton's death he was succeeded by P.S. McCallum until 1913, and W.H.C. Clay, who went on to serve the LMS.[25]

It is of interest to compare six principal companies' rent income with their estate staffs in 1913.[26]

Company	Rents £	Salaried Staff	Wages Staff	
London & North Western	313,299	140	34	(including building tradesmen)
North Eastern	178,355	73	1	(messenger)
Midland	175,000	53	7	(chainmen)
Great Western	121,161	48	4	(chainmen)
London & South Western	103,672	23	8	(messengers and caretakers)
Great Central:				
(excl London)	89,504	20	2	(building inspectors)
(London)	22,859	4	21	(20 tradesmen and one inspector)
	112,363	24	23	

Railways owned considerable areas of land in many towns. This map shows its extent in the built-up area of Chester, a city generally better known for its historical associations than for railways. Most of the railway-owned canal land passed to British Waterways Board in 1963.

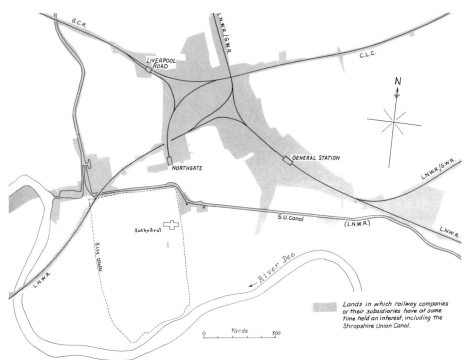

Lands in which railway companies or their subsidiaries have at some time held an interest, including the Shropshire Union Canal.

In 1902 the Great Central's Estate Department was situated in Manchester under Edwin Barker when it was decided to establish a separate London department following the opening of the London Extension to Marylebone, where the company had acquired a considerable amount of surplus property. A.J. Brickwell of the Great Northern gained the appointment but did not take it up, preferring to stay where he was, so the job went to A. Puleston in 1903 at £500 a year. He had no formal qualifications but undertook to take the Surveyors' Institution examinations and qualify within 18 months. As the figures show, he built up a small staff of building tradesmen, which helped to put the company's London property on a more profitable basis.[27]

Estate department offices were usually at stations or in station chambers, although the Great Western's Cardiff office was for a time in the Central Hotel. When

The LMS Railway's deed room inside the pediment of the Euston Arch in 1961. Custody of deeds is an important Property Board function, and the wooden storage cabinets are still used in the London deed room at St Pancras. (National Railway Museum)

Shelmerdine was appointed architect and estate agent to the Lancashire & Yorkshire he at first occupied the company's London office in Mincing Lane before moving to the Manchester headquarters. The drawing office at Euston was a smoky place alongside platform 6 and the deed room was in the pediment of the Doric Arch, gained by a spiral staircase inside one of the columns, cold and poorly lit by grimy skylights.

Land Plans
In chapter 5 we saw something of the diversity of railway property. Its extent probably made the railways collectively the country's largest single landowner. In the historic centre of Liverpool, for instance, Kellett has shown that they owned 9 per cent of the land in 1900, more than in any other large city, including London. Simmons (*The Railway in Town and Country*) suggests that on average every mile of railway required 11 acres of land. In a sample of 20 agricultural counties in England and Wales the railways' proportion of the total acreage in 1873 was only 0.24 per cent, but the rental value was far greater, on average 3 per cent overall and in six of the counties as much as from 7.3 to 9.2 per cent. In populous counties the proportions were much higher.

The key to the management of such large and varied property holdings was, and still is, the railways' survey or land plans, or line plans as they are sometimes called. Drawn to a scale of 2, 3 or 4 chains to the inch, and bound in volumes which the London & South Western Railway called 'terriers' (from the Old French for rent-roll), they form a cartographical record of all land and occupancies, mile-by-mile, with details of purchases and sales. Coloured and tinted, the older plans invariably were beautiful examples of the highest order of draughtsmanship. Many are still in use, although the steady spread of the 1/2500 (25in to 1 mile) Ordnance Survey plans in the last century enabled those to be used for later revisions. Two very fine early sets at 2 chains to the inch were prepared by Binns & Clifford of Birmingham for the London & Birmingham Railway in 1840.[28] Each had an elaborate tinted title page, respectively portraying the Euston Arch and Curzon Street station at Birmingham. They were in use and updated until 1863. A similar set of Birmingham & Derby Junction plans of the line from Derby to Hampton-in-Arden was drawn at 3 chains to the inch in 1837, probably by John Hornblower.[29]

As amalgamations proceeded, so did the need for standard plans, and in the 1850s and 1860s most lines found that extensive resurveys were necessary, as we have already seen on the Great Western, providing work for a number of firms of surveyors, some of which started to specialise. The North British used their former engineer, John Miller, in 1848, and Charles Jopp in 1853; the Glasgow & South Western James Horne in 1852 and Hugh McClure in 1858. A man with one of the largest practices in this field was Henry Fowler, one of the many engineering Fowlers, who had offices in London, Manchester and Rugby. A son of the leading engineer Charles Fowler of Leeds, he was one of Frederick Wood's assistants from

181

LONDON DIVISION.

CORRECTED AND REVISED BY F. WOOD, RUGBY, 1863.

EUSTON STATION.

Binns and Clifford Surveyors, Birmingham.

1840

Part of the title page of a set of land plans for the London Division of the London & Birmingham Railway, drawn by the Birmingham surveyors Binns & Clifford in 1840, and updated by Frederick Wood in 1863. The Birmingham Division volume was prefaced by an equally delicate title page depicting Curzon Street station. The originals are finely aquatinted. (Public Record Office)

about 1860 to 1880, when he set up on his own. He carried out many resurveys, producing plans for the Manchester, Sheffield & Lincolnshire, Great Northern, London & North Western, North Eastern and North Staffordshire railways, among others.[30] Another Henry Fowler, of Birmingham, did similar work, and a third Fowler, Frederick of Sheffield, was the younger brother of the famous engineer Sir John Fowler and surveyed many lines.[31]

In 1863-7 Frederick Wood engaged Atherton Selby of Leigh, Lancashire, to resurvey the Liverpool–Manchester and Stockport–Stalybridge lines of the London

& North Western. On the former the original Liverpool & Manchester Railway 7-chain plans were still being used, by now considerably out of date. Selby charged 5 guineas (£5.25) a mile for the Liverpool line survey, using the odd scale of 1 chain to ¾in, and 6 guineas (£6.30) for the other, at 2 chains to the inch. So much for standardisation. Selby fell badly behind, invoking curt demands from Wood: 'We are greatly inconvenienced for want of completion of this survey. We were to have had them six months ago'; and three days later, 'Your letter of yesterday as to the state of these plans is very *indefinite* and *unsatisfactory* . . . send at once [those] that you have completed.' Despite having to correct some mistakes spotted by the meticulous Wood, Selby was asked to resurvey the Crewe–Chester line.[32]

Other companies used their own surveyors, notably the Midland, London, Brighton & South Coast, London & South Western and, later, the North Eastern. J.R. Wright's land plans prepared for the Lancashire & Yorkshire in 1855 provoked a row with the East Lancashire Railway, joint owner of the line between Salford and Clifton Junction. Typically, the East Lancashire disputed the ownership of the retaining wall of the canal which ran alongside and which belonged to the Lancashire & Yorkshire, averring that only where it held up the railway should the cost of the wall's maintenance be charged to the joint account, the remainder being the LYR's sole responsibility.The Lancashire & Yorkshire managed to find evidence that the whole of the wall had been built to support the line.

In 1934 the LMS Estate Department was having difficulty in keeping its plans up to date after reductions were made in staff, so when a new one was needed at Upminster a trial aerial survey was made of 1½ miles of line. Not only was it successful, but it was less expensive. The cost was only £16 per mile, saving 40 per

When a landowner sold land to the Birmingham & Gloucester Railway at Eckington, he reserved to himself the shooting and hunting rights on the embankment, subject to adequate rights of support for the safety of the railway. Hence the boundary fences along the top instead of the usual position along the bottom. (Author)

cent on a field survey. It was the first successful large-scale railway plan produced by this method, and more were undertaken.

Boundaries

The maintenance of boundaries has always been an important function of most railway estate departments, not only to delineate the company's property but to comply with the statutory obligation to keep lines securely fenced. Posts and rails were the most usual — in 1846 an enterprising timber merchant from Painswick, Gloucestershire, gained a contract with the Taff Vale Railway — although some companies used quickset hedges supplied by a firm at Melbourne, Derbyshire, which sent men out to plant them. Later, post and wire fences became almost universal, with posts made from old sleepers and sometimes old rails; nowadays they are of concrete.

Along the line, boundaries usually follow the edges of cuttings or the foot of embankments, although there is at least one instance of boundary fences along the top of an embankment, near Eckington on the Birmingham & Gloucester line, where in 1838 the vendor reserved to himself all rights on the slopes, which still apply. In cases of encroachment, a dispute or where, for some reason, a fence was not desirable or possible, boundary markers were erected, usually of cast iron bearing the company's name or initials, although on some early lines they were stone. Even as late as 1878 the London & North Western's Permanent Way

Two boundary markers.
Stockton & Darlington Railway stone on Crawley Bank on the site of the Stanhope & Tyne Railway in 1989. (Author)

Restored cast-iron post from the North Union Railway, made to a standard pattern of the London & North Western which became a joint owner of the line in 1846, although the North Union remained in existence as a company until 1888. Up to half of the post would be sunk into the ground. (Author)

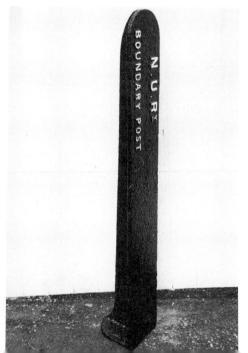

Committee ordered boundary stones to be erected on the Cromford & High Peak line, where stone was plentiful.[33]

In 1888 the Surveyors' Institution discussed railway boundaries, which at that time extended over some 36,914 miles and were a frequent source of contention. A boundary was often lost because the railway first marked it with a fence, inside which it dug a ditch and then planted a hedge, the object of the fence being to protect the line while the hedge grew. Over the years the fence fell to pieces, cattle trod the ground and debris from ditching was thrown in the hedge, forming a mound which was then thought by adjoining owners to be the boundary. Some members favoured iron fences, Edward Ryde a double hedge, and it was noted that the Great Western used old rail about every 100yd (there is still some of it about), while between Redhill and Ashford the South Eastern erected short iron rail stumps which were not always visible. Fences on the actual boundary were the only answer.[34]

The meeting might also have considered the contribution made to boundary disputes by missing or incomplete deeds. In 1870 the Great Eastern was still trying to trace over 130 deeds executed by absorbed lines, including some by the Eastern Union Railway which had ceased to exist as a separate company in 1862, thought to be held by Peter Bruff who had been the Eastern Union's engineer.[35]

In 1894 the rector of Ormside in Westmorland had the entrance to the village school improved, under the impression that it belonged to the newly formed district council of which he was a member, but was sent a bill for 1s (5p) nominal rent by the Midland Railway's estate agent, P.S. McCallum, together with an agreement. After much argument the rector reluctantly signed it, but only after the company sent him a 6d stamp (2½p) to make it legal.[36]

Boundaries between railway companies were equally important, as they often formed the basis of tolls and charges for running powers by one company over the lines of another, and for the maintenance of junctions. Special plans showed the juxtaposition of land and brief particulars of the agreement, such as that made for the Furness & Midland Joint line where the Midland maintained the junction at one end and the Furness at the other.[37]

Estate Management

The management of a large estate covers many activities, none more so than on the railway. Valuation, arbitration, letting and rents have been touched upon, but space precludes mention of more than some of the others that were contended with, including a few of the more unusual.

The disposal or letting of surplus land intermittently exercised railway companies from the outset, particularly when economies had to be made. The Aylesbury Railway in 1837, for instance, invited tenders for renting lineside land as gardens or paddocks, to be given up on short notice if the company required, in return for compensation for 'Crops and Acts of Husbandry at a fair Valuation'.[38] Most surplus land was acquired as a result of severance or unavoidable conditions made when lines were built or enlarged. Other land was obtained when it came on the market, as a deliberate policy against the day when it might be needed for a new line, widening or other improvements, sometimes for schemes which were little more than a twinkle in a chairman's or chief officer's eye, in anticipation of an advantage that could be taken of a rival company or for warding off potential competition. All the major companies took this policy, and against it there was a system of periodical review of unused saleable assets. Under the pre-emption provisions in the Lands Clauses Act, 1845, the original owner was entitled to first refusal or, failing him, adjoining landowners. In practice, only when revenue was down were committees of investigation formed. The Great Western appointed one in 1867, but in its two years' existence it achieved very little.[39]

The Caledonian's enquiry in 1902-5 was more effective. In general there was satisfaction with the factor's performance, but one or two startling circumstances were uncovered, like the 5½ acres near Larbert on which £60 a year feu duty was being paid but of which the company had never taken formal possession. But the old attitude prevailed regarding Rutland Place and Rutland Square in Edinburgh, where houses were not to be sold but added to 'in readiness for an extension of Princes Street station'.[40] It never happened, and one wonders just how realistic the forecasting was. In 1924 the Cheshire Lines Estate Committee discovered that, on 1922 values, their non-railway property was worth the massive figure of £1,146,470, much of it empty land at Otterspool, Liverpool, where it was thought new docks might one day be built. Arrangements were made to sell as much as possible, with other surplus property, as opportunity might arise but, as always, 'to retain ample land for all possible future requirements'.[41]

Surplus land was excluded from the 1897 agreement by which the Great Western bought the bankrupt Banbury and Cheltenham Direct Railway for cash. Although the line was completed two years before, a considerable number of accommodation works had not been carried out or were unsatisfactory, requiring renewed negotiation with landowners by the GWR. Then there were arguments with the liquidators over what was and was not surplus. It was a good example of the muddles that had to be sorted out when small, ailing companies were taken over. That one took three years to resolve.[42] Conversely, when the Great Eastern was trying to sort out its inheritance of land holdings in 1870, the estate surveyor discovered that many holdings purchased in earlier years were no longer in the company's possession, yet there were no records of sales.[43] To anyone familiar with the early history of that company, it is not surprising.

Considerable work was involved in the granting of easements or rights of way over or under the railway, particularly for footpaths and, later on, road or bridge widenings, sewage schemes and other public services. When the Great Western wanted to rebuild Stafford Bridge over the River Exe near Exeter in 1904, the question arose of liability to maintain the Earl of Iddesleigh's private road which ran across it alongside the railway. The GWR agreed to reconstruct and maintain the entire bridge and allow the earl a right of way across it, and to relinquish its fishing rights (which the earl maintained it never had) in return for two parcels of land and a payment of £300.[44]

Until the repeal of the Tithes Act in 1935, the recording and paying of mostly small sums was an archaic, time-consuming and inescapable job. The Great Western was one of the largest tithe payers in the south of England, to the tune of over £5,500 a year in 1934, but nearly all in sums of only a few shillings or even pence. From the outset railways had to maintain accurate records; the East Lincolnshire Railway's tithe book of 1847 showed against each plot of land purchased the name of the previous landowner, area, tithe rent payable and any title rent payable to a lay impropriator, in respect of 39 parishes. There were 36 separate plots in Louth alone.

The Estate Department was responsible for settling fire claims. In the days of steam locomotives, fires were frequent in dry weather, and under the Railway Fires Act, 1905, railways were liable for damage to agricultural land caused by sparks from engines, up to £100. They also had a right to enter land to extinguish a fire and to reduce the risk by clearing undergrowth. Claims work was a major occupation, with many false fire claims to be investigated. It was significant that there was a considerable reduction in the latter after steam operation ended. The estate surveyor also arranged insurance, the extent of which varied over time and between companies. Some insured nearly everything against fire, particularly the smaller railways; others were selective, increasingly so as expansion enlarged their financial reserves, progressing to the creation of their own insurance funds which were steadily built up by annual allocations, accompanied by progressive reductions in commercial insurance.

The Edinburgh & Glasgow in 1865 carried fire insurance on nearly all its buildings and some of its rolling stock, although two years earlier it decided to stop insuring locomotives.[45] The Great North of Scotland Railway carried extensive insurance of all kinds right up to the end of its existence in 1923. There were contractual obligations to insure, too, in respect of leased or rented property, or under agreements like the Great North of Scotland's with the Caledonian over the junction at Ferryhill, Aberdeen, and with the Highland at Boat of Garten, where the GNSR had to insure the other company's signal-boxes.[46] The Midland decided to start its own fund in 1876, and by 1903 it had grown to £460,000, earning 4 per cent interest and paying the cost of the company's fire brigade at Derby. By 1883 only leasehold property was insured commercially.

The letting of retail premises and advertising on stations was an early development, starting with refreshment rooms. In the days before dining cars and corridor trains, the refreshment stop was an important feature of travel, and contracts for the rooms at stations where meal halts were made were particularly prized. For some years, for instance, all London & North Western expresses stopped at Wolverton, immortalised by Sir Francis Head's description in *Stokers and Pokers* (1849) of periodic invasions by passengers endeavouring to be served, eat and drink in 10 minutes. Compulsory stops were included in the terms of the lease for rooms at stations like Wolverton, Swindon, York, Normanton, Preston and Carlisle, but with the gradual introduction of dining cars from 1879 they became an anachronism and were either discontinued when leases expired or were withdrawn by negotiation and suitable compensation.

The Great Western had a particular difficulty at Swindon where, as noted on p138, the refreshment rooms were built and maintained by a contractor who, as part of the agreement, also built the houses at Swindon in return for the refreshment room profits. At a time when the railway's construction costs were soaring, a deal which saved the expenditure of yet more capital was attractive to the company, and in 1841 it was embodied in a 99-year lease at a peppercorn rent, including a compulsory 10-minute stop by all regular trains. No other refreshment stop was to be made between London and Bristol. It was a foolish move. Within a week the contractors had sub-let the refreshment rooms for seven years for £6,000 and an annual rent of £1,100, at the end of which they sold the lease outright for £20,000. When the Great Western tried to cut the stop to 1 minute for some trains in 1845 they were taken to court and lost the case. The lease changed hands again in 1875 for £45,000, in 1880 for £35,000 and in 1881 for no less than £70,000. The hapless Great Western was unable to pay out the lessees and get rid of the useless stop until 1895, when it cost the then enormous sum of £100,000, which remained a charge on the revenue account until 1920.

As the railways entered the hotel business, some companies handed over refreshment rooms to the Hotels Department, although several used the specialist catering contractors Spiers & Pond. Their first contract was with the Metropolitan Railway for Farringdon refreshment room in 1863, quickly followed by one for all the London, Chatham & Dover's rooms which lasted until 1905. In 1888 they gained the London & South Western's contract and in 1899 the South Eastern's, both of which continued into Southern Railway days, ending in 1930, and they also managed several individual rooms at large stations. By that time, most of the main refreshment rooms were under the railways' own control, with only some of the smaller ones let to local contractors, except on the Southern where Frederick Hotels were contractors. In 1932 the LMS looked at the possibility of its Hotels Department taking over Finlays' sweets and tobacco kiosks on the ex-North Western lines and Graham & Co's in Scotland, being prepared to exclude sweets and tobacco from Wymans' and Menzies' bookstall contracts as well in order to secure the trade, but despite a strong recommendation from the Land and Rating Committee the idea was not proceeded with.[47] There was competition between Wymans and Finlays; the Great Central, in particular, played one off against the other.[48]

The long history of railway station bookstalls is bound up with the rise of W.H. Smith & Sons.[49] The first station bookstall was let to Horace Marshall & Son at Fenchurch Street in 1841. They went on to open stalls on the Great Western and in South Wales. It was a competitive business and at first the contracts were small, the companies' estate committees letting selling rights to the highest bidders on a piecemeal basis with little attempt at control. The result was that the London bookstalls became notoriously scruffy and untidy, with cheap and offensive literature mixed up with bottles of ginger beer, buns and cakes, kept as often as not by a former railway employee or a widow and regarded as a sort of unofficial pension. Smiths changed all that in 1848, when they offered the London & North Western an exclusive contract to sell newspapers at all their principal stations for £1,500 a year. It marked the beginning of Smiths' transformation from being a wholesale distributor to the country's largest newspaper and book retailer, but was not without trouble when the previous vendor at Euston had to be expelled forcibly, and unsuccessfully sued the railway company. The North Western's earlier lack of acumen was revealed when the court heard that the vendor had made £1,021 profit in ten months on a rental of £60 a year.

The other railways were no better, but the case quickly made them realise the opportunities they were missing, and by 1852 Smiths had contracts with ten other companies, six of them worth more than £600 a year. The Great Western came into the fold in 1863. The North Western renewed its contract in 1851 on a scale rising from £3,500 to £4,200 over seven years. In 1876 for the first time rents were agreed on a percentage of receipts, subject to minimum guarantees of £10,500–12,000 a year, which in 1886 rose to £26,000 for ten years. It was good business for the railways, and for Smiths even better. The North Western also gave the lead in insisting on very tightly drawn contracts, with strictly enforced clauses setting out the sort of literature Smiths could sell or advertise on their stalls. Anything the company considered indecent, immoral or seditious it was empowered to remove and

W.H. Smith's bookstall on Skipton station in 1907.
Two railway hotels are advertised on the rear wall,
the North British's at Glasgow and the Midland's at
Manchester. (Courtesy D. Joy)

prohibit, including advertising trade union activities and dubious medicines for 'complaints or ailments of an indecent or indelicate nature'.

Smiths also offered to take over general station advertising. Combined contracts were negotiated, and advertisement boards on station walls and fences had to be of approved pattern. Smiths found the advertisers and, from the mid-1860s, rents comprised 50 per cent of revenue, Smiths paying all expenses. Their activities were restricted to England and Wales, although they did open a bookstall at Edinburgh Waverley in 1851. In the same year the Edinburgh & Glasgow let its Glasgow Queen Street bookstall for £40 a year and received an offer from Green & Prince of London for 'hanging internal space of the stations on the line'.[50] Smiths made no move to expand and when the Edinburgh contract ended in 1856 they were outbid by Thomas Murray, who in time gave way to John Menzies who became monopolist booksellers on Scottish stations. Smiths withdrew and never went back.

When, towards the end of the century, the railways were finding it harder to make profits and bookstall rents increased with each renewal, Smiths cautiously began to diversify into shops, and vigorously into wholesale warehousing, printing, bookbinding and selling stationery. They acted wisely, for in 1905 the Great Western announced that at the end of the year its contract with Smiths would be terminated. The estate agent, Williams, persuaded his directors that bookstalls and advertising were capable of generating more revenue than Smiths were paying and that if negotiations broke down the company should look elsewhere. But it was the London & North Western that took the lead: its contract with Smiths expired around the same time and was not renewed, the bookstalls going to Wymans and advertising to Kershaw. The Great Western, which had discussed the matter with the North Western, gave both its contracts to Wymans, who already did printing work for the company.

The reasons for the changes are obscure. They made the columns of the press and created a great upheaval in Smiths, who immediately speeded up their programme of opening shops. Wymans had no experience of bookstalls and advertising and, in fact, had to be supported by both companies by reducing rents, which was still going on in 1918. Spite at a high level has been suggested on the part of the North Western; possibly patronage on the GWR. Whatever their motives, the change did little for the two railways while Smiths, once they had recovered, continued to prosper.

Fruit and flower stalls, hairdressing saloons and boot blacks were allowed on some of the large stations, where the management of the lavatories was also let out; Faulkners, for example, looked after those on the Midland. The Estate Department was also responsible for contracts for automatic vending machines. In the present century a few other trading outlets like Boots the Chemist and one or two post offices appeared on some of the biggest stations, and in the 1930s at least three news cinemas, at Waterloo, Victoria and the new Leeds City station, but they were exceptions. Until recent years bookstalls remained the main traders. One of the smallest station trading activities must have been the arrangement under which the Neath & Brecon, and later the Great Western, left a local landowner's daily newspaper at Aberbran station for a shilling (5p) a month, which was duly collected by the Estate Department.

Estate Departments had wide-ranging and sometimes peculiar issues to resolve. In 1877 a dispute arose between the Furness Railway and landowners and lessees on Walney Island off Barrow, who alleged that the railway's harbour works had destroyed two ancient fords across the tidal channel. The Furness must have realised that it had no case to answer, and instructed its estate agent and engineer to provide a steam-operated chain ferry. It ran until the Walney Bridge was opened in 1908.[51] The same company owned extensive marshland near Grange-over-Sands where sea-washed turf was abundant. In 1935, the LMS allowed a firm of Glasgow landscape architects to remove 40,000 square yards over five years for £370, to be taken away by rail from Meathop siding nearby. The Cambrian Railways owned the wooden toll bridge across the Dovey estuary at Penmaenpool, and the Great Western owned the Kingswear–Dartmouth ferry.

The 1870 Education Act introduced local School Boards, financed from the rates, to build new schools in areas where church schools were absent or inadequate. In such instances railway companies, as large ratepayers, would be called on to make a major contribution, and it became the practice of church schools to seek donations from railways towards repairs or extensions in the knowledge that the companies would invariably pay up rather than see a School Board set up and an annual rate charged. The Cheshire Lines Committee estate minutes give numerous examples, at first lump sum donations and then in proportion to those made by other ratepayers. In 1906 the Great Central calculated that it would have to pay a rate of at least 2¾d (1p) in the pound for 30 years if a School Board were set up at Haydock to meet the demands of the Education Department. It was a lot cheaper to donate £20 15s 11d (£20.79).[52]

The electric telegraph was first installed in 1838, on the Great Western between Paddington and West Drayton where it attracted great public interest. The spread of the telegraph went hand-in-hand with railway expansion so that by 1852 there were some 4,000 miles of wire in Britain. The main company was the Electric Telegraph Company whose wires were carried mostly along railways, which provided ready-made routes. Soon a nationwide system was operating and no railway line was without its poles and wires. The usual arrangement was for the telegraph company to provide the system, and often the clerks, with lines reserved for exclusive railway use. In 1854, 8 out of the 17 London telegraph offices were at railway stations and by 1868 1,226 stations were public telegraph offices for the sending and receipt of telegrams. Under the 1868 Telegraph Act the private companies were taken over by the Post Office, including public telegraph services operated by the railways. Compensation was claimed for loss of wayleave payments and rents, and as their agreements with the telegraph companies were for different periods there were considerable variations, although in general compensation was based on an estimated 20 years' net profit from transmitting public messages, including allowances for projected increases. It was a complicated business, which the estate departments negotiated. The Great Eastern, for instance, claimed £271,000 for its 965 miles of telegraph line. When the Great Western's claim was settled it went on to receive £5,500 a year; the London & North Western was paid £6,000 a year, plus £1 extra for each mile of wire above 6,000.[53] As time went on many of the railways took over the maintenance of their installations, which the Post Office used.

The South Eastern Railway owned a beach. In 1873 it had ideas about building a new port at Dungeness and bought a large part of the shore. The scheme went no further and the shingle was used to provide ballast. The Great Northern dredged ballast from the Trent at Newark, and in 1925 its successor, the LNER, bought 2 acres of the gravel bed from Lord Middleton for £50. Since the company also extracted water at this point, for its troughs at Muskham on the main line which crossed the river there, the supply was secured. A number of companies owned ballast quarries, notably the London & South Western which, in 1897, acquired one of the largest at Meldon in north Devon where, as we have seen in chapter 6 (p162), a small community grew up. It still provides ballast under BR ownership. The little Isle of Wight Railway owned St Boniface Down quarry at Ventnor, from which for some years it made a modest profit selling stone and providing itself and its neighbour, the Isle of Wight Central Railway, with ballast.[54]

The oldest railway-owned quarries were at Caldon Low, which the North Staffordshire Railway inherited when it took over the Trent & Mersey Canal in 1846. A tramroad was laid from the canal to the quarries some time after 1776 (p21)[55] and the canal and railway companies went on working them, including an internal narrow gauge railway, some of the output being hard limestone ballast. Parts of the workings were leased out, and in 1934 the LMS, finding the retained portion no longer profitable, leased it to Sheffield steelmakers. When the Euston rebuilding was to commence in 1938, the LMS President, Lord Stamp, blasted out 100,000 tons of stone by remote control from the shareholders' room, but the war intervened before the scheme could proceed. British Rail still owns the quarries, which continue to be leased, not without certain historic problems.

The Great Central's estate agent also had to manage quarries that came from a canal company, at Doveholes in Derbyshire. They came to the railway in similar circumstances to Caldon, resulting from the Manchester, Sheffield & Lincolnshire purchasing the Peak Forest Canal in 1846. Here, too, there was a tramroad linking the quarries to the canal. The railway did not own all the quarries, and those which it did it leased. The tramroad lingered on until 1925, and even at that relatively late date there were protests at its closure from some of the users.

Estate departments usually looked after the property interests of absorbed canal companies, which formed a significant portion of the total railway estate and were equally varied. Towards the end of the nineteenth century the Great Western's estate agent had a senior member of his staff permanently engaged on canal work, based at the Kennet & Avon Canal offices at Bath, but in 1899 canal estate affairs were transferred to the various canal engineers, who reported to the estate agent at Paddington. Where railways had been built on canals, loops and bends too sharp for

At Waterford, Ireland, the London & North Western, Midland and Lancashire & Yorkshire railways shared an enquiry office at 12, The Quay. Evidently there was insufficient business to justify each company having its own office. (BR Property Board)

the line were rarely capable of being sold, but because they often performed a drainage function required minimum maintenance. Unforeseen developments long afterwards could cause problems, as happened in 1944 on the Glastonbury Canal. It had been partly built on by the Somerset Central Railway in 1852 and the remainder became a drain, for 3 miles of which the Lower Brue Drainage Board subsequently accepted responsibility. When water was taken for a Second World War ordnance factory at Bridgwater, Highbridge locomotive department found itself running short and the LMS Estate Department and the Drainage Board had to unravel some complicated history before satisfactory arrangements could be made.[56]

Following the failure of the contractors supplying its coke ovens at Bristol (until about 1860 locomotives burned coke), the Great Western bought Gyfeillon Colliery near Pontypridd in 1854, which it operated until 1865. In 1874 the company again decided to secure its own coal supplies and bought Cilely Colliery in the Ely valley, which it kept until 1896, and leased Avon Colliery in the Llynvi valley until 1912.

During the First World War the Great Eastern went into the poultry business. It purchased Dodnash Priory estate at Bentley, near Ipswich, where it established a poultry farm, partly to encourage the wartime poultry industry, with government approval, and partly to supply the company's hotels with eggs. Under the land agent's enthusiastic management the undertaking became quite extensive, in 1920 producing over 42,000 eggs. A demonstration train toured East Anglian stations and station-masters attended lectures on poultry management. To promote the better quartering of birds, hen houses made by local firms were displayed at stations, and in conjunction with the National Utility Poultry Association annual national egg-laying competitions were held, sponsored by the *Daily Mail* newspaper. The Great Eastern sold accredited eggs for breeding purposes to ex-servicemen and allotment holders who could not afford good birds, in an endeavour to improve the country's laying stock. The estate was also farmed for grain, potatoes, sugar beet, timber and cattle, but less profitably. The LNER sold the estate in 1924, retaining 16 acres for egg-laying tests which were finally sold in 1928.[57]

The railways which operated shipping services had offices at Irish and continental ports, and some of the larger companies also had tourist offices in capital cities as well, all of which fell within the estate departments' portfolios. After the Grouping an Associated British Railways office was opened in New York, which was administered by the LMS on behalf of the LNER and the Southern. The Great Western did not participate, but the office sold its tickets on a commission basis. In 1961 British Railways had 19 overseas offices and two in the Channel Islands.

Railway Rating
There is neither the need nor the space to go into the complexities of railway rating, although, in view of its importance in property management, it cannot be ignored here. The railways always considered that they bore an unfair share of the local rates burden. The original system of parish rating was totally inapplicable to railways, but following case law in 1841 and 1844 a uniform, but cumbersome, method of calculation was devised, although it did nothing to reduce the burden. Kellett cites Huyton, a parish of 2,615 acres near Liverpool, where the railway occupied 25 acres, or just over 1 per cent, yet paid £5,267 out of a total rate income of £15,039, or over 35 per cent. It was laid down that rates should be based on the notional rent that a theoretical tenant would pay to the railway for use of its track, including fixed equipment but not rolling stock. But, unlike buildings which could be used for something else, railway track had no rental value, so instead railways were uniquely assessed on net receipts. What constituted net receipts gave rise to much legal argument, but the railway still paid up to 20 times more than industry, per employee.

We have seen how leading surveyors like Edward Ryde became specialists in rating appeals, and numerous text books appeared. Charles Lee, another leading rating surveyor, made £120,000 during his lifetime.[58] In 1878 a paper on the subject was given at the Surveyors' Institution.[59] One of the reasons why railways were reluctant to encourage suburban growth by providing new stations was because they would also increase their rates contribution. After a good deal of legislation, which tended to make the position rather worse, and continual appeals against assessments — often unsuccessful — the Railways (Valuation for Rating) Act was passed in 1930, which in effect attempted to codify accepted practice in valuing net receipts. The Bill was strenuously opposed by the companies, and Showers of the Great Western appeared as expert witness on behalf of the 'Big Four'. The Act immediately set off another round of appeals through the Railway and Canal Commission and the courts, and in 1935, for example, the Southern Railway distributed £1,000 to its estate and legal staff involved in getting the valuation reduced from £2,180,000 to £1,077,131.

Rating valuation and negotiation entailed a large amount of estate department work. A separate assessment had to be agreed for every parish through which the railway passed, requiring special plans, the whole purpose of which was to ensure that the railway paid no more than it could possibly escape with. The Great Western in 1913, for instance, paid around £1 million in rates, £2¼ million in 1921, and £1.3 million during the depression in 1932.[60]

Site Development
Although restricted by statute, a certain amount of site development was ventured by certain railways in the first half of the present century. In 1900 the Great Central bought some 95 acres adjacent to Metropolitan Railway land at Wembley Hill when building its Neasden–Northolt line, to avoid having to provide expensive accommodation works because the new railway would cut off access. From 1923 to 1925 some 64 acres were let by its successor, the LNER, for the British Empire Exhibition, for which roads and services were laid. After the exhibition had finished the company took them over in lieu of restoration of the site, together with some of the exhibition buildings. The railway developed them as an industrial estate, although a lot of the land remained vacant.[61]

When the Royal Agricultural Society decided not to have a permanent showground on the site of its 1903 show at Park Royal, Acton, the Great Western bought the land and built a football stadium on part of it, which it let on very generous terms to Queen's Park Football Club with the idea that traffic would be encouraged to what was then a thinly populated area. The Rangers had it from 1907 to 1915, when the site was requisitioned by the government for munitions storage. After the war the GWR developed the site as a trading estate, alongside which they had a large goods depot, and in 1934 the estate agent declared the results so far to be 'highly satisfactory'.[62] Part of it went back to the government in 1941 for war use, and most of the remainder was sold in 1952 and 1975. A smaller industrial estate was developed on the Great West Road at Brentford on land bought in 1928-30 that was surplus to a new goods depot. Most of that was sold in the 1970s and 1980s, but some is still leased out by BR Property Board.

The controversy about the desirability of railways having powers to develop lineside land continued. In 1920, F.R.E. Davis argued that the Act setting up a permanent Ministry of Transport in 1919 put control of land acquisition under the Acquisition of Land Act of the same year, instead of the Lands Clauses Act of 1845. He went on to claim that the railways were misguided in opposing town planning schemes that local authorities were now starting to produce, on the grounds that by so doing they were less likely to gain support for relaxation of statutory restrictions.[63] That the railways did oppose planning is borne out by the comments of F.C. Hockridge, who succeeded Showers on the Great Western, on the Acts of 1925 and 1932 and proposals that would adversely affect that company's interests.[64]

In 1928 the LMS set up an Estate Development Committee, and in 1930 the chairman, the estate surveyor W.H.C. Clay, and the Scottish Divisional estate agent went to the USA to gain ideas for increasing estate revenue from reconstruction schemes on which the company was about to embark. Station car parks were one of the results.[65] The visit led to the LMS and the LNER taking the bull by the horns in 1933 and gaining clauses in their general powers Acts giving them authority to invest in companies for developing land 'in the vicinity of a railway or owned or worked by the company'. The LMS promptly set up a wholly owned subsidiary company called Lineside Estates Ltd, initially to develop 130 acres between Elstree and Radlett in Hertfordshire which had been bought in 1931, partly for a new station and partly in the hope of developing it for light industry. The Estate Department carried out the management. It was also suggested that it might, among other things, acquire the bed of Windermere when it came on the market in 1936. The company operated steamers on the lake and owned the piers at Ambleside, Bowness and Lakeside, where it had dredging powers derived from the Furness Railway, but the LMS decided not to enter the underwater property business. Lineside Estates did purchase The Grove estate near Watford from the Earl of Clarendon, however, which proved invaluable as dispersal premises in the war and went on to become British Rail's management centre; it also bought Willow Grange, nearby, which after the war passed to British Waterways, and several other smaller properties in the same area.[66] But otherwise it seems to have done very little. Part of the Elstree land was eventually sold to the Greater London Council for housing, but some of it remains greenbelt farmland still owned by BR.

The LNER waited until 1937 before forming a development subsidiary called Railway Sites Ltd, which appears to have been even less active. In 1961 the British Transport Commission had the name changed to Renel Sites Ltd, in order to preserve the 'paper' company and to allow registration of a new Railway Sites Ltd, of which more in chapter 8 (p201).

The Southern Railway does not appear to have acquired powers, probably because it was too occupied with its extensive electrification programme, but the Great Western did, to somewhat greater effect, in its Additional Powers Act, 1936. As a result, Western Enterprises Ltd was formed jointly with the Provident Mutual Life Association. The board comprised two directors from the City and two from the

GWR, with the Great Western's vice-chairman, Charles J. Hambro the banker, as chairman, and Showers as managing director. Hambro was also a director of Provident Mutual. A considerable tract of land was bought through nominees at Aldermaston, Berkshire, in 1933, 1939 and 1940, on both sides of the Kennet & Avon Canal which the GWR owned. During the war part was used for a rail-served government depot, and after nationalisation the land south of the canal was sold to the Docks & Inland Waterways Executive, but nothing was done with the remainder which is still in BR ownership and, again, is designated agricultural land.

In the late 1930s the Great Western set up a joint company with a South Wales pleasure park proprietor to develop for recreational purposes the disused inner basin at the company's Porthcawl Dock, but the war stopped progress. As noted in chapter 5 (p119), hostilities also halted work on the Looe scheme. Land was bought from 1935 onwards, some of it by Western Enterprises for development and the rest, for railway, hotel and golf course, by Hambro and Showers as nominees of the GWR itself. Western Enterprises was wound up after nationalisation.

In the early 1920s the Metropolitan Railway began a programme of station rebuilding and development, the latter aimed at meeting the board's required return of 6 per cent. Its 1906 Act gave powers to build property to let over stations and lines. At Farringdon a new entrance building faced a matching row of shops built on a raft adjoining the opposite side of the bridge. Many others followed, and by 1914 commercial rents had increased from near £67,000 in 1908 to over £171,000. In the following year R.H. Selbie persuaded his board to embark on an ambitious scheme of building a large seven-storey block over and alongside Baker Street station. So arose Chiltern Court, C.W. Clark's great neo-Edwardian block of flats and offices that dominates the junction of Marylebone Road and Baker Street. Completed in 1930, it contained shops, a 250-seat restaurant, the Chiltern Hall for functions, 198 apartments and 30 maids' rooms. The desired 6 per cent was achieved but Spiers & Pond, who reluctantly took the lease of the Chiltern Hall and the restaurant, made a loss, despite the popularity of the *thé dansant* they held.

The main line companies followed the Metropolitan's lead, but slowly. The Great Western built some shops and flats on station approaches and bridges in the late 1920s and the 1930s, including West Acton, Tilehurst and Ealing Broadway, and the LNER next to its new Shenfield station in 1934. The LMS selected 16 sites, including Watford High Street, Wembley and other stations in North London, Walsall and St Annes, although some were on bridge approaches and not over the railway. The Southern included shops at a few of its new stations, such as Horsham and Kingston. Unwanted parts of station frontage buildings in urban areas were let off, particularly on the Southern, often insensitively to the particular detriment of those with architectural merit like North Dulwich and Kew Bridge. All development work stopped during the war, of course, and afterwards there was little opportunity before nationalisation. However, in 1945 the well-known architect Clough Williams-Ellis prepared a scheme for the Southern for a hotel colony — it would now be called a holiday village — at Farringford on the Isle of Wight.[67]

Little organisational change in estate departments resulted from the Grouping, except on the LMS which went in for centralisation. The number of Estate Department districts was reduced, but a separate Scottish Division was created, with its own sub-committee responsible to the Scottish chief officer. In 1933 W.H.C. Clay was made chief estate manager, on the same level as the commercial and operating managers. Rating continued to have a separate agent under the Finance Department, which lasted until 1946 when the estate manager took over.[68] The LNER adopted a system of three area managements, one covering Scotland, and the Estate Department followed the same pattern under H.W.J. Powell who succeeded Brickwell of the Great Northern in 1935 but, as on the LMS, did not include rating until quite late in its independent existence. The Southern's Estate Department was arranged in two divisions, the Eastern under W.J. Clayton from the South Eastern & Chatham, whose territory it mainly comprised, and the much larger Western Division covering the former Brighton and South Western lines, under W.I. Selwyn, who came from the latter company.[69] They were under the direct control of the general manager, Sir Herbert Walker, but in 1936 the departments were combined under Clayton after Selwyn retired. After Clayton's retirement 18 months later, Albert Endicott, from the Ministry of Works, took over.

The Second World War

For some months before the outbreak of war in 1939, the railway estate departments were hard at work seeking dispersal premises for headquarters staff from London. The Southern went to Dorking, the Great Western to Aldermaston in Berkshire, and the LMS to The Grove at Watford. Traffic control offices were also moved out. The LNER adopted complete dispersal over a widespread number of premises, westward as far as Gerrards Cross and as far north as Peterborough where the Estate Department itself went. The process was accentuated by wartime bombing, when provincial offices had to be moved. The residence of the LNER chairman, Aston Hall at Waleswood near Sheffield, was taken for the city's goods, engineering and minerals departments at a nominal rent of £100 a year. With the end of the war the procedure was reversed as damaged premises were repaired.[70]

Fourteen major new connections and spurs were constructed between various lines, some up to a mile long, to provide alternative emergency routes. Certain sections of single line were doubled, and double tracks quadrupled. Most of these works required land, which was taken under wartime emergency powers. They were carried out at government expense and the lines remained government property until after the war when most came under railway ownership.[71]

Chapter 8

Cinderella to Market Leader

Moves towards Change

By the time the railways were grouped into four large companies in 1923, many of the larger ones had combined the post of land agent and estate surveyor, some including rating as well, which brought all aspects of land and property management under unified control. The estate surveyors of the 'Big Four' ranked as chief officers.

Although, as we saw in the last chapter (p196), three of the companies levered themselves out of the statutory strait-jacket that for so long had prevented the development of land for non-railway purposes, there was a marked failure to take any significant advantage of the new freedom. The companies were investing what capital they could raise in modernisation, through their new works programmes, stimulated by the Development (Loan Guarantees & Grants) Act of 1929, making heavy demands on all departments at a time of falling receipts, staff cuts and reductions in pay and salaries during the slump years of the 1920s and early '30s. Investment was reserved for schemes that would produce quick and obvious returns, based on a strict order of priorities in which property development was low. By the time the LMS, LNER and GWR had formed their development subsidiaries there were few financial reserves to activate them, particularly in the case of the LNER, and the long-term outlook was heavily clouded by the imminent prospect of war. Had legislative sanction been obtained earlier, followed by vigorous action on the pattern set by the Metropolitan, the railways could have capitalised on their surplus land holdings.

The severe monetary restrictions served only to reinforce long-standing attitudes: lineside land continued to be seen as an asset to be safeguarded for possible future use, while other land and property was regarded as a long-term investment, even though much of it was of low value. Emphasis remained on the 'safe' management of property, and estate departments were regarded as a back-room operation which rarely saw the limelight. Indeed, in 1934 F.C. Hockridge, assistant estate surveyor on the Great Western, self-effacingly acknowledged in a lecture that his department was the 'Cinderella' of the company which 'has to do a lot of hard work and is not usually invited to the ball'.[1] The same could be said of the other companies, and a similar article appeared in the *Southern Railway Magazine* for September 1932.

At the end of the railways' independent existence in 1947 the chief estate surveyors were Hockridge, who had succeeded Showers on the Great Western, A.P.J. Ball who was Clay's successor on the LMS, W.S. Barnes as successor to Powell on the LNER, and Endicott on the Southern. When transport was nationalised on 1 January of the following year, the railways came under the control of an executive board of the British Transport Commission. In place of the four main line companies the Railway Executive set up six operating regions, each of which had an estate surveyor. Endicott was made chief estate and rating surveyor at the Executive, responsible for co-ordinating policy and practice but with no administrative function, the regional men being responsible to their chief regional officers. Otherwise, property management continued much as it had before.

One of the first tasks at Railway Executive level was to define the boundaries between the railway estate and that of the other executives which had been established to run what were termed 'ancillary' functions, which hitherto had been part of the railway system: Docks & Inland Waterways, Hotels & Refreshment Rooms and parts of Road Transport. Boundaries between Railway Executive and London Transport Executive property already existed, as they had been established long before by the old companies and the London Passenger Transport Board.

The result has been called 'tidying up', aimed at ensuring that the Railway Executive was confined to running the railway,[2] but in reality it was a time-consuming exercise in agreeing operational and physical demarcation lines, many of them artificial, and putting them into appropriate forms of words. Where there was overlapping or joint use, the principle of 'prime user pays' was introduced. After the operation was over it was still not particularly tidy. The transfer of railway-owned canals to the Docks & Inland Waterways Executive was relatively simple, and the railways were not sorry to be rid of them, but only the railway-owned general ports were transferred. As railway shipping remained under Railway Executive control, the railway packet ports which it used remained likewise. Hotels that were integral parts of stations, as many were, also presented problems. Boundaries defined for legal, financial, administrative and maintenance purposes were often meaningless for practical working, and simply created paperwork.

In 1953 the Commission formed a property committee. Before that, there were differences in approach among the regional railway estate departments, stemming from pre-nationalisation practices. Even then the committee dealt only with policy and the more important transactions. When the Railway Executive was disbanded in 1955 and area boards were formed, reporting direct to the BTC, the chief surveyor's function was transferred to the Commission under W.S. Barnes, but still with few administrative powers and, indeed, no staff to perform them. Not until 1960-1, nine years after the post-war Labour administration was displaced by the Conservatives, did the financial potential of the railway's property assets begin to be recognised, and that but dimly. But it was enough to establish a formal policy.

The new policy had two principal objectives: the rapid disposal of low-value property, such as disused branch lines, and as large a part of the railway's housing stock as possible; and raising money from letting, selling or developing higher-value property. There were at that time some 37,000 railway-owned houses, but rent control made them uneconomic and the steady change in social attitudes since the First World War had made them unfashionable. Both strategies were seen as a means of producing much-needed revenue to support the main railway business which, apart from 1951 and 1952, had been in continuous deficit since nationalisation. That this was not new thinking we have seen; the difference was in urgency and scale. It was one of the more immediate results of the report of the Special Advisory Group set up by the Transport Minister, Ernest Marples, in March 1960, the so-called Stedeford Group after its chairman, Sir Ivan Stedeford. The group was instructed to report on the BTC's activities and make recommendations on future transport policy.[3] Significantly, the members were four businessmen, including Dr Richard Beeching, Technical Director of ICI, and two civil servants, but no railwaymen.

Unable to reach a concensus on the reorganisation of the Commission, the group produced two alternatives. The one chosen by Marples advocated decentralisation, with no holding organisation but individual autonomous boards reporting direct to the minister. A railway board's non-railway activities would be placed under subsidiary companies, including one for property. Marples appointed its principal proponent, Beeching, to implement the railway provisions. The BTC was wound up and the British Railways Board was created under the 1962 Transport Act, effective from 1 January 1963. Among other changes, the Act replaced the Docks & Inland Waterways Executive with two other autonomous boards, British Waterways and British Transport Docks, while the Hotels Executive, which included train and station catering, became British Transport Hotels. While these new arrangements did not affect railway property, they did entail work in amending demarcation agreements.

Railway Sites Ltd

In the interim, while legislation was going through Parliament, Beeching had been made chairman of the BTC, and Railway Sites Ltd (see p196) was used to form a subsidiary to develop railway property interests. The idea had, in fact, emanated from the BTC some three years earlier, but was deferred when the Stedeford Group was set up. Hitherto, the regional estate surveyors had prepared their own development plans after the post-war building controls were relaxed in 1954, and a number of schemes were under way, mostly by way of leases to development companies. But there was little co-ordination by the Railway Executive or the BTC, and regional general managers were given no direction on, for instance, the release of financial potential locked up in operational railway land. So each region went its own way and possible profitable avenues remained unopened. The onset of the development boom in the mid-1950s, however, generated growing awareness of the dormant potential.

The new Railway Sites Ltd was put together with difficulty in the first seven months of 1961. The government's intentions, although known, could not be implemented until a Bill had been drafted and passed by Parliament. In the meantime there was the usual jockeying for position among members of the soon-to-be-defunct BTC, creating an atmosphere of uncertainty in which officers were trying to plan for a future of which only the broad outlines were at all certain, and at the same time continuing to run the railway. At this stage members of the Property Committee were far from unanimous about, for instance, the stage at which outside developers should be brought in — whether before or after planning consent was obtained for a scheme. There were differences over the future role of the committee itself, or whether it should be disbanded. Then, when Beeching was appointed BTC chairman in June, he had to be consulted, but as he had not yet revealed his plans in detail the committee was working mainly in the dark. Barnes drew up a list of 500 possible sites for development, and the committee decided to recommend dividing the railway Estate Department into two sections, placing development under central control and leaving estate management to the regions, with emphasis on passing the financial benefits of development directly to them. Railway Sites Ltd was seen as the co-ordinator of joint operations by the department's development arm and private developers. Beyond that the committee felt it could not go until Beeching revealed his detailed intentions, but when Barnes put it to him that further planning should wait, the response was 'No, get on with it.' So Barnes was set to prepare a draft organisation and the new company came into existence in September.

The chairman was Maj Gen G.N. Russell, chairman of the Eastern Area board. H.L. Matthews, chairman of Crosse & Blackwell, was his deputy and the other directors were Sir Reginald Wilson, who had been the BTC Comptroller, and two property men, F.J. Howe, ex-chairman of the Liverpool Victoria Friendly Society, and Harold Samuel, a Crown Estates Commissioner, director of Land Securities Investment Trust and a chartered surveyor. Barnes became managing director, and R.G. Henbest from the Western Region succeeded him at the BTC until it was dissolved, when he became chief estates surveyor at the new British Railways Board.

Beeching chose a number of non-railwaymen for his new railways board, prominent among them Philip H. Shirley, an accountant and chairman of Batchelor Foods. A powerful and controversial figure, Shirley headed several board committees, including property which took Railway Sites Ltd under its wing, and in 1965 he took over from Russell as chairman. He was then also vice-chairman of the Railways Board.

It was the intention that Railway Sites should concentrate on site development from a central base, employing a common policy.[4] The idea of joint companies with developers was upheld, the latter to hold a 51 per cent share interest and provide expertise and finance, while Railway Sites contributed the land on a basis that ensured a continuing share of the profits. The new company was given wide publicity and its brief was described by one developer as 'the biggest development programme this country has seen or is ever likely to see'. Schemes already started in the railway regions were taken over and completed and others launched, but, despite the initial euphoria, Railway Sites was not a success. Although 19 consortia were organised, the work was hampered by disagreements between developers so that only one joint company was actually formed. The prices BR wanted for its land were too high and there was reluctance to offer developers a commercial return, while the regional estate surveyors disliked the scheme because it took away their most interesting work.

Then in 1964 came another change of government, and Harold Wilson's Labour administration brought different political thinking. Measures to control office development were introduced, and in London British Railways were instructed to give London County Council and its successor the GLC first refusal on surplus land, for housing. Not least, the railway's continued financial deterioration brought a change in emphasis from development to outright sale as part of a campaign to raise money quickly from unwanted assets. As a result, early in 1965 Railway Sites was made moribund and property development was put in the hands of a reorganised BRB Estate Department answerable to the Board's Property Committee. Henbest and Barnes retired and C.R. Smith became manager.

June 1965 saw Beeching back in ICI, but not before implementation of his controversial report, *The Reshaping of British Railways*, had started. The most contentious proposals were for the reduction of passenger routes by some 5,000 miles, 40 per cent of the whole system, and the closure of 2,100 of the existing 4,300 stations (in 1947 there had been approximately 7,000), accompanied by drastic rationalisation of freight services and depots. Severe pruning was well under way, and although the new government slowed it down, Beeching's insistence that the railways had to be more positively commercial had registered. The result was a sudden and massive increase in redundant land.

That year, the Railways Board set a land sales target of £20 million. It was not reached. Indeed, the reorganised Estate Department had hardly time to organise itself, and the £12.7 million it managed to raise, in the circumstances, was very creditable. In 1966 over £24 million was put into BR's coffers from property sales, a large proportion from London. In that time the requirement to offer London land to the GLC was extended to all provincial local authorities, to which the bulk of the land went. In all, between 1964 and 1968 some £58 million was raised from surplus land sales, with no loss of rental, which itself increased from £10.6 million to £11.3 million. Meanwhile, the development work already started was continued, notably the reconstruction of Birmingham New Street station and the shopping centre above it, the first big scheme to realise the potential of station 'air space'.

Further legislation ensued. In fact, it can be said that Labour's Transport Act of 1968 brought more changes to the railways than any other legislation. Not least on the property front was the establishment of a separate National Freight Corporation, which took over the railway's freight sundries business under its National Carriers Ltd and Freightliners Ltd subsidiaries, requiring yet more demarcation agreements for warehouses and yards. Frequently National Carriers warehouses formed awkward property 'islands' in BR freeholds, causing problems which in some places remain today.

Creation of British Rail Property Board
Following a report from management consultants, a further structural change took

place on 1 January 1970 when British Rail Engineering took over the railway workshops and the BR Property Committee was reconstituted as the British Rail Property Board, operating in the manner of a professionally managed property company. Its remit from BRB was clear enough: 'to exercise on behalf of the British Railways Board responsibility for, control of and advice on, all property matters for the whole of the Railway Board's undertaking, with particular regard to the commercial development of its properties, including the air space over stations, and other areas, either in association with other parties, or, where appropriate, by directly financing development schemes.' The importance of the new organisation was emphasised by the BR chairman, Sir Henry Johnson, when he elected to take the chair of the Property Board himself. C.R. Smith became managing director.

The new board assumed responsibility for the sale or management of all non-operational property and, where possible, for earning maximum revenue from operational property. The latter function was shared with the regional general managers or subsidiary company boards, which otherwise relinquished their property responsibilties. The regional estate surveyors now became regional managers under the Property Board, responding direct to their own managing director.

'Operational' land was defined as that which was needed for current or future operational purposes, obviously needing continuing involvement of the region or the subsidiary in daily management. Here, the Property Board's role lay in negotiating and managing commercial transactions with outsiders on behalf of the operator. 'Non-operational' property, on the other hand, comprised land and structures no longer required by the railway for its business. When Sir Henry Johnson retired, J.M.W. Bosworth, a BR Board member, briefly occupied the chair until 1972 when R.L.E. Lawrence (later Sir Robert Lawrence) took over. P.R. Dashwood, who had been the eastern regional surveyor and then, on the formation of the Property Board, Chief Estate Surveyor, was made property director. Smith retired and for the first two years Lawrence combined the positions of chairman and managing director until 1974, when Dashwood assumed the latter post. Considerable organisational changes took place which served the new organisation well for a number of years, but before looking at its work it is necessary to record some of the major development schemes that were completed before the Property Board was formed.

Property Development, 1961-74

Railways have always attracted varying degrees of public criticism, with equally varied degrees of justification, or none at all, and during the late 1960s, following the demise of Railway Sites Ltd, British Rail was blamed for lack of an enterprising land development policy. A leading Scottish developer declared that urban railway buildings worth thousands of pounds were becoming derelict because buyers would not accept BR's terms. Another prominent figure called the railways 'the scourges of city centres', owning 'industrial poison left by their property departments', which were accused of being lazy and inefficient.[5] For a hitherto back-room department that rarely came to public notice, this was strong stuff. Transport and environmental pressure groups used a different form of attack, alleging that private groups interested in taking over lines threatened with closure, or lines already closed, were prevented from doing so by being quoted inflated prices for land and installations. In the case of the Waverley Route, BR retorted that it had waited six months for evidence of financial backing which in the end was not forthcoming, and had lost £60,000 for its pains. While some of the strictures were justified, the Estate Department, as with the railway as a whole at this time, could not really win. With changes of government policy, not to mention governments, three Transport Acts and four changes of chairman, all in the space of 12 years, the entire railway industry was in a state of constant change in the struggle to achieve ever-elusive profitability.

Even so, a considerable amount of valuable development work did take place in the years up to 1974. A number of important stations that were reconstructed incorporated commercial elements. The more notable included Holborn Viaduct, Cannon Street and Blackfriars in London, and Manchester Piccadilly, Birmingham New Street, Wembley, Walsall, Southport and Harrogate elsewhere. The new Euston should have had offices above it and an hotel but, just one week after the proposals were submitted for planning consent in 1963, the government announced controls on office development in central London, with the result that only offices for BR's own occupation were permitted. It was 1979 before the two office blocks on the station piazza were completed, and today the station still awaits the superstructure it was designed to carry. Delays also beset the rebuilding of Cannon Street, first announced in 1955. The scheme to retain the old hotel was discarded a year later when structural faults dictated its demolition. In the event, failure to obtain planning consent from the City Corporation meant starting again, and it was 1963 before E.M. Barry's hotel was demolished. The new building was opened progressively between 1962 and 1965, although the temporary wooden offices at the front remained until the street was widened and a new Underground station entrance and ticket office could be completed. The final phase was finished in 1974, 19 years after the scheme started.

Birmingham New Street was completed in 1967 and, with Cannon Street, marked the era of partnership schemes that Railway Sites Ltd had been set up to promote. New Street was financed by Norwich Union Insurance and Cannon Street by Town & City Properties. Two new stations of this period, Leeds and Bradford Exchange, did not include commercial development but incorporated railway offices and a bus interchange respectively. The site of Liverpool Central, on the other hand, was virtually a total commercial development, in association with Viking Properties. The main line station was closed and the only remaining railway operational requirement was enlargement of the underground station and a new ticket hall for Merseyrail. Other early major station reconstructions like Plymouth, Coventry, Sunderland and Stafford included relatively little commercial development, although successful schemes were carried out at or close to stations at Barking, Bracknell, Gunnersbury, Richmond, Cardiff Queen Street, Bristol, Southampton and Southend. What could have been profitable participation in development on the old Victoria station site at Nottingham was a victim of BRB's campaign to raise cash from sales.

A start was made on selling railway houses, accelerated after Beeching, and the upsurge in surplus land resulting from his policy enabled between 6,100 and 7,000 acres a year to be disposed of between 1968 and 1973. The years 1970-3 saw £64 million realised. Some railway hotels had already been sold as part of post-nationalisation thinning out, but largely at the insistence of Philip Shirley, who brought in American consultants, a new one was built by British Transport Hotels. The first new railway hotel for 30 years, the Old Course Hotel erected on the site of former engine sheds at St Andrews was opened in 1968. With 68 rooms, all *en suite*, it was much the largest and most up-to-date hotel in the district and should have been a success, but it wasn't and in 1982 was sold as part of British Transport Hotels privatisation. The closure of the railway to St Andrews in 1968 is unlikely to have been a significant factor in the hotel's failure, as motorways were then spreading through Scotland and in 1964 the Forth road bridge gave vastly improved access to Fife, so the time should have been ripe. The main cause, it appears, was failure to obtain golfing rights or package terms on the public courses, which in a place like St Andrews would seem to be essential.

The Lawrence Decade
Robert Lawrence went to the Property Board from being general manager of the railway's London Midland Region. He was a professional railwayman, having started as a traffic apprentice on the LNER in 1934. He was also chairman of a number of BR subsidiaries: in 1978 he chaired British Transport Hotels until it was wound up, and National Freight Corporation from 1979 to 1982. He sat on the main BR board from 1971 until his untimely death in 1984, having been a vice-chairman from 1975 to 1981, and was knighted in 1980. But it was as chairman of the Property Board that he probably made his greatest contribution, for it was his enthusiastic advocacy that finally brought Cinderella to the ball by breathing new financial life into BR.

Primarily Lawrence was an operating man, brought up in the long tradition that the railwayman's first priority was running the trains, with the timetable as his Bible. He was a wise choice. Lawrence entered his new world with zest, seeing his operating background as a positive advantage when combating railway management's long-established and somewhat uninterested attitude to ancillary activities like estate. To railway property management he brought a new, dynamic approach. To gain the results the government and BRB were demanding, Lawrence realised that the Property Board had to take the initiative. The slow emergence of the regional estate departments from their traditionally passive role had to be accelerated, quickly. Property was booming, and he could see that in its legacy of disused city centre freight yards and, to a lesser extent, its large passenger station sites, British Rail was sitting on a potential gold mine that he was determined to exploit. In that sense, he was the right man at the right time.

Lawrence immediately set about restructuring his new organisation to shape it for its revised role. Having established a close working relationship with P.R. Dashwood, he strengthened regional managements and gave greater delegation, tightened up the budgeting system and generally created a more enthusiastic outlook. In 1974 the property regions were increased from the five (originally six) that corresponded with the railway regions to seven. With the exception of Scotland and the Southern Region, this put regional estate surveyors into smaller administrative areas that gave closer contact with local business and municipal communities. Staffing was reorganised to provide a full range of services and expertise in each region, and promotion prospects were improved in order to help retain senior surveyors by providing more challenging work. The Board's financial function was changed and it became fully self-accounting at the beginning of 1975.

The newly formed Property Board had a big challenge in getting its philosophy accepted inside the railway industry, and in building a new image in the outside world. It was essential that it should not be seen as a revived Railway Sites Ltd under another name. Hardly had the new programme been announced than there was more criticism, this time for 'giving away' valuable assets. In 1973 Richard Marsh, the then BRB chairman, published his Policy Review in which he asked the government for a £1,700 million investment grant over ten years. Within days, the *Observer* of 8 July published a long article on the Property Board's proposals for developing London's termini, contending that if only the Board did its own development work, instead of in partnership with the private sector, the railways would not have to share the proceeds which, in total, could well exceed the figure for which Marsh was asking. Dashwood, in what must have been an unenviable interview, explained the need for outside entrepreneurial expertise; the authors did not accept it, pointing to the current Blackfriars scheme which the Property Board was successfully doing itself. Although they acknowledged that the particular circumstances were unlikely to be repeated elsewhere (see p218), they still argued that Blackfriars was a clear demonstration that the skills were there, obliquely suggesting that only numbers were missing. They might have added that the BR salary scales within which the Property Board operated possibly had some bearing on it. The article concluded that the blame lay in a governmental policy which did not allow a nationalised industry to engage directly in commercial development. In reality, it was a revival of the old argument about the advisability of giving a railway powers to develop its own land.

Lawrence's organising ability was accompanied by a dominant personality which he did not hesitate to use in overriding his former general manager colleagues when he felt that BR's financial considerations warranted it. This approach was particularly necessary when negotiating the transfer of surplus operational property to the non-operational portfolio; in other words, he persuaded the operators and the engineers that in property terms they could manage with less, whether in giving up a piece of land with high development potential in favour of some with lower value, or realising the commercial value of a prime station site by transferring non-essential railway activities to a less significant location, thereby releasing space for letting or land for sale. Lawrence saw that the £20 million a year being contributed to BR's accounts from land sales in the 1970s could not go on indefinitely without a drastic review and thinning out of operational land requirements. In the years 1978 to 1983, for instance, sales outstripped transfers from the operational estate to the extent that the stock of non-operational land for disposal was down by about one-third. Achievement of his objective needed persuasion of a high order, which is where his first-hand experience of railway working proved to be invaluable.

In 1979 there was renewed government pressure on British Rail to keep within public expenditure cash limits. Estate policy at that time was one of 'Optimum Management', a professionally based, prudent policy that combined sale, where it was seen to be in the best interests of the railway, with retention and development where long-term income and capital appreciation indicated a better return. But there was now heavy political influence to increase sales for short-term advantage and British Rail turned to the Property Board to contribute in excess of £15 million a year towards its finances.

The government's privatisation policy also dictated the sale of British Transport Hotels, the railways' shipping and hovercraft interests and other subsidiaries, calling for yet more complicated demarcation arrangements, and in 1980 BR decided to set up a wholly owned subsidiary called British Rail Investments Ltd as a vehicle for their disposal in a manner that would enable them to expand and develop free from public sector controls on investment. BRIL was also instructed to take over the sale of existing non-operational railway property, together with 10 major post-war developments that were built on or over operational land, including London Bridge, Blackfriars and the Euston office blocks. Disused lines were excluded from the non-operational remit, but the inclusion of what had hitherto been considered operational property, because of its proximity to the working railway, forced the operators into a drastic reappraisal of their criteria. It also meant that provisions to safeguard the railway had to be carefully written into contracts of sale.

The story of the disposal of the hotels has been recorded elsewhere,[6] and in retrospect there seems little logic in setting up a separate property-selling arm of BR, leaving the relatively recently created Property Board — which had hardly been unsuccessful by any yardstick — with a residue of non-operational property, mainly disused lines, that were either hard to sell or of low value. Ostensibly, BRIL was intended to prepare the way for the introduction of private money into the property placed under its wing, but in practice the work was done by Property Board staff anyway, as BRIL comprised only a board, with few personnel. It seems probable that the creation of BRIL was a political manoeuvre to show that something positive was being done to comply with government demands. At all events, as selling agent for BRIL the Property Board quickly placed greater emphasis on its sales policy, to the extent that in October 1984 BRIL was declared a moribund company and the Property Board was again securely in control.

Most of the hotels went in 1983, when a record £71 million was earned from total sales — twice that of the previous year — and letting income increased by 9 per cent, netting a total of £103 million for BR. Hovercraft and shipping interests were also sold in the following year.

From the outset there had been no non-executive directors on the Property Board, but to assist this rapid change in attitude Lawrence brought in several figures from the property world outside the railway, to strengthen his board and senior management. Up to this time he had concentrated on improving the standing of his surveyors, within the railway service and in the professional field. To do this required a change in attitudes not only of the surveyors themselves, but those of the railway managers, particularly operating men and civil engineers. Lawrence encouraged the estate surveyors to take a more positive approach, and as it grew apparent that the result brought in more cash for BR the railway surveyor's reputation rose steadily, inside and outside the industry.

New external influences brought new ideas and revived old, long-forgotten ones. Property auctions were organised, unheard of in railway disposals since 1937-8 when the LNER and the LMS held some. Indeed, in many ways the Property Board revitalised the land auction business. Its first auction in Scotland, for instance, was also the first large-scale property auction of any kind to be held there for fifty years, and in 1986 the sale of West Ealing good yard and some adjoining land realised the then highest single lot price in Great Britain. For the Property Board there were several advantages: the whole system of disposals was speeded up, creating a faster flow of sales which in turn created a steady cash flow for BR and a big improvement in financial forecasting, all with existing resources. This happy state was not achieved, though, without more hard bargaining and persuasion directed at railway management.

One of the biggest stumbling blocks was the system of obtaining clearance for the transfer of operational land to non-operational status, preparatory to its transfer to the Property Board for disposal. 'Clearance' meant securing the agreement of every department that had any conceivable interest, a process that by the traditional written memorandum took many months. Instituting round-the-table meetings expedited the operation, and when the railway managers realised that the entire aim was to generate cash for the railway that would not be forthcoming from elsewhere, with a good chance of helping their own projects forward, they took a much more flexible attitude to land disposal.

In March 1980 Dashwood retired and was succeeded by Gavin Simpson, a Property Board director who had previously been Southern regional surveyor. Then, on 8 October 1984, Sir Robert Lawrence died suddenly. On 1 January 1985 he was succeeded by Sir James Swaffield, as non-executive chairman. Sir James was a former Director General of the Greater London Council, and had a distinguished career in local government as well as being a member of public advisory bodies. He took over at a difficult moment. In September 1984, a few weeks before Sir Robert's death, the Monopolies and Mergers Commission was instructed by the government to enquire into the efficiency and costs of British Rail's property activities. For the next seven months BR's property management, particularly the Property Board, was under the closest scrutiny.

The Monopolies & Mergers Commission Report

The Commission reported to the Secretary of State for Trade and Industry in April 1985 and its report was published in June.[7] Its terms of reference were summarised as 'requiring us to review and assess the Board's husbandry of [its] large estate of land and property', including the use of air space over land. The report's 190 pages gave a detailed account of the Board's activities, in which a number of criticisms were made, together with 43 specific recommendations for improvement. Overall, however, the shortcomings were not deemed to be sufficiently serious to operate against the public interest. Despite a high turnover of professional staff in the middle levels — largely due to difficulty within the BR framework of meeting external salary levels and conditions, and, at lower levels, a considerable volume of routine work that was unattractive to potential high-flyers — the Property Board's staff was found in general to be conscientious. Higher up, it was felt that staff risked being 'outgunned' by their opposite numbers in the private sector, resulting in a somewhat cautious and defensive approach. To some extent, therefore, the Property Board's sales and development record, while attracting a degree of commendation, was thought in some areas to be patchy. The injection of more outside marketing skills, possibly by using private sector estate agents, could, it was considered, be beneficial.

In the Commission's view the key to improvement lay at the top, within the British Railways Board. There the Commission found that the railway was, in effect, run by a group of board members and senior directors known as the Railway Executive, on which the Property Board was not represented, a feature which the Commission flatly described as 'not good enough'. Indeed, the lack of a direct line of communication between the Executive and the Property Board, and failure by the executive to appreciate the need to direct property strategy at that level, attracted explicit criticism over and again. Between the lines of the report was a fairly powerful implication that, provided the annual flow of cash was maintained, the Property Board generated little interest except when more money was needed. This attitude applied particularly to the Property Board's declared policy of Optimum Estate Managment, causing the Commission to wonder whether pressure from the government, through BR, to raise cash from quick sales was being applied at the expense of steady long-term income. BRIL sales were cited as a case in point. An arbitrary schedule was set by the Railways Board, but was later modified when it was realised that it put the Property Board at a bargaining disadvantage. 'It is difficult to believe that these sales so far have yielded as much as they might have done.' Similar issues arose over the portfolio of residual property in which BRB accepted the Property Board's need for flexibility, 'provided again that their cash requirements are met'. The Commission was careful to emphasise that although the Property Board's policy could not override the government's, and that in any case a consideration of that policy was outside its terms of reference, the issue was not simple. Scope for enhancing values by not selling immediately required analysis, to make BRB and the Department of Transport fully aware of the effect of timing on BR's finances. In the Commission's view, BR tended to exaggerate the importance of property sales in meeting government targets for state subsidies, suggesting that they did not really affect the outcome.

British Rail's cash objectives should be flexible enough to absorb variations in annual property income in order to gain the full benefit of using maximum market advantage: 'BR's short-term cash needs can be pressed too far . . . they should not see themselves . . . needing cash so urgently that they are justified in liquidating property immediately at almost any price.' Again, 'to dispose of surplus land and concentrate on the main business is sensible; to do so in an ill-considered way and risk unnecessarily incurring loss is not.' In short, Optimum Property Management received implicit approval from the Commission, with more than a suggestion that the Property Board's professional advice should be more closely heeded. At the top of its list of recommendations, the Commission advocated the appointment of a Director of Property as a full member of the Railway Executive, 'responsible for maximising the return from the whole estate'.

A second implied but no less recurrent theme recalled Sir Robert Lawrence's struggles with the railway establishment. The Commission remained unsatisfied that surplus land was promptly indentified and transferred to the Property Board. 'There is substantial evidence that in the regions the need to obtain clearances from numerous operational interests has been a common cause of serious delay and sometimes of negative attitudes.' Property strategy should be 'actively managed rather than left to an interplay of interests.' Progress, the Commission declared, lay in 'adequate motivation of the operational interests in British Rail', and emphasis on regional and area managers' responsibility for making the most of the property in their charge. The 'clumsy and protracted' procedure for releasing land was criticised, as were the restrictive conditions that on occasions might be imposed, for instance, on customers using BR sidings in which they were asked to accept a long-term rental agreement in exchange for a short-term undertaking to provide a rail service, pin-pointed as a weakness in co-ordinating freight service marketing with the necessary property transaction.

The Commission's approval of the Property Board's successes in sales and development was tempered by the suggestion that on occasions the Board seemed to prefer the easy way, being 'too ready to enter exclusive arrangements', instead of going for 'a greater element of competition'. The report pointed out that a high proportion of sites was developed in this way instead of being put out to competitive tender, and that development briefs could have greater impact if common private practice were followed in gaining outline planning consent before a site was placed on offer, instead of leaving it to the developer. But, in general, the Property Board was found to be exploiting its opportunities, although the Commission was not convinced that the full potential was being explored, and recommended that independent valuations should be obtained for the more valuable sites rather than risk being put at a disadvantage by accepting a potential developer's estimate.

The Board's initiatives in station trading and refurbishing viaduct arches (p232) were commended, although there seemed to be scope for 'improved marketing', and there was general approval of the management of the 'linear estate' — the use of the railway for pipelines and cables. Again, as elsewhere in the report, greater use of the private sector received firm advocacy. The Commission gave thoughtful consideration to the Board's liabilities for what it sympathetically called 'Burdensome Properties', in the possession of which BR is unique. These comprised non-operational land with little or no development or sales potential, such as closed lines for which the railway has a continuing statutory responsibility to keep adequately fenced and drained, to maintain in safety structures such as bridges, tunnels and viaducts — particularly the last — and works involving bridges carrying roads not transferred to the highway authority. The onerous effect of listing by the Department of the Environment, the Welsh Office or the Scottish Office, and the whole issue of the railway's responsibilities in this field was questioned. The Commission saw a clear analogy with the Public Service Obligation grant for uneconomic passenger services. The Board's policy of selling such property at a loss if future relief made it worthwhile was approved as the only possible solution in many cases, but the policy of 'minimal maintenance' was felt to be possibly short-sighted. A more sophisticated maintenance policy based on estimated whole-life costs was suggested as perhaps being better in the long term, and the accuracy of current estimated future liabilities was questioned. Small rents, that is those up to £50 per year, mainly wayleaves, produced revenue of over £0.5 million a year less than the cost of collection, an unsatisfactory position that nevertheless had to be accepted. Beyond welcoming the Board's new guidelines and urging it to do everything possible to improve the net return, the Commission was unable to offer a solution.

Turning to internal management affairs, the report recommended improved costings and common planning and control systems in the Board's regions, improved staff supervision (complaints about delays seemed to be well-founded) and better performance measurement. The Commission concluded that the Board was not achieving good value for money under its purchasing system, which should be based on wider tendering. The report's final recommendations concerning personnel management were rather woolly; it admitted that pay relativities made it difficult to compete with the private sector, particularly in the senior ranks, but could offer little by way of remedy within overall BR policy beyond hoping that British Rail's job evaluation scheme would afford some relief, and — again — suggesting greater use of the private sector.

The fact that the government ordered the enquiry did not imply that the Property Board was thought to be inefficient or was operating against the public interest.

Within the public sector the Commission is commonly used as a form of check. As part of the democratic process the nationalised industries have periodically undergone its scrutiny, either wholly or in part, although inevitably the terms of reference have reflected the attitudes of the government of the day. In that sense, therefore, it was the Property Board's turn. Viewed in retrospect against the background of the historical attitudes the Property Board inherited and encountered during its 15 years in business, the Commission's overall verdict can be seen as one of qualified approval. The strongest criticism was directed at the British Railways Board; the rest of the recommendations, although numerous, hardly amounted to a serious indictment. Most were relatively mild, some were leavened with sympathy and others were clearly influenced by terms of reference over which the Commission had no control. Having regard to the sheer size and diversity of BR's estate — it ranks among the twelve largest — its countrywide spread and large volume of low-value property, the report, while not providing grounds for complacency, gave the Property Board a reasonably clean bill of health.

Optimum Estate Management
Despite the main Railway Board's periodic moves to override the Optimum Management policy when cash demands became acute, the Property Board managed to keep it more or less intact, a course which received underlying endorsement by the Monopolies Commission. As the Commission appreciated, the big problem lay, and still lies, in the huge imbalance of the railway's estate, of which only 10 per cent can be compared with the bulk of property commercial holdings and from which, moreover, the Property Board derives some 85 per cent of its income, producing yet further imbalance.

In exercising this policy the Property Board has to consider three principal alternative forms of action, of which the first, to sell, is applicable only to non-operational property. Here, opportunity is the key: finding a purchaser to whom the site in question is attractive. This is easier said than done. If the land is a depreciating asset or has expensive liabilities, sale is the obvious answer but presents equally obvious difficulties.

Taking a closed line as an example, its linear nature, often in a relatively remote location, means that unless by good fortune the highway authority has an eye on it for a new road or an improvement scheme, the only likely buyers are farmers. Even then the site is only of value if it forms a useful means of access or can be easily incorporated into adjoining land without bulldozing embankments and filling in cuttings; this is not often the case, and so the railway may have to pay the landowner to relieve it of the liability. Otherwise, disused country railways may be suitable only for a footpath or cycle track, given sufficient local authority enthusiasm, as we shall see in the next chapter (p253). Some sections of old line have been incorporated into realigned or widened roads, although generally they are fairly short sections with no major engineering structures, for even a double-track railway is far too narrow for a trunk road. One of the first was the Heads of the Valleys road in South Wales which

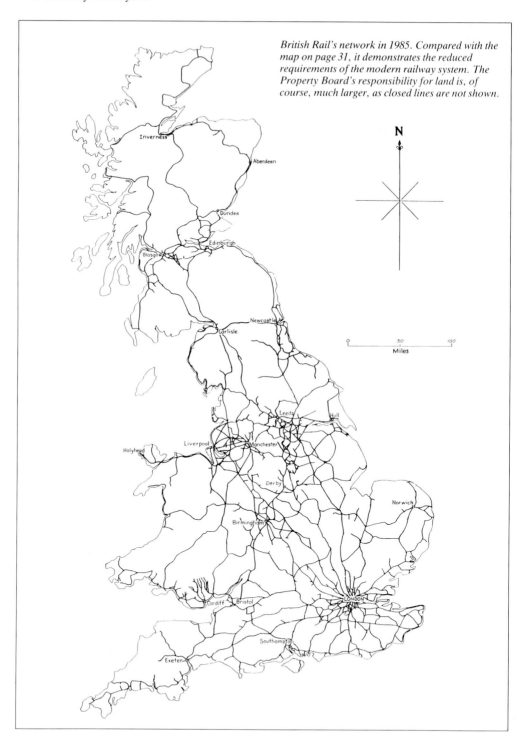

British Rail's network in 1985. Compared with the map on page 31, it demonstrates the reduced requirements of the modern railway system. The Property Board's responsibility for land is, of course, much larger, as closed lines are not shown.

uses part of the Abergavenny–Merthyr line — but not, significantly, sharply curved sections, viaducts and tunnels — while straight, well-graded portions of the line between Tebay and Ravenstonedale made an ideal replacement route for several miles of the narrow, winding A685 trunk road between the M6 and Kirkby Stephen. Recently, much of the North Wales coast road has been built on railway land alongside the line which, in some instances, has been realigned to make space. At Lenton, Nottingham, it was possible to relocate some sidings to release land for a new road.

Even a broad tract of land may be commercially unsaleable if, as in the case of Alloa marshalling yard in Fife, it comprises 70 acres of poor, unattractive, marshy land with the added disability of being zoned as green belt. Also in Scotland, green-belt zoning affects the sale prospects for the former Cadder yard east of Glasgow, while the nearby Lenzie yard, also afflicted by poor ground conditions, has the added problem of no access. Such sites may be suitable for a country park, as has been done at Aberdare in South Wales, or as a nature reserve, which will be considered in the next chapter (p253). Absence of access is usually due to the land being 'rail-locked', and is a particular difficulty that can be overcome only by building a bridge over or under the railway, with associated road works. The successful £16.5 million sale of former Great Central land for a hypermarket at Neasden in north-west London was dependent on new roads and access bridges, although here the proximity of the North Circular Road helped to make the site sufficiently attractive for the developer to carry out the works, once the Property Board had secured planning consent and executed the design work. Land enclosed within a triangular junction poses the same problem, to overcome which usually needs a combination of the right circumstances. This happened at Portsmouth where suitable ground, in an area of high economic growth possessing good external communications, induced the developer and the local authority to finance jointly a bridge. In all cases of commercial sales, the Property Board endeavours to retain a financial interest by means of a 'claw-back' clause in the conveyance, linked to any future financial gain the new owner may make.

In 1986-7 a major rationalisation of BR's London headquarters released for sale the offices at 222 Marylebone Road (the former Hotel Great Central), and disposal of leases on Melbury House nearby and, at Euston, Rail House, Stephenson House and a building in Cardington Street. This was done by concentrating the headquarters' offices at Paddington station and Euston House, the old LMS headquarters in Eversholt Street, and by sending the Western Region head office to Swindon and the London Midland to Birmingham. All the new locations were on BR freeholds.

The creation of the Tyne & Wear Metro involved sales of a unique kind: the transfer of complete sections of working railway from BR to the Tyne & Wear Passenger Transport Authority under the Tyneside Railway Act, 1973. The Act gave the PTA powers of acquisition, but left it to the parties to agree terms. By taking over BR tracks the PTA was saved the cost of building its own and, therefore, in

BR's eyes was acquiring a valuable asset. The PTA saw it differently; it was relieving BR of a loss-making liability which it was already subsidising. A compromise was agreed whereby the PTA compensated the Property Board for loss of future estate revenue. Even so, there were many complications to overcome before railway departmental clearances could be given and the statutory rights and responsibilities transferred. The transaction was caried out in six phases, each of which was treated as a separate legal entity, and the fourth was signed only a week before the official opening by the Queen in November 1981. On part of one of the lines an added complication was created by the Newcastle & North Shields Railway Act of 1836. Under it the Duke of Northumberland and other landowners were granted a share of the tolls on coal, a measure intended to protect their wayleave interests in wagonways which the railway threatened to supersede. In return the railway company was granted a 999-year lease. Failing sufficient coal traffic to cover the payments, passenger traffic receipts could be called on to contribute. The present Duke still owned some of the freehold, a difficulty which had to be resolved before the transfer could be made. A somewhat similar procedure was followed when operational lines and disused viaducts in east London were transferrred to the Docklands Light Railway in 1984-5. Where the light railway runs alongside BR tracks on viaduct, BR continues to carry out structural maintenance.

The second of the Optimum Management alternatives comprises two specific options — to retain or to manage — and in general is applied to land on or alongside the railway. If the land is already leased or let, the management option requires potential for income growth, or development potential if it is not. A policy of retention requires a high degree of inspired foresight, political awareness and persuasive argument to justify keeping property, on the grounds that the railway itself may need it at some time in the future. It was fortunate that this policy had been followed in respect of the two Snow Hill lines, both disused and trackless for close on twenty years but now brought back into use, the one in London to make the new 'Thameslink' between main lines north and south of the river in 1988, its Birmingham namesake in 1987 to form part of BR and the West Midlands Passenger Transport Authority's cross-city 'Midline'. But these were exceptional, and in any case consisted of virtually inaccessible viaducts, cuttings and tunnels, although the Birmingham scheme was accompanied by above-ground development of the Colmore Court office complex on the site of the old station (p236).

Retained land, whether for management or for future railway use, frequently carries so many disabilities as to make retention virtually obligatory. They range from historic statutory liabilities, rights of way, lack of services, redundant structures and low rental potential resulting from poor past investment, to operational restrictions that have to be imposed to ensure safe working of the railway; these will be more fully discussed in chapter 9.

Property Development, 1974-90

The third alternative under Optimum Estate Management combines retention and

Railway revival in Birmingham: the new Snow Hill station with a multi-storey car park above and the Property Board's Colmore Court office development in the background. Part of the PTA's Midline, it is planned to continue the tracks in the foreground along the former Great Western Railway trackbed to Smethwick. Snow Hill is an example of property development paying for a new station.
(BR Property Board)

development, either commercially when there is sufficient prospective income growth, or to meet a clearly proven need for additional railway infrastructure as opposed to possible need under the second alternative. The increasing pace of commercial partnership schemes since the 1970s, accompanied by the regeneration of derelict land, has been accompanied by a growing collaboration with local authorities, in some cases as a third partner. One of the first local authority joint schemes, in 1981, comprised a small industrial estate on the site of Sutton-in-Ashfield goods yard and locomotive depot in Nottinghamshire, a collaborative venture by the Property Board and the district and county councils, and the forerunner of more. Liaison with other public bodies has followed, notably the Scottish Development Agency, which has led to a variety of projects, like the rebuilding and development of stations such as Oban, and outright purchase of the old Great North of Scotland Railway station at Elgin (a listed building). A partnership of the Property Board, the SDA and local authorities has resulted in the establishment in Glasgow of STRIDE — the St Rollox Industrial Development Enterprise. Financial assistance by the SDA and local councils enables small businesses to set up in the old Caledonian Railway works. The Property Board has refurbished them and undertaken maintenance, and lets the units at low rents.

Similar work has been done at the former Horwich works in Lancashire in conjunction with local authorities, at Ashford and at Swindon, at all of which the Property Board acted on behalf of British Rail Engineering.

Commercial partnerships of all kinds and sizes increased during the 1970s and '80s. An early scheme was the replacement of Blackpool North station by a new, smaller one on the site of the old excursion platforms in 1974, enabling the station site to be sold to a supermarket chain, thus providing money for the new station, a method that has been repeated elsewhere. At Weston-super-Mare the opposite happened. The station has been retained and the excursion platforms in Locking Road have been released for supermarket development. Smaller parcels of land have been relinquished at Henley-on-Thames, where in 1985 a new station was financed by selling surplus goods yard land for an office block, and at Windermere where the passenger train shed was converted into a supermarket and a new station built at the rear. At some places it has been possible to cut back a station at the end of a branch line to release land and generate cash for a new station, as was done at Epsom Downs, St Ives and Looe. Developing former goods yards in town centres has been particularly attractive to property companies, among them Hull Priory and Keighley in Yorkshire, both for supermarkets, and Birmingham Hockley for industrial use. Many have been developed as part of inner-city regeneration and renewal schemes, notably Vermont Street, Glasgow, where 1.6 acres of the old Kinning Park goods station was reopened as an industrial estate in 1980, in this case wholly designed, financed and managed by the Property Board with the aid of British Rail's Scottish Region architects. Direct investment was introduced into the conversion of 10 acres of the former Barrow Road locomotive depot at Bristol for light industry and warehousing, including the removal of a bridge. In Birmingham, the former Central Goods station site now contains Post Office and Mercury telecommunications offices, and Stanier House accommodates BR's London Midland Region headquarters. Top of the list in financial terms are Aberdeen, where a new shopping centre was completed in 1984 at a cost of £20 million, and in the same year Preston Butler Street, at £17 million including station improvememts.

These years saw further steps taken in developing the commercial potential of stations themselves, among which Blackfriars was a landmark in being the only such scheme which British Rail has funded direct. In this case there was an adjoining landowner anxious to develop — King's College, Cambridge — and a customer for a new office building on the combined sites, neither of which individually was large enough. Special government permission was required for BR's direct investment in property it did not already own, which, because the financial argument was indisputable, was granted, enabling the Property Board to form a partnership with King's. The government acquiesced because the circumstances were unusual and not likely to be repeated. The building incorporates a new station entrance and concourse.

Next in the capital came London Bridge, not before time. Almost since the first station was built in 1836 it had been a byword for inconvenience that grew worse

Typifying a modern Railfreight terminal is Theale in Berkshire, where the commodities handled by rail include petroleum and lubricants, cement, limestone and sand. The leasing arrangements, handled by BR Property Board for Railfreight, bring in rentals of over £300,000 a year. (BR Property Board)

with each successive change, so that when work finally started in 1970 the station was by far the most confusing and disreputable in London. Oldham Estates had already built a tower block on the forecourt in the mid-1960s, and now a leasing deal was made with Peachey Properties for a new entrance, concourse, bus station and office tower, accompanied by some rearrangement of the platforms. The basic layout could not be changed, but a new footbridge, linking for the first time all the platforms, gave London Bridge some cohesion.

The use of air space over a station, pioneered in this country at Birmingham New Street in the 1960s but which failed to materialise at Euston, was revived at Victoria. The station was only slightly less chaotic than London Bridge and, like it, at the 1923 grouping had consisted of two stations side by side which the Southern Railway tried to make into one. Work following the Second World War was piecemeal, what with planning problems, indecision over the Channel Tunnel, use as a terminal by successive airlines, development of the Gatwick Airport link, and above all, the station's historic role as the principal terminal for the Continent. In 1980 work started on phase one of the Property Board's largest development scheme up to that time, when a concrete raft was built over part of the western side of the station platforms between the concourse and Eccleston Bridge, half way down the station, to carry Victoria Plaza, a six-storey office block and shopping mall, in partnership with Greycoat London Estates at a cost of £45.5 million, including £8.6 million for the station works. A £13 million office block was also built on the Wilton Road side of the station. Phase two continued the raft eastwards as far as the listed arched roof which stopped further extension. Later phases in progress cover the air space between Eccleston and Elizabeth Road bridges and at the outer end of the eastern side roof.

Fenchurch Street was next for the air space treatment where, in association with Norwich Union, a £28.5 million scheme for a five-storey block of unusual pyramidal

The listed front of Fenchurch Street station in the City of London has been restored in connection with the provision of a new station for Network SouthEast and offices above, which discreetly appear behind the façade. (BR Property Board)

design was finished in 1987. The new concourse and ticket hall made a big improvement. By far the biggest scheme so far promoted by the Property Board is the 4 million square feet Broadgate development at Liverpool Street, using the air space of the eastern side of the station and the site of Broad Street station next door to finance the much-needed modernisation. Broad Street had seen a steady decline in traffic for some years, but the frontage block was listed, as were the offices and the western train shed at Liverpool Street. Strong controversy arose over the proposals. Battle was joined with conservation groups anxious that both stations should be retained intact; ultimately Broad Street and most of the Liverpool Street frontage buildings had to go, but the unique western train shed was not only kept but is being extended southward in similar style, using modern materials, to cover an enlarged concourse. The work enables the barrier line to be straightened and the old confusing platform layout will disappear. The office complex is the largest ever undertaken in Europe and was carried out by Rosehaugh Stanhope Developments. It generated not only money for the station works and a substantial surplus for BR, but paid for the new Graham Road spur that brought North London line trains into Liverpool Street, allowing Broad Street to be closed in 1986. It is anticipated that the entire scheme will be finished by the end of 1991. It is a successful demonstration of how, given the initiative and will, a compromise can be worked out between site development, station improvement and conservation, with cash from the first paying for the other two. Although in some ways it was a pity to lose the Broad Street frontage, in historical terms it was far more important to retain and, as seems likely, enhance the western train shed at Liverpool Street.

Two new factors came into play at Liverpool Street. The boom in demand for City office space following the 'Big Bang' of the mid-1980s was accompanied by the start of the Canary Wharf development in London Docklands, which the City planners feared might tempt firms to move out. So they were more sympathetic over granting planning consent for the development, a final reversal of the policies that bedevilled Cannon Street 20 years earlier. In fact, the final scheme for Broadgate was larger than was originally hoped for. The latest air space schemes are now under way at Charing Cross, again with a shop and office complex over the platforms, and over the northern entrance to the North or Monument Lane Tunnel at Birmingham, linking developments on either side of the line.

It has proved much more difficult to do something about the largest single area of railway land in central London, the combined King's Cross and St Pancras sites, which are unusual in containing two large, listed passenger termini still very much in use. Besides extensive former goods, coal and mineral yards at the rear of each station, the area is intersected by lines into St Pancras station and King's Cross Freightliner terminal, roads and the Regent's Canal, and contains pockets of private property and a number of listed structures. Railway lines also form two of the boundaries. One of the largest plots was formed by Somers Town goods station, alongside St Pancras, and after some years as a very scruffy car park and a coach station it is now being transformed into the new British Library. Smaller parcels of

The new passenger concourse at Liverpool Street station under construction as part of a £125 million investment, which forms part of the proceeds of the 4.2 million square feet Broadgate development. At the end of the train shed is a 468,000 square feet office building, constructed on a huge arch over the platform ends, designed by Skidmore Owings Merrill and developed by Rosehaugh Stanhope Developments Plc. (Wordsearch/Alan Williams)

land have gone to local authorities for residential and light industrial development, not all of which has been proceeded with. The largest remaining area is occupied by the former York Way goods depot of the Great Northern Railway, virtually intact and comprising large, down-at-heel Victorian railway warehouses and sheds occupied by a variety of tenants. The difficulties are great. Ambitious overall development schemes were submitted by three consortia of developers, all exhibited at a public showing. The chosen scheme, which also needs the acceptance of other property owners involved, also has to take into account the proposed Channel Tunnel terminal and the cross-London rail link, both of which add to the complexities and are the subject of a parliamentary Bill. So all that is certain at this stage is that the controversy the proposals have raised will undoubtedly continue, at a considerably higher intensity than at Liverpool Street.

Meanwhile, refurbishment and development of the numerous arches under the Midland lines and St Pancras station is actively proceeding, while after many years of neglect an imaginative scheme has been produced to convert the listed former Midland Grand Hotel that fronts the station back into an hotel. After planning delays it now (March 1990) seems likely to proceed. Rightly considered to be Britain's finest Victorian secular building, it is to be hoped that this latest plan will give St Pancras the sympathetic restoration it needs and deserves.

While the largest station development partnership schemes have been in London, there has also been a number of important ones in the provinces. Swindon, Watford Junction and Reading are among the largest, while air space over the platforms and cutting at the north end of Aberdeen station has been used to create part of the 180,000 square foot Trinity Shopping Centre. Reading has been the largest outside London so far, with 200,000 square feet of floor area developed in association with Prudential Assurance. Opened by the Queen, it incorporates the listed station building. A number of major developments started at stations in 1988 included retail space of 200,000 square feet at Welwyn Garden City and 20,000 square feet at Ilford.

How have these large station developments been received? Those built in the 1960s comprise mainly multi-storey office blocks typical of the contemporary functional style which is now receiving criticism. Birmingham New Street has been condemned by rail users. The old narrow platforms on the north side were retained, reached by equally narrow stairs and escalators. The way to them from the shopping centre above is difficult to find, and as it is at first-floor level while the platforms are literally in the basement, passengers have to go up from the street and down twice to reach the trains. Externally, there is hardly anything to indicate that it is the station for Britain's second city.

There has been criticism, too, of the loss of the traditional lofty train sheds that air space use brings about. Platforms beneath rafts produce a sense of confinement that even ingenious lighting cannot entirely dispel, particularly noticeable at New Street, Wembley and Victoria, and which one commentator has likened to arriving by train at a cellar, repeated at Fenchurch Street and Liverpool Street. At the latter it contrasts strangely with the lofty, cathedral-like proportions of the retained area of roof. Because air space has not been used at London Bridge, the station is the most successful in that sense. The arched roof over one half has been kept, and over the other new, generously proportioned awnings have replaced the old ones. The design of the concourse and forecourt, too, is successfully original.

Flanking Buckingham Palace Road, behind the restored hotel and offices that front Victoria, the dignified stone colonnade is listed and therefore had to be retained; it sits uneasily beneath the overpowering mass of glitzy stainless steel and reflective glass that makes up Victoria Plaza. Fenchurch Street is immeasurably better. The offices over the platforms are stepped back with increasing height so that, while maintaining a distinctive outline from a distance, they are almost unseen behind the listed 1856 façade that was restored in a remarkably successful manner, retaining the essential charm of Railway Place, the small, intimate square fronting the station off Fenchurch Street proper. It is too early to comment on the post-modernism of Broadgate, but the extension to the western train shed at Liverpool Street and the design of the new entrance towers that set it off look set fair to complement handsomely the Great Eastern Hotel and the new development.

At both Victoria and Liverpool Street the train-shed roofs are boxed in by the tall buildings alongside, with no great aesthetic loss, but it seems a pity that the ones across the outer ends block the view that was so important a part of their perspectives. When Charing Cross is finished the platform area will be all 'cellar' — indeed, the air space could not otherwise have been used — and the design at platform level has already been likened to a 'letter box'. But at least, from across the river, the arched glass roofs over the shopping complex preserve the classic railway station outline, even if they do not light the platforms, forming an interesting throwback to the original roof that so disastrously collapsed in 1905.

The latest scheme for a London terminus, announced in January 1990, links a new office and residential development on surplus land and the site of Melbury House with the refurbishment and improvement of Marylebone station. Melbury House itself, a typical 1950s building that has encountered structural problems, will be demolished. The keynote of the new building is stated to be harmony with the surrounding area, which includes a number of listed buildings and is dominated by the former Hotel Great Central, currently undergoing restoration. The station frontage will be cleaned, the elaborate iron-and-glass *porte cochère* renovated, and the decorative iron railings and gates that originally enclosed the forecourt replaced.

The Property Board has been linked with several Civic Trust and other awards for new developments, notably King's Reach at Chelsea, built on the site of the old West London Railway basin, Cannon Street and Aviemore.

Organisation and Results
In September 1986, having seen the Property Board through the Monopolies and Mergers investigation, Simpson retired and Douglas Leslie became managing director. He was one of the men brought in by Lawrence from outside the railway

The new development above Charing Cross station, Embankment Place, seen from across the River Thames. A raft built over the station supports nine levels of accommodation with an area of 347,000 square feet. Designed by Terry Farrell & Co, the development has been undertaken in conjunction with Greycoat plc. (BR Property Board)

Members of the BR Property Board, the body responsible for estate management policy and administration, photographed at head office in Hamilton House, part of the Broadgate development in the City of London. From left to right, standing: David Lawrence, John Mayfield, Robert Gardner, Patrick Scutt, Peter Moakes, Alison Murray. From left to right, seated: Ian Northen, Einion Holland, Sir James Swaffield (chairman), Douglas Leslie (managing director), Peter Spriddell, Philip Chappell. Geoffrey Powell was not present.
(BR Property Board)

service, and had successively been regional estate surveyor in Scotland and in the Eastern Region before becoming deputy to Simpson. He took charge of an organisation which by 1989 was administering an estate of 173,500 acres with a gross rental of £82.5 million a year. That, as *The Times* of 24 June 1989 put it, made British Rail Property Board one of the top five, maybe even three, landlords in Britain. The organisation which had worked well for 12 years was now streamlined further, in order to serve British Rail even better.

Mammoth schemes like Broadgate and Charing Cross were being undertaken, and early in 1989 controls of these and similar developments in the provinces was centralised. The key Eastern and Southern Regions of the Property Board, between which London had been split, were put together under a single director. Close involvement with the private sector was strengthened by the decision to use private resources for up to one-third of the corporate services the Property Board provides for British Rail, part of the change to competitive tendering that was brought in at the same time, and removing its exclusive rights to act for BR.

The results for the seven years up to 1988-9 are shown in the accompanying bar charts and speak for themselves. The 1987-8 figures came from 1,702 separate sales and 95,100 separate tenancies, leases or wayleaves, impressive figures when balanced against a staff that had been reduced to 737 from 944 five years earlier; a

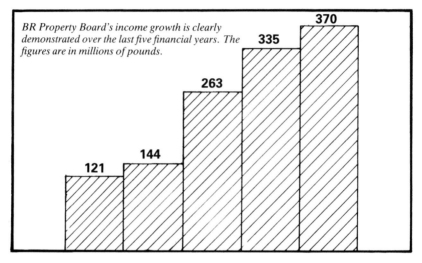

BR Property Board's income growth is clearly demonstrated over the last five financial years. The figures are in millions of pounds.

work-force in 1988 that was handling a country-wide development programme of £957 million. British Rail Property Board now operates virtually autonomously within BR, making a life-supporting contribution to its balance sheets. In that sense, Cinderella has indeed found her glass slipper.

As one of Great Britain's leading developers, the Property Board shares part of the collective responsibility for the dramatic changes in our towns and cities over the last three decades, which now provoke arguments approaching the Victorian 'Battle of the Styles' that was so fiercely fought in the days when earlier railway managements were prominent patrons of architecture. There the similarity ends. The new railways of the 1840s and '50s, conscious of their emerging power, were prepared to spend money on prestigious buildings to display their intense pride in achievement. Now it is the other way round. The tower blocks and shopping malls that are covering the yards and stations built by the Victorians provide investment money that helps to develop the railway. As in all modern commercial developments, every square foot is vital. The point was made to some purpose by the architect Richard Rogers in an address in March 1990.[8] Whatever the present-day arguments, the visual, social and environmental results will receive a true and detached assessment by posterity.

Chapter 9

The Working Property Board

Gavin Simpson had been largely responsible for building up the Property Board's sales programme. On his succession Douglas Leslie's main task was to consolidate and accelerate the work done by Lawrence, Dashwood and Simpson in establishing the successful dual strategy of skilful private-sector marketing while converting railway operators and technical staff to new thinking on the use of property, as highlighted by the Monopolies and Mergers Commission. Most managers now appreciated the benefits to be gained from giving up valuable operational land where alternative sites were available; some were starting to advance their own ideas for Property Board approval. Meanwhile, estate management and sales remained core regional activities, supported by a range of technical services that included building maintenance, land survey and drawing office work, the custody of deeds, personnel, finance and, of course, the traditional but vital land management services to the railway regions on subjects like wayleaves, leases, statutory rights, legal agreements and town planning. Property development, dealt with in the last chapter, was centralised at headquarters, with regional representation, together with station trading which was seen as needing new impetus.

Incorporating a modern newsagent, stationers and bookshop into Crewe station was a challenge successfully achieved by John Menzies, providing a facility much used by changing passengers as well as those starting their journeys at this famous mid-Cheshire junction.
(BR Property Board)

Station Trading
Historically, station trading comprised bookstalls, refreshment rooms and little else, except for sweets, tobacco and fruit kiosks, and a few other businesses at larger stations (see p187). The increasing number of station modernisation programmes from the early 1970s led to some modest expansion of the kiosk-type unit, like theatre ticket agencies, bureaux-de-change and heel bars, but it was close to the end of the decade before station trading was looked at with an entirely fresh eye that saw it as a major source of revenue which, with imaginative handling, could improve a station environment and add life to the concourse. When Travellers' Fare was divorced from British Transport Hotels the opportunities increased. In 1976-80 shops on stations were bringing in £800,000 worth of new income a year, marking the beginning of a new concept that proved profitable to the railway and to traders alike.

Station trading was made a separate Property Board division in 1985, with emphasis on service, not just convenience to passengers. A marketing campaign called 'Action Stations' promoted the idea of flexibility, whereby traders could operate under licence, a negotiated tenancy or a lease, although the officially preferred method was rental as a percentage of turnover, reviving the system pioneered in 1876 (p189). Shops built into new barrier lines between the concourse and the platforms replaced the old railings and advertising hoardings. The first of

*The modern demand for fast food is illustrated by the
new Travellers' Fare Foodcourt at London's
Liverpool Street station.* (BR Property Board)

Maximising station income: a former toilet beneath the concourse at London's Waterloo station makes an attractive bar/bistro, providing an excellent service for home-going commuters as well as a regular clientele.
(BR Property Board)

these new features appeared at Waterloo, followed at the same station by conversion of redundant areas under the offices opposite, including a smart French restaurant in what had been a basement 'Gents'.

These small units have proved popular with specialist traders concentrating on high-volume sales in a small space, like Tie Rack and Sock Shop, which started on stations and have now spread into the high street, becoming well-known names. The traditional bookstall has become a walk-in self-service store, and at a number of large stations it is now possible to buy a wide range of goods, from pictures and computers to fast foods and records. Several multiple traders have been persuaded to come in from the high street, part of the drive to encourage the use of stations as shopping centres for the general public as well as the traveller.

The process continues, although not all concourses are adequate for more than one or two shops, while others have unsuitable layouts, and barrier lines are not necessarily an improvement for the hurrying passenger trying to identify a platform. Euston now has an attractive combination of peripheral and free-standing units which is a big improvement on the former, somewhat haphazard layout. The row of shops on one side of the broad island platform at Edinburgh, which has no concourse as such, is less so. The bright red moulded plastic and glass units are fairly tasteless, do nothing for their surroundings and have not been a commercial success. On the other hand, the Caledonia Centre on the concourse at Glasgow Central is an environmental triumph. The dignity of the listed curved wooden structures has been enhanced by careful conversion to shops, restaurant and bar, with new additions entirely in keeping, and is the greatest credit to the Scottish railway architects who designed it. Small though it may be by shopping mall standards, it is one of the Property Board's most successful station concourse schemes. Others are nearing completion at Reading and Manchester Piccadilly at the time of writing, with more planned. In 1988-9 the Board earned over £26 million in gross rentals from over 2,000 trading outlets on and alongside stations, a three-fold increase in three years, and the policy is rapidly being extended to smaller stations such as Lincoln and Beverley, with considerable success.

Underneath the Arches

Alongside the prestige development schemes that caught the headlines, the Property Board embarked on a smaller but no less enterprising plan to remedy the dreadful legacy of disreputable arches carrying urban viaducts. The letting of such arch space goes back to the London & Greenwich Railway, which was built entirely on a viaduct and let its first arch, probably the first to be finished, in 1834. The intention was to use arches as houses for families dispossessed by the railway, and two six-room demonstration dwellings at Deptford were completed in the following year. Rectilinear façades hid the curves of the arches and, to avoid a row of chimneys along the line, they were heated as well as lit by gas. The company received an offer for the whole of the arches, which would be sub-let, but it was refused, unwisely as it turned out, because the houses were a failure, not least from the noise of trains and penetration of water from the track. Noise also seems to have deterred commercial tenants, as by 1852 only 52 arches had been let out of some 850 available.

Railway viaducts undoubtedly brought about or hastened the decay of districts through which they passed, dominating the smoky slums portrayed by Doré and Tait, and the shady underworld described by Dickens and Henry Mayhew, producing the familiar image of sleazy backwaters occupied by disreputable characters running businesses of doubtful legality, which could be only too real.

British Rail has some 8,000 arches in built-up areas across the country. In 1985 they produced about £14 million in rents. An earlier examination of the rent roll had revealed that income could be improved if arches were made more attractive, with environmental improvements that could well generate further growth. Two initial schemes quickly proved the potential. In 1982 the refurbishment of 20 arches at a coal yard off Walworth Road in south London, complete with a new road called Robert Dashwood Way, had paid for itself in three years, and in 1985 the Grand Vitesse Industrial Centre in Southwark received a Civic Trust award. There, in a triangle of viaducts once occupied by the continental express freight depot, after which the new development was named, seven arches were refurbished and a new building erected on the acre of land in the middle. The Property Board thereupon embarked on a £60 million, 10-year rolling programme covering the whole country.

Above:
Typical of the novel approaches made to arch refurbishment by the BR Property Board is this scheme at Cook Street in Glasgow's Gorbals district. Note the successful integration of security grills as a feature of the trading area, which incorporates a sub-station for BR on piers at the rear of the scheme. Glasgow Central signalling centre towers above.
(BR Property Board)

Below:
The interior of a refurbished arch on the Eglinton trading estate in central Glasgow, in use as a photographic retail outlet, illustrating the versatility of arches. (BR Property Board)

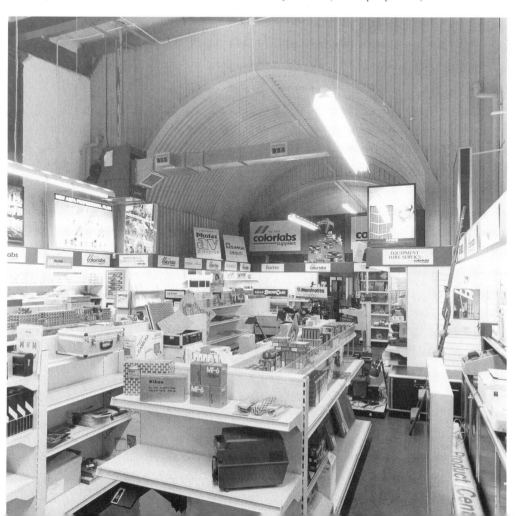

Above:
The Caledonia Centre at Glasgow Central is a major example of the Property Board's development of retail trading on stations. The scheme transformed the well-known 'Torpedo Building', which contained the train indicator, into shops and restaurant.

Below:
The scheme included the construction of a new matching structure with a bullet lift. As the station concourse is used by pedestrians from adjoining streets, the shops and kiosks trade well.

Very appropriately, one of the early ones, the Apollo Business Centre at Deptford, was under part of the old London & Greenwich viaduct, and in 1989 one of the largest schemes to date included 60 arches under the same line at Bermondsey.

These programmes provide premises at low rents for small businesses needing a fairly central location, usually for light industrial use or storage, although in the latter instance care has to be taken to ensure that nothing is done by a tenant that could present a hazard to the railway above. Arches receive attention as leases fall due for renewal, with emphasis on access, services and improved appearance that attract a good class of tenants. Significantly, motor repairers are excluded. Local authorities and government welcome these schemes as fitting into their inner city programmes and job creation schemes, and in a number of places refurbishment has sparked off other improvements. Birmingham quickly realised the implications and offered £12,000 towards listed arches in the city. Grant aid has followed elsewhere, now amounting to some £3 million nationally, locally and from the European Regional Development Fund. So far over 500 arches have been improved out of a total of 1,000 programmed for the immediate future. Not only large cities such as Glasgow, Manchester and Liverpool have benefited, but smaller places like Bath, Worcester and Leamington Spa.

New Stations and New Uses
A large new station on a virgin site is not often built these days. There have been two between 1976 and 1990, Birmingham International and Milton Keynes Central, but there has also been a considerable number of new small stations and the reopening of old ones on a scale that, little more than a decade ago, was thought to be wishful thinking on the part of rail enthusiasts and transport integration ideologists. Birmingham International, opened in 1976, had the advantage that it was built under the terms of the planning consent for the National Exhibition Centre and the land was acquired for a nominal figure. Milton Keynes was a joint project between BR and Milton Keynes Development Corporation in 1982, incorporating a six-storey office block with the station offices on the lowest two floors.

The concept of the parkway station began at New Pudsey, between Bradford and Leeds; it was opened in 1967 to cater for motorists joining long-distance trains without having to drive into either of the city centres. The 'Parkway' name was first used for the new station on the north side of Bristol, strategically placed at Stoke Gifford close to three motorways and opened in 1972. Others followed at Tiverton Parkway close to the M5, replacing the old Tiverton Junction station, and at Southampton. The initial success of Alfreton & Mansfield Parkway, on the site of the former Alfreton station, has not been sustained, largely due to changes in train routing; Bodmin Parkway was simply a new name for Bodmin Road station.

A surge of new stations has come about through the initiative of the Passenger Transport Authorities serving the provincial conurbations. There have been around 90, notably in the West Midlands, West Yorkshire, Greater Manchester and Strathclyde, principally small ones and unstaffed halts built jointly by the PTAs and

BR and usually fitting within existing railway boundaries. They include a fair number of reopened stations on sites that have been brought back into use. In Tyne & Wear the emphasis has been on the Metro system, part new and part on former BR tracks, and in Merseyside on Merseyrail, an extension of the existing BR electrified system with new lines as well, run by BR and the PTA in collaboration.

Tyne & Wear Metro presaged a remarkable development of urban Light Rapid Transit projects. In Greater Manchester the first phase, which will use BR lines from Bury to Altrincham, linked by tramway-type tracks through the central streets in continental fashion, is now under way. A metro scheme in the West Midlands will use part of the former Great Western line, already reopened for BR trains from the south to Birmingham Snow Hill station which, a few years ago, no one thought would ever see a railway again. The station was closed in 1972 and, after some years of dereliction, was finally razed. Fortunately BR retained the site, with the approach tunnel and viaduct, over which has risen the Colmore Court office complex, developed by the Property Board in association with Viking Properties and Sun Alliance Assurance. It incorporates a new four platform station in what might be called the basement, and a further phase, with Speyhawk, is in progress. Close by, a new Moor Street station on the through lines has released the old terminus, the future use of which has still to be determined. Sheffield, Bristol and Edinburgh are also actively promoting LRT, and many others are seriously investigating the possibilities.

Joint projects which release land for development, which in turn pays for the reconstruction of a station, as at Swindon, Watford Junction and others already mentioned in the last chapter (p205), have also been successfully employed at smaller places. Egham station, for instance, has been rebuilt and offices erected on adjacent surplus land, and a similar scheme has been started at Epsom.

The same strategy is pursued at stations which have buildings far larger than are now needed, but which otherwise are perfectly good for continued use. A rearrangement of operational requirements can often release portions for letting, thereby providing revenue that helps to meet the cost of overall refurbishment. If station buildings are listed, careful treatment is called for. Restaurants, wine bars and pubs are popular occupancies – there are widely separated examples at Acton Central, Bearsden, Broadbottom, Denmark Hill, Hadfield and Swanwick. The station house at Horsforth is now a pottery, and there are many examples of conversions to offices — Crowborough, Hale, Wareham and West Worthing among them — while trains continue to call at the platforms. The west wing at Chester's historic station is occupied by the architects responsible for the restoration work. At Gobowen, the charming Florentine station has been excellently restored in conjunction with the local authority and amenity groups after many years of neglect. The waiting room and ticket office have been moved into the former level-crossing gatehouse, which provides ample space, and the main buildings are tenanted.

When a smaller station was built alongside North Woolwich station, the handsome terminal building, which is listed, became surplus. A fire worsened its chances of

Broadbottom station, near Manchester, is an example of a joint venture by the Property Board and private commercial interests. After fire gutted the station house, it was tastefully refurbished by Thornhill Leisure Developments Ltd, at a cost of around £400,000. Too large for current operating requirements, the building was extended in matching style to house a restaurant, pub and tenants' living accommodation, while providing a new waiting room for rail users alongside the booking office, and a car park on the old goods yard. The development won a Railway Heritage Award in 1988.
(BR Property Board)

reuse until the London Borough of Tower Hamlets took it over and converted it for use by the local Passmore Edwards Museum Trust as extension premises, appropriately devoted to exhibits from the Great Eastern Railway. Although very different, two of the most ambitious schemes at operational sites reflect historical themes. Brunel's original terminus at Bristol Temple Meads, again a listed building, has for years been surplus to operational requirements and became a very sad-looking car park, a poor fate for such an important historic station. Full restoration was estimated to cost £2 million, a seemingly impossible task until 1981 when a local group secured financial sponsors, set up the Brunel Engineering Heritage Trust and embarked on a long-term programme of restoration. The local authority helped, and BR Property Board gave £100,000, some professional assistance and 99-year lease at a £1 peppercorn rent.

Above:
Great Malvern station was deliberately designed to integrate into a wider setting. The station, bridges and frontage gardens date from 1862 and form a complete entity which complements the spa town. After a serious fire in 1986 the station was attractively restored with aid from the local council and the Railway Heritage Trust. Most of it is now let to tenants, including the tea-room which, in summer, puts tables out on the platform in continental fashion. This contribution by the Property Board provides income to help the viability of restoration. (A. Davies)

Below:
The Great Western Railway rebuilt Windsor & Eton Central station in readiness for Queen Victoria's Diamond Jubilee in 1897. Now the part that is no longer required for railway purposes, including the former Royal waiting room, has been let by the Property Board to Madame Tussaud's for their 'Royalty & Empire' exhibition, which includes this representation of the Queen and her guests leaving for Windsor Castle. (Royalty & Empire)

Windsor & Eton Central, a station having strong associations with Queen Victoria, was another that had become too large for its traffic. Madame Tussaud's came up with an ingenious plan for a waxworks and audio-visual exhibition portraying events leading to Queen Victoria's diamond jubilee in 1897. It took two years to overcome the opposition of the local council, which seemed to think that Windsor had sufficient attractions in the castle and the river. Then £600,000 was spent by BR on repairs and new rail facilities so that the rest of the station, including the Victorian booking office, large covered cab drive and former Royal waiting room, could be handed over on a 50-year lease. 'Royalty and Empire' opened to the public in 1983.

Planning obstacles had to be overcome in order to convert Ashley station, in north Cheshire, to offices. It was a small rural station, but because it was in a green belt consent was not forthcoming from the planning authority. However, the parish council gave support; they wanted to see the building kept as part of the local scene, not to mention a modest means of creating employment, so the application succeeded, although a later application for extensions did not.

Langley station, on the Western Region main line in Buckinghamshire, is one of the Property Board's latest restoration schemes to provide modern, upgraded passenger accommodation. The redundant portions have been refurbished with assistance from the Railway Heritage Trust, for letting as business premises. (BR Property Board)

London, Chatham, and Dover Railway.

BLACKFRIARS WAREHOUSE.

The DIRECTORS are prepared to receive Tenders for the exclusive use and occupation of one of the Floors of these commodious premises, for a period of not less than six months, commencing August 8th, or such other date as may be fixed upon.

The area of the Floor is upwards of 30,000 feet, it is immediately connected with the Sidings of this Company and the Great Northern and Midland Railways, and there is unbroken communication between it and the Great Eastern, Great Western, London & North Western, London Brighton & South Coast, South Eastern, and London & South Western Railways, and all Railways reached by any continuation of these Lines.

The Floor is provided with ample Hydraulic Machinery, by which Goods are lifted and dropped from and into Railway Trucks on the one side, and it possesses superior street frontage, also fitted up with Hydraulic Cranes, in Holland Street, Southwark Street.

The accommodation is suitable for Warehousing Furniture, Grain, Flour, Hops, Wool, Rags, &c., &c.

Permission to view the Floor can be obtained upon presentation of business card to Mr. W. WALLIS, Superintendent, Goods Department, Blackfriars Station.

Form of Tender can be had upon application to the Secretary, L. C. & D. Railway, Victoria Station.

(By ORDER).

VICTORIA STATION, PIMLICO.

July 12th, 1875.

A London, Chatham & Dover Railway advertisement of a warehouse to let.
(BR Property Board)

This listed former grain warehouse at Burton-upon-Trent has been excellently restored in conjunction with the local council, and now houses small businesses, forming a good example of imaginative conversion of a redundant building.
(BR Property Board)

While it is not easy to find tenants for stations, disused goods warehouses are much more difficult. A number of small ones have found new uses, and one of the best examples in the middle range is the Midland No 2 Grain Warehouse at Burton-upon-Trent, as the repainted lettering proudly displays. Built in 1850, it was sold to East Staffordshire District Council and, after restoration to its original appearance, it is now managed by Burton Enterprise Agency as a series of small workshops and offices. Another, at Huddersfield, is leased to the National Children's Centre. The giants are the most difficult and, if they are listed, even though no alternative use can be found, they cannot be demolished without consent. The huge Deansgate warehouse in the centre of Manchester has now been sold, but the problem remains. It still awaits a use, although not for want of suggestions. Quite apart from its size, the massive construction and the costs of conversion are major deterrents.

Some of the many non-railway buildings that came into railway ownership in the past are listed, too, and require sensitive treatment. A small shop in the Canterbury Conservation Area, dating back to the sixteenth century, was bought by the South Eastern & Chatham Railway in 1901 together with some land it wanted. Liaison between the Property Board, council and a prospective tenant produced a workable restoration scheme that earned a diploma from the Canterbury Society. At Belper, Derbyshire, the Board collaborated with the council by improving a bridge over the line and laying setts, as part of the restoration of what is stated to be the oldest

241

surviving street of industrial housing in England. Close to Watford, one of London's surviving coal dues obelisks standing next to the railway was moved to a new site to prevent vandalism and collapse into the river, half the cost being met by BR's Environment Fund.

A recent and welcome development in station refurbishment is a scheme to improve a series of six stations between Guildford and Hampton Court Junction in a single, co-ordinated exercise. London Road, Clandon, Horsley, Cobham, Oxshott and Claygate were built in a matching style, typical of the London & South Western Railway in 1885, that gives character to the line, worthy of comprehensive rather than piecemeal treatment, embodying respect for distinctive styling and its place in the local environment. The work will release excess accommodation for trading purposes, thereby helping to meet the cost.

Wherever possible, BR seeks the involvement of local communities through its Community Unit, which has been set up to promote and strengthen local links and partnerships, backed by a Corporate Community Fund. Where there are no commercial possibilities, the Property Board is not averse to letting premises for social or community use at an appropriate rent. A form of local association which has proved fruitful to both parties is a station sponsorship scheme, begun at Godalming which was renovated in partnership with the brewers Friary Meux, whose headquarters is opposite. The station was repainted in the brewery's house colours and their name and logo were displayed beneath the name boards.

New use for an old station: Lartington, County Durham, on the old line from Barnard Castle to Tebay, in 1984 has become an attractive private house, with a lawn filling the space between the platforms. The attractions of living in a former station are so high that the Property Board cannot satisfy the demand, particularly as there have been few closures in recent years. (Author)

Subsequently Basingstoke was sponsored by Provident Life Assurance which, like Godalming, won a Railway Heritage Award, and Andover by TSB and Hampshire County Council. Similar schemes are under way elsewhere.

New Lines

When the Euston to Manchester electrification was planned to include the loop line through the Potteries, it was found that the three Harecastle tunnels north of Stoke-on-Trent were in poor condition and had insufficient clearance for overhead wires. So it was decided to bypass them with a new line, 2½ miles long and the first stretch of new main line built for many years. Four new bridges, a 250yd tunnel, a new reservoir and an embankment across two more had to be built, land purchased and, as part of the agreement with the local authority, part of it landscaped as a country park. The new line opened in 1966.

That apart, very little new construction was done in the 1950s and '60s; the emphasis was on closures. But the next two decades saw a small but welcome resurgence of new railways which has brought the Property Board's purchasing powers into play, hitherto not in great demand for a long time. Most of the new lines have been industrial branches, like those to the Ford Motor Company's plant at Bridgend in Glamorgan and, further west, the Milford Haven oil terminal. New running lines needed land to form the Graham Road spur to give access to Liverpool Street from the North London line, the Hazel Grove chord that provides a new route from Manchester to Sheffield via Stockport, and in the same area the long-needed Windsor Link that enables trains from the north west to run through to south and east of Manchester via Piccadilly station, previously possible only by a very roundabout route via Victoria. Although it is only a short line, the dense urban area it traverses required involved negotiations to acquire land that cost £2.8 million. The 3½-mile line to Stansted airport, due for completion in 1990, is the latest major project, including a mile-long tunnel. Manchester airport rail link of 1½ miles is now proceeding and a Bill for a Heathrow link is before Parliament at the time of writing.

The 14½-mile Selby diversion was quite different. It takes the East Coast main line across open country clear of the new Selby coalfield and cost the National Coal Board £60 million in order to allow unobstructed mining under the old line. It was cheaper than having to leave a broad pillar of coal to support it and risk subsidence claims. The Coal Board was offered the old line for disposal, but as they had no expertise in that field the Property Board did it for them, including a substantial acreage bought for materials handling and storage that became surplus after the job was finished in 1983 (see p56).

New works of a kind not encountered for a long time were undertaken when the new Merseyrail tunnels were built beneath central Liverpool in the early 1970s, for which BR obtained a special Act on behalf of the PTA. Liverpool Central main line station had already closed and large-scale redevelopment was proceeding, but the low-level station had to be enlarged. The new line enabled Exchange station to be closed, but the listed street façade had to be retained and, after the site was sold, was eventually incorporated into a new shop and office complex behind it.

A tunnel diversion in completely different circumstances was needed when Penmanshiel Tunnel collapsed in 1979, tragically killing two men working inside it. Although much shorter than Harecastle, the work involved the sudden and unforeseen closure of the East Coast main line north of Berwick while a new 1,100yd line was constructed through a deep cutting, with a temporary realignment of the A1 trunk road pending major reconstruction, all in the space of five months during which work went on around the clock. To meet local authority requirements the cutting sides were landscaped.

BR's long-distance linear land holdings make ideal routes for telecommunications. Here Mercury Communications have erected a transmitting tower on railway land once occupied by Barrow Road engine sheds, Bristol. (BR Property Board)

Another feature of recent years has been the reopening of freight lines to passenger traffic. In one instance, part of a disused line from which the track had been lifted has been reopened for freight traffic. The section of the Whitby–Redcar line from Whitby to Carlin How, on the coast of Cleveland near Skinningrove, was closed during 1958-60. Then valuable potash deposits were discovered at Boulby, near Staithes, and in 1974 Rio Tinto Zinc opened a mine and paid for the relaying of track over some 5 miles from Carlin How, requiring the repurchase of parts that had been sold. The same will be necessary if, as seems probable, British Coal sinks a new super pit at Hawkshead Moor, near Coventry, which will need the reopening of several miles of the Berkswell–Kenilworth Junction line, closed in 1965 and partly sold to the county council. Similarly, the proposal to restore passenger services between Nottingham and Mansfield will need the reinstatement of 5 miles of abandoned railway, ½ mile of which has been obliterated by dumped colliery waste, including the short Kirkby Tunnel. Former railway land will have to be repurchased, more land bought for a new connecting line, and the tunnel will need unearthing, although after one end was dug out the interior was found to be in surprisingly good condition.

Railways can provide lines of communication by other means, too. The attraction of a continuous linear estate under one occupier from Cornwall to Caithness is as obvious to the telecommunications industry today as it was to the telegraph companies in the nineteenth century. Mercury Communications already makes use of British Rail, which is in a strong position to offer long-distance easements for cable laying.

Railways and Local Authorities
Historically, relationships with local authorities were concerned principally with rating, followed by roads, public rights of way and wayleaves. The railway companies tended to regard the authorities as financial predators who saw them as a prolific source of rate revenue, while parishes, local boards and then local councils successively considered that railways were too ready to ride roughshod by invoking their statutory powers. There was considerable justification for both attitudes. Arguments over rating assessments frequently led to arbitration and long-standing, strained relationships.

It was not until the passing of the 1948 Local Government Act that there was any real simplification of the railway rating system, when the principle of standard overall values was introduced in respect of operational railway property, subject to periodic revision, although the normal valuation procedure continued to apply to non-operational property, and appeals are still made. The 1988 Finance Act, which replaced domestic rates by the community charge, also acknowledged the special place of railways by valuing them on a percentage of turnover, to which the national business rate poundage figure is applied, with an adjustment factor.

Since the Second World War, the railways have had to pay attention to planning legislation. Towards the end of the last century most large cities acquired powers for public works which the railways had to heed when they were proposing new lines and stations. But these special Acts were limited in application; it was not until 1909 that the first general Town Planning Act was passed, and only the 1932 Act had any significant impact on railways, bringing estate surveyors into contact with newly appointed planning officers. The far more comprehensive 1947 Town and Country Planning Act formed the basis of post-war planning.

From the beginning of planning legislation, statutory undertakings have enjoyed favoured treatment, including exemption from planning controls for works executed under parliamentary powers or government order, and for minor works on operational land. Certain works are now subject to planning approval, respecting affected roads and certain kinds of structures, and there are restrictions covering new lines, bridges, stations and other buildings, and alterations to the exterior of existing structures. In practice, since the 1947 Act local planning authorities have been consulted on all major works, irrespective of the statutory position, although not, in the past, without criticism of dilatoriness by both sides. For many years the railways were accused of hoarding land by planners who wanted to designate it for more socially useful purposes, not without cause until the railways' attitude changed. Equally, the authorities themselves held up some railway land disposals by procrastinating over decisions on whether to buy it, on which by government decree they had first refusal, and by political indecision over establishing structure plans and local transport policies that were just as frustrating to the railway. In Edinburgh a decade passed before the Property Board was able to dispose of 140 acres of surplus land to the local authorities because they would not make up their collective mind. Delays, from whatever sources, result in vandalism of buildings and general dereliction.

To the general public, one of the most noticeable signs of the railway's favoured treatment is adverse; the number of former goods yards used for what at its kindest can only be called environmentally unfriendly purposes. At how many stations, still used or not, does one see in the adjoining yard an untidy scrap dealer, road haulier or builder's merchant? If it is now closed, the station itself may have disappeared, but is readily identifiable as a site by a blot on the landscape that was once the goods yard. They can be seen everywhere, in town and country, conservation areas, national parks, areas of outstanding natural beauty, or simply spoiling a pleasant landscape. Some may be completely disused and acting as a dumping ground.

The reason lies in the past practice of claiming that tenants' activities fell within the conditions applying to 'existing use', in this case storage, which the railway maintained is what goods yards were used for and which, in broad terms, had not changed with the end of operational use and the letting of a yard to a tenant. This argument has not been overturned. More recently, however, the Property Board has recognised that such locations reflect very poorly on BR and do nothing to promote the environmental image it has been successfully pursuing elsewhere. Unfortunately, it is still frequently blamed for a problem which is no longer the railway's, but the result of past policies of selling surplus yards with little or no development potential, as often as not to sitting tenants. Yards still owned by the railway are now subject to a positive policy of environmental improvement.

The Legacy of History

History is always present at the Property Board. Much of the daily work is governed by legislation, agreements and other legal constraints imposed during more than 150 years of railway operation, reflecting, as they do, the complexities of British land and property tenure that have grown over the centuries. Rights of way are one example from the many interests and obligations that have to be recognised.

When they were first built, the railways were required to provide certain occupation and accommodation works to the requirements of owners and occupiers of adjoining land, as already outlined in chapter 4. They included, among other things, level crossings, gates, bridges, culverts, fences, ditches, drains and watering places for cattle, and were intended to reduce the effect of severance of land by the railway. As an interesting sidelight on the obligation to fence railways, the Animals Act of 1972 made owners responsible for livestock escaping on to a highway, putting on them the onus for keeping their land securely fenced, but not in the case of railways.

Occupation bridges and crossings were required where the railway crossed an existing private road or footpath. Nowadays, when alternatives are available, the railway seeks to abolish accommodation and occupation crossings by agreement, in order to reduce maintenance and attendance costs, while the majority of public road crossings have now had their gates replaced by remotely controlled or automatic lifting barriers. Electrification and resignalling work provide opportunities when this is particularly desirable, although negotiations have to be started well in advance. For example, when the West Coast main line electrification north of Crewe was being planned and resignalling dramatically reduced the number of signal-boxes, the railway wanted to abolish Lambrigg Crossing box on the Lancaster & Carlisle line. It was no longer needed as a signalling block post, and the signalman's only other function was to operate the gates on a very minor public road that saw little use. Negotiations went on with the county council for several years, culminating in the railway agreeing to pay for a replacement road under the nearby Docker Viaduct, at a cost of £38,000, which was cheaper than building a new bridge or, long term, than continuing to pay a crossing keeper or installing and maintaining lifting barriers. The single payment enabled the railway to be rid of a liability once and for all.

Where station approach roads and footpaths were built by the railway, the responsibility usually remains, either by statutory provision or by agreement, and sometimes includes lighting. Railway-owned bridges on approach and other roads are sometimes called side bridges; there are two at Hebden Bridge station, in West Yorkshire, crossing the Rochdale Canal and the River Calder. In Lancashire, the Midland Railway in 1911 replaced a footbridge over the River Lune alongside Halton station, on the line from Skipton to Morecambe. Ironwork conveniently recovered after rebuilding a bridge at Lancaster, not far away, was used to make a

*The signalman unlocks the gate at Lambrigg
Crossing on the West Coast main line north of
Oxenholme, Cumbria, in 1972. In order to close this
little-used crossing, Property Board surveyors faced
the challenge of persuading the highway authority to
divert a public road — not easy, even for a very
minor one — and agreed to pay for a replacement
road beneath a nearby viaduct.*
(BR Property Board)

road bridge and thus improve access from Halton village on the opposite bank. Tolls were charged, collected by the station staff, and although it was narrow and of light construction the bridge was perfectly adequate for the traffic of the day. When the station was closed in 1966, the railway had the choice of employing a toll collector or freeing the bridge which, as traffic was light, was the cheaper option. The bridge still belongs to BR but now carries more traffic than was ever intended, as it forms a convenient short cut to the M6 motorway, with consequent increases in maintenance costs. The Property Board would like to hand it over to the county council, but negotiations so far have been inconclusive.

A classic case concerns the four-arch stone bridge across the River Swale built by the York & Newcastle Railway to connect Richmond, North Yorkshire, with its new station, which was opened in 1846. Nowadays the bridge carries a main road. The county council maintains the structure, but BR is still responsible for the cost. Yet the railway to Richmond closed in 1969 and the nearest is now 12 miles away. At Derby the railway was more fortunate. The ornate iron bridge that took the Great Northern line across Friargate became redundant after final closure in 1967. Because of its decorative features it was listed and the town council took it over for a nominal £1, with a lump sum endowment from BR towards future maintenance.

Not far from the bridge at Halton an accommodation bridge across the West Coast main line south of Lancaster is twice the normal width. It was built at the boundary of two properties, where both owners insisted on separate bridges, so it was cheaper to build one broad one with a third parapet along the middle as a demarcation line. When the headroom had to be raised for electrification, the bridge was rebuilt in the same manner. Oddly, there is a similar one across the Lancaster Canal less than 3 miles away; perhaps it prompted the idea to the railway in the first place.

Several important railway bridges carry footpaths as well. Best known, perhaps, are Charing Cross railway bridge over the Thames and Barmouth Viaduct, where the footpath provides panoramic views of the estuary and the mountains. Until the new road bridge was built alongside it, Runcorn Bridge across the Mersey carried a footpath. It is still there, but now closed, the original rights having been extinguished under the Act for the new bridge. Teviot Viaduct, in the Borders, carries an unusual early wrought-iron footbridge at the base of the piers. The former East Lancashire Railway bridge crossing the River Ribble at Preston has not carried trains since 1972, but British Rail is still responsible for the footpath, which the 1847 Act stipulated should be constructed 5 feet wide on the east side. It is a good example of how legislation concerned to establish a public facility in return for large-scale private works has, by its very attention to detail, restricted a public body in making sensible changes a century and a half later. BR wishes to move the footway on to the main deck of the bridge and alter the steps at each end, which have become unsafe, but to do so it has to seek parliamentary repeal of the original powers.

The railway does not always own the land crossed by bridges and viaducts. To save money a few were built by obtaining an easement from the landowner, in return for a wayleave which is still paid by BR. The London, Chatham & Dover Railway viaduct at Strood, in Kent, is a case in point, where BR does not own the land beneath the arches. Sometimes the landowner insisted; the influential Bridgewater estates in Lancashire and Cheshire for long refused to sell freeholds to railways in respect of bridges, insisting on wayleaves which BR still pays to the present owners. The Castlefield viaducts in Manchester, and parts of the approach viaducts to the Runcorn Bridge, cross what was Bridgewater land and are subject to wayleaves; in the case of Runcorn other portions of the viaducts are freehold.

Most railway-owned piers were sold when BR disposed of its shipping interests, but a few ferry piers were retained. New Holland pier became redundant when the Humber Bridge was opened, and has been leased as a jetty, with a conveyor laid over the old railway tracks. Starcross pier in south Devon has been sold to a local firm that operates the ferry to Exmouth, and Gravesend Town pier, dating from 1834 and bought by the London, Tilbury & Southend Railway in 1884 for its Tilbury ferry, was bought at auction for conversion to a restaurant after the ferry moved to the nearby West Street pier. The small stone pier alongside Loch Awe station on the Oban line had been disused since the early 1930s and the station closed in 1965. Both have now been brought back to life, the station in 1985 in partnership with a holiday association which owns a guest house close by, and two years later the pier, which was leased to a local enterprise that has brought a steam launch back to the loch as a tourist attraction, connecting with the trains in traditional fashion.

For many years the railway owned a short pier at Arnside in Cumbria, built by the Furness Railway after a court action by local shipping interests following widening of the viaduct and permanent closure of the opening span that formerly allowed vessels up the Kent estuary to the little port of Milnthorpe. The railway also built a new road and sea wall along the shore. Eventually the highway authority adopted the road and the parish council bought the pier in 1983, leaving BR still owning the sea wall, which has only recently been taken over by the county council.

The recent introduction of Radio Electronic Tokenless Block signalling on lightly used single lines has required access agreements for radio masts erected off railway land. The agreement for a mast on the slopes of Ben Wyvis, overlooking the Kyle of Lochalsh line in the western Highlands, prohibits access at certain times during the grouse-shooting season.

Ancient rights periodically surface. Every five years the Property Board receives a bill for its share of the repair and insurance charges on the chancel of Steeple Claydon church in Buckinghamshire, together with 16 other local landowners. Their liability originates from an enclosure Act of 1795 granting exemption from tithes in return for assuming the upkeep of the chancel. A somewhat similar provision at Melton Mowbray, Leicestershire, in 1760 gave rise to a court case in 1980 in which all the 'rectorial owners', including British Rail, were deemed liable to contribute to church repairs. In examples like this the liability passes down from one landowner to another, in the railway's case from the original purchaser of land for the line.

Legal obstacles to the closure of certain stations were noted in chapter 4 (p100). They can also affect a proposal to close a whole line, among which the most celebrated case is the Bluebell line in East Sussex, part of which is now operated as a preserved railway. The Act of 1878, which authorised the amalgamation of the local company building the line with the London, Brighton & South Coast Railway, contained a clause calling for at least four trains a day at stations at West Hoathly, Horsted Keynes, Sheffield Park and Newick & Chailey. Stations at these places were duly built, but when services were withdrawn in 1955 local residents took action to enforce the clause and a year later services had to be resumed. British Railways had to obtain another Act before it could close the line in 1958.

The Cornwall Minerals Railway Act, 1873, was even more onerous. If the railway closed the Treamble branch, it was required to reinstate and restore the land to its original state within 12 months should the adjoining landowner, Lord Falmouth, so desire. The question first arose when the line was closed in 1917, but in 1925 the Great Western decided to relay the track and reopen it. The point cropped up again in 1952, more than two years after the last train, although the track was not lifted until 1956 when the British Transport Commission paid £100 under a deed of release, enabling the land to be sold as it stood.

Defective legal work in the past can create present embarrassment. It has caused difficulties in two instances in Scotland, and in one case deprived BR of a considerable amount of money. When the Portpatrick Railway bought land from the Earl of Stair in 1857-8 it appears that the railway's legal entitlement was not properly documented, which was not discovered until BR came to sell the land after the line was closed. Fortunately, the Act empowering the Portpatrick Railway to purchase and take possession was accepted as proof of entitlement. The railway was not so fortunate when it came to selling part of the Speyside Railway back to the successors to the original owner, the Earl of Seafield. The lawyers discovered that although the Great North of Scotland Railway in 1863 had paid £4,190, a deed to transfer ownership was never executed. In 1984-5 BR contended that the provisions of the Strathspey Act of 1861 and the payment gave a right of ownership, but the court thought otherwise and the land reverted to Seafield Estates gratis.

The tendency of the courts to uphold old agreements, despite changed circumstances, was illustrated in 1971. In 1920 the Midland Railway let 100 square yards of land at Luton for £1 a year 'for the term of one half-year and so from half-year to half-year'. The agreement contained provision for termination by either side by giving three months' notice, but the railway could only exercise it if it needed the land for its undertaking. BR wanted to charge a more realistic rent in line with 1970 values and took the case to appeal on the ground that a valid tenancy agreement required certainty as to its duration, which clearly was not present here, but the court ruled that payment of the rent in accordance with the terms automatically renewed the agreement for six months and, as BR freely admitted that it did not require the land for its undertaking, the railway could not otherwise terminate it.[1]

The Problem of Closed Lines

Only about 852 route miles of closed lines remained unsold in 1989, out of an original 11,000. About half of that residue represents a hard core of unuseable linear estate. Structures, earthworks or pieces of valueless land make it almost impossible to give away. If one adds the accompanying legal obligations, the result is a continuing problem that seems unlikely to be fully resolved. Certainly Parliament would not relieve the railway of statutory obligations bearing on public safety, represented by disused bridges, tunnels and viaducts, without there being an equally responsible body to hand them on to, of which at present there is no sign.

In the light of these disabilities, therefore, and the awkward, often unattractive shapes of quite a lot of the land, the disposals so far have been no mean achievement and have exercised considerable ingenuity. The sheer number of landowners fronting on to a stretch of line has accentuated the task. The 10 miles from Peasmarsh Junction to Slinfold, in Surrey, for instance, had 253 separate adjoining owners with whom to negotiate. Help with piecemeal sales has been arranged by forming consortia of purchasers for a bulk sale, as the National Farmers Union did on two lines in Somerset, and estate agents have been used for the same purpose elsewhere.[2]

In all cases care has to be taken to ensure that in ridding itself of one liability, the railway does not create another. This has happened in the past, particularly over access. At Catesby Tunnel on the old Great Central line through Northamptonshire, land sold at one end left BR with access only at the other, which subsequently caused difficulties in dealing with flooding in the tunnel from drains damaged when the ballast was removed.

The Property Board has sold old trackbeds for a variety of uses. Examples are the tyre-testing tracks for Dunlop on 4½ miles of the Leicester–Rugby line, several touring caravan sites where stations once stood, such as Notgrove in the Cotswolds and Aberbran near Brecon, refuse disposal sites (not altogether popular), a shooting gallery in Devizes Tunnel, while at Woodhead, between Manchester and Sheffield, one of the tunnels has been used to carry a high voltage power line to avoid damaging sensitive landscape. Tunnels, in fact, although posing problems of their own, as often as not can simply be sealed which, if made vandal-proof and subject to periodic inspections, is an inexpensive and safe enough means of resolution, although the liability remains.

One of the disused Standedge tunnels through the Pennines between Manchester and Huddersfield has postulated a unique problem. There are four parallel tunnels over 3 miles long and comprising, briefly, a canal tunnel opened in 1811, the original single-line railway tunnel slightly above and to one side of it, opened in 1849, a second single-line tunnel and a subsequent double-line tunnel, on the same level. All are interconnected by cross passages, and the canal tunnel serves to drain the railway tunnels and to provide ventilation by means of its vertical shafts. Only the double-line tunnel is now in use (one of the single-line tunnels carries a fibre optic cable), and since the ending of steam traction ventilation is not so important. The canal and the railway were both owned by the LMS before nationalisation, after which, for some reason, no demarcation agreement was made between the Inland Waterways and Railway executives. The railway went on maintaining the shafts, presumably because it was the prime user after the canal closed in 1944, although the canal tunnel clearly belongs to the Waterways Board which carries out what maintenance is necessary. Then in 1986 a proposal was made to investigate the reopening of the canal tunnel as a tourist attraction in connection with the work being done by a restoration society, thus raising the question of which nationalised body was responsible for the shafts. BR said it no longer needed them and suggested that the cross passages might be a joint responsibility. If the tunnel does come to be reopened, British Waterways will require statutory authority to amend the Act of abandonment, for which proper demarcations will be a prerequisite.

In recent years a number of sites have become important wildlife habitats, and the Property Board has collaborated in a big way with conservation bodies to ensure that they are safeguarded for the future. This policy was publicly launched in 1986 when the chairman, Sir James Swaffield, handed over 10 recognised wildlife sites to Sir David Attenborough on behalf of the Royal Society for Nature Conservation. They ranged from 5 acres in a triangle on lines at Syston, near Leicester, to 17 acres of the Humber foreshore at Brough, 13 acres of marsh forming a Site of Special Scientific Interest at Stafford and the deep Goldicote cutting near Stratford-upon-Avon. Five more followed, making a total of 190 acres, and the process is still continuing.

As long ago as 1937 the LMS set a precedent for turning a disused railway into a footpath, when it handed over the track of the narrow gauge Leek & Manifold Light Railway to Staffordshire County Council to form 8½ miles of splendid walking through the spectacular Manifold Valley on the edge of the Peak District. The same area was in the forefront of post-Beeching conversions, led by Derbyshire and the Peak Park Planning Board in making the High Peak Trail on 17½ miles of the old Cromford & High Peak Railway, the Tissington Trail on the Ashbourne–Buxton line, and the very fine walk from Rowsley through Monsal Dale on the old Midland main line to Manchester, which with others adds up to well over 50 miles of paths. County Durham has bought over 70 miles of disused lines for long-distance paths of high scenic value. There is the Wirral Country Park which uses the West Kirkby–Hooton line as a 12-mile spine; at Stoke-on-Trent the Tunstall Greenway on part of the North Staffordshire Loop Line, an urban lung for walkers, cyclists and equestrians; and an 18-mile footpath between Shoreham and Baynards in West Sussex. In all, 32 English counties have railway footpaths or bridleways, amounting to well over 400 miles. There are less in Wales, which seems a pity considering the beautiful routes taken by many of its former lines, although the path along the Mawddach estuary from Morfa Mawddach to Dolgellau deserves mention for its panoramic views. Scotland has a number, including the 16-mile long Speyside Walkway from Ballindalloch to Dufftown, and 15 miles in the western Highlands from Dunblane to Lochearnhead.

To an organisation called Sustrans goes much of the credit for turning old railways into cycle ways. It aims at a country-wide network. A registered charity, Sustrans works with the Property Board, local authorities and national organisations like the Countryside Commission and, first, the Manpower Services Commission and now the Employment Training scheme, to promote and manage conversions. The physical work was often done by Community Programme Teams, and the local authorities took over the responsibility for bridges and other structures. One of the first successful schemes was the conversion of the line from Bath to Mangotsfield, north of Bristol, into an easy cycle route between the two cities. Part is now a railway again, run by a preservation society, with the cycle path fenced off alongside. Others have followed, including a start on 13 recommended in the Scottish Railway Path and Cycle Route Project Report published by the Scottish Development Association in 1985. One, from the centre of Glasgow to the foot of Loch Lomond, uses a disused railway and a canal towing path. Sustrans also has a long-term scheme for a route from Glasgow to Killin, using old lines for part of the way. The portion from Callander to Strathyre was started in 1987.

The best-known single co-operative project between the Property Board and Sustrans has been the conversion of the abandoned portion of the East Coast main line between Selby and York after the Selby diversion was completed (p 243). The section between Selby and Riccall was taken by the Department of Transport for a new bypass, leaving a purchaser to be found for the 7 miles onward to the outskirts of York. The biggest obstacle was the swing bridge over the Ouse at Naburn, which, although fixed for many years, was still in its original form and represented a heavy liability. Local councils showed no interest, so it was decided to dismantle the swing bridge and transfer the others to the highway authority, so that the land could be sold to landowners, with whom negotiations were well advanced. Then, at the

*Railway to cycle-way on the former Midland
Railway between Bristol and Bath, the Property
Board's first joint venture with Sustrans. Track has
also been relaid alongside 1½ miles of the cycle-way
by a preservation group to form the Avon Valley
Railway, based on Bitton station.*
(BR Property Board)

Above:
The former Penmaenpool station on the closed line alongside the Mawddach estuary in north Wales, seen here in 1989, exhibits four different features of disposal. The wooden toll bridge on the left, once owned by the railway, has been sold to a private owner; the signal-box in the centre distance is now an RSPB wildlife centre; the station building on the right has been incorporated into an adjacent hotel; and the trackbed itself is now a public footpath, while the signals are an interesting reminder of the site's original purpose. (Author)

Below:
The disused Smardale Gill Viaduct, formerly on a North Eastern Railway penetrating line in Cumbria, is a classic example of the problem of maintaining a remote Grade II* listed structure that over 130 years has become an integral part of the landscape. Now a local trust has been formed to acquire and restore it, with substantial financial help from the Property Board, English Heritage and the Railway Heritage Trust, under a scheme which will be the forerunner of others. (Author)

The restored Ingrow station on the Keighley &
Worth Valley Railway in West Yorkshire, the first
fully equipped line to be sold outright to a
preservation group, in 1990. The station was
dismantled and transported from Foulridge,
Lancashire, and re-erected here. The Property
Board contributed additional materials.
(David C. Rodgers)

eleventh hour, when contracts were being prepared, Sustrans produced a proposal to acquire the line for a footpath and cycle way. The overriding question of liability for structures was solved by Selby District Council agreeing to act as guarantor for the legal obligations and convenants, while Sustrans organised MSC labour. The Property Board was able to fund capital works from the sale of surplus land and negotiated an astute bargain with a contractor working on York ring road to concrete the swing bridge deck in return for a free supply of ballast from the line. On these terms the line was sold for a nominal £1, producing an asset to the area that satisfactorily met all legal requirements.

The most appropriate disused railway transfers are those that have been made to preservation societies. There are now 44 organisations operating significant stretches of line, and a number of museums and steam centres operate at former BR depots and yards. The oldest, the Bluebell Railway, has run a public service since 1960; the longest, the West Somerset Railway, at 20 miles, began in 1976. Originally regarded, perhaps, as amateurs playing with trains, that has never been the case. The Department of Transport agrees to grant a Light Railway Order only when it is sure that onerous conditions of public safety can be fully met. Collectively the private railways are now big business, some of them sizeable companies in their own right in the worlds of tourism and 'heritage'.

The preserved lines' representative body, which sets standards and arranges collaboration, the Association of Railway Preservation Societies, also organises the prestigious annual Railway Heritage Awards for outstanding work in structural restoration; the sponsored scheme is open to volunteer, private, public and commercial interests alike, including BR, which also gives major support and has won many awards.

The Railway and Conservation

In 1961 Britain's first and finest railway monument, Philip Hardwick's Doric Arch at Euston, fell to the demolition men, an act of corporate vandalism which an appeal to the Prime Minister in person did not prevent. Other notable stations, large and small, disappeared at this time: Glasgow St Enoch, Dundee West, Nottingham Victoria, Tamworth and Shalford, to name a very small number, all with their own individual characteristics. Others were closed and left to deteriorate. But, like most catastrophies, Euston marked a turning point. The national outcry at its destruction without doubt saved many other historic railway buildings, notably St Pancras, and in the early 1970s a marked change took place in BR's attitude to its heritage. There was increasing external pressure to have important railway structures listed as being of historical or architectural importance by the relevant government departments in England, Scotland and Wales. Some were even declared Ancient Monuments, giving them the highest form of statutory protection. British Rail realised that in many instances repair and conservation were cheaper than rebuilding, and won it friends into the bargain, so the Property Board set about seeking new occupancies for redundant buildings. As a result, the past 15 years have seen a growing number of excellent restoration schemes, often in collaboration with other bodies such as local authorities, civic amenity groups or commercial interests. By the early 1980s British Rail, although by no means perfect, was among the leaders in corporate conservation in this country. The list includes not only stations, but viaducts, bridges, tunnel portals, signal-boxes and all manner of ancillary structures.

Today, BR has well over 1,000 listed structures of all kinds. It means that they cannot be altered, much less demolished, without ministerial consent. It may be that in some cases the process of listing has now gone too far the other way. There are listed structures, mainly stations and bridges, that are of standard design or of no overriding historical or architectural merit, similar examples of which can be found elsewhere, sometimes in better condition. While it is important that environments and landscapes should be taken into account, and local interests and wishes respected, a nationwide assessment could have been made with the object of retaining the best out of similar types. After all, in this context the railways are somewhat unusual in the extent to which standardisation in design was applied from about the 1870s onward. Instead, somewhat random, unrelated choices have been imposed on a nationally owned organisation, part of which is still publicly subsidised and which has to meet ever more stringent government financial demands. They are choices, moreover, that by statute take no account of the owner's needs or, as in many railway cases, lack of them. Preservation orders, of whatever kind, are, after all, of little practical value without money for upkeep, which for a commercial railway means that the structure must have a purpose and a use.

British Rail did three important things to push forward its conservation policy: it set up an Environment Panel at headquarters, charged with ensuring that environmental considerations form part of corporate planning; it backed up the panel with a Corporate Environment Fund to help managers establish constructive relationships with local communities in a meaningful manner, usually on a partnership basis; and it established the Railway Heritage Trust as an independent

The Grade II listed former signal-box on York station has been ingeniously converted into a walk-in book store for W.H. Smith & Son, with railway staff accommodation on the upper floor where the signalmen used to work; typical imaginative reuse of a listed structure. (BR Property Board)

company limited by guarantee, to make grants for work on historic operational structures, with an initial funding of £1 million for the first year. The Trust was also given the equally important role of liaising, where possible, in the transfer of disused listed structures to other parties, like local councils, preservation groups, civic societies and commercial organisations, acting as a catalyst between interests. It now has a rapidly growing number of excellent restoration schemes to its credit, from stations large and small to bridges, tunnels and viaducts. The Property Board plays an active part in all three developments.

The number of restored sites continues to grow. Some have already been mentioned. One of the first and, historically, most important was the original Liverpool & Manchester Railway terminus in Liverpool Road, Manchester, where a remarkably complete set of passenger and goods buildings has survived, the oldest in the world. Now it forms the Greater Manchester Museum of Science and Industry. Central station, in the same city, is an important example of the arched iron train shed, second in this country only to St Pancras, and now an exhibition hall. The classical entrance building to Curzon Street station, Birmingham, the counterpart of the Euston Arch at the other end of the line, happily survives, restored, used and winner of a Civic Trust award. Bath Green Park station, a fine combination of a classical front and an arched train shed, has been restored thanks to a combined effort by the local authority and Sainsbury's supermarket chain, winning a Railway Heritage Award. Kelvinside, a disused station in Glasgow in handsome Renaissance style, presented a particular problem because it stands on top of a shallow tunnel used by trains, which for operational reasons precluded its sale, so it was restored and let for use as a restaurant. There are many more. Among other things, restoration actually helps in finding a use, conveying a certain air of originality and prestige that attracts potential buyers or tenants.

The reduction of railway-owned houses from some 37,000 to 765 between 1960 and 1989 has been accompanied by refurbishment and modernisation by many of their new owners, although they still tend to remain recognisable. In addition to the restoration of the New Town houses at Swindon and the few remaining early ones at Crewe by the local authorities, bold action by the Derbyshire Historic Buildings Trust and Derby Civic Society saved a group of houses near Derby station from demolition. Built by Francis Thompson, a designer of many fine early stations, including Chester and Derby itself, they formed an equally important example of early railway housing. The Trust carried out a first-class restoration, producing attractive small dwellings. The cottages at Pilmoor referred to in Chapter 7 (p159) form a similarly attractive example of house restoration, this time by private owners. Another row at Welton in Northamptonshire, dating from around 1839 and probably the only surviving London & Birmingham Railway houses, has been sympathetically restored externally, along with a much later standard London & North Western Railway house that was tacked on to the end of the terrace.

Stations on closed rural lines are increasingly popular for conversion to homes, and many attractive houses have resulted. Some, indeed, have been painstakingly restored by their new owners to include a full complement of railway fittings to provide appropriate atmosphere and also qualifying, perhaps, for a Railway Heritage Award into the bargain. Tintern station, in the Forest of Dean, is now an interpretative centre for tourists, including the signal-box, a role also played by Cefn Junction box near Bridgend and now on a nature trail, and Penmaenpool box near Dolgellau which is used by the Royal Society for the Protection of Birds as a wildlife centre. The old box on York station, listed Grade II, houses the station bookstall. Wisely, signal-boxes have received more selective treatment for listing than stations, ensuring that a representative sample is retained, together with some of the more unusual ones.

The Redundant Viaducts Problem

British Rail Property Board is responsible for 27 disused listed viaducts in England and Wales and 24 in Scotland. The Monopolies and Mergers Commission recognised this onerous liability when it recommended government aid for maintaining disused listed structures, either by removing the statutory liability from the railway or by separate funding. The government disagreed and instead, so far as viaducts were concerned, suggested that the Property Board should set up an advisory committee as a forum for considering the future and priorities of English and Welsh viaducts, in the same way as it had already done in Scotland. The threat to the exceptionally fine Leaderfoot Viaduct in the Borders Region, which was becoming unsafe, was the spur behind the Scottish committee's formation, chaired by the Scottish Civic Trust and with members representing local authority associations, the Countryside Commission for Scotland, the National Trust for Scotland, Scottish Historic Buildings and Monuments, and the Scottish Railway Preservation Society.

A similar committee was accordingly set up for England and Wales, with comparable representation, including English Heritage (which is responsible for protected building inspections and surveys) and its equivalent in Wales, CADW. By their nature, viaducts present a unique problem. John Ruskin bitterly attacked the building of a railway through his beloved Monsal Dale, particularly the viaduct. Yet when, some years ago, demolition was proposed, the same thing happened but for the opposite reason. The viaduct was held to be an essential part of the landscape of the dale and a campaign was mounted for its retention. Eventually Derbyshire acquired it for the Monsal Way footpath.

More recently, something similar happened in Cumbria when Smardale Gill Viaduct, a fine structure of 13 arches in a dramatic but remote location 2 miles from the nearest road, became unsafe and there were falls of masonry. BR applied for listed building consent to demolish, which was refused on appeal to the Secretary of State following a public enquiry. Estimates of repairs varied between £150,000 and £350,000. Demolition was estimated at £66,000 if the stone could be left where it fell, and £175,000 if it had to be taken away.

Meanwhile, in Scotland negotiations over Leaderfoot were slowly but positively moving forward and, emboldened by these results, the English & Welsh Committee met a small group of people, including a civil engineer and a solicitor, interested in forming a trust to take over and repair Smardale Gill. The Property Board and the Railway Heritage Trust were prepared to give grants, while the upgrading of listing status helped in securing funding from English Heritage, local government and other bodies. There have been other problems to surmount, including access for contractors' plant — part of the area is a Site of Special Scientific Interest — but the outlook for Smardale Gill and Leaderfoot is distinctly encouraging. It is hoped there may be work in progress by the time this appears in print and that other viaducts can be similarly transferred. Meanwhile, the first transfer of a redundant viaduct to a local authority took place at the end of 1988, when Balmossie Viaduct was ceremonially handed over to the Lord Provost of Dundee, on behalf of the city council, with a cheque for £75,000 to be held in a maintenance trust fund. An endowment of this kind is based on a negotiated percentage of the cost of repair and future maintenance to a standard appropriate to conservation and public safety.

In the Somerset town of Shepton Mallet there are two redundant viaducts. One was taken over by the local firm of Showerings some years ago, and the land beneath it made into an attractive factory garden; the other continued to moulder but now may be taken over by the district council, with a substantial endowment from the Property Board, probably under the auspices of a local trust. So Shepton Mallet looks like producing two different answers to a common problem.

Bennerley Viaduct, linking Derbyshire and Nottinghamshire across the Erewash Valley, is an iron trestle structure, one of only two surviving and therefore historically important. The other is Meldon Viaduct in north Devon, and still in use. Bennerley has been out of use and steadily corroding for 22 years, alienating local opinion which a recent tragic fatality made worse after a child who had trespassed on to the viaduct fell off. However, again a local trust is in formation and, after several false starts, progress is being made although the cost of restoration will he high.

These problems are best highlighted in Devon and Cornwall, which possess a series of unique railway structures in the stone piers that supported Brunel's original timber viaducts. Gradually they were replaced by stone or girder viaducts, in most cases alongside, leaving lofty stone stumps standing, a number of which are listed and therefore cannot be demolished without consent. At present they do not constitute risks, but obviously will need maintenance at some future date. Of great historical importance, they nevertheless form particularly useless liabilities.

The public's attention was drawn to the viaduct problem by an advertisement which appeared in the *Sunday Times* homes section in 1985 headed 'Viaducts with Vacant Possession'. Six were illustrated and described in estate agent's terms. Here is Hengoed: 'An exceptional 15 semi-circular arched viaduct on tapering pillars constructed from local materials. Last tenant a Dr R. Beeching, vacated 1964. One of the Wonders of Wales.' There were no takers, but it raised a few laughs and publicised the general issue.

*   *   *   *

This book has been mainly concerned with history, which in railway property management is ever-present in some form, demanding attention. Like the viaducts, it will not go away but is always there, whether as a relic from the past, currently in the making or, by repeating itself as it nearly always does, as a guide to the future.

In the 30 years since the turning point of Euston, BR has developed a steadily growing social awareness which has become manifest in its environmental attitude and recognition of its stock of historic structures. There is still a great deal to be done, for which resources are slender and have to be self-generated, and mistakes are still sometimes made. But the will to find a way is clearly there.

The enlightened policies of BR displayed by the Property Board, the Department of Architecture and Design, the civil engineers and the Community Unit have been demonstrated by much admirable work, ranging from major reconstructions to routine repainting jobs, frequently with the aid of the Railway Heritage Trust, and much goodwill has been generated.

But an up-to-date account of the railway's efforts in conservation would be incomplete without reference to the King's Cross Railways Bill — already mentioned in Chapter 8 (p224) — presented to the 1989-90 session of Parliament and, at the time of writing, undergoing its scrutiny. Opposition is heavy, particularly to the contentious Clause 19 which 'seeks to remove all listed building, conservation area, and ancient monument statutory controls from the development proposals' contained in the Bill.[3]

In evidence to the Commons Select Committee and in a supporting memorandum, British Rail holds in essence that, in seeking to override existing town and country planning legislation, Clause 19 simply invokes Section 423 of the Local Government (Miscellaneous Provisions) Act, 1976, which, BR contends, reserves to Parliament the right in certain exceptional circumstances to make an exception to planning legislation; this discretion the Railways Board now asks Parliament to exercise. BR's case is that, because at so important a site as King's Cross transport and conservation issues are so interlocked, Parliament itself should form a view on the merits of the scheme, balancing the case for preservation of listed buildings and conservation areas against the need to create a Channel Tunnel terminal and interchange of national and international importance, in the full knowledge that to achieve it demolitions and alterations are inevitable.

Five listed buildings are proposed for demolition: a lock-keeper's cottage on the Regent's Canal, a Victorian gasholder in the group close to St Pancras, the Great Northern Hotel, a public house and a shop. Alterations to King's Cross station comprise the demolition of the later suburban station and the *porte cochère* on the western side, and at St Pancras some alterations to the platforms. The Board points out that if listed building and conservation area consents were sought through the normal channels from the local authorities they would, by virtue of the authorities' opposition to the Bill, be unlikely to be granted, resulting in an appeal to the Secretary of State for the Environment, a process which could take two years or more, causing a delay which BR considers it must take all possible steps to avoid.

During the Commons Committee stage BR has subsequently given an undertaking to, among other things, lessen the impact on listed buildings by moving and then returning the lock cottage intact to, or close to, its existing site; to dismantle, store and later re-erect the King's Cross *porte cochère* on a suitable site elsewhere; and to effect certain important modifications regarding building works that might otherwise affect the two main line stations.[4]

The local authorities and conservation bodies are among the main opposers of the Bill, and Clause 19 has drawn particular opposition from English Heritage in its capacity of statutory adviser to the Secretary of State on ancient monuments and listed buildings with, in London, authority to direct local authorities on the exercising and enforcement of protected buildings legislation. The core of English Heritage's objection is the fear that if Clause 19 removes these public functions in relation to a development by Private Bill so large as King's Cross, a precedent will be set for other promoters who wish to avoid statutory conservation controls. Government departments, it is assumed, would in such circumstances be unlikely to oppose such a clause once a precedent had been established.

In support, English Heritage points to three other Bills containing similar clauses, deposited in 1989 and waiting in the wings at Westminster. The implications of Clause 19 for conservation in general it calls 'monumental',[5] a view with which, at the time of writing (July 1990), the Commons Committee has agreed. The Bill will now be debated by the full House and then, if approved, will proceed to the Lords.

Postscript

Since this book was started events have moved swiftly, requiring a number of revisions to make it as up-to-date as publishing schedules allow. Foremost is the Channel Tunnel, which has produced fiercely debated proposals for a high-speed link, the King's Cross terminal and, in many quarters, the need for improved rail communications beyond London. To paraphrase comments by BR's immediate past chairman, Sir Robert Reid, much depends on the speed and vigour with which the opportunities the tunnel presents are grasped.[6]

During the first half of 1990 the fortunes of these schemes have changed rapidly. Having failed to gain private capital for the link, in June British Rail was told that government funding would not be available either, which might also affect the King's Cross Railways Bill. As these events follow closely on the High Court's ruling that, under the pre-emption provisions of the Great Northern Railway Act of 1846, BR must offer the King's Cross surplus lands back to the original owners' successors at the price paid 144 years ago, Sir Robert's words seem unlikely to be implemented just yet.

However, this cannot be for long. Despite these and other well-publicised setbacks, positive moves like East Coast main line electrification, the recently announced investment in the West Coast and other lines, the numbers of new or reopened stations in recent years, and proposals to reopen closed lines show that, gradually, railways are again coming to be regarded as a national resource.

Add rapidly increasing road congestion, the blossoming of Light Rapid Transit schemes in our cities, the effects of atmospheric pollution and the public's growing environmental consciousness, and there seems little doubt that railways are about to undergo a resurgence. The question is now becoming transmuted from 'if' to 'when'. Political responses on all sides are moving unmistakably in that direction, albeit slowly, and to a considerable extent progress is governed by the parliamentary process outlined in chapter 2 and highlighted by the King's Cross Bill; at last the need for something better than the Private Bill procedure now seems to be appreciated. Leaving that aside, however, it seems clear that for the railway estate surveyor of the future, land disposal could well be subordinated to acquisition, signalling something of a reversion to the role of his predecessor of a century and more ago.

References

Abbreviations

JTH	Journal of Transport History
PRO	Public Record Office, Kew
RCHS	Railway & Canal Historical Society
RICS	Royal Institution of Chartered Surveyors (see note below)
RO	(County) Record Office
SRO	Scottish Record Office, Edinburgh
Note:	For simplicity, RICS is used to include the Institution's successive name changes from Institution of Surveyors (1868-81), to Surveyors' Institution (1881-1930), Chartered Surveyors Institution (1930-46) and Royal Institution of Chartered Surveyors.

Chapter 1 — ANTECEDENTS

1 D. Chilton, 'Land Measurement in the Sixteenth Century', *Trans Newcomen Soc*, vol XXXI, 1957-9
2 T.K. Derry & I. Williams, *A Short History of Technology*, 1960
3 A. Clapham, 'A Short History of the Surveyor's Profession', *Trans RICS*, vol LXXXII, 1949-50
4 F.M.L. Thompson, *Chartered Surveyors: the growth of a profession*, 1968
5 Thompson
6 Much of the following on wagonways and wayleaves is based on M.J.T. Lewis, *Early Wooden Railways*, 1970
7 T.G. Cumming, *Illustrations of the Origin & Progress of Rail and Tram Roads*, 1824
8 Northumberland RO, 725/F17
9 F.A. Sharman, 'The First Railway Act?', *Journal RCHS*, vol XXI, no 3, Nov 1975
10 Lewis
11 J. Farey, *General View of the Agriculture of Derbyshire*, 1817 — quoted in Lewis
12 C. Hadfield, *The Canals of the West Midlands*, 1966
13 Northumberland RO, 725/F17
14 C. Hadfield & G. Biddle, *The Canals of North West England*, vol 1, 1970
15 C. Hadfield & A.W. Skempton, *William Jessop, Engineer*, 1979
16 C. Hadfield, *The Canals of South & South East England*, 1967
17 Lewis
18 A.W. Skempton & E.C. Wright, 'Early Members of the Society of Engineers', *Trans Newcomen Soc*, vol XLIV, 1971-2
19 Thompson
20 Skempton & Wright

21 H. Malet, *Bridgewater, the Canal Duke*, 1977
22 Skempton & Wright
23 Quoted in C. Hadfield, *British Canals*, 7th edn, 1984

Chapter 2 — PROMOTING A RAILWAY

 1 *An Account of the Proceedings of the Great Western Railway . . . .*, 1834, Somerset RO, DD/Fs/45
 2 Lincolnshire RO, HIG 16/2
 3 J.F. Curwen, *Kirkbie Kendal*, 1900
 4 P.J. Long & Rev W.W. Awdry, *The Birmingham & Gloucester Railway*, 1987
 5 Lancashire RO, UDC1 8/28
 6 PRO RAIL 69/26
 7 PRO RAIL 299/2
 8 *Pictorial Times* supplement, 1845, Bodleian Library, Oxford, John Johnson collection (folder)
 9 J.S. Holden, *The Manchester & Milford Railway*, 1979
10 P. Stevenson, 'For Sale or Exchange — Railway Surveys', *RCHS Journal*, vol X, Nov 1963
11 Bulmer & Gillan, *Practical Instructions to the Promoters of Private Bills*, 1839
12 D.J. Hodgkins, 'The Origins & Independent Years of the Cromford & High Peak Railway', *JTH*, vol 1, no 1, May 1963
13 A. Doull, *Random Hints on Railways & Railway Legislation*, 1848
14 See note 11
15 Printed Report on Committee Proceedings, 28 April 1846, Bodleian Library, Oxford, John Johnson collection
16 Somerset RO, DD/FS/45

Chapter 3 — PREPARING THE ROUTE

 1 J. Bailey Denton, *The Future Extension of the Railway System*, Trans RICS, 8 Feb 1869 (discussion)
 2 SRO BR/1/2
 3 D.G. Moir (ed), *The Early Maps of Scotland*, 1983
 4 PRO RAIL 2/6
 5 Prospectus in John Johnson collection, Bodleian Library, Oxford
 6 Hampshire RO, 10MS/TR7
 7 PRO RAIL 1005/81
 8 PRO RAIL 1005/81
 9 PRO RAIL 667/958
10 PRO RAIL 631/15
11 *The Builder*, vol 3, 5 May 1845
12 *The Builder*, vol 5, 18 Dec 1847
13 *John Brunton's Book, 1812-1899*, 1939
14 Cumbria RO (Kendal)
15 PRO RAIL 2/6
16 Northumberland RO, ZMD129
17 PRO RAIL 313/21

18 Dorset RO, 9389/F11
19 Liverpool RO, 385 LIV 5/6
20 L.T.C. Rolt, *Isambard Kingdom Brunel*, 1957
21 Cumberland RO (Carlisle), D/Sen/Silloth/3
22 PRO RAIL 1008/69
23 Sheffield Central Library, Fairbank Collection, CP-51 (6)
24 PRO RAIL 384/56
25 PRO RAIL 357/66
26 *Personal Recollections of English Engineers*, 1868, reprinted as *The Men who built Railways*, J. Simmons (ed), 1983
27 Extensive papers are in the Fairbank Collection (note 23) and PRO RAIL 1153
28 Liverpool RO, 385 JAM 1/6/2
29 Liverpool RO, 385 LIV 1/6/2
30 PRO RAIL 699/8
31 Vol 3, 6 Dec 1845
32 A full account appears in P.A. Stevens, 'The Midland Railway's Syston & Peterborough Branch', *RCHS Journal*, vol XIX, no 1, March 1973
33 Fully quoted in *The Builder*, vol 3, 6 Dec 1845
34 *Report on the Sanitary Condition of the Labouring Population of Great Britain*, 1842
35 F.M.L. Thompson, *Chartered Surveyors: the growth of a profession*, 1968

Chapter 4 – LAND FOR THE LINE

 1 P.S. Richards, 'A Geographical Analysis of Surveys made for the London & Birmingham Railway', *Trans Birmingham Archaeological Soc*, vol 80, 1965
 2 See J.R. Hepple, *The Influence of Landowners' Attitudes on Railway Alignment in Nineteenth Century England*, PhD thesis, Hull Univ, 1974
 3 'The Lands' Clauses Consolidation Acts', *Trans RICS*, vol VI, 1873-4
 4 Hampshire RO (Winchester), 25M61/10/3
 5 See 'The Struggle to obtain Parliamentary Sanction for the building of the London & Birmingham Railway', *Stephenson Locomotive Soc Journal*, vol XLI, Nov 1965; P.S. Richards, 'Railways, Landowners & Farmers', *RCHS Journal*, vol XXIII, no 1, Mar 1977; F.A. Sharman, 'The Influence of Landowners on Route Selection', *RCHS Journal*, vol XXVI, no 2, July 1980
 6 F.M.L. Thompson, *English Landed Gentry in the 19th Century*, 1963
 7 Stevens (chapter 3, note 32)
 8 PRO RAIL 315/5-7 & 15
 9 See W. Hodges, *A Treatise on the Law of Railways*, 7th edn, 1888-9
10 SRO BR/CAL/1/100
11 Buckinghamshire RO, 39/52D/DU/6
12 Hampshire RO (Winchester), 44M69 G1/113-117
13 PRO RAIL 384/277
14 PRO RAIL 46/40
15 D. Whomsley, 'A Landed Estate and the Railway: Huddersfield, 1844-54', *JTH* new series, vol II, Sept 1974
16 Devon RO (Exeter), 961 M/54, B961M/M & B21-22
17 Dorset RO, D86/E32

18 F.M.L. Thompson, *Hampstead: Building a Borough, 1650-1964*, 1974
19 'A Country Cockney', *Railways & Commons*, 1881
20 Lincolnshire RO, MEASURE 5/672-735
21 *The Oxley Parker Papers, from the Letters & Diaries of an Essex Family of Land Agents in the Nineteenth Century*, 1964; Essex RO, Transcript 326
22 *Railways in Essex*, Essex RO Teaching Portfolio no 10
23 *The Railway in Town & Country, 1830-1914*, 1986
24 PRO RAIL 491/708
25 A. Bennett, *The Great Western in West Cornwall*, 1988
26 Suffolk RO, HA93/3/453
27 See C. Croughton, R.W. Kidner & A. Young, *Private & Untimetabled Stations*, 1982
28 PRO RAIL 418/37
29 PRO RAIL 527/1867
30 PRO RAIL 527/1867
31 PRO RAIL 236/1006
32 PRO RAIL — see numerous collections under headings of NER and absorbed companies
33 SRO BR/CAL/4/27/39
34 Devon RO, 3424Z/L
35 PRO RAIL 1057/2846
36 R.B. Grantham, 'Private Agricultural Railways', *Trans RICS*, vol V, 1872-3
37 J. Bailey Denton (chapter 3, note 1)
38 S.C. Brees, *Railway Practice*, appendix, 1839
39 F. Clifford, *A History of Private Bill Legislation*, vol 1, 1885
40 E. Ryde, 'Results of Land Purchase of the Tunbridge and Dartford Railways', *Trans RICS*, vol III, 1870-1
41 *Report from the Select Committee of Lords on Compensation to be made to Owners of Real Property, Land &c, compulsorily taken for Public Railways, with Minutes of Evidence*, 1845
42 Cumbria RO (Carlisle), D/SEN/RIS/MCRy/19
43 PRO RAIL 110/71
44 See, eg, J.R. Kellett, 'Urban & Transport History from Legal Records: an example from Glasgow solicitors' papers', *JTH* new series, vol 6, 1964
45 *JTH* vol 4, 1960
46 SRO/BR/FBR/1/2 & 4/2
47 Clifford
48 PRO RAIL 631/180
49 Lancs RO DDC1 1197/46
50 Thompson, *Hampstead*
51 J. Simmons, 'The Pattern of Tube Railways in London', *JTH* vol 7, 1965-6
52 R. Berkeley, 'Electric Railways & Street Compensation', *Trans RICS*, vol XXXIV, 1901-2
53 Hampshire RO, 10M57/TR7
54 PRO RAIL 236/238
55 SRO BR/CAL/4/36
56 PRO RAIL 226/33 & 34
57 F.M.L. Thompson, *Chartered Surveyors* (chapter 1, note 4)
58 Bedfordshire RO, RR8 *et seq*
59 Buckinghamshire RO, AR76/82, item 3, and AR170/79 DX682/37

Chapter 5 — THE INFLUENCE OF THE RAILWAY

1 C. Kidson, 'Dawlish Warren: a Study of the Evolution of the Sand Spits across the mouth of the River Exe in Devon', *Trans Inst of British Geographers*, 16, 1950
2 PRO RAIL 377/33
3 J.M. Theaker, *Coastal Change and Man in the Grange–Silverdale Area of Morecambe Bay*, BSc dissertation, Huddersfield Polytechnic, 1981
4 John Gough, 'An Unused Railway: Hinckley to Stoke Golding', *RCHS Journal*, vol XXVII, 1, Mar 1984
5 Cumbria RO (Kendal), WDX/426 and WDB/35 (464)
6 *The Railway Gazette*, Sept 1937
7 J.M. Bestall, *History of Chesterfield*, vol III, 1978
8 J.M. Prest, *The Industrial Revolution in Coventry*, 1960
9 J. Hassall & D. Baker, *Bedford: Aspects of Town Origins & development*, no date
10 C. Chapman, 'The Growth of Watford', *RCHS Journal*, vol XVII, 3, July 1971
11 D. Possee, 'The Development of Braintree between 1820 and 1900', *Essex Journal*, vol 21, 1986
12 S.A. Pearce, *The Impact of the Railway on Uckfield in the 19th century*, Sussex Archaeological Collections, 122, 1984
13 R.H. Selbie, 'Railways and Land Development', *Modern Transport*, vol 5, 11 June 1921
14 H.C. Binford, 'Land Tenure, Social Structure & Railway Impact in North Lambeth, 1830-61', *JTH* (new series), vol II, 1974
15 J. Simmons, *St Pancras Station*, 1968
16 H.J. Dyos, 'Railways & Housing in Victorian London', *JTH*, vol 2, 1955-6, and 'Some Social Costs of Railway Building in London, *JTH*, vol 3, 1959
17 PRO RAIL 527/1682
18 [Robert Thorne], *Liverpool Street Station*, 1978
19 Tenders in PRO RAIL 227/223
20 PRO RAIL 390/873
21 PRO RAIL 226/178
22 Specification in PRO RAIL 463/129
23 PRO RAIL 390/873
24 PRO RAIL 226/178
25 Leicestershire RO, Desposited plans 2989 and 3639
26 PRO RAIL 390/873
27 'The Estate Department', *Southern Railway Magazine*, Sept 1932
28 SRO BR/CAL/4/36
29 PRO RAIL 418/39
30 *Essex Standard*, quoted in A.F.J. Brown, *English History from Essex Sources, 1750-1900*, 1952
31 C.H. Dingwall, *Ardler. A Village History: the Planned Railway Village of Washington*, 1985
32 H. Carter, 'Aberystwyth: The Modern Development of a Medieval Castle Town in Wales', *Trans Inst of British Geographers*, 25, 1958
33 PRO RAIL 313/9, 10 & 11
34 PRO RAIL 226/33
35 PRO RAIL 390/984

36 J.D. Marshall, *Old Lakeland: Some Cumbrian Social History*, 1971
37 J.K. Walton, 'Railways & Resort development in Victorian England: the case of Silloth' *Northern History*, vol XV, 1979

Chapter 6 — RAILWAY COMMUNITIES

1 R. Young, *Timothy Hackworth & the Locomotive*, 1923
2 George Weight, *Sermons and Tracts* (nd) in M.A. Bird, *The Development of Wolverton, Bucks, from Railway Town to New City (1838-1974)*, ms thesis, Buckinghamshire County Library, Aylesbury
3 Buckinghamshire RO, AR49/88
4 M.A. Bird; P.S. Richards, 'The Influence of Railways in the Growth of Wolverton, Bucks, *Record of Bucks'*, vol XVII, 1976; S.F. Markham, *The Nineteen Hundreds in Stoney Stratford and Wolverton*, 1951
5 Bristol University Library, Brunel private letter book, 2b, fol 249, Brunel to F. Thompson, 10 Jan 1842
6 K. Hudson, 'The Early Years of the Railway Community in Swindon', *Transport History*, vol 1, no 2, July 1968
7 W.H. Chaloner, *The Social & Economic Development of Crewe, 1780-1923*, 1950
8 J.D. Marshall, *Furness & the Industrial Revolution*, 1981
9 B.J. Turton, 'The Railway Towns of Southern England', *Transport History*, vol 2, no 2, July 1969
10 E.C. Vollans, 'Derby: A Railway Town and Regional Centre', *Trans Inst* of *British Geographers*, 15, 1949
11 R.A. Dane, *The Railways of Peterborough*, 1978
12 D. Barber, 'The Concept of the Railway Town and the growth of Darlington, 1801-1911', *Transport History*, vol 3, no 3, Nov 1970
13 F. Worsdall, *The Tenement a Way of Life*, 1979
14 *Railway & Travel Monthly*, vol 4, no 24, April 1912
15 *Railway & Travel Monthly*, vol 4, no 21, Jan 1912
16 G. Turner, *Ashford, the Coming of the Railway*, 1984
17 PRO RAIL 220/10
18 A.E. Grigg, *Town of Trains, Bletchley and the Oxbridge Line*, 1980
19 C.S. Bagley, *Boston, its Story & its People*, 1986
20 N.R. Wright, *The Railways of Boston*, 1971, and *The Book of Boston*, 1986
21 R.S. Joby, *The Railwaymen*, 1984
22 J.W. Anscombe, 'Woodford Halse, the Village with a Heart of Steam', in *Northamptonshire Past & Present*, vol 6, 1982-3; also *The Railway at Woodford Halse* and *Woodford Hulse and the GCR*, mss, nd, Northants Studies Section, Northampton Library, 16850/312 and 17721/312; *Woodford Halse District Plan*, Daventry District Council, 1975
23 J.E. Roberts, *The Changing Face of Carnforth*, [c1974]
24 PRO RAIL 667/273
25 SRO BR/CAL/4/4/150
26 P.W. Kingsford, *Victorian Railwaymen*, 1970
27 PRO RAIL 509/125

28 Sources: Col 2, Railway Yearbook, 1922 (1921 figures); Col 3, companies' annual reports in PRO RAIL 116/167 and 117/118; total numbers of houses, all purposes, Board of Trade Returns, 1921

29 PRO RAIL 418/35

30 P.S. Richards, 'A Note on the Early Life of Robert Benson Dockray (1811-1871)', *RCHS Journal*, vol XXIX, part 6, no 140, Nov 1988

31 PRO RAIL 418/35

32 F. McKenna, *The Railway Workers, 1840-1970,* 1980

33 SRO BR/HR/49

34 PRO RAIL 50/6

35 PRO RAIL 527/1783

36 PRO RAIL 527/1145

37 PRO RAIL 487/97

38 PRO RAIL 411/660

39 A. Platt, *The Life & Times of Daniel Gooch,* 1987

40 PRO RAIL 667/273

41 Buckinghamshire RO, AR49/83

42 A. Vaughan, *A Pictorial History of Great Western Architecture,* 1977

43 Quoted in Chaloner

44 PRO RAIL 410/289

45 Dorset RO, D611/11

46 Lincolnshire RO, SHER G/77

47 Sir George Findlay, *The Working & Management of an English Railway,* 6th ed, 1899

48 PRO RAIL 410/115

49 R.W. Miller, 'Cheshire Lines Railwaymen's Cottages', *Historical Model Railway Society Journal*, vol 4, no 10, Oct 1979

50 Cheshire Lines Committee Estates minutes, 2 Oct 1894 *et seq*

51 PRO RAIL 253/509

52 PRO RAIL 220/35

53 SRO BR/SCC/4/5

54 J.H. Proud, 'Stockton & Darlington House Number Plates', *NER Assoc Journal,* Aug 1974 (appendix)

55 PRO RAIL 410/97 and 410/333

56 Chaloner

57 PRO RAIL 220/10

58 Platt

59 SRO BR/EGR/1/78

60 W. Minchinton, 'Industrial Housing in the West Country', *Southern History,* vol 8, 1986

61 PRO RAIL 491/330-332

62 PRO RAIL 411/660

63 SRO BR/CAL/3/6

64 PRO RAIL 261/308

65 PRO RAIL 390/39

66 PRO RAIL 390/39

67 PRO RAIL 418/35

68 PRO RAIL 645/16

69 PRO RAIL 250/243-4, 267/308. *Railway Gazette,* vol 86, no 22, 13 June 1947

70 PRO RAIL 390/357, 1058/1
71 PRO RAIL 390/41
72 PRO RAIL 418/35
73 PRO RAIL 1007/620
74 Kingsford
75 PRO RAIL 418/38, 1007/620

Chapter 7 — RAILWAY PROPERTY MANAGEMENT, 1830-1946
 1 PRO RAIL 384/27
 2 PRO RAIL 220/10
 3 SRO BR/SCC/1 22A, 22B & 23
 4 SRO BR/EGR/1 78-82
 5 PRO RAIL 386/17
 6 PRO RAIL 157/4
 7 PRO RAIL 176/16
 8 PRO RAIL 39/6
 9 PRO RAIL 343/523-32
10 Surrey RO (Guildford Muniment Room)
11 PRO RAIL 635/148
12 PRO RAIL 1057/2859
13 PRO RAIL 855/6; also Charles Hadfield, *The Canals of the East Midlands,* 1966, and *The Canal Age,* 1968
14 PRO RAIL 410/36, 410/1854
15 *Trans RICS*, vol 1
16 PRO RAIL 410/709, 1057/2804
17 PRO RAIL 207/125
18 PRO RAIL 207/163
19 PRO RAIL 207/125
20 PRO RAIL 258/272
21 PRO RAIL 207/125
22 PRO RAIL 258/272
23 Obituary, *The Builder,* vol CXLIX, no 483, 13 Sep 1935
24 PRO RAIL 258/272
25 PRO RAIL 491/330-332
26 PRO RAIL 258/272
27 PRO RAIL 226/33-37
28 PRO RAIL 384/191
29 PRO RAIL 36/7
30 *Trans RICS,* vol XLIII, 1910-1 (obit)
31 *RICS Journal,* Nov 1921 (obit)
32 Lancashire RO, DDLi Box 217
33 PRO RAIL 410/110
34 *Trans RICS,* vol XX, 6 Feb 1888
35 PRO RAIL 227/139
36 Cumbria RO (Kendal), WPR/2
37 PRO RAIL 213/5

38 PRO RAIL 15/3

39 PRO RAIL 250/252

40 SRO BR/CAL/4/36

41 CLC Estates Committee Mins 13 May & 29 July 1924, 9 March 1926

42 PRO RAIL 18/40

43 PRO RAIL 227/139

44 Devon RO (Exeter), 527/A/11/13

45 SRO BR/EGR/1/2 & 78

46 SRO BR/GNS/42

47 PRO RAIL 418/38

48 PRO RAIL 226/37

49 This account is based on C. Wilson, *First with the News: the History of W.H. Smith, 1792-1972,* 1985

50 SRO BR/EGR/1/78

51 PRO RAIL 214/58

52 PRO RAIL 226/33

53 J. Kieve, *The Electric Telegraph: A Social & Economic History,* 1973, and PRO RAIL 227/139

54 PRO RAIL 328/33

55 C. Hadfield, *The Canals of the West Midlands,* 1966

56 Somerset RO, DD/X/WLH c/2141

57 PRO RAIL 227/200 & 390/537, 578 & 658

58 F.M.L. Thompson, *Chartered Surveyors,* 1968

59 T.F. Hedley, 'The Rating of Railways', *Trans RICS,* vol XI, 9 Dec 1878

60 F.C. Hockridge, 'The Work of the Surveyor's & Estate Department', *GWR (London) Lecture & Debating Soc,* no 282, 8 March 1934 (RAIL 253/300)

61 PRO RAIL 390/718

62 Hockridge

63 'Railways & Real Property: a Glance into the Future', Auctioneers' & Estate Agent's Inst, reported in *Modern Transport,* 20 Nov 1920

64 Hockridge

65 LMS Estate Agents' Annual Report, 1930

66 PRO RAIL 418/39; LMS Estate Agent's Annual Report, 1932

67 PRO RAIL 648/121

68 PRO RAIL 418/38 & 1057/2804

69 [M.J.I. Greenleaf] 'The "Estate Office", an important but little-known department', *Southern Railway Magazine,* Sep 1932

70 PRO RAIL 390/1161

71 C.E. Lee, 'New Works for War Time Traffic', *Railway Magazine,* vol 92 March/April & May/June 1946

Chapter 8 — CINDERELLA TO MARKET LEADER

1 Hockridge (chapter 7, note 60)

2 M.R. Bonavia, *British Rail: The First Twenty-five years,* 1981

3 For an exhaustive account of the first 25 years of BR, see T.R. Gourvish, *British Railways, 1948-73: A Business History,* 1986

4 See P.R. Dashwood, *Property Development in British Rail,* 1974, for detail
5 *Daily Telegraph,* 18 Oct 1968
6 P.A. Land, *Sauce Supreme: the Annihilation of British Transport Hotels Ltd,* private publication, c1988
7 The Monopolies & Mergers Commission, *British Railways Board: Property Activities,* Cmnd 9532, June 1985; see also M. Harris, 'The British Rail Property Board Today', in *Modern Railways,* Aug 1985
8 Walter Neurath Memorial Lecture, London University, March 1990

Chapter 9 — THE WORKING PROPERTY BOARD
1 *Financial Times,* 1 Feb 1971
2 See J.H. Appleton, *Disused Railways in the Countryside of England & Wales,* HMSO 1970
3 English Heritage, *Conservation Bulletin,* No 10, Feb 1990
4 King's Cross Railways Bill: promoters' memorandum, evidence and undertaking to Commons Committee, session 1989-90
5 English Heritage (above)
6 *Modern Railways,* vol 47, no 500, May 1990

Bibliography

Primary and documentary sources, and articles in magazines and journals are given as references in the text.

Allen, C.J. *The Great Eastern Railway*, 1955

Appleton, J.H. *The Geography of Communications in Great Britain*, 1962

Atthill, R. *The Somerset and Dorset Joint Railway*, 1970

Bagley, C.S. *Boston, its Story and its People*, 1986

Barker, T.C. & Robbins, M. *The History of London Transport* (2 vols), 1963 & 1974

Barnes, E.G. *The Rise of the Midland Railway* (2 vols), 1966 & 1969

Barty-King, H. *Scratch a Surveyor*, 1975

Baughan, P.E. *The Chester & Holyhead Railway* vol 1, 1972

Baughan, P.E. *The Midland Railway North of Leeds* 2nd edn, 1987

Bestall, J.M. *History of Chesterfield* vol III, 1978

Biddle, G. *Great Railway Stations of Britain*, 1986

Biddle, G. & Nock, O.S., and others. *The Railway Heritage of Britain*, 1983

Bigg, J. *Public & General Acts for the Regulation of Railways, 1830-1911* 16th edn, 1912

Binns, D. *The 'Little' North Western Railway*, 1982

Binns, D. *The Scenic Settle & Carlisle Railway*, 1982

Bennett, A. *The Great Western in West Cornwall*, 1988

Bonavia, M. *The Four Great Railways*, 1980

Bonavia, M. *British Rail: The First Twenty Five Years*, 1981

Boucher, R.T.G. *James Brindley, Engineer, 1716-1772*, 1968

Bowtell, H.D. *Over Shap to Carlisle*, 1983

Boyes, J. & Russell, R. *The Canals of Eastern England*, 1977

Brees, S.C. *Railway Practice* 2nd edn, 1837, 3rd edn, 1847

Brunton, J. *John Brunton's Book, 1812-1899*, 1939

Bulmer & Gillan. *Practical Information to the Promotors of Private Bills in Parliament*, 1839

Butcher, A.C. *Railways Restored* (1989-90 edn), 1989

Carlson, R.E. *The Liverpool & Manchester Railway Project, 1821-1831*, 1969

Chaloner, W.H. *The Social and Economic Development of Crewe*, 1950

Channon, B. *Bristol and the Promotion of the GWR*, 1985

Christiansen, R. & Miller, R.W. *The Cambrian Railways* (2 vols), 1967

Christiansen, R. & Miller, R.W. *The North Staffordshire Railway*, 1969

Clifford, F. *A History of Private Bill Legislation*, 1885

Clinker, C.R. & Firth, J.M. *Register of Closed Passenger Stations and Goods Depots, 1830-1970*, 1971

Collier, R.P. *The Railways' Clauses, Companies' Clauses and Lands' Clauses Consolidation Acts*, 1845

Conder, F.R. *The Men who Built Railways* (ed J. Simmons), 1983

Copeland, J. *Roads and their Traffic, 1750-1850*, 1968

'A Country Cockney'. *Railways and Commons*, 1881

Croughton, C., Kidner, R.W. & Young, A. *Private and Untimetabled Stations*, 1982

Cumming, T.G. *Illustrations of the Origin and Progress of Rail and Tram Roads*, 1824

Curr, J. *The Coal Viewer and Engine Builder's Practical Companion*, 1797

Dane, R.A. *The Railways of Peterborough*, 1978

Davies, H. *A Walk along the Tracks*, 1987

Dendy Marshall, C.F. *History of the Southern Railway* (2 vols) revised R.W. Kidner, 1963

Derry, T.K. & Williams, T.I. *A Short History of Technology*, 1960

Dingwall, C.H. *Ardler, A Village History: The Planned Railway Village of Washington*, 1985

Doull, A. *Practical Hints on Railways and Railway Legislation*, 1848

Dow, G. *Great Central* (3 vols), 1959-65

Dyos, H.J. & Aldcroft, D.H. *British Transport: An Economic Survey from the Seventeenth Century to the Twentieth*, 1969

Faulkner, J.N. & Williams, R.A. *The London & South Western Railway in the Twentieth Century*, 1988

Findlay, Sir G. *The Working and Management of an English Railway* 6th edn, 1899

Fowler, J.K. *Recollections of an Old Country Life*, 1894

Fox, F. *Road, River and Rail: Some Engineering Reminiscences*, 1904

Francis, J. *A History of the English Railway, Its Social Relations and Revelations, 1820-1845*, 1851 (reprint 1967)

Fuller, A.H. *The Preparation of Parliamentary Plans for Railways*, 1897

Gaunt, A. 'The Law Relating to Railways' (in *Modern Railway Administration*, 1921)

Gourvish, T.R. *British Railways, 1945-73; A Business History*, 1986

Gray, A. *The London Chatham and Dover Railway*, 1984

Gregory, R.H. *The South Devon Railway*, 1982

Greville, M.D. & Spence, J. *Closed Passenger Lines of Great Britain, 1827-1947*, 1974

Grigg, A.E. *Town of Trains: Bletchley and the Oxbridge Line*, 1980

Hadfield, C. *The Canals of South Wales and the Border*, 1960

Hadfield, C. *The Canals of the East Midlands*, 1966

Hadfield, C. *The Canals of the West Midlands*, 1966

Hadfield, C. *The Canals of South and South East England*, 1967

Hadfield, C. *British Canals* 7th edn, 1984

Hadfield, C. & Biddle, G. *The Canals of North West England* (2 vols), 1970

Hadfield, C. & Norris, J.E. *Waterways to Stratford*, 1962

Hadfield, C. & Skempton, A.W. *William Jessop, Engineer*, 1979

Harper, D. *Wilts and Somerset, A Railway Landscape*, 1987

Hinchliffe, B. (ed). *The Hull and Barnsley Railway* vol 2, 1980

Hodges, W. *The Law of Railways* 2nd edn, 1855

Holden, J.S. *The Manchester & Milford Railway*, 1979

Hoole, K. (ed). *The Hull & Barnsley Railway* vol 1, 1972

Hoole, K. *The Stockton & Darlington Railway*, 1975

Hovendenden, T.K. *New Railways and New Streets*, 1872

Howat, P. *The Lochaber Narrow Gauge Railway*, 1980

Jackson, A.A. *Semi-detached London*, 1973

Jackson, A.A. *London's Termini* 2nd edn, 1985

Jackson, A.A. *London's Metropolitan Railway*, 1986

Jackson, A.A. & Croome, D.F. *Rails Through the Clay*, 1962

Joby, R.S. *Forgotten Railways of East Anglia*, 1977
Joby, R.S. *The Railwaymen*, 1984
Johnston, C. & Hume, J.R. *Glasgow Stations*, 1979
Kellett, J.R. *The Impact of Railways on Victorian Cities*, 1969
Kieve, J. *The Electric Telegraph: A Social & Economic History*, 1973
Kingsford, P.W. *The Victorian Railwaymen*, 1970
Klapper, C.F. *Sir Herbert Walker's Southern Railway*, 1973
Lee, C.E. *The Evolution of the Permanent Way*, 1937
Lewin, H.G. *Early British Railways*, 1925
Lewin, H.G. *The Railway Mania and its Aftermath*, 1936 (new edn 1968)
Lewis, M.J.T. *Early Wooden Railways*, 1970
Lidster, R.J. *The Scarborough and Whitby Railway*, 1977
Lindsay, J. *The Canals of Scotland*, 1968
Long, P.L. & Awdry, Rev W. *The Bristol and Gloucester Railway*, 1987
MacDermot, E.T. *History of the Great Western Railway* vols 1 & 2, 1927 & 1931
M'Dermott, F. & Gairns, J.F. 'The Constitution of Railway Companies: their Finance and Legal Status' (in *Modern Railway Administration*, 1921)
McGovern, J.H. *How to Assess the Value of Land and Property Compulsorily Taken by Railway and Canal Companies*, 1887-8
McKenna, F. *The Railway Workers, 1840-1970*, 1980
Madsen, A.W. *Why Rents and Rates are so High*, 1938
Malet, H. *Bridgewater, the Canal Duke*, 1977
Marshall, J. *The Lancashire and Yorkshire Railway* (3 vols), 1969-72
Marshall, J. *A Biographical Dictionary of Railway Engineers*, 1978
Marshall, J.D. *Furness and the Industrial Revolution*, 1958
Marshall, J.D. *Old Lakeland: Some Cumbrian Social History*, 1971
[Mewburn, F.] *The Larchfield Diary: Extracts from the Diary of the late Mr Mewburn, the First Railway Solicitor*, 1876
Mitchell, J. *Reminiscences of my Life in the Highlands* Vol II, 1884
Moffatt, H. *East Anglia's First Railways* [the Eastern Union Railway], 1987
Monopolies & Mergers Commission. *British Railways Board: Property Activities*, 1985
Nock, O.S. *The Caledonian Railway*, 1961
Nock, O.S. *History of the Great Western Railway* vol 3, 1967
Norris, J.E. *The Stratford and Moreton Tramway*, 1987
O'Dell, A.C. & Richards, P.S. *Railways and Geography* (2nd edn), 1971
O'Flaherty, C.A. *Highways* vol 1 *Highways and Traffic*, 1974
Ottley, G. *A Bibliography of British Railway History* (2nd edn), 1983
Ottley, G. *A Bibliography of British Railway History* Supplement, 1988
Parr, H.W. *The Great Western Railway in Dean*, 1971
Paar, H.W. *The Severn and Wye Railway*, 1973
P[aine], E.M.S. *The Two James and the Two Stephensons*, 1862
Parris, H. *Government and the Railways in the Nineteenth Century*, 1965
Pease, Sir A.E. (ed). *The Diaries of Edward Pease*, 1907
Perkin, H. *The Age of the Railway*, 1970
Platt, A. *The Life and Times of Daniel Gooch*, 1987
Pollins, H. *Britain's Railways: An Industrial History*, 1971
Pratt, E.A. *A History of Inland Transport and Communications*, 1912 (reprint 1970)

277

Prest, J. *The Industrial Revolution in Coventry*, 1960
Radford, B. *Rail Centres: Derby*, 1986
Ransom, P.J.G. *The Archaeology of Railways*, 1981
Reader, W.J. *MacAdam*, 1980
Reed, B. *Crewe to Carlisle*, 1969
Reed, M.C. *Investment in Railways in Britain, 1820-1844*, 1975
Riddell, H. *Railway Parliamentary Practice*, 1846
Robbins, M. *The Railway Age*, 1962
Robbins, M. *The Isle of Wight Railways*, 1963
Robbins, M. *Points and Signals: A Railway Historian at Work*, 1967
Roberts, J.E. *The Changing Face of Carnforth* [c1974], nd
Robertson, C.J.A. *The Origins of the Scottish Railway System*, 1983
Rolt, L.T.C. *Isambard Kingdom Brunel*, 1957
Rolt, L.T.C. *Thomas Telford*, 1958
Rolt, L.T.C. *George and Robert Stephenson*, 1960
Simmons, J. *St Pancras Station*, 1968
Simmons, J. *The Railway in England and Wales: 1 The System and its Working, 1830-1914*, 1978
Simmons, J. *The Railways of Britain* (new edn), 1986
Simmons, J. *The Railway in Town and Country, 1830-1914*, 1986
Skeat, W.O. *George Stephenson, The Engineer and his Letters*, 1973
Smith, D.L. *The Little Railways of South West Scotland*, 1969
Steel, W.L. *History of the London and North Western Railway*, 1914
Thomas, J. *The Callander and Oban Railway*, 1966
Thomas, J. *The North British Railway* (2 vols), 1969 and 1975
Thomas, J. *The West Highland Railway*, 1970
Thomas, R.H.G. *London's First Railway, the London and Greenwich*, 1972
Thomas, R.H.G. *The Liverpool and Manchester Railway*, 1980
Thompson, F.M.L. *English Landed Gentry in the Nineteenth Century*, 1963
Thompson, F.M.L. *Chartered Surveyors: the Growth of a Profession*, 1968
Thompson, F.M.L. *Hampstead: Building a Borough, 1650-1964*, 1974
[Thorne, R.] *Liverpool Street Station*, 1978
Tomlinson, W.W. *The North Eastern Railway, its Rise and Development*, 1914
Tooley, R.V. *Maps and Map Makers*, 1978
Trinder, B. *The Making of the Industrial Landscape*, 1982
Turner, G. *Ashford, the Coming of the Railway*, 1984
Turner, J.T. Howard *The London Brighton and South Coast Railway* (3 vols), 1977-9
Turnock, D. *Railways in Britain: Landscape, Land Use and Society*, 1982
Vallance, H.A. *The Highland Railway* (revised edn), 1963
Vallance, H.A. *The Great North of Scotland Railway*, 1965
Vaughan, A. *A Pictorial History of Great Western Railway Architecture*, 1977
Vignoles, K.H. *Charles Blacker Vignoles*, 1982
Webster, N.W. *Joseph Locke: Railway Revolutionary*, 1970
Webster, N.W. *Britain's First Trunk Line* [the Grand Junction Railway], 1972
Welch, H.D. *The London Tilbury & Southend Railway* (2nd edn), 1963
Whitehead, R.A. & Simpson, F.D. *The Story of the Colne Valley* [Railway], 1951
Whittle, G. *The Newcastle and Carlisle Railway*, 1979

Williams, F.S. *The Midland Railway, its Rise and Progress*, 1876

Williams, F.S. *Our Iron Roads* (3rd edn), 1883

Williams, R.A. *The London and South Western Railway* (2 vols), 1968 & 1973

Wilson, C. *First with the News, the History of W.H. Smith, 1792-1972*, 1985

Wood, N. *A Practical Treatise on Rail-Roads* 3rd edn, 1838

Wooler, N. *Dinner in the Diner*, 1987

Worsdall, F. *The Tenement: a Way of Life*, 1979

Wright, N.R. *The Railways of Boston*, 1971

Wright, N.R. *The Book of Boston*, 1986

Wrottesley, A.J. *The Midland and Great Northern Joint Railway* 2nd edn, 1981

Wrottesley, A.J. *The Great Northern Railway* (3 vols), 1979-81

Young, J.N. *Great Northern Suburban*, 1977

Young, R. *Timothy Hackworth and the Locomotive*, 1823

A Regional History of the Railways of Great Britain series

Vol 1   *The West Country* D.St J. Thomas, 6th edn, 1988

Vol 2   *Southern England* H.P. White, 4th edn, 1982

Vol 3   *Greater London* H.P. White, 1963

Vol 4   *The North East* K. Hoole, 3rd edn, 1986

Vol 5   *The Eastern Counties* D.I. Gordon, 1968

Vol 6   *Scotland — The Lowlands and the Borders* J. Thomas, 1971

Vol 7   *The West Midlands* R. Christiansen, 2nd edn, 1983

Vol 8   *South and West Yorkshire* D. Joy, 1975

Vol 9   *The East Midlands* R. Leloux, 1976

Vol 10   *The North West* G.O. Holt, 2nd edn (revised G. Biddle), 1986

Vol 11   *North and Mid Wales* P.E. Baughan, 1980

Vol 12   *South Wales* D.S.M. Barrie, 1980

Vol 13   *Thames and Severn* R. Christiansen, 1981

Vol 14   *The Lake Counties* D. Joy, 1983

Vol 15   *The North of Scotland* J. Thomas & D. Turnock, 1989

Acknowledgements

A work of this kind can be written only with considerable help from others. First I must thank Douglas Leslie, Managing Director of British Rail Property Board, for providing access to the Board's working records, particularly plans and deeds, and his fellow directors for their ready assistance, especially David Lawrence, Property Director (Provinces), who has been my main source of help and advice at the Board. I must express my gratitude to the regional Chief Estate Surveyors and their staffs who dealt patiently with my many queries, especially those members who acted as my specific points of contact: Dick Bassett, Derek Whitcher, Ayleen Ledger, Mike Greenwood, Keith Whitehead, Steve Denmark and Richard Dean who also drew the maps; also former managing directors Cyril Smith and Bobby Dashwood, together with other retired members of the Board's staff who dredged deep into their memories to set me off into unsuspected areas of research.

Above all, I have to acknowledge my gratitude to Professor Jack Simmons for his interest and advice throughout the work. I discussed the project with him initially, he read the original drafts of chapters 1-7, and offered valuable comments and suggestions without which this book would be the poorer.

I am indebted to the Public Record Office at Kew and the Scottish Record Office, Edinburgh, for their unfailing helpfulness in giving me facilities to inspect material on which so much of this book is based, to all the county record offices who replied to letters, and the following which I visited: Cumbria (Kendal and Carlisle), Lancashire, Devon, Hampshire, Somerset, Dorset, Buckinghamshire, Suffolk, Leicestershire, Northumberland, Bedfordshire and Surrey (Guildford); also Liverpool Record Office. The assistance of the following libraries is gratefully acknowledged: The British Library (Bloomsbury) including the Map Library, Manchester, Liverpool, Northampton, Aylesbury, Chelmsford, Birmingham, Sheffield and Bedford; the Mitchell Library, Glasgow; the Royal Institution of Chartered Surveyors, the Institution of Civil Engineers, the Royal Institute of British Architects; Springburn Museum Trust; the National Railway Museum; the universities of Manchester (John Rylands Library), Bristol and Hull; and Brunel University. Also Robin Linsley, BRB Records Officer, and his staff were very helpful.

Numerous individuals have given freely of their time and knowledge: Rex Christiansen, R.W. Miller, Geoffrey W. Knight who let me loose on the Railway & Canal Historical Society's records index, Peter E. Baughan, Bill Simpson, John Norris, Peter Fells, E.W. Cornall, Bill and Mary Atkin, Hugh Compton, Harry Paar, Tom Richards, J. Burrows of the Railway Housing Association, Robin Leloux, John Langford, Rodney Lines, P.A. Land, J. Robin Lidster, Ron Dickson, Douglas Thompson, David Joy, John Edgington, D. Hewins and R. Ward (BRB Assistant Secretary). Lastly, but not least, I must also thank my editor, Anthony Lambert, for his advice and help, and Judith Ashford who typed the final manuscript and good naturedly endured so many 'last' amendments.

Index

Page numbers in *italics* refer to illustrations